T0329124

Public Debt Dynamics of Europe and the US

Public Debt Dynamics of Europe and the US

Dimitris N. Chorafas

AMSTERDAM · BOSTON · HEIDELBERG · LONDON · NEW YORK · OXFORD
PARIS · SAN DIEGO · SAN FRANCISCO · SINGAPORE · SYDNEY · TOKYO

Elsevier
The Boulevard, Langford Lane, Kidlington, Oxford, OX5 1GB, UK
225 Wyman Street, Waltham, MA 02451, USA

Notices
Knowledge and best practice in this field are constantly changing. As new research and experience broaden our understanding, changes in research methods, professional practices, or medical treatment may become necessary.

Practitioners and researchers must always rely on their own experience and knowledge in evaluating and using any information, methods, compounds, or experiments described herein. In using such information or methods they should be mindful of their own safety and the safety of others, including parties for whom they have a professional responsibility.

To the fullest extent of the law, neither the Publisher nor the authors, contributors, or editors, assume any liability for any injury and/or damage to persons or property as a matter of products liability, negligence or otherwise, or from any use or operation of any methods, products, instructions, or ideas contained in the material herein.

British Library Cataloguing in Publication Data
A catalogue record for this book is available from the British Library

Library of Congress Cataloging-in-Publication Data
A catalog record for this book is available from the Library of Congress

ISBN: 978-0-12-420021-0

For information on all Elsevier publications
visit our website at store.elsevier.com

  Working together
to grow libraries in
developing countries

www.elsevier.com • www.bookaid.org

Contents

Part Two   Destiny in the Land of Homer

Part Three   Case Studies with Teetering Sovereigns

Part Four   Who Killed the Golden Eagle?

Preface

Niels Bohr, the quantum physicist, once said that every statement should be taken by a scientist as a provisional hypothesis that has to be tested. This holds true not only of physics and engineering but as well of finance and economics whose theories are too often accepted without scrutiny by chiefs of state, ministers of finance, central bankers, economists, analysts, and common citizens.

An example is the theory (or, more precisely the myth) that high leveraging is good for a person, a company, or even a nation. If accepted, this leads to the *DEBT syndrome* and its disastrous aftereffects. The fallacy that "debt is good" is the subject of this book. In each of its 15 chapters, the evidence emerges that piling up public debt can lead to an unmitigated disaster. This is documented through case studies on Greece, Spain, Italy, France, and the United States—in short, those western countries that nowadays lost control of their senses and of their economy.

Bohr's thought demolishes the generally held opinion that scientific, economic, or social "truths" and "theories" are forever. By extension, it dissipates the widely prevalent delusion that books in science and in economics contain only eternal wisdom. Books are learning tools written by people who are fallible. As such, they may include impractical theories like:

- The reign of debt, and
- The gates of nirvana.

Written for professionals, academics, and researchers, the book the readers have in their hands provides the documentation and describes the implications of current policies by sovereigns and central banks, in dealing with the *debt abyss*. In so doing, it brings in perspective the diversity of opinion reigning in modern economics and finance. It also outlines themes which, among themselves, are defining the society in which we live.

"Authors are the engineers of the human soul," Stalin once said, adding that: "If you want to know the people you deal with learn about what they are reading."[1] In this, the Soviet dictator was right. Ideas and arguments contained in books are basic to culture and civilization. They are eye-openers to the wisdom of the past and help in positioning one's mind in a way confronting present challenges by making use of assumptions, interpretations, and extrapolations.

Usually, though not always, when the author succeeds in his or her mission, books become living entities aimed to both inform and provide the grounds for a discussion where different, contradictory opinions can be heard. "I completely

---

[1] Montefiore SS. Staline. Paris: Editions des Syrtes; 2005; London: Weidenfeld & Nicolson; 2003.

disagree with you but will fight for your right to state your opinion," said Voltaire to Jean-Jacques Rousseau. Like Voltaire's writings, this book brings to the reader contrarian opinions, but its intention is not polemics. It is a reflection of the dynamics of social, economic, and financial life which are almost entirely built on contradiction.

Contradiction and diversity enlightened the past centuries and permitted different philosophies to develop. By contrast, our world has been flattened by the steamroller of the nanny state. Margaret Thatcher was right when she said: "... too many people have been given to understand that when they have a problem it is the government's job to cope with it. ... They are casting their problems on society. And you know, there is no such thing as society. There are individual men and women and there are families."[2]

There are individuals and families who in the post-World War II generations have been taught that "debt is good" and they are accumulating it crazily. Individuals and families depend on entitlements to enlarge their income, and if they are homeless, the government must house them. Run by politicians who are no better than second raters, western governments are happy to oblige no matter how illogical are their citizens' demands.

- The cost goes to increase the already ultrahigh public debt, and
- Not even a thought is given to the fact that, at the end of the day, debt means slavery.

Deception is far from being unheard of in politics and in society at large. In 1957, at the time of the Treaty of Rome, the "European dream," embraced by the majority of the old continent, promised a middle-class lifestyle for most people. But delays and bickering made this almost impossible. The more public debt rose, the less was the prospect of secure jobs for the young as financial crises:

- Destabilized the politicians, and
- Created a widening gap between social classes.

No wonder that the majority of Europeans have deep cynicism toward their governments, national institutions, and political leaders. To make educated guesses about *how long* this will last, we must appreciate *what* has happened and *why*.

Part of the answer can be found in drift, which always accompanies a rich society misled to believe that the good times last forever. Another part of the answer is wrapped in the comic thinking that "*debt* is an asset." That's the concept which led to wrong-way policies by chiefs of state and their cohorts, all the way to common citizens. We will see *why*.

Hopefully, this wrong-way thinking could be corrected through decisions which are factual, motivating, and able of changing the direction of future events. The potential of a correction is increased by nonmainstream books able of showing how to think out of the box, inciting their reader to:

- Examine alternatives,

---

[2] Financial Times, April 19, 2013.

- Challenge the "obvious", and
- Organize to get out of the trap.

Along this line of thinking, this book provides a probing discussion on the state of the economy, the reasons why we came into the trough in which we reside for over 6 years, and what it takes in terms of effort to get out of it and get moving again. The text makes plenty of critical thoughts public, relying on the right to freedom of opinion and of expression, as well as on the obligation to provide thinking people with contrarian arguments and information different to the one that so often is being heralded by politicians and the media.

* * *

The book divides into six parts. Part One provides the reader with a snapshot of the economic, social, and financial world today which, as different commentators suggested, is a *casino society*. This includes the globalization without limits which started in earnest in the 1980s and the "kingdoms of debt" which it created, practically in all western countries. No attention has been paid to the fact that both public and household debt is in the upside, and it is very difficult getting up from under *if* this could be done at all.

The theme of Part Two is an answer to destiny by the land of Homer: The Greek economy and its fall to the abyss can teach very valuable lessons on what "not to do" if you wish to keep your freedom and your independence. But is anybody listening?

Part Three presents to the reader more case studies on self-wounded economies: Spain, Italy, and France. These are brought to the readers' attention in an *as is* way, with every effort made to avoid the political and bureaucratic romanticism that "the worst is behind us." The worse is still ahead of us and nobody can tell for how long it will last.

Part Four attempts to answer a daunting question: "Who killed the Golden Eagle?" When WW II came to an end, the US economy was supreme and it continued being so for over a decade. But slowly its mighty weight was eaten up from within. Like ancient Athens, American citizens listened to the fallacy propagated by weak politicians that, no matter how fast you used them, your assets last forever.

One thing that we learned during the past half a dozen years is that events which appeared unimaginable do sometimes occur. Therefore, we need to enlarge our mental map of how the world works and how conditions change. Part Five adds to the names of troubled economies those of the BRICs, even if a couple of them are still bystanders. Can anyone prognosticate what will be their future?

The answer is "yes!" and this in several respects, from sovereign governance to the unexpected aftermath of an aging society. I strongly recommended paying attention to the words of Taro Aso, the Japanese minister of finance in Section 5 of Chapter 13, about *longevity risk*.

Part Six has two chapters complementing one another. The first is constrained by the fact that there are so few cases of economies which have been successfully deleveraging—and therefore improving their creditworthiness. Both are small countries: Iceland and Latvia, but what they have accomplished can teach the big ones about what is required to take hold of oneself and change course while it is still time. I also added to this chapter case studies on Ireland and Britain (though with mixed feelings); as well as on Germany for being able to walk since 2007, the very beginning of the deep debt crisis, at the edge of the abyss without falling into it.

The book's last chapter has a polyvalent objective, starting with the viewpoint of those who believe that the higher is the public debt, the better. True or false? Have this theory's proponents duly considered the effects of *ineptocracy* when it comes to judge, for example, how unfunded liabilities will be managed? What will be the effect of higher public debt on our living standard? Why matters get worse because of the lack of ethics, all the way to sovereigns adopting the policy of grabbing money out of common citizen bank accounts? And, not to be forgotten, what should be done with parliaments voting in favor of democratic cleptocracy?

* * *

Because the best way to convey a message is through facts and figures which can be understood and appreciated, this book is full of real-life examples. It has been a deliberate choice to depend on case studies as evidence of good and bad approaches to social, economic, and financial life. Live events also help as undisputable demonstrators of successes and failures in the search for solutions in getting out of the hole western governments find themselves. As Denis Healey, a former British chancellor of the Exchequer, once said: "The first law of holes is that if you are in one stop digging."

In conclusion, in the course of the last six years, political, social, and economic events have been crowding one another. A prolonged financial crisis opened the door to all instincts. At sovereign level, tragedy alternated with comedy, for the same reason that in life the sublime is mingled with petty and with self-deception. Governance admits errors, but errors are magnified when they are hidden. The first requisite for success is to hide nothing—weaknesses least of all—and to call everything by its right name.

This book has been written on that principle. The evidence is provided through the case study presented to the reader as a Conclusion. The trickery associated to the birth of the Euro.

* * *

I am indebted to a long list of knowledgeable people, and of organizations, for their contribution to the research which made this book feasible; also to several senior executives and experts for constructive criticism during the preparation of the manuscript. Dr. Heinrich Steinmann, Dr. Nelson Mohler, Eva Maria Binder, and Souzy Capoyannopoulos-Biris have made a significant contribution of out-of-box ideas, double-checking on facts, and review of text samples.

Let me take this opportunity to thank Dr. Erin Hill-Parks for suggesting this project, Dr. Scott Bentley for seeing it all the way to publication, and Vijayaraj Purushothaman for Production.

September 9, 2013

Valmer and Schlössli   **Dr. Dimitris N. Chorafas**

Part One

The West Today

1 Globalization of a Casino Society

1.1 "My Lord," Answered Solon to King Croesus, "You Are Asking Me What I Think of Human Life"

"My Lord," answered Solon (640−599 BC), the Athenian lawmaker, to a question by King Croesus of Lydia, "You are asking me what I think of human life. How can I answer you otherwise than by judging people only after their life is over, when I know that divinity is jealous of the happiness of human beings and it makes it pleasure to upset it. *Man is subject to a thousand accidents*."[1] How true.

Established by Solon, the laws of the Republic of Athens formed the basis of what we are used to call Western civilization. Solon did much more than setting the code of social morality and of social order. Through laws which were tough but more liberal when compared to the laws of Dracon, who preceded him as lawmaker of ancient Athens, Solon aimed to assure social and financial stability. He also initiated important monetary reforms, including:

- The introduction of coinage into Attica,
- Rules against female luxury to reduce luxury imports,[2] and
- Monetization of agricultural commodities to offset usury's destructive effect on farmers.

To a large measure, Dracon had adopted Hebraic laws, adapting them to the early society of Athens.[3] The concepts on which he based himself followed the legal policies of Hammurabi of Babylon (1792−1750 BC), particularly in establishing severe sanctions for violation of the laws. This is a practice our society has more or less abandoned (presumably for "humanitarian reasons") replacing it with nearly total impunity. In restructuring Dracon's laws, Solon took a broader and somewhat more liberal approach and also set the basis for evolution of economic thought.[4]

Contrasted to the ancient times when law setters were philosophers, today's law setter, and not only in monetary policies and finance, is the financial elite: City of London and Wall Street. (The latter is also known as Eastern Liberal Establishment.[5]) According to Anthony C. Sutton, this is populated by American *corporate socialists*.[6] The Eastern Establishment has also been:

- The motor behind the virtual economy, and
- An important promoter of globalization.

As in ancient Carthage, the Eastern Establishment's criterion of excellence is wealth and competitiveness—the latter being based on financial systems, private

Public Debt Dynamics of Europe and the US. DOI: http://dx.doi.org/10.1016/B978-0-12-420021-0.00001-4

institutions, infrastructures, skills, educational performance, flexible labor markets, and (until recently) monetary stability. Together, these make the "free economy," though rules, beliefs, and criteria vary widely by country and so does the per capita gross domestic product (GDP).

If at the time of King Croesus a huge amount of wealth was rare exception, today from America to India and China there is no lack of billionaires.[7] In 2010 (latest available statistics), global GDP amounted to over 60 trillion dollars, an income divided up in the most unequal way between 7 billion souls on planet Earth— to each, according to his or her effort and (sometimes) to his or her connections.

Using per capita gross domestic product[8] per year as basic criterion, a study by UBS divided the world population into three layers: The top 1 billion people are largely living in Western countries, including Japan. The next billion people is a class on its own interfacing between the top and bottom layers. The lower layer is populated by 5 billion people, those of low income and the really poor.[9] This strati- fication makes it easier to compare not only annual earnings but also:

- Investments,
- State of development,
- Products in demand, and
- Externalities, for instance CO_2 emission.[10]

On an average, the wealthier people in the first billion enjoy a per capita GDP of close 40,000 US dollars per year. People living in the richest countries of this first bil- lion, such as Luxembourg, Norway, or Qatar, enjoy an average per capita GDP close to 100,000 dollars per year.[11] South Korea, the bottom country in this first billion has a per capita GDP of 17,000 dollars. Always talking of averages, the per capita GDP in the United States is 45,000 dollars and that of Europe and Japan is 40,000 dollars.[12]

As these statistics document, per capita GDPs vary from country to country and, as well, within each of the three layers, for instance, within the top billion of the Earth's citizen. Always in average income terms, the population of this first billion people is homogeneous enough when compared to the (country-by-country) income averages of the second billion and, most evidently, to those of the third layer of 5 billion people.

In this lower stratum of 5 billion in terms of average per capita GDP, people live under conditions of poverty to extreme poverty compared to western standards. Within each country, however, the range between higher and lower income is wide. This hap- pens even if in the course of the last three decades large stretches of population have benefited handsomely in terms of per capita GDP—particularly in countries which are energy and mineral producers.

At the top of the 5 billion people bottom layer is Iran, with average per capita GDP 4500 dollars; China, 3700 dollars; India, 1200 dollars. At the bottom's bottom lies Niger with 300 dollars average per capita GDP per year and Congo with 170 dollars. Yet, the Congo is a relatively rich country in minerals, but its wealth distribution is awfully skew.

The reader will be right if he or she thinks that a global comparison of per capita GDP averages resembles *Fata Morgana*. Average dollar values are illusory; they tell nothing of the cost of living and other conditions. At the same time, however, in an age of globalization, the magnitude of aforementioned "average" differences has to be kept in perspective because it leads to an interesting pattern permitting comparisons.[13]

Plotting the scores against average per capita GDP in each of the aforementioned three layers reveals some interesting facts which override what is usually looked at as "common economic wisdom"[14]: *competitiveness brings wealth*, and the richer countries can best afford to be competitive as long as they remain "the richer."

The model of per capita GDP per year distributions one derives from differences between 100,000 dollars and 170 dollars—or over 58.800 percent in average—is that inequality is at an all-time high and even greed has gone global. While a major reason for this discrepancy is explosive birth rates in poorer countries and ill-focused daily human effort, the reader should not forget Solon's dictum that divinity is jealous of well-being in human life, and it makes itself pleasure to upset it. Chapters 4−6 explain what has happened in Greece while subsequent chapters focus on Spain, Italy, France, and the United States. The common thread behind these studies consists of:

- Spending more than one earns, and falling deeper into debt,
- Creating incentives for private households to borrow more through low interest rates,
- Designing and selling toxic financial products, which are sure to hurt their owner and the economy, and
- Having central banks buying the bonds of overly indebted sovereigns so that they persist with their budget deficits, instead of trying to reduce the burden.

This common thread also explains how the casino society marches on and looks as being unstoppable. "The list of measures to curb the gambling is already long," one could read in *The Economist*.[15] Yes, but under the lobbyists' massive impact, the trumpet heralding government action gives an uncertain sound, and no one prepares him or her for the battle.

Beyond the sovereign and household debt, there is a swarm of companies with fragile balance sheets who have been able to bide their time and avoid potential bankruptcy in 2012−13, thanks in part to the voracious investor appetite for high-yielding debt. That helped keep default rates low, as managements pushed out toward 2014 and 2015 a debilitating wall of debt maturities. We are just entering that time frame.

Divinity has its own, largely secret, criteria for judging people and nations while the wheel of fortune continues turning. Those best known are hard work, thrift, and discipline. King Croesus might have been the richest man of the then known world when Solon visited him, but years later destiny changed. Fortune which had lifted him to the crest washed him away as hostage in the hands of King Cyrus.

1.2 Globalization Worked As Long As It Worked[16]

As contrasted to the internationalization of trade which dates back to the second millennium BC, as the twentieth century neared its end, three decades of economic and financial globalization sailed seamlessly through the world's economic fabric. Then, things began to change. Something like a U-turn is now championed—at least in the West—by a crisis which has been moving from US mortgages to the slow-motion breakup of the euro.

"Globalization worked as long as it worked, now it does not work anymore," said George Soros in an interview he gave to Bloomberg News on July 27, 2012. Then he added, "We have global markets, but we don't have global governance of markets. The markets are unstable as global regulation conflicts with national sovereignty. Hence, deregulation is the dominant force."

As time goes on, the lack of global financial regulation, and therefore of discipline, creates an environment of growing uncertainty where everyone does whatever he or she likes. This leads to anarchy and eventually to chaos. The wave of novel financial instruments, many of which are beyond the regulators' ability to compete in terms of establishing checks and balances, has aggravated an already bad situation created by wide swings in cross-border capital transfers. The silver lining of the crisis we are in is that it made many people aware of the severe consequences associated to unregulated globalization.

International trade itself is falling. An obvious cause is the global economic slowdown. Trade often tracks quite closely worldwide GDP. Exports are sales to other countries, and they tend to weaken when buying power is low or (even worse) in reverse gear. Patterns of trade match the fortunes of economic prosperity or lack of it. At least in recent years, trade has typically grown faster than GDP; then, the curve ebbed.

In 2011 and 2012, imports into the European Union have fallen by 4.5 percent, but in oil-rich Middle East, imports increased by 7.4 percent. The International Monetary Fund (IMF) thinks that trade will grow by 5.1 percent in 2013 because of a strengthening economy; this, however, is still to be seen. Shipping data are an early indicator and statistics hold out little hope for rapid rebound. On September 5, 2012 a survey by Lloyd's indicated that container volumes from Asia to Europe plunged by 13.2 percent year-on-year to July 2012.[17]

A growing number of economists now think that the ongoing economic reversal may have deeper roots than simple *malaise*. For several decades, following World War II, worldwide business transactions increased and globalization created a new phenomenon of tighter integration of markets. This has been further promoted by global companies with research centers, production facilities, sales, and service networks. Such an expansion, however, has not been followed by sophisticated:

- Governance structures able to look after the problems confronting globalizing economies, and
- Political and civil institutions at global level required to control excesses and unwanted externalities.

The Group of Twenty (G20) chiefs of state has not delivered the expected benefit in global business guidance; neither did it bring forward an effective structure of management planning and control. Some efforts aimed to make sense out of globalization, and the leveraging it brings along (Section 1.5) turned into a sea of paper. Take the capital adequacy rules of the banking industry as an example:

- In the late 1980s, Basel I rules on bank capital had just 30 pages.
- In the late 1990s, early twenty-first century, the paper volume of Basel II rules rose to 347 pages.
- In 2012, Basel III featured 616 pages and not yet everything is in place, as full implementation comes in 2019.

The tendency to beef up the size of volumes on rules and regulations prevails in practically all domains. In the United States, the Glass−Steagall Act of 1933, which separated commercial and investment banking, required 37 pages; the Dodd−Frank Act of 2010 ran up to 848 pages, and experts say that it may go to 30,000 pages of detailed rule making when various agencies provide their input. If so, this will become a bureaucratic mega book sinking under its own weight.[18]

A few but clearly stated and cutting rules of behavior—like the Ten Commandments—are urgently needed in global finance, and in other industries. They should provide a stable global business framework, like the laws of Hammurabi and Dracon did at their time (Section 1.1). In their absence prevailed negative paradigms of business, social behavior and wealth distribution.

The way Zanny Minton Beddos had it in a recent essay: "A majority of the world's citizens now live in countries where the gap between the rich and the rest is a lot bigger than it was a generation ago...[19] (in the US) the portion of national income going to the richest 1 percent tripled from 8 percent in the 1970s to 24 percent in 2007."[20]

The economic crisis we are going through, and most particularly the high unemployment, saw to it that times have changed. The era when the swallowing sea lifted all boats is now a memory. As Gideon Rachman reminds his readers James Callaghan, the Labor Prime Minister of the late 1970s, had said: "There are times, perhaps once every 30 years, when there is a sea change in politics."[21] Not only in politics, of course, but also:

- In economics,
- In social behavior, and
- In the attitude one has toward his work, if he or she finds a job.

The free reign (therefore also lust and greed) lasted too long. Now has come the time for discipline in order to get out of the tunnel. An old proverb says that to move "the human donkey must see a carrot in the front and feel a stick in the back." The carrot in the front is standard of living. The stick in the back are the laws Dracon and Solon set in ancient Athens, and before them Hammurabi in Babylonia. Let's face it: society has turned against itself. To be lasting, the change must be both:

- Cultural, and
- Legislative.

Successful regulatory frameworks always have a cultural quotient which holds together complex and highly fragile standards of interdependence. The right financial legislation and regulation can have a profound impact on the way commercial systems, investment plans, and capital markets work. Only a cultural change can assure that political, economic, and social thinking follow a line which defines the limits within which stakeholders should behave.

Culture is promoted through education, and education Socrates said is more than teaching. Its aim is not to feed his students with information but to make them *think* and, therefore, make them better persons. In a frequently quoted passage Cicero, the Roman senator, orator, and author, says that Socrates was the first to bring philosophy down from heaven. To Cicero's mind, Socrates:

- Took it into the men's cities,
- Introduced it to their homes, and
- Forced philosophy itself to inquire about life and morals, as well as about good and evil.

Globalization has never been up to Socratic standards of enquiry, a reason why over several decades, a long roster of scandals have made matters worse than they were earlier on. An example is the so-called *Geithner doctrine*[22] which professes that the preservation (with total impunity) of self-wounded big banks is an obligation of the state—and therefore, of the taxpayer—no matter which might be the consequences. In full moral hazard, this constitutes the globalization of:

- Too big to fail, and
- Too big to jail.

This double-whammy perverted the justice system. Critics say that Geithner's doctrine also demolished the American criminal justice system turning it into a two-tier framework which assures "more excessive risk, more crime and more crises." That's what writes Neil Barofsky, former inspector general of the Troubled Asset Relief Program (TARP), in an article in the Financial Times[23] (see also the discussion on Barofsky's book *Bailout* in Chapter 2).

Rather than providing service to their community, global banks have been pursuing their self-interests offering a poor, indeed very poor, public service. This created public anger. The bank, particularly the big bank, became the global casino losing a torrent of money from its gambles, while its executives and traders are awarded fat bonuses.

In a speech he gave in 2010, Hector Sants, of the British Financial Services Authority (FSA), said that trust has been lost between the financial community and the rest of society. This is compounded by different around the world scandals which followed the financial debacles from 2007 to 2014 and beyond.

The LIBOR scandal, which surfaced in 2012 (for greater detail see Chapter 3), revealed a culture in which bankers knew they were doing something wrong but did not fear being caught—or, if caught, punished. It is not that regulatory rules have been missing, but they have not been applied. No wonder, therefore, that the aftermath of this attitude is the global casino society and continued erosion of public confidence.

In conclusion, the culture of too big to fail and too big to jail creates a global climate of uncertainty which destabilizes persons, companies, and nations—at least those who would rather like to live in an environment they can understand and trust. We are at an inflexion point. "Man is subject to a thousand accidents," as Solon aptly remarked more than 2500 years ago. In the following sections, we will look at the most immodest.

1.3 The Web of Debt Has Led to Slavery

A popular French proverb says: "Un banquier bon est un banquier con." This roughly translates into: "A banker with a good heart is nuts." Nuts, however, are not only the good-hearted bankers but also those who become loan addicts and continue sinking into debt. They have no idea of what they are getting into—from taking loans to accepting economic assistance programs with strings attached to them.

Economic assistance which followed WWII, says John Perkins, did not target swift economic recovery. It aimed to assure, or at least encourage, that countries become part of a network promoting the commercial interests of industrial nations.[24] And because debt is addictive, in the end the highly indebted sovereign becomes *paignion*—a plaything.

To Perkins' opinion, after WWII ended, country after country became ensnarled in a *web of debt*. This has been built over decades by international banks recycling money, big corporations colonizing a market, as well as sovereigns eager to have a say on the way other countries manage their procurement and how they vote in the United Nations. According to this opinion, the foreign aid program set for itself two objectives:

- To make the politicians running a country's fortunes rich and popular so they continue being in charge, and
- To stack up the country's economy with debt which may never be repaid, but keeps on providing good income to the lenders.[25]

This strategy works in a way fairly similar to that of the late nineteenth century European nations which used sovereign default of their borrowers as an excuse to invade foreign countries. It is as well the strategy employed by rogue creditors, known as *debt vultures*, who actively prey upon people, companies, and countries likely to default, buying up significant portions of their debt and then storming in to demand that they repay their debts at 100 cents on the dollar.

If they are successful, debt vultures make impressive gains because they have bought the debt in the secondary market at huge discount, a price arrived under the assumption that the debt would never be redeemed at face value. Not only countries but also their currencies may be repeatedly attacked, in full knowledge that, more often than not, defenses are ill-thought-out, poorly planned, and weak.

Pure debt is not the only game in town. A more polished debt-upon-debt trick, at sovereign level, takes the form of loans to develop power plants, industrial factories, universities, highways, ports, airports, and other infrastructural projects. Repayment conditions aside, the loans carry the requirement that contracts will be given to engineering, construction, and consulting companies from the country providing the aid.

Interestingly enough, disbursements are limited because money is simply transferred from the banks to the engineering and other firms, and then back to the banks as the recipient country is required to pay the loan with interest. To a large extent, this is a con game based on the assumption that:

- All countries like to develop their infrastructure, and
- All men in power are corruptible.

John Perkins introduces an interesting hypothesis on how the world's economy is being run nowadays. It starts with the assumption that no major power looks at nuclear warfare as the way to gain or sustain global dominance. Instead, it prefers debt-based covert operations with global banks acting as interfaces.

Punishment for trying to get out of the con game can be severe. Strategies modeled along the line of a palace coup, or an organized but unexpected uprising from within, have been used throughout history. This time around, however, they have been restructured to take advantage of globalization which:

- Significantly amplified the impact of debt, and
- Enlarged as well as strengthened the geopolitical effects.

An early example dates back to the late 1950s with the overthrow of the Mossadegh regime in Iran, which opened the way for another two decades of the Shah's reign. The uprising in Teheran was organized by Kermit Roosevelt who was in CIA's payroll. The way Perkins has it: "Had he been caught, the consequences would have been dire. He had orchestrated the first US operation to overthrow a foreign government, and it was likely that many more would follow, but it was important to find an approach that would not directly implicate Washington."[26]

That's where the international web of debt came in, incarnated by global banks, mammoth manufacturing companies, marketing corporations as well as supranational organizations such as the World Bank and IMF. A whole constellation of consultancies and other service industries revolved around them. They were not directly paid by the government but drew their financing from firms in the private sector. If they did dirty work and this was exposed, it could be nicely attributed to corporate greed rather than the policy of a sovereign.

The role played by money without frontiers was further promoted by the freedom to print currency which is internationally accepted as legal tender. This gives to sovereigns, and central banks in their jurisdiction, immense power because the webs of debt are multiplied as commercial banks and governments continue to make loans that know they will never be repaid. (See in Chapter 2 the discussion on European Central Bank's (ECB's) Outright Monetary Transactions, OMT.)

Banks can make loans to countries with full knowledge that the chance of seeing their money back is slim or nonexistent. They do so because they appreciate that the sovereign, and its central bank, stand behind them. In fact, the sovereign does not really want that the borrowing countries honor their debts. Nonpayment gives him an inordinate amount of leverage.

Simon Bolivar, the liberator of the Andean Spanish Colonies (roughly Venezuela, Colombia, and Ecuador) had stated in his time: "I despise debt more than I do the Spanish." Mao, too, knew enough of the racket associated to the web of debt to be eager to repay China's loans from Moscow. Mao understood that loans from other governments come at huge political cost:

- Binding countries to each other, and
- Creating a dependency that first establishes and then reinforces existing power asymmetries.

Therefore, China's leader had insisted on repaying the Soviet loans quickly. He saw that the cost of debt cannot *only* be measured in financial terms, and he did not want to risk being so dependent on the Soviet Union that he lost political maneuverability, while at the same time he endangered his own sovereignty.

If China could lose its freedom of action because of debt to its Soviet neighbor, *then* imagine what happens with small countries which fall into the "easy money" trap and, from there, become victims of long-term financial woes leading them into subservience and/or virtual bankruptcy. The billions advanced by their "aid" benefactor and the banks' sovereign loans have been used to import consumption goods, buy oil, hire more bureaucrats, and sign contracts with engineering and construction firms for consumption purposes. Either way, it is no more available to repay the loans.

The more dramatic part of all this is that the misguided, highly indebted country continues to contract more loans and spend more money on entitlements which are unaffordable. The net result is falling even deeper into debt. Politicians are not known of being able to calculate the consequences of their decisions, and therefore, they are ever prone to look at the public debt racket as an "opportunity."

In an article he published in *The Four Pillars*, of the Geneva Association, Milton Nektarios presented an excellent example of how political leaders fail to protect their country's interests and longer term well-being. "The politics of irresponsibility practiced by successive Greek governments since 1975," Nektarios writes, "have resulted in the effective bankruptcy of the country and the request for international financial assistance in the form of a joint European Commission/International Monetary Fund/European Central Bank":[27]

- Financing ever growing budget deficits, and
- Supporting unsustainable economic policies.

To the opinion of Nektarios, without any serious preparation, the Greek Ministry of Labor and Social Insurance started producing successive drafts of legislation trying to meet two contradictory objectives: appease the citizens and labor unions and, at the same time, satisfy the demands of the European Commission (EC)/IMF/ECB (the Troika) on pension reform.

That has been misguided. Pensions, salaries, and public health care costs had to be downsized because they were unaffordable. A weak Greek economy could not really honor them, as its virtual bankruptcy documents. But this had to be done by an overall economic plan, not by following orders. This case of accumulated bad government decisions underlines the fact that countries strangle themselves by:

- Spending money beyond their means,
- Stacking up their economy with loans they can ill afford, and
- Subsequently having to devote a huge chunk of their national budget simply for servicing and paying-off debts.

The reader should appreciate that this situation is by no means a "Greek exception." As far as the global economy is concerned, *it's the rule*. It is a process that has occurred in history as a matter of course bringing countries to an unsustainable condition because of living under the steady stress of debts. The most tragic part of living literally on debt is that it becomes a habit which is difficult to eradicate. Ironically, there is more resentment against those who advise to kick the debt habit, than against those who created it and sustained it.

1.4 Policies That Brought Us to a Mess

One of the principles of Taoism is that in order to follow in one direction you have to start from the opposite. This finds an excellent field of application with globalization, as countries have to examine their strengths and weaknesses by first studying those of their competitors, then compare themselves to their competitors, some of which may be at the other side of the globe. Having sized up themselves at world scale, they have to carefully:

- Feed their strengths, and
- Strangle their weaknesses.

Both require a thorough internal restructuring which may be painful, but the alternative is decay. Sovereigns who fell on hard times should be keen to enact reforms, from structural changes of the labor market to cutting the tentacles of the nanny state. Both are doable, but attempts fail when they are half-baked and/or give rise to fierce opposition by an ill-informed public and by special interests.[28]

In times of crisis, relatively generous and constructive impulses which come with a rising standard of living give way to increasing enmity between "haves" and "have-nots," and not just in terms of money or employment. Measures which might soften the edges of a society of rising differences are being put in the time closet, while the gaps between people benefiting from the economy and those suffering from it increase. Experts say that the years ahead will be rocky, marked by:

- Chronic financial volatility, and
- An widening economic divide which cannot be closed just by rhetoric.

To a substantial (and unexpected) degree, globalization of the economy and worldwide communications led to a widening economic rift both internationally and within the same jurisdiction. As the "highs" and "lows" of living standards (particularly the latter) became more visible than they used to be, differences in income as well as in wealth have been shown to be extensive with wide parts of the population confronted by:

- Economic stagnation, and
- Cultural alienation.

Political instability is believed to be the reason behind the paradox that even when world trade prospered some countries fell into deeper rooted economic troubles. At his time, Adam Smith had made reference to "the principal architects" of global policy, "our merchants and manufacturers" who sought to assure that their own interests have "been most peculiarly attended to." Nothing really changed over the centuries, except that nowadays the East is master of income and wealth while the West finds it difficult to recover its past position.

Even some of the formerly upcoming countries in the BRIC (Brazil, Russia, India, and China, see also Chapter 12) have fallen way behind, because their leaders have been singularly incapable to keep them in a course of global competitiveness. A case in point is India, which during the last few years seems to turn into a violent do-as-you please social environment with gang rape of young women becoming a sort of sport.[29] This would have never happened under Indira Gandhi. Personal security aside, like India the West confronts itself with a double deficit:

- Fiscal, and
- De-competitiveness.

When the system of competitiveness crashes, the person responsible is not just the latest chief of state but a tandem of them who have been unable to see that when quality takes a dive, mistrust increases almost exponentially. Under these conditions, hopes that problems can take care of themselves are awfully misplaced, because bad news continues coming from declining fortunes while prudence and personal responsibility take a leave.

For a consumer/producer society which most unwisely confined itself to consuming alone, the price paid by the West has been steep. Starting in the late 1980s and continuing into the 1990s and the twenty-first century all the way to the present day, the Western standard of living stagnated then fell, particularly for middle class households. Income redistribution which benefited high income earners lifted the averages, and this gave a misleading picture of greater wealth. The true condition is an increase in relative poverty.

The boom of the 1990s and of the first years of this century has bypassed most common people in western countries, who were kept quiet by a rapid but unafford-able increase in obligations toward them through entitlements, assumed by the sovereigns. These increased the public debt by leaps and bounds.[30] Past a point, it led to the economic and social crisis in which we landed.

The taxes the state collects are no more sufficient to pay salaries and pensions for its swallowed mass of bureaucrats,[31] over and beyond the endowments and other free lunches it offers. To make ends meet, even formerly serious sovereigns have joined the speculators in high gearing while the common citizens are crashed. Euroland's member states are now planning to leverage to euro 2 trillion, the euro 500 billion of European Stability Mechanism (ESM), the fund set up to help those over-leveraged sovereigns to come up from under. (The ESM funds are insufficient, but throwing them to profligate governments is simply silly.)

As for the shrinking standard of living, a study by the Federal Reserve released in June 2012 shows that between 2007 and 2010 the median net worth of American families fell to level last seen in 1992—except for the top 10 percent of earners, whose wealth rose.[32] While most of the decline was attributed to the collapse in the housing market, it is no less true that the gap between the better off and those worse off has increased to levels which are difficult to justify.

The reader should also know that even within the top 1 percent of US citizens exist enormous differences in income. In 2011, Ray Dalio, head of Bridgewater, a large hedge fund, made 3.9 billion dollars—or 480 times the 8.1 million dollars received by Brian Moynihan, CEO of Bank of America. Compare either and both of these to the income of 8.3 million people unemployed in the United States, and you see what's the size at the gap's edges.

This gap pattern characterizes as well other Western countries (even if it is less dramatic). Leveraged sovereigns have become accustomed to live with a poorly planned and ill-thought-out system of income and expense, which will unavoidably crumble with the cost paid by the worst off common citizens. Take Italy and its public debt at 127 percent of GDP as an example. In early September 2012, Professor Johnson of MIT said that Italy's debt is the most unsustainable of Euroland[33] —in spite of the other basket cases at both shores of the North Atlantic.

On August 20, 2012 *Le Figaro*, a Paris daily, published an interview by Nouriel Roubini, the economist, who stated that the only effect of delaying the breaking-up of Euroland is the continuation of the crisis. To Roubini's opinion, the bailout strategy adopted for sovereigns, like the financing of Greece and Portugal, and (eventually) through OMT for Spain and Italy, will (in the near future) lead to the destruction of the ECB's balance sheets.[34]

In addition, highly indebted sovereigns who are being offered manna from heaven are not likely to take the necessary but painful steps of pruning the economy and putting it back on its feet. Their demand that the taxpayers of other Euroland nations pay for their debts lacks ethics, makes no economic sense, and is as well politically unrealistic. It is unthinkable that the Germans would pay part of the French debt when the French have cut their retirement age to 60 while Germans retire at 67.

"German voters have every reason to feel misled about the euro," writes Gideon Rachman in the Financial Times. "They were once promised that the single currency involved a no-bailout clause that would prevent German taxpayers from having to support other eurozone countries. But Germany has already had to accept potential liabilities of euro 280 billion to fund Europe's various bailouts — and there will be further demands to come."[35]

Not only highly leveraged nations should look at public debt as their citizen's and their own enemy No. 1, but also tough measures are needed reversing "liberalizations" of the last three decades which promoted high gearing at global scale. In

Bretton Woods, John Maynard Keynes considers as the most important achievement of the conference the establishment of the right of governments to restrict capital movements.

Keynes has said that cross-border finance should be regulated at *both ends*. In the case of the American economy: margin requirements, the Volcker rule and the Dodd−Frank Act have the potential to stem outflows. However, since Dodd−Frank implementation has exempted foreign exchange derivatives and bank branches from the Volcker rule, the gates are wide open for gambling in the global financial market, including wide capital movements.

In sharp contrast to a policy of restraint, globalization looks at free capital mobility as its "important entitlements," if not "fundamental right." It is indeed curious that the self-proclaimed Neo-Keynesians make no reference to this and other important policies of Keynes. They only spouse deficit spending, which Keynes had advised as an exceptional measure—not as permanent policy. Guess why.

Bretton Woods also restricted financial speculation as well as attacks on currencies, which today have become a second religion. Let me be clear on this issue. The more free reign is given to speculation, the more skewed becomes income and wealth distribution to the disadvantage of common citizen. This has serious consequences, particularly as lobbyists are busy protecting the interests of high earners and of the different excesses which characterize the 1 percent of society at the expense of the other 99 percent.

1.5   Leveraging and Getting Deeper into Debt

Leverage is debt. As the level of gearing grows that of assumed, risk increases exponentially. Leverage exists everywhere in the economy, but at very different degrees and for different reasons. Sometimes debt is used to start a new firm or to better the productive capacity of a company or of an industry. The practice of leverage is not always negative but it:

- Must not become the only policy, and
- Should be done in a way providing tangible results without damaging the future.

Leveraging is done by means of loans and trading. Derivative financial instruments[36] are, in principle, geared. To explain the sense of leverage, Wall Street analysts use the paradigm of cracking a whip. A force applied in the snap of the wrist results in multiples of that initial effort discharged at whip's end. In a similar manner, as derivative financial instruments exploded all over the globe, two things have happened:

- Leverage conjured vast amounts of virtual (not real) value, and
- This resulted in a higher rate of growth than could otherwise be possible, till the system went belly up.

A leveraged nation, a leveraged company, or a leveraged family can survive as long as the environment continues to grow in the *virtual world*. A geared entity's biggest fear would be a long period of calm and stability in the markets and in society at large, lulling companies and investors into slowing their trading activities.

The worst of all worlds for those who are geared is a marketplace where nothing happens. The most important risk, in this case, is not that a high volatility will hit the market, but that in a market which is calm and stable customers are less susceptible to continue entering into risky contracts. Then something big happens to the economy followed by sharp rise in volatility leading to destruction.

At the G20 Washington economic conference of November 15, 2008, after the collapse of Lehman Brothers, leverage was blamed for having wrecked the American and the global economy. The third paragraph of the communiqué which has been issued after that conference states: "[W]eak underwriting standards, unsound risk management practices, increasingly complex and opaque financial products, and consequent excessive leverage combined to create vulnerabilities in the system."

In his book *Secrets of the Temple*,[37] William Greider gives an example on an alternative to leverage: "As a banker who understood leverage, (Marriner) Eccles[38] argued that the government could have more impact on housing through direct spending." The funding for public housing, he said, "was just a drop in the bucket so far as need went." Washington, Eccles suggested, could stimulate millions of housing starts by:

- "Knocking a percentage point off mortgage interest rates, and
- Providing government guarantees to induce lenders to make long-term mortgages."[39]

Buying one's own house is an investment, provided that he or she is not doing it for speculation. Investments have a return. For the typical household, leveraged investments are risky; when leverage filters largely into consumption, with too much money chasing a finite amount of goods, it pushes up inflation. In principle,

- Productive investments have a longer term return.
- Debt incurred to cover shortfall in income and in sovereign budgets has only a short-term effect, leaving behind it a liability.

Leveraging makes a mockery of financial staying power, and it obliges the speculator: person, company, or sovereign to shorten his or her horizon. Money is always invested. Somebody is financing somebody else's leveraging by extending credit and assuming counterparty risk. The more leveraged an entity is, the less the likelihood that it can face up to its financial obligations, particularly in times of crisis.

When adversity hits, a leveraged entity enters a phase of *reverse leverage*, a vicious cycle of disposing assets at fire-sale prices to confront margin calls or the demand to repay loans that have become due. Reverse leverage is particularly dangerous because speculators have assumed an inordinate amount of debt to capitalize on a projected upside in securities and commodities prices. But the doors of risk and return are adjacent and identical. Paraphrasing Mao: "The market is the sea. We are only the fish in it."

In the banking industry, leverage is often associated with large off-balance sheet liabilities as well as questionable corporate governance. Mid-May 2012, an article in the *Financial Times* put it this way: "Chesapeake Energy ticks all of the boxes for a company that investors should beware of." The article stated that according to analysts Chesapeake will have to go further to bring its debts under control. "Chesapeake is fixable," said Jon Wolff of ISI Group, (but) management needs to make clear that reducing leverage is a much bigger concern than funding growth."[40]

A record with leveraging was set in 1998: 5000 percent, when Long-Term Capital Management (LTCM) crashed. That crisis was averted at the twelfth hour through the intervention of the New York Federal Reserve, which brought LTCM investors into the rescue plan. This 5000 percent leverage was a high water mark in the 1990s, but today, it is in its way to become rather common.

The LTCM experience says Henry Kaufman, the economist, has shown that international diversification worked in bull markets but failed in bear markets.[41] More recently, alert analysts have detected broad structural changes in the financial marketplace due to the wide use of derivatives and the increasingly global nature of investments. Both have made small game of diversification—which is a sound principle, but it has been turned on its head.

In theory, the highly leveraged LTCM reduced its risks by scattering its investments among many markets and types of instruments. But in practice as anxiety began to spread through the global landscape (after Thailand's currency collapse in the summer of 1997) these instruments and markets correlated with one another. Prices fell and businesses failed all along the Pacific Rim. In response, by early 1998, investors worldwide began seeking a haven in US Treasuries.

The gamblers had leveraged themselves expecting a windfall of profits, but what they got was a torrent of red ink. This has plenty of similitude to governments loading themselves with debt and granting unsustainable entitlements to please the voters, then penalizing these same voters through austerity measures. Sovereigns gear themselves up to pay the bills of the nanny state, and by so doing, they hurt the common citizen.

One of the risks with leverage, particularly with high gearing, is that it becomes addictive leading to the pyramiding of debt. Sovereigns, companies, and households get deeper into debt to live beyond their means. That's the mentality of the State Supermarket[42] into which has drifted western democracy toward economic and social chaos. Shakespeare had given the right answer when in one of his plays *Polonius* advised his son: "Neither a borrower nor a lender be" (let alone a leveraged borrower).

Bringing leverage under lock and key is good advice for people, companies, and sovereigns particularly in times of "risk-on." Organizations, and society at large, are misguided by the existence of several fallacies about the practice of gearing. Here are three examples:

Leverage suggests that one is clever enough to use a tool that multiplies his or her financial power.

Such frequently heard bad advice does not even mention the fact that leverage weakens one's financial *staying power*, and this is true in practically any case. Debt has to be repaid. The alternative is bankruptcy.

Using leverage is something to boast about, not to conceal.

This type of argument conveniently forgets that who steadily uses leverage, particularly high leverage, becomes credit-impaired, and the day comes when the mountain of debt drives a country, company, or family against the wall.

After you file for bankruptcy protection you are viewed as good credit risk, because you become debt-free.

Bankruptcies, including filings for bankruptcy protection, reduce an entity's creditworthiness. Its credit rating plummets. Serious banks don't court borrowers who have caused them (or their competitors) to lose money in the past, though derelict banks may.

High leverage has disastrous effects on financial stability. The longer term value of a dominant currency should be questioned when the central bank of their jurisdiction keeps its printing presses busy to pay for huge sovereign deficits. Still, several central banks in the so-called *advanced economies* have violated their charter by pursuing unconventional policies: quantitative easing (QE), pseudo-assets purchases, and large liquidity provisions to self-wounded big banks, without accounting for the fact that "more of the same" implies:

- Destabilizing the currency, and
- Decreasing the efficiency of expected results.

Like any other leverage, the rapid printing of paper money becomes addictive—and it debases the currency. It is wrong to believe that the only challenge is technical: to provide hundreds of millions of perfect copies of a product that is difficult to fake but cheap to make. The real challenge is financial stability, which has taken a leave. Since the gold standard has been repealed, there is no strict formula on how to taper this massive money printing process which has become one of the casino society's better known follies.[43]

1.6   Tic, Tac, Tic, Tac ... The New Bubble Builds Up

"Money exists not by nature but by law," said Aristotle. Well before Aristotle, the Laws of Solon (Section 1.1) have been the first on record to target monetary stability. The lawmaker of ancient Athens was thinking for the long term. By contrast, sovereigns who have been leveraging themselves are short-termists. They are thinking too much of their present problems and too little or not at all of the future.

The public debt of Japan currently stands at 240 percent its gross domestic product, largely due to over 20 years of continuing but unsuccessful efforts to jump start the economy. Italy's public debt is 127 percent of GDP, that of the United States 110 percent of GDP with the raising of the nation's debt ceiling having become an almost annual business.

Spending is running ahead of income. Even if taxes rise and rise what enters into government coffers is not enough to cover bloated budgets. Both sprawling bureaucracies and entitlements are fed through tax money. In the United States, aside federal taxes there are state and city taxes. A major part of city taxes is earmarked for financing the school system. But as education has become an increasingly costly chapter, in some states, the citizens have voted to put a ceiling on local taxes.

Politicians are lying when they say that the government provides "free" education and "free" health service. The public is not dupe; it knows that there is no "free" lunch. As Thomas Jefferson (1743–1826) had it: "He who permits himself to tell a lie often finds it much easier to do it a second and third time, till at length it becomes habitual. He tells lies without attending to it, and truths without the world's believing him."[44]

Free education is a lie even when taxes are not rising because, helped by banks, school districts now use derivatives to leverage themselves and mortgage their future. In the process, they are feeding the next bubble. Few school districts have an idea of how to control their expenses, let alone how to be in charge of risk. If they had, they would not embrace derivative financial instruments as a way to ease their budgetary constraints.

Let me offer some hindsight prior to going on with this case study. Since 1990, the use of derivatives increased the complexity of the financial system, and nowadays, risk controllers who know what they are doing are very few. The crisis of 2007 which is still around has been promoted by instruments like collateralized debt obligations (CDOs) and credit default swaps (CDSs) which (during the 2007–2014 crisis) held many surprises for their issuers and users because of:

- Unexpected traps associated to the way the instrument itself has been designed,
- Pricing structures chosen for providing high commissions, but paying lip service to the pricing of risk, and
- Instruments which are tough to unwind and become even more complex and opaque as they travel through intermediaries.[45]

Instead of being financed through taxes and keeping their expenses at or below their income, American school authorities started to issue a swelling volume of leveraged bonds to supplement tax money. School administrations don't know, and therefore cannot appreciate, the intricacies of derivatives. If they could understand the risks being involved, they would not even touch the new generation of derivatives designed by investment banks for the US school system (of all places).

Experts say that in the background of this silly policy of leveraging then crashing the educational system lies the fact that following the 2007 bust of the real estate market, property tax revenues (largely used to fund schools) have declined. As fiscal controls have been imposed by voters on educational boards, schools searched for and found some "innovative" but highly risky solution to financing. California led the pack.

In 2011 Poway Unified, a San Diego educational district, issued over $100 million worth of *capital appreciation* bonds to finance previously planned projects. These are similar to zero-coupon bonds; hence, the district does not need to start repaying interest (or reimbursing capital) until 2033. But the risk is enormous. To attract investors and compensate for payment deferral, such bonds are paying double-digit interest rates with the result that:

- When the bond is repaid, the total bill will be some *10 times* the initial loan, and
- It's a sure bet that the school district will not be able to confront its obligations; most likely it will go bust.

At present time, it is not possible to know how widely such a crazy 20-year school bond has spread. The Securities and Exchange Commission (SEC) stated, in early August 2012, that the $2.7 trillion municipal bond market is extremely opaque. The Poway case, however, is far from being unique. Others (albeit less extreme leveraging schemes) exist at several San Diego school authorities, and they are also based on derivatives:

- Oceanside Unified has borrowed $30 million, but will need to repay $280 million (including interest),
- Escondido Union, borrowed $27 million but faces $247 million repayments, and
- San Diego Unified, borrowed $164 million, and will have to repay an astronomical (for school district) $1.2 billion.[46]

An important question is how fast this sort of dynamite bond will establish a national pattern in the United States and then spread over the global economy. In some states, like Michigan, public entities are banned from capital appreciation bonds, but not every state takes that attitude. Lack of firm rules to stop high stakes gearing leaves residents, investors, and school districts exposed to a nasty future shock of a bubble whose bust may be the most destructive ever.

What can be stated with certainty is that the culture of spending more than one has and going beyond the limits of rational behavior has taken roots because there is money to be made in decadence (Chapter 2). As new huge debt is created, the crisis moved seamlessly from US mortgages to other domains. Today the most important is the high indebtedness of sovereigns. But school districts and companies, too, compete in bubble making.

A recent case is the Facebook Bubble. The price/earnings (P/E) multiple is a good indicator of two things in one shot: how much a given equity is sought after, and what's the state of the economy. By contrast, a way to look at a growing bubble is how a company's workers are valued in terms of annual income.

- Each Goldman Sachs banker masters an impressive $1.7 million; a high level.
- Googlers were valued at $12.9 million each when the company was floated.
- From secretaries up to the boss, each Facebook worker was worth $31.25 million when the company became public.

This is a bubble, given that what bubbles have in common is the drive to extremes. No wonder that Facebook's capitalization fell by half a couple of months after the initial public offer (though it subsequently recovered part of the loss). One does not need to be a Taoist to appreciate the dictum: "Don't go to the extreme; if you do so you will fall."

There is a risk of contagion with to bursting bubbles. Researchers at the University of California, Berkeley, and Geneva's Graduate Institute who looked at 20 currency crises in industrial economies (between 1959 and 1993), found that a crisis in one country increases the probability of crises in others. When an economy sours, its trading partners pay a price, as demand for their exports falls. Contagion also spreads through financial channels transmitting severe losses in income and unpaid bank loans across borders.

In the globalized economy, indirect links via common creditors play a crucial role. In the late 1990s, Japanese banks had lent to companies in booming Thailand and Indonesia. When Thailand went bust, Japanese banks found out the hard way that their Thai customers would never repay their loans. To compensate, they cut credit to Indonesia and other economies. As contagion spread engulfing the "Asian tigers," economists said that abruptly retracting credit was reckless.

Bubbles follow a similar pattern with more pronounced financial and trading characteristics than other types of contagion. Subprimes sold by American banks to European banks brought a massive amount of unstable debt across the Atlantic; the European banks' fuses blew shortly after the subprimes bubble burst in the United States. As these examples show, speculation, leveraging, and greed are the viruses infecting financial systems and feeding bubbles. Weak regulation in one country promotes contagion between countries, and it fails in its duty of punching the bubble when it is still small.

End Notes

1. D'Andrezel L. Extraits des Auteurs Grecs, Paris: Imprimerie et Librairie Classiques; 1836.
2. Zarlenga S. The lost science of money. Valatie, NY: American Monetary Institute; 2002.
3. Cohen R. Athènes, Une Democracie. Paris: Fayard; 1936.
4. Apart from the introduction of money, he also significantly reduced the farmers' debts.
5. *Anglo-Saxon* is still another name for it, not necessarily an accurate one.
6. Antony CS. Wall street and the rise of Hitler. San Pedro, CA: CSG Publishers; 2002.
7. The way a Bloomberg News ticker had it on September 26, 2012, there are as well 100 hidden billionaires in Africa, generally considered to be a poor continent.
8. This means the gross domestic product of a country divided by the number of citizen living in this country.
9. UBS CIO WM Research. Equity markets, August 23, 2012.
10. In this section, we will only be concerned with incomes.
11. Unless otherwise indicated, "dollars" refer to US dollars.
12. UBS CIO WM Research, August 23, 2012. The posted per capita income averages are as of 2009 (latest available statistics).
13. See also in Chapter 10 for the huge differences existing between jurisdictions in health care costs (also on a per capita basis).
14. "Common sense is the most widely distributed quality," says a French proverb, "that's why each of us has so little."
15. The Economist, September 15, 2012.
16. Chorafas DN. Globalization's limits. Conflicting national interests in trade and finance. London: Gower; 2009.
17. The Economist, September 8, 2012.

18. This is in no way a critique of the Dodd—Frank Act which became necessary as the banking industry turned itself into a king-size casino. But as Campenella wrote centuries ago, the rules must be few and clear. Large paper volumes decrease the rules' impact. They don't improve it.

19. See also Section 1.1.

20. Rachman G. Financial Times, August 7, 2012.

21. *Idem.*

22. Geithner was up to early 2009, when he became US Treasury Secretary, the president of the Federal Reserve Bank of New York, and he is debited with the moral hazard of refilling the treasury of big banks with public money.

23. Financial Times, February 7, 2013.

24. Perkins J. Confessions of an economic hit man. Penguin, London: Plume Books; 2004.

25. *Idem.*

26. *Idem.*

27. The Geneva Association. The four pillars. No. 50, March 2012.

28. Particularly those who have a job and take as hostages those who haven't.

29. In 2013 Egypt run by the Moslem Brotherhood, supposedly a theocratic party, massive rapes have become commonplace. They did not happen under Mubarak.

30. Chorafas DN. Household finance, adrift in a sea of red ink. London: Palgrave/Macmillan; 2013.

31. As an example of swollen bureaucracy, the US Home Security, a department instituted under George W. Bush, allegedly has 315,000 people work for it.

32. The Economist, June 16, 2012.

33. Bloomberg News, September 5, 2012.

34. Roubini was joined in this warning by Niall Ferguson, of Harvard University, who warns that Europe is perilously close to repeating the disasters of the 1930s.

35. Financial Times, June 6, 2012. Three months after this article was published, the ECB did it again with a September 6, 2012 announcement of the OMT policy and "unlimited" sovereign bond buying program (Chapter 2).

36. Chorafas DN. An introduction to derivative financial instruments. New York, NY; McGraw-Hill; 2008.

37. Greider W. Secrets of the temple. New York: NY: Touchstone/Simon & Schuster; 1987.

38. Chairman of Federal Reserve in the 1930s under the Roosevelt Administration.

39. At the time, home mortgages were limited to 7 or 10 years which meant high monthly payments.

40. Financial Times, May 18, 2012.

41. International Herald Tribune, December 8, 1998.

42. Kratos Bakalis.

43. De la Rue (which literally means "from the street") is one of the foremost companies printing money for central banks eager to rapidly increase the monetary base in their jurisdiction, no matter which may be the consequences. With plants in Britain, Kenya, and Sri Lanka de la Rue switched to a 7-day week to meet deadlines and chartered 27 Boeing 747s to deliver the freshly printed bank notes (The Economist, August 11, 2012).

44. Filton RA (editor). Leadership: quotations from the military tradition. Boulder, Colorado: Westview; 1990.

45. In early September 2008, largely because of underwriting CDSs, AIG was exposed to an estimated $2.7 *trillion* worth of perilous financial contracts. Its luck has been that it was "too big to fail." Therefore, almost at the twelfth hour it was bailed out by the US government, using taxpayers' money for the rescue.

46. Financial Times, August 10, 2012.

2 Kingdoms of Debt

2.1 Debt and Growth

To assure their election or re-election, several EU chiefs of state have been repeatedly saying that (by using a magic wand) they will relaunch growth and wipe out public debt, all in one go. There exists an interesting precedent to those statements of "having your pie and eating it, too" dating back to François Mitterrand shortly after he was elected the President of the French Republic.

Jacques Delors, then minister of Finance, was sent by Mitterrand to Washington to measure how and how well the Reagan Administration was relaunching the US economy. Donald Regan, then Treasury secretary, told him that a great boom was lying ahead in America. But when Delors went to New York where he met Anthony Solomon, president of the New York Fed, and asked him what the outlook was for the American economy, Solomon told him precisely the opposite: The New York Fed was predicting a contraction.

Delors reported his findings to Mitterrand and the latter chose the optimistic version, announcing that his government would pursue an expansionist policy since the American economy would be booming. The US Treasury, to his opinion, had given irrevocable assurances. This was a gamble; the forecast of Solomon not of Regan proved to be the right one. The French government went ahead anyway and got clobbered. Thereafter, the franc was devalued 3 times.

"Growth" deprived of fundamentals, and being largely based on theories, does not deliver anything tangible. It does not lead to unambiguous and uncontroversial guidance or benchmarks. Trying to kill two birds with one well-placed stone may cost dearly to the economy. Solomon understood what really lays ahead, though the US Treasury secretary and the French president did not. *Understanding* is the name of the game, prior to:

- Saying big words,
- Believing one's own comments, and
- Reaching the wrong decisions.

Hopes that things will fall in line on their own accord because one has been selected as president are a harbinger to potentially disastrous developments. A recent example of inconsistent crisis management has been the often repeated call for joint liability on government debt by European Union member states through *eurobonds*, which is explicitly ruled out in the Lisbon Treaty. Article 125

Public Debt Dynamics of Europe and the US. DOI: http://dx.doi.org/10.1016/B978-0-12-420021-0.00002-6

forbids joint liability for public debt, and article 123 forbids the funding of such debt by the European Central Bank (ECB).

If unsound and undocumented "solutions" to the growth crisis are left aside—and the Mitterrand example talks volumes on why they should be discarded—then draconian measures for debt reduction will come as the only option for insolvent sovereign debtors. Debt keeps growth away, but all alone repayment will not restore trust on a longer term basis.

- Austerity measures are necessary to stop the debt hydra's heads from multiplying is one thing, and
- Labor restructuring as well as other measures to spur growth through a consistent effort over the medium to longer term are just as necessary.

This effort to relaunch the economy should be properly planned from the start, and it is inseparable from the needed sharp reduction in public debt. A mid-2012 study by Bloomberg has shown the interesting relationship between public debt and the economic growth in a dozen countries, over the last couple of decades. A public debt below 40 percent of GDP is no problem and is normally accompanied by high growth rates of the economy. Notice that in many developing countries, public debt is below that rate.

By contrast, an increase of public debt from 40 to a maximum of 67 percent can temporarily boost economic expansion, but the effect is not lasting in all of the cases studied by Bloomberg. Its weight turns the economy into negative territory. Moreover, as the public debt grows beyond 67 percent, there is a clear negative correlation to growth: the higher the debt, the lower the real growth rate.

François Hollande should take note because the French economy has passed to 90 percent of GDP benchmark in public debt. Another very interesting Bloomberg finding is that in cases the debt exceeds 95 percent of GDP, there has never been a lasting growth rate of the economy. In those cases, all growth rates above 2 percent had their origin in excessive money printing or massive external help—and were followed by deep recessions.

A wise statesman, who wants to leave a name in history, would learn from his own travails, as well as those of others, to avoid repeating the same mistakes in relaunching the economy. The economy's contraction and citizens suffering are an inevitable consequence of past excesses. The question is whether it is better to suffer it in the short term or continue living in a morose economic environment in the long run. Neither the central bank nor foreign governments can rescue a country's economy without the latter's:

- Restructuring, and
- Debt repayment.

Both are by more than 80 percent, political not technical decisions. The other 20 percent is cookbook economics, with academics divided between those who are believers in "this" or "that" past theory (Keynesian, monetarism, Austrian school) and those who have become doubters. The way an economist had it: "... the crisis has made the academic establishment fractious and vulnerable. Highly credentialed economists now publicly mock each other's ignorance and foolishness."[1]

Past economic theories cannot provide guidance at a time when and with only a few exceptions,[2] in the stagnating economies of the West the total debt to GDP ratio keeps on increasing. It does not take a genius to understand that this is very bad for the future. Neither is the *public* debt to GDP ratio revealing the *total* depth of a nation's debt. Summing up sovereign, corporate, and household debt,[3] in order of magnitude in 2011, the 10 most indebted countries have been:

- Japan at 460 percent of GDP[4]
- Portugal, 370 percent of GDP
- Spain, 360 percent of GDP
- Britain, 325 percent of GDP
- France, 320 percent of GDP
- Canada, 315 percent of GDP
- Italy, 310 percent of GDP
- United States, 270 percent if GDP
- Greece, 270 percent of GDP[5]
- Germany, 240 percent of GDP[6]

Though Germany has nearly half the *total* debt exposure to GDP when compared to Japan, the difference is a mere 12 percent when compared to total American and total Greek debt. There goes the myth that Germany can pull all the overleveraged countries of the EU out of the abyss into which they have fallen[7] and, following that, lead them to a garden of roses.

An important criterion in evaluating the risks associated with the 10 most indebted countries in the world is their ability to refinance debt coming to maturity. For totally different reasons Germany, the United States, and Japan have (at least at the present time) no real problem with rollovers. To this small group might be added Britain and Canada—while the other five: Portugal, Spain, France, Italy, and Greece are at razor's edge.[8]

It is improper to accuse only Greece for economic mismanagement when—in terms of total debt—the other four Mediterranean countries are worst off. Curiously enough, the amount of money that, in the first 4 months of 2012, the largest Euroland countries alone needed to refinance more than euro 370 billion ($500 billion) was mastered without a trauma in market psychology, in spite of the challenge which it has represented. Let's wait and see what happens when to the end of 2014 Italy is confronted with bond redemptions of euro 426 billion ($564 billion), with Spain coming right behind.

A long list of factors tends to suggest that no matter what some chiefs of state may be saying in contemplating conditions favorable to growth, these will not show up till the economy can find a new base. In the mean time, increases in public and other debt contribute even more uncertainty in a word beset by doubt, while delays in deciding which way to go work to the detriment of western nations because:

- Risks are hovering ominously over their economies, and
- Indecision plays dirty games with excessive public and private debt, particularly at a time of global economic crisis.

Chinese economic growth may be slowing down somewhat, but it still leaves the American, European, and Japanese economies in the dust. In a lecture which he gave on January 18, 2013 to Assya, the asset manager, in Monte Carlo, Dominique Strauss-Kahn, the former president of IMF, expressed the opinion that the Chinese leadership is worried—and this for two main reasons:

- Capital is leaving China, and
- There is a risk the country splits into two: one part centered on Shanghai, the other around Beijing.

Strauss-Kahn attributed this to American politics and a strategic plan targeting the country's division into two weaker constituencies not necessarily friendly to one another. It needs no explaining that this will work to the detriment of the Chinese zone of influence, as well as of global growth. (It may as well correlate with the drain of capital from China, as sometimes investors have an extra sense politicians are lacking.)

What about debt and growth in the European continent? A study by UBS takes as proxy Swiss exports. In a year-on-year comparison, in 2011, Swiss exports to Europe stagnated. To the contrary, exports to many emerging markets have enjoyed double-digit growth rates.

Still, today, less than 20 percent of Swiss goods exports are targeted for Brazil, China, India, Russia, and other ex-China Asian emerging markets, but this share is increasing as these countries' economic momentum is far from being saturated. Swiss export growth to developing economies has outstripped export growth to Europe.

But even Switzerland's economy, which has a reputation of being very robust compared to those of other European countries, is not invulnerable because of steady rise in health care costs and in pensions. As far as entitlements are concerned, the same challenges practically confront every western nation, and therefore, failing to implement overdue reforms could have drastic effects on the economy (more on the disparity of health care costs are discussed in Chapter 10).[9]

2.2 Debt and Decline

According to several sociologists, nations decline because of the lobbying power of distributional coalitions, which represent special-interest groups. Their growing influence fosters economic inefficiency and inequality, suggests Mancur Olsen.[10] Eventually, both inefficiency and rising inequality become powerful motors of public debt.

Like any other organization, nations decline because they are living beyond their means over long stretches of time. This is precisely what is happening nowadays in the western world—specifically in the European Union and the United States. Worst yet, there is no plan on how to come up from under and get out of the debt crisis.

The European people and their elected officials are wondering what would happen *if*, as the crisis intensifies, one or more countries leave the Euroland—or the currency union simply disintegrates. Even if Euroland's structures do not collapse in the near future, the prevailing policy of muddling through (see Chapter 3) is more reactive than proactive. This makes the problem of finding a solution very complex. The same is true of establishing the basis for a new departure.

"... It will be harder to kick the can down the road," wrote Nouriel Roubini, the economist, "A few eurozone members may need to coercively restructure their debts and even consider exiting the currency union... Markets in the US may become more concerned about the political gridlock that perpetuates unsustainable twin deficits."[11] By 2013 at latest, we could face:

- "A double-dip recession in the US,
- A disorderly scenario in the Eurozone, and
- A hard landing in China."[12]

The slope of *decline* increases as debt, which feeds a mare's nest of economic and financial problems, becomes second nature, and the eradication of bad spending habits is no more a strictly national or even regional project. Neither it is possible to reach valid solutions by accepting *a priori* that sacred cows will not be spared the clean-up effort; for instance, health care and pension costs paid fully from public money. Everything across the board should be on the table, subject to restructuring and to budget cuts.

Short of a holistic solution limiting expenses below the level of sovereign income, the economy first of Euroland and then of America and Britain will risk collapsing in whole or in part. At an interview, he gave to Bloomberg News on January 25, 2012 in Davos, Switzerland, during the World Economic Forum, Roubini said that Euroland's debt problems are spreading to the core. That's to Germany, because he would consider France a peripheral country.

According to this line of reasoning, to help the economy of the old continent recover, there should be euro/dollar parity. The downside is the risk of American-style leverage in Europe, trying to correct the ills of debt with more debt—which is evidently a very risky strategy with lots of unexpected consequences. One of them is that of revising downward economic forecast for economic growth.

The concept of euro/dollar parity is challenging, particularly so as it is a serious error to forget about the impact of exchange rates. One of the effects of globalization has been that, other things equal, a cheap currency imports inflation. As Chapter 1 brought to the reader's attention, globalization has helped up to a point, but as (since the start) it has lacked guideposts and limits, it turned into a runaway train:

- Decimating jobs in western countries,[13] and
- Prodding western citizens to rely on cheaper imports.

Don't count on the G20 and its heralded aims of global coordination. To the opinion of Gideon Rachman, "...Efforts to rescue the world economy will be afflicted by a perilous political paradox. The more that international co-operation is needed, the harder it will be to achieve."[14] Despite G20, every country is looking inward; neither is there much purpose of searching around for global leadership. The world is divided into two groups:

- Countries which have become *consumer only*, financing their consumption through debt, and
- Countries which are, to a large extent, *producers only* and exporters, a strategy which has global consequences.

The almost exponential rise in industrial output of emerging economies has been fed by the growing western economies indebtedness. According to Goldman Sachs, however, the decade of the BRIC may become history. While China might have a soft landing, India and Brazil (particularly the former) are facing major economic problems (Chapter 12)—while Russia looks like entering a time of political instability.

Several economists now suggest that another sort of déclinisme in the offing. The trend toward a multipolar world which manifested itself with the projection that emerging markets will be eventually contributing 75 percent of global output which, by now, looks like an overestimate. If historical precedence is of any value, there are fewer and fewer reasons for being so cheerful about developing economies.

At end of the nineteenth century, the world's biggest manufacturer was Britain. Two world wars bent Britain's economic, financial, and industrial might. A great deal of deindustrialization has happened in the Thatcher years (1980s). Britain lost its markets abroad. The British industry (like the French and other western industrial economies) also got penalized through an inordinate amount of social costs. This wrong-way policy is now infiltrating developing countries.

The changes referred to in the preceding paragraph are not going to happen overnight, but neither will they take several decades. Things move faster these days, thanks to global communications while, for their part, western labor unions do their best to export the western brand of entitlements to developing countries. By so doing, they are raising the social costs of companies in developing countries.

After the Iron Curtain fell, Renault, the French automobile manufacturer, bought control of Dacia, Romania's automaker. This gave it access to low-cost labor which showed all the way to the car's price tag. Renault profited handsomely by exporting low-cost Dacias in the different countries it operates till, prodded by their French colleagues, Romanian workers at Dacia went on strike:

- Social costs significantly increased, and
- The cost of Dacia's production went up.[15]

Cross-border penalizing through a movement, which at the base raises labor costs in developing countries, has a chance of being more effective than betting on technology to revolutionize the production process and bring western manufacturing costs down. Theoretically, technology does not know frontiers. Practically, new ideas and discoveries, which have been a very important cause of sustained productivity (hence economic growth), originate from an intensive basic research effort which nowadays has declined. In the last couple of decades of the twentieth century and in the first one-and-a half decades of the twenty first:

- Innovation waned, and
- The rate of invention slowed because of lack of funding related to the accumulation of sovereign debt.

In retrospect, the high point of new ideas and new inventions was the late nineteenth and first half of the twentieth. Among them, they produced electric light, the electric motor, the internal combustion engine, telephony, radio, phonograph, television, refrigerators, vacuum cleaner, man-made chemicals, artificial fertilizers, as well as the airplane, computers, telecommunications, new pharmaceuticals, (the basics of) space exploration and systems of mass production, mass distribution, and logistics.

Both individually and collectively, the practical applications of these inventions transformed lives. In the late twentieth and early twenty-first centuries, by contrast, apart from the seemingly "magical" services of Internet and the mobile phone, life in broad material terms is not so different from what it was in 1950. Biotechnology has made plenty of promises, but expectations are still below of what it was thought it could deliver. While there may always come a major breakthrough, this is still expected. We shall see.

2.3   The Debt Reduction Pact for Europe, Real or Fancy?

Debt's ugly progeny is inequality, injustice, and poverty, yet these same issues are called upon to justify, even legitimize, acts of financial trickery by sovereigns who do not want to live according to their income. This is, of course, indefensible but it has curiously found a widening circle of adherents. Euroland's Mediterranean countries, the so-called Club Med, and the United States are examples.

Countries featuring chronic budgetary deficits justify them by making reference to social pressures which are behind their inability to observe budgetary constraints. This is merely another manifestation of the more fundamental problem of irresponsibility in governance. Social demands are infinite, but since the resources we have at our disposal to satisfy them are finite, the responsibilities a government assumes should not exceed the resources to see them through—even if this means we have to do something "unpleasant" like:

- Working harder,
- Sell something we own, or
- Go without some of the entitlements.

Getting in debt to buy time in making tough and urgent decisions attests to a much greater pain: that of a head-on collision with reality. This spirit also underlines requests and propositions to pay other peoples' debts to be a "nice chap." Here is a real-life example on how this wrong-way strategy is used to sugar-coat poorly planned initiatives.

In 2011, the German Council of Economic Experts thought to be an opinion leader among German economists, presented its plan for a *Debt Reduction Pact for Europe* (DRPE). According to this plan, the debt of Euroland member states above 60 percent of a jurisdiction's GDP would be financed by common bonds, under strict conditionality.

While so far DRPE has remained a theoretical paper, precisely because nearly everyone understands that a "strict conditionality" clause is not going to be fulfilled, it is quite instructive to dwell into its logic to learn from its fallacies. To start with, it does not make any sense to sign treaties, like the EU's Lisbon Treaty, and then throw them to the waste basket for ill-conceived "rescue" purposes. Second, the rush to come up with money for Euroland's profligate member states has significantly reduced the incentives to:

- Cut expenditures,
- Balance the budget,
- Pay the outstanding loans, and
- From now on maintain sound public finances.

Third, the 60 percent of GDP criterion makes funny reading. The way this DRPE proposal wants it, the public debt of every Euroland country above 60 percent of GDP will be shared. *If* this becomes the rule, *then* for every country every year there will be a deficit of over 60 percent to be mutualized. This is like giving all governments carte blanche to go on "as usual." Let's recall that in the 1993–2003 time frame, when Euroland membership was decided, *creative accounting*[16] had a field day.

- In Italy and Portugal gimmickry stood at 8 percent,
- In Spain it was somewhat below 8 percent, and
- In Greece it was well above it.[17]

Instead of upholding the important link between liability and risk control,[18] the proposal by the German Council of Economic Experts is opening the valves of the former, while dropping the latter by the way side. This means eliminating altogether responsibility for fiscal discipline. Over and above that come different schemes for an extensive mutualization of liabilities resulting from sovereign debts, which are made by magic to disappear through the debt reduction fund and *other* gimmicks.

It is not only German taxpayers who revolt against such unwarranted plans to legalize a *transfer union*, with the result that money will freely run from those who work and produce to those who enjoy the sunshine and simply consume, smaller countries, too, are fed up. "Taxpayers here are extremely angry," said Timo Soini, the leader of True Finn, whose party got 19 percent of the vote in the last election, "There are no rules on how to leave the euro but it is only a matter of time. Either the south or the north will break away because this currency straitjacket is causing misery for millions and destroying Europe's future. It is a total catastrophe."[19]

Warnings were also echoed by Miapetra Kumula-Natri, chairman of the Finnish parliament's Grand Committee on Europe, who said bailout fatigue is nearing its limit. She added that Finland can be pushed only so far: "There is a feeling on the street that there has to be a limit. I can't say whether it is 10 percent of GDP, or what. It's not written. But it is obvious that a small country can't help big countries eternally."[20]

What proposals and plans like DRPE aim to establish is an eternal nirvana for profligates—a permanent perpetual motion machine transferring money from Finland and other small Euroland member countries to much bigger ones like Italy and Spain. When Mario Monti went to Helsinki hat-in-hand to convince the Finns "to give," the world saw a country of 55 million people (third economy in Euroland) begging support from a country of 5.4 million people—but well-managed. When it becomes permanent, eleemosynary help is no more welcome by the donors.

Avoiding to throw money to the four winds, which means protecting the savings and pensions of hard-working people in the better managed Euroland member countries, is also synonymous to taking care of moral risk which abounds in Euroland. It does not look like the German Council of Economic Experts includes among its members experts in moral risk management. If this were the case, it would not have proposed that:

• The portion of the Euroland member states' sovereign debt that exceeds 60 percent of GDP would be gradually transferred to a Euroland-wide "debt redemption fund," and
• New bond issues by individual states would be *jointly* (!!!) guaranteed, with a member state's debt exceeding 60 percent of GDP being mutualized.

The more curious part of this fancy proposal is that at the end of the day the higher is a member country's debt ratio to its GDP, the larger the benefit it will derive through the *jointly* guaranteed debt. And the more economically sick a country is, the more it will featherbed in the covert bailout scheme. It did not occur to those who wrote the DRPE that money does not grow on trees. Where will the other Euroland countries find the money to feed the imaginary patient hand-to-mouth?

The pros say that this critique is not right because of DRPE's conditionality clause. But as already stated, this argument forgets that, as past experience documents, conditionality clauses are for the birds. Sovereign countries are not prone to accept conditions unless these are hard-wired in the loan; there is steady supervision of their budgetary chores and penalties which cannot be negotiated or overrun.[21] This is true whether we talk of bailout or mutualization of debt. The curious thing is that the authors of DRPE pride themselves that their proposed Pact:

• Envisages an extensive mutualization of debt over the next few years, and
• It does so without obliging Euroland member countries to relinquish enough of their national sovereign rights.

The second bullet is another sugarcoating. Most states believe that supervisory control clauses infringe national sovereignty. Their negative reaction also includes the case imposing a premium on a national tax and using that revenue for direct debt redemption as well as of pledging national gold and foreign currency reserves. As for DRPE's clause of ending mutualization should commitments not be met, with so much money already run under the bridge, this clause guarantees that DRPE never gets into action.

Other demands included in the same proposal are equally unrealistic. DRPE asks for collateral and that's precisely what it cannot get from a country whose public debt to GDP ratio is 123, the case of Italy. Even if the conditionality outlined in the proposal by the German Council of Economic Experts were fulfilled, what remains has many characteristics of a free lunch, and not because the majority of Euroland's member states have or are nearing a public debt above 60 percent of GDP.

Let me add this in conclusion: As annual deficits continue to weigh heavily on budgets of Eurolands' members, this 60 percent-to-GDP rule would mean that big spender governments can keep adding to their 60 percent and in return for their profligacy are offered an interminable motion machine with collective liability taking care of their mounting debts—no questions asked. In addition, as no rights of sovereignty would or could be transferred to European level under the DRPE proposal, there is no way to intervene in trimming the excesses of national budgets. That's not an economic pact. It's a Disneyland.

2.4 Outright Monetary Transactions Mean Debt to Infinity

On September 16, 2012, the ticker on Bloomberg News read: "Financial industry warns of *cliff effects*[22] in ECB's bond pricing." Ten days earlier, on September 6, when he announced the ECB's *Outright Monetary Transactions* (OMT) Mario Draghi stated that he is right with "unlimited" purchasing of bonds by highly indebted Euroland countries because his mission is to support the currency. He probably forgot about the cliff effects. Lapsus?

These two statements, by Draghi and by the financial industry, contradict one another. In addition, with OMT, the ECB positioned itself as *lender of last resort* for governments. The positive side is that, at least temporarily, this announcement reduced Euroland's tail risk and may be for some time it removed some of the contagion risk from the Greek bailout (but not from eventual Greek exit from the euro). There exist contradictory opinions on this "unlimited" bond intervention.

Spain and Italy have already been featherbedded by Euroland and the EU with the *Troubled Countries Relief Program* (TCRP) of June 28/29, 2012[23] as well as on-and-off buying of their bonds by the ECB. In one go, the ECB violated Articles 123 and 125 of the Treaty of the Functioning of the European Union (Lisbon Treaty) as well as its own.

Spain, whose banks are bleeding cash, has already benefited from a loan of up to euro 100 billion ($130 billion) authorized by Euroland's ministers of finance after talking a couple of times on the phone. Nobody really knows the depth of the abyss of the Spanish banking industry. Some estimates talk of euro 300 billion ($390 billion).[24]

All these disasters did not happen overnight. Chapter 7 will explain how the Spanish economy has been shaken by the bursting of the real-estate bubble, which pulled down the country's banking industry. As for budgetary overruns at sovereign level, the Spanish budget deficit is still alive and kicking, even if its rate of growth has been somewhat reduced.

Italy's economic situation is not much better than Spain's. For both, the only bright star in the horizon is that they benefit from the ECB benevolence without limits. Hopes that the Santa Klaus will be visiting daily got a boost when just 10 weeks after TCRP Draghi announced the OMT program—an intervention ECB's president considers as necessary because of "severe distortions" in the bond markets. Draghi added that:

- The country which wants to benefit from OMT must ask ESM for financial help,
- The ECB would only buy bonds with maturities of up to three years,
- The purchases would be "sterilized," meaning the central bank would mop up the extra liquidity that was created,[25] and
- The central bank would not have seniority over private creditors, thereby abandoning one of its privileges.

Draghi's action, which has not been based on a unanimous decision by the central bank's governing council, underlines the opacity and lack of an institutionalized mechanism for dealing with member states' debt crises. According to the ECB chief, troubled Euroland countries either could choose a full bailout or a precautionary program, adding that bond buying would include strict conditionality and would happen only in concert with the European Financial Stability Facility (EFSF) and the ESM—Euroland's bailout funds.

Jean-Claude Juncker, then head of Eurogroup (Euroland's council of finance ministers), commented that the meeting of the ECB's Governing Council went well and there was "no trouble." No reference was made to the fact that Jens Weidmann, president of Germany's Bundesbank, strongly criticized the sovereign bond buying plans and the central bank funding of state budgets by the ECB.[26]

This is not Draghi's opinion, who says that (to his viewpoint) he is strictly within his mandate to maintain price stability over the medium term. No assurance was given that these short-to-medium term sovereign bonds will not be exchanged some time later with long-term sovereign bonds in an ECB version of the Fed's "Twist." To cover itself from unavoidable slippages, reportedly the ECB would seek IMF involvement for:

- The design, and
- Monitoring of any aid program.

OMT may be a different ball game than TCRP and the suggested DRPE (Section 2.3), but all three share two facts: They definitely lack endgame characteristics, and they risk remaining "nothing but initials" if they don't find the torrent of money to have any effect on Euroland's economy. Pertinent has been the advice general George Marshall, the US Army's Chief of State in WWII, gave to the nuclear scientists who, at president's Roosevelt's request, met him to ask his opinion about the atomic bomb project.

Marshall asked the visiting scientists, "That projected factory of yours, how many nuclear bombs will it produce: One per week, per month or per year?" The scientists had not thought of this subject and found it difficult to answer this general's question. "Remember, gentlemen," Marshall said, "the power of the military rests on its ability to deliver." The same principle applies with the power of the central bank and with any other economic authority. There are six reasons why OMT may end up as a fiasco:

1. The "unlimited" bond buying policy to stabilize Italian and Spanish bond yields, raises German, Dutch, and Finnish fears over excessive money printing by ECB.

   It is nobody's secret that the ECB has been buying sovereign bonds since May 2010 through its Securities Markets Program (SMP). Supposedly it did so for monetary purposes but in reality to bring down yields of Italian and Spanish government bonds. With OMT, SMP is being closed. That leaves the RCB with a stock of debt worth euro 209 billion ($272 billion) which may be never paid.

   In addition, as far as bond yields stabilization is concerned, the ECB has not specified Italian and Spanish yield caps for its OMT program. This leaves open its commitment "to do what it takes" (read: to intervene without limits) in violation of Winston Churchill's principle that one does not jump into the sea to fight the sharks.

2. The Outright Monetary Transactions program of ECB cannot maintain order in troubled bond markets taking "sterilized" action by borrowing money from the banking industry at close to zero interest rates to fund these purchases.

   The statement that such "sterilization" will avoid major expansion of ECB's balance sheet, and associated monetization of debt in the near term, is unfounded. There are contradictions in it. In December 2011 and February 2012 with the long-term refinancing operation (LTRO), the ECB handed out to Euroland's banks more than euro 1 trillion ($1.30 trillion) to restructure their balance sheet and start lending. Instead, Spanish and Italian banks bought their government debt.[27]

3. Though right, OMT's "conditionality" clause cools down timid government efforts in highly indebted countries, dissuading them from asking for assistance.

   For a Euroland member state's debt to be considered "for purchase," that country must attach itself to an appropriate EFSF/ESM program. Such programs have strict fiscal targets and require structural reforms. The fact that the IMF will be included in designing the terms of conditionality is welcomed by many economists, but profligate countries don't like the IMF's intervention.

   Only after conditionality is met, the ECB will begin purchasing the sovereign's bonds in the secondary market, and it can terminate such purchases should the country fail to comply with the program's strict conditions. Or, alternatively, the "lender of last resort" judges that interest rates for the country have been brought in line with its objectives.[28]

4. In highly indebted countries and those in current disarray, there is no economic motor to get the economy moving again. Hence, it is doubtful they will ever buy back their bonds purchased by the ECB.

   As the economy of countries swimming in a sea of red ink goes down and down, the EFSF/ESM funds and newly minted money will also become damaged goods. The fiasco will be even greater if the ESM leverages itself, since its euro 500 billion fund is totally inadequate to confront a simultaneous bailout of

Italy and Spain. Private investors understand not only the magic of compounding long-term returns but also the tyranny of compounding risks.

High indebted countries are not being helped by the current Euroland-wide and global slowdown. In fourth quarter 2012 private sector economic activity contracted at the fastest rate since 3 years earlier France had the steepest drop in business and also, German economic statistics were negative. This defied ill-founded hopes that the ECB's unlimited bond buying plan would:

* Boost confidence, and
* Help reignite growth in the single currency's economic and industrial landscape.

"The eurozone downturn gathered further momentum in September, suggesting that the region suffered the worst quarter for three years," said Chris Williamson, chief economist at Markit. "We had hoped that the news regarding the ECB's intervention to alleviate the debt crisis would have lifted business confidence, but instead sentiment appears to have taken a turn for the worse, with businesses the most gloomy since early 2009 due to ongoing headwinds from slower global growth."[29]

5. The OMT plan could trip up on a number of implementation risks relating to both the profligate countries benefiting from it and those providing the funds, including the ECB.

Critics say that OMT has been poorly studied in terms of its design, benefits, shortcomings, implementation risks, and aftereffects. There exists as well exposure to political issues. An evident hurdle is Spanish politics. *If* OMT is to work, *then* Mariano Rajoy, the Spanish prime minister, has to quickly swallow his pride and that of his country, publicly accepting the need for a sovereign bailout in parallel to the banking bailout.[30]

To make matters bleaker, there exists as well an inherent inconsistency in ECB's stance. Would it really stop buying bonds from a country that fails to comply with stipulated conditions? *If* it does so, *then* the ECB would precipitate the market panic it intends to prevent. If it does not, it will collect a great lot of potentially unpayable debt. That dilemma adds to the tension between the ECB and the Bundesbank.

6. There is plenty of *moral risk* associated to the "unlimited" sovereign bond buying by the ECB.

Not long ago, 10-year Spanish bonds commanded over 7 percent interest rates. After ECB's OMT announcement, the rates fell well below 6 percent. The gap has been around 150 basis points. Investment banks and hedge funds who bought these bonds at more than 7 percent interest made a hefty profit by selling them. Has any supervisory authority investigated if there has been insider trading?

Indeed, there might have been a case of selling Spanish bonds to bring home profits as by September 17, 2012—a mere 11 days after Draghi's announcement —Spanish interest rates for 10-year bonds rose above 6 percent. Or, alternatively, the effect of Draghi's decision was ephemeral and did not leave much of a footprint in the market. Far from being a "masterstroke" that decision was another blip—a "solution" which cannot work in the long run. Neither can it really "help" highly indebted Euroland countries.

2.5 The End of ECB As We Knew It

"The Fed's effects (with QE3) are fading," read a financial news dispatch in late September 2012. "Fading" has anyway been the course many economists expected from the "new and improved" version of unlimited money printing by Ben Bernanke's Federal Reserve. Three months after that dispatch, in December 2012, came QE3.5 as substitute to the Fed's *Twist*.

Many economists suggested that by continuing the same medicine without practical results, Bernanke's reputation for competence is badly strained. As for the effects of the ECB's unlimited buying of (useless or devalued) sovereign issued by Euroland's profligates, we are still waiting to see if and when it becomes popular. Yet, at the time of its announcement it was hailed by many analysts as an "ideal solution."

The impact of "unlimited" profligate bond purchases by the ECB has been wearing out even before OMT handouts started, though the populist rhetoric (as well as the political and social risks) remain. So far politicians and central bankers have managed to avoid the storm of popular reaction which is, by all evidence, negative. Nobody wants to take the responsibilities for having the ball rolling. God, the father, is not the first in line, said an analyst. It's his son who dies on the cross.

Contrary to the years which followed the devastation of World War II, there is no Italian or Japanese miracle to lift these economies. In a way quite different from the Bernanke strategies fixed on printing money and spending, Draghi of ECB is opening his eyes. On February 15, 2013, he was quoted by Bloomberg News as having said that: In the eurozone you cannot create growth simply by inflating the budget—even for social reasons.

Quite an important element in defining Draghi's behavior as central banker is the position he is taking in regard to the ongoing *currency wars*. In a press conference on February 7, 2013, he issued a veiled rebuke to François Hollande, the French president, who a few days earlier had called for managed exchange rates.

"President Hollande. Well, we should always remember that the ECB is independent," Draghi said. "We heard all over the world now talking up, talking down currencies. The ultimate judgment of the effectiveness of this strategy is to see what markets make of these statements."[31]

Regarding euro's rise against the US dollar, Draghi commented that the central bank's mandate is to target inflation, or maintain price stability, not the exchange rate. It is no less true, however, that the strength of the euro has alarmed European politicians since a sustained rise could kill early signs that Euroland might return to growth in 2013. Not every Euroland chief of state, however, looks at the stronger euro with disdain. The Germans like it because:

• It keeps inflation in check, and
• Lowers the cost of imports,

while German competitiveness sees to it that a stronger euro's impact on exports is limited. Despite the interminable EU summit tourism and proliferation of those "summits" labeled "last chance," a common ground among the 17 on stronger or weaker euro has not yet been formal.[32]

Those participating to the "summits" are typically defensive and deprived of out-of-the box ideas. This makes hard to learn from past mistakes. Recent political developments have shown that the process of Euroland's integration has entered a phase of institutional stagnation, at least in the short to medium term. This:

- Brings under focus the questionable economic fundamentals, and
- Motivates the search for a free lunch by Euroland's big spender member states.

Tiny Slovenia is the new basket case. At Iron Curtain times, as part of Yugoslavia, Slovenia used to be the envy of Eastern Europe. In 1991, it declared independence from a disintegrating Yugoslavia, joining the European Union in 2004 and Euroland in 2007. At independence time, Slovenia was the richest of the former Yugoslav republics.

Times have changed, and so did the will to be ahead of the curve. Like the Club Med countries, Slovenia has been slow to reform and now seems to need Euroland's help to keep its banks afloat. Since 2007, and despite promises made, there has been remarkably little restructuring of Slovenia's labor market and of the banking system (which is primarily in public ownership). The privatization process itself was sluggish, and most importantly, living standards in this country of 2 million grew faster than productivity, resulting in:

- Loss of competitiveness, and
- A boom in public debt.

As bad loans proliferated in Slovenia's banking system, the government came up with a bailout plan equal to 11 percent of GDP, increasing the public deficit by an equal amount. In addition, like Spain, Slovenia has one of the European Union's most unsound pension systems. In 2011, a proposal to raise the retirement age to 65 was overwhelmingly defeated. Add to this excessive entitlements and what you get is a miniature version of Spain and Greece—as well as an expanded firefighter role for the ECB.

Since it is well-known that one misfortune never comes alone, Jens Weidmann has plenty of reasons in warning the ECB against buying "addictive" sovereign debt. When Draghi decided to massively buy "unlimited" amounts of worthless sovereign bonds (Section 2.4, OMT), he should have thought that Spain and Italy don't stand alone in the queue for handouts which, in modern parlance, have been called *monetary financing* (a misleading term).

It is indeed quite curious that, with the exception of the Bundesbank, no other of Euroland's central banks objected to this destabilization of the common currency through a policy which rather than "saving" the euro is killing the euro. Several analysts are now expressing the worry that by using blank checks the ECB may be limiting its own room for maneuver.

Blank checks by the ECB were the main reason why Jürgen Stark, known as a hawk in monetary policy, quit as the ECB's chief economist.[33] Former Bundesbank president Axel Weber, who had been front runner to succeed Jean-Claude Trichet at the ECB's pinnacle, also resigned in February 2012 in protest at the same policy.

Critics say that no matter how careful Draghi may be in building up his defenses, these defenses risk to crumble. For instance, he would not have taken the initiative to buy Italian and Spanish bonds if this was not a move Merkel had tacitly approved, allegedly giving her consent in exchange for having voted the *fiscal compact* by the parliament of Euroland's member states. If so, this was a very bad deal, indeed.

Aside the fact that Euroland's fiscal compact, Angela Merkel's darling, is nothing more than a beefed-up version of the penalties foreseen by the Stability and Growth Pact—which have never been applied—"unlimited" buying of sovereign bonds and fiscal compact bite one another. This reflects a contradiction embedded in Euroland's policies, many experts see as forerunner of huge problems to be confronted by the central bank.

Germans, Dutch, and Finns clearly face challenges with the direction the ECB has taken. Economists who care for financial stability and for the value of the currency warn that, as experience teaches, excessive hope that unlimited buying of sovereign bonds will solve Euroland's debt problem is bound to end in disappointment. This is particularly true when the profligates "hope" is that someone, with supposedly very deep pockets, to come along and pay the bills.

- The ECB does not have deep pockets.
- What it has is paper money which turns to ashes by irresponsible actions, and
- A failure due to uncontrollable common currency risk may well signal the end of ECB, as we knew it.

As we will see in Chapter 13, small Latvia had the political courage to take a different road to economic recovery: *Internal devaluation*, and after 3 years of steady effort, it succeeded in getting out of the tunnel. In Euroland, too, references have been made to the need for internal devaluation, but that issue has been discussed in a half-baked and unconvincing way.

The expectation of a strong decline in wages in Greece and Portugal was deceived, and by all evidence the same will happen in the case of Italy and Spain. Greece and Spain also have the highest levels of youth unemployment in Euroland, with more than 55 percent of under-25-year-olds in the labor force out of work in Spain and 61 percent in Greece. Neither have the EU's, ECB's, and IMF's calls to stimulate job creation by opening up some professional sectors been respected. The political backing is missing *as if* governments don't understand that attacking unemployment requires:

- Relaxing job protection,
- Reducing minimum wages,
- Abolishing wage indexation, and
- Rethinking and downsizing unemployment benefits.

Critics have also noted a sharp deterioration in markets' assessments of businesses' credit risk, particularly in Italy. Neither is there a pan-European agreement on which course to take. Italy and Spain don't like the internal devaluation solution having found that with the ECB's "unlimited" purchasing of sovereign bonds

Germany will, at the end of the day, be paying their bills even if German taxpayers lose their money in this transaction.

In addition, as long as Spanish and Italian banks can remain solvent, thanks to massive financial help by Euroland, they can obtain liquidity from the ECB which will continue buying highly risky bonds issued by these countries. The funny thing which defies sound lending practices is that these bonds can then be used as collateral for other ECB funds. That's the daisy wheel in ECB money.

Just as funny is the fact that financial markets have been cheered by the ECB's buying of short-term government debt, albeit on the condition that ailing governments first ask for help from Euroland's rescue funds. The euphoria of vulture funds, which make billions from this unprecedented mismanagement of European finances, is so great that some market players are pushing for LTRO III while others, the more sober, are unconvinced by the need for another LTRO, given that liquidity is no longer the main issue for banks.

Still another of the proposals made not long ago by commercial bankers is that the ECB can use more effectively its program to buy banks' covered bonds (debt backed by a pool of collateral, usually mortgages). Many analysts, however, look at this option as unlikely given that some banks have been buying back debt and repackaging it to pledge as collateral with the ECB—which is another version of the perpetual motion machine.

2.6 Still, the Big Short Is Europe

Mid-April 2012, John Paulson, the only hedge fund manager who made it big by betting on the 2007 debacle of the subprimes,[34] said, "The new big short is Europe."[35] In half a dozen words he described Europe's plight and his strategy for the next couple of years. Paulson is not alone in following that line of thinking. Josef Stiglitz of Columbia University also says that Europe's window of opportunity (to put its house right) is closing.

What Paulson and Stiglitz did not say is that their opinion about sovereigns in the sick bed applies hand-in-glove also to America, and for good reason. America has abandoned its strengths of hard work, flexibility, and persistence in reaching a goal. Instead, it adopted Europe's weaknesses which add up to a moribund economy.

There exist good reasons why bankers, hedge fund managers, and bond investors are still betting on economic weakness in major western countries ranging from America's stalling economy (Chapters 10 and 11) to Europe's not so stable common currency as well as repeated demonstration that the old continent can pull defeat from the jaws of victory.

Euroland's currency union, whose longer term survivability is being questioned in many quarters, has its roots in the agreement signed in 1992 known as the Maastricht Treaty. This set in motion the rules for creating the euro and for screening the countries wanting to join Euroland. Everything done in this connection is imperfect. Moreover, the Maastricht Treaty stopped short of telling chief of state how to handle:

- Fiscal issues: spending, taxation, and
- Budget deficits to avoid hurting one another.

The Lisbon Treaty, which followed Maastricht, did not close the many gaps which were left open, and in the few cases it did so the letter of the law is not being observed by Euroland's chiefs of state and the ECB. An example is the Treaty articles which forbid joint liability for public debt. The same criticism is valid of the agreement establishing the ECB, with the responsibility for currency stability and for managing interest rates much like the original pact of the US Federal Reserve (early twentieth century). Unfortunately, the ECB also copied the Fed's bad habits—downplaying its main mission: monetary policy, and:

- Substituting itself for sovereigns in their responsibilities and duties connected to fiscal policy, and
- Exposing its authority, independence, and prestige by getting a long way from its original role as a Bundesbank-like guarantor of price stability.

It is nobody's secret that the ECB takes inordinate risks (including reputational) by trying its hand at tasks to which, as *The Economist* put it: "...(are) ill-adapted and on which its 23-strong governing council, made up of the heads of the 17 national central banks and a six-member executive board finds it very hard to reach consensus."[36]

There are good reasons why the market is and will remain nervous about the perils of overindebtedness in government, which in other times might have raised no eyebrows, but this is no more the case today. For their part, banks are unsure about their huge loans to sovereigns after the haircut of 73.5 percent on Greek debt (PSI, Chapter 4), and are afraid that more haircuts will come in desperate effort to solve Euroland's crisis.

With the absence of a global western leadership, power has been accruing to upcoming nations like China, each of which exerts its own gravitational pull. One of the reasons this is important is that nearly every issue the world presently faces requires negotiation, which on one hand spurs greater uncertainty and amplifies risks while on the other it diminishes most significantly western influence.

There is no great surprise regarding the disastrous effects of this drift because, as documented through the ages, no society can flourish in which the greater part of its members are uncertain about tomorrow, as is the case in the diminished and impoverished West, the United States included. Western countries have been hit by a double whammy which is undisputedly their own doing.

1. They are sinking under mountains of debt largely due to piling up unaffordable upon unsustainable entitlements and silly salvaging of badly wounded businesses, like the big banks.

   According to Masaaki Shirakawa, governor of the Bank of Japan, the maintenance of "zombie" companies largely explains his country's failure to adapt its productive structure to the requirements of growing competitiveness of emerging Asian countries and those of an aging population. Both Europe and America should have learned from Japan's failure, but they have not.

For any practical purpose, the main uncertainty in this curious initiative in having good money run after bad is whether the banks took the sovereigns to the cleaners or vice versa. There is a message in the statistics that debt held by the American banking industry grew from $2.9 trillion in 1978, which represented 125 percent of US GDP to $36 trillion in 2007 when the worst economic, financial, and banking crisis in post-WWII years started. The latter figure corresponds to about 260 percent of US 2007 GDP, and it has been growing ever since.

2. Chiefs of state and central bankers have spent trillions to ignite robust economic growth and employment accompanied by new lending in the banking system, but they have failed in all of these tasks.

William White has been economic advisor to the CEO and head of the monetary and economic department at the Bank for International Settlements (BIS). Among his many contributions to economics and finance is his exploration of unintended consequences of a protracted super easy monetary policy. White outlines as follows the ways in which steady rapid increase in western nations' monetary base:

- Tends to lower potential growth rates,
- Creates a perpetuating misallocation of resources, and
- May lead to serial bubbles that produce declining credit standards coupled by expanding debt accumulation.[37]

Let's face it. Economic, fiscal, and monetary policies in the West have got off the track, while populism has taken their place, and rational thinking, particularly about the consequences, is in permanent stagnation. Those responsible for fiscal policy and monetary policy are doing anything else but their job and even that "other job" they are doing it badly.

In a paper "Seeking Growth in a G-Zero World" published in mid-2012, Ian Bremmer and Lisa Shalett bring attention to the fact: "In the years since the financial crisis, the largest emerging economies, such as China and Brazil, have gone through two complete monetary cycles—easing in 2008 amid the global recession followed by tightening as growth heated up in 2011–2012, with easing resuming again in 2011–2012. During the same period, the developed world, led by the United States, largely remained stuck in the ultra-low-interest-rate doldrums."[38]

There exists an interesting parallel between monetary base overshooting and military adventures. McGeorge Bundy, national security advisor under presidents Kennedy and Johnson, observed in retrospect that "our effort" in Vietnam was "excessive" after 1965, when Indonesia was safely inoculated.[39] Precisely the same can be said about the monetary policies individually and collectively followed by Bernanke of the Fed, and his colleagues at Bank of England and ECB after the results of the first quantitative easing (QE1) waned, QE2 failed, QE3 has been a nonevent, and still in December 2012 Bernanke went ahead with QE3.5.

In Euroland, the basket case of economic malaise is Spain. Spanish banks repeated the same mistakes Japanese banks did in the 1980s applying low standards in granting loans while they themselves got overleveraged. By wide margin, the market thinks that the stress tests of Spanish banks have been manipulated. At the same time, the Spanish economy is unable to diversify and therefore remains in very bad shape.

The irony with the euro's weak fundamentals and ECB's spending habits is that in the first 40 days of 2013, the euro has been the strongest G10 currency, while the pound has declined more than 7 percent against the euro. Analysts and economists ask themselves whether this is a reversion of the "save haven" flows of 2012.

The answer is not at all clear. While diversification flows supported the pound in 2012 from both the private and central bank sides, there are reasons to believe that the current move of the euro against most of it crosses as overdone. Euroland's economy is only slowly recovering and the ongoing political risks in Greece, Spain, and Italy are not supportive of a strong euro. As an article on global financial markets had it: "... While the OMT has reduced euro tail risks, at the same time it has increased the risk that the ECB may need to implement a sort of quantitative easing program..."[40]

When Draghi was still a new face in the ECB, an old hand like Mervyn King, the governor of Bank of England, had cautioned that the ECB's decision to buy Italian and Spanish debt had "gone to the outer limit" of what a central bank should do. The onus for handling the debt crisis should lie with the eurozone's governments, King aptly said at that time, adding that:

> You cannot expect a central bank to engage in credit allocation decisions and to be a substitute for the inability to deal with the fiscal problems facing the euro area. That is a problem for governments.[41]

Rightly so. At the World Economic Forum, Davos 2013, Ignazio Visco, governor of Bank of Italy, put his thoughts in a similar way: "The objective of monetary policy is to provide financial stability. You cannot rely only on monetary policy to fix the current economic situation and restart growth."

That's precisely what ill-advised central bankers and chiefs of state in the western democracies are trying to do. Not unexpectedly, they are unsuccessful. The following paragraph explains how Dominique Strauss-Kahn, the former head of IMF, looks at Euroland's future.

Current European policies will not lead to resolution of the crisis whose roots can be found in the absence of economic growth. Tensions have temporarily subsided, and this masks the fact that the underlying problems are still unsolved. There are plenty of negatives due to absence of confidence by the public and the market—which persist. European growth, including growth in Germany, is too weak. In a few months, the hidden problem will resurface and reignite the crisis. In the end, Paulson's dictum "The new big short is Europe" may prove right.

*   *   *

There is no international standard defining *debt sustainability* and its limits. To study this issue, economists are often using scenarios, hypotheses, and answers to some critical questions. The most important question is: Can the country *afford* the debt it has contracted? But the response is usually qualitative, which means subjective.

While it is indeed impossible to separate sharply what is sustainable and what is unsustainable, I have found in my studies a danger zone of sustainability which tends to fall in the band of 8 percent to 10 percent of interest cost to government revenues. Ratios beyond 10 percent are unsustainable. Ireland, Italy, and Greece are in that area above 10 percent. For Portugal and Spain the ratio of interest cost to government revenues falls between 8 percent and 10 percent. Both governments try to keep a tap on their ratio. *If* it falls below 8 percent, even better below 6 percent, *then* the chances are good that it will be sustainable.

End Notes

1. The Economist, December 31, 2011.
2. Over the last 15 years, the exceptions have been Australia, Norway, Sweden, and Switzerland in that order.
3. In practically all cases in this list of highest indebted countries, which are mainly western, household indebtedness is elevated—adding so much more to the already high public debt ratios to GDP.
4. Half of that is public debt.
5. Notice that Greece and the United States have the same statistics on total depth of debt. Greece is nearly bankrupt. What one should think of the United States?
6. Statistics by UBS Wealth Management Research, February 6, 2012.
7. A strength and at the same time a weakness of Germany is that the exports share of its GDP rose from about 25 in 1995 to 45 percent in 2010—half of it outside Euroland. This 45 percent makes the economy vulnerable to a global slowdown.
8. True enough, France *presently* finds no problem in refinancing. This shows that there exists a gap in the market's knowledge.
9. Increasing life expectancy is one of the key reasons for worry; with it come inordinate costs. A little over three decades ago, in 1981 in Switzerland, average life expectancy after retirement for men was 14 years and for women 18 years. In 2012, these averages have grown, respectively, to 18.6 years and 22 years.
10. Olsen M. The rise and decline of nations. Yale University Press; New Haven, Connecticut; 1982.
11. Budgetary/fiscal and current account. In 2011, the current account balance of the United States was negative by $473 billion, that of Italy by $70 billion, of France by $62 billion, and of Spain by $55 billion.
12. Financial Times, December 21, 2011.
13. Chorafas DN. Globalization's limits. Conflicting national interests in trade and finance. London: Gower; 2009.
14. Financial Times, January 3, 2012.
15. Dacias are still low cost, but not as low as they used to be.
16. The misrepresentation of accounting information by manipulating statistics and other facts.
17. Société Générale. Cross asset research: popular delusions. May 12, 2012.
18. Chorafas DN. Risk accounting and risk management, for professional accountants. London and Boston: Elsevier; 2008.
19. The Daily Telegraph, August 17, 2012.

20. *Idem.*
21. The Stability and Growth Pact envisaged penalties for sovereigns when budget deficits exceeded 3 percent. Has anybody paid such penalties? None that I know, yet there has been a horde of overruns.
22. A term emulating the US *fiscal cliff*, a simultaneous cancellation of the Bush tax relief and reduction in public expenditures.
23. Chorafas DN. The changing role of central banks. New York, NY: Palgrave/Macmillan; 2013.
24. And practically everyone knows that 1 out of 10 loans by Spanish banks has to be written off.
25. Reportedly by selling these bonds to banks (more on this later).
26. Revealing is the title of one of published articles: "Spanish Pull Out Cash and Leave Country." Spain's citizens don't trust their government. Why should the ECB and other Euroland members trust it?
27. By late January 2013, an estimated amount of euro 150 billion has been returned by the better off banks to the ECB, about year after year they borrowed it.
28. OMT will be considered for countries presently under Euroland's bailout program only when they are in a position to regain access to markets. This requires further clarification, and at present exist no details about it.
29. Financial Times, September 21, 2012.
30. The same is true of the political government which follows Mario Monti's, after Italian elections.
31. Financial Times, February 8, 2013.
32. Chorafas DN. Breaking up the euro. The end of a common currency. New York, NY: Palgrave/Macmillan; 2013.
33. Edgar Meister, a former senior executive of the Bundesbank, attacked Merkel's government for failing to give Stark sufficient support. She faced more criticism after Weber's resignation.
34. Chorafas DN. Financial boom and gloom. The credit and banking crisis of 2007–2009 and beyond. London: Palgrave/Macmillan; 2009.
35. Bloomberg News, April 17, 2012.
36. The Economist, October 22, 2011.
37. www.dallasfed.org/assets/documents/institute/wpapers/2012/0126.pdf/
38. www.ml.com/greatglobalshift. Bremmer is president of Eurasia Group; Shalett is chief investment officer at Merrill Lynch Global Wealth Management.
39. Chomsky N. Failed states. New York, NY: Owl Book/Henry Holt; 2006.
40. UBS CEO WM Research. Global financial markets, February 7, 2013.
41. Financial Times, August 11, 2011.

3 Options for this Decade

3.1 Three Main Options for the Next Years

In an interview he gave on February 8, 2013 to CNN, Mohammed El-Erian, the CEO of Pimco, said that there is a big gap between the economic fundamentals which are low and the market expectations which stand high. To Richard Quest's question on what makes that gap, El-Erian answered that the wedge is made by central banks, their excessive liquidity and its impact. There is no better description of the bubble economy in which we live.

To the opinion of Dominique Strauss-Kahn, the real question is what will happen *if* the dollars drop out of the screen of global currencies. As long as confidence in the US dollar persists, even a weak level of confidence, Strauss-Kahn said in his Monte-Carlo lecture of January 18, 2013 America is able to balance its accounts with the rest of the world. But the internal problems, particularly the challenge of huge and growing deficits, continue being gigantic.

According to the former boss of the IMF, the twelfth hour accord on *fiscal cliff* was, so to speak, mandatory; but it was not useful. Obama gained a few months till the debt calamity hits again with a lot of unwanted consequences. On January 1, 2013 the United States avoided bankruptcy as the Republicans agreed to join in kicking the problem to a later date. Neither party, however, did much to:

- Improve the US economy, or
- Answered the worries of the American people.

Economists think that there is a deeper message hiding behind the sluggish pace of the current recovery,[1] which follows the most severe recession since World War II: countries are not doing what it takes to lift themselves up. This is particularly true in western countries. Leveraging by money printing is the wrong remedy given the magnitude of the downturn.

Heavy public debt has been one of the most important reasons why over 5 to 6 years the economic and social structure of western society has been under stress. Unemployment zoomed and then remained at high level, while national income at end of 2012 was lower than what would have been expected in an average recovery. In an interview he gave to Bloomberg BusinessWeek mid-August 2012, Nouriel Roubini, the economist, stated that as far as the coming couple of years are concerned, there are three alternative scenarios.

A. Meddling through, characterized by a 55 percent probability,

Public Debt Dynamics of Europe and the US. DOI: http://dx.doi.org/10.1016/B978-0-12-420021-0.00003-8

B. A global "perfect storm" for 2013, with a likelihood of 35 percent, and

C. A slow, very slow, improvement of the economic situation to which Roubini gave the remaining probability of 10 percent.[2]

Less than a week earlier, on August 9, 2012 CNBC had conducted a poll focusing on investors' view of the economy. Of course economists and investors are different populations and their opinions may also differ. This has indeed been the case, but still the likelihood of indecision and meddling through came up in first position, followed by a worsening projection on economic development. Here is in a nutshell this poll's result:

- There is no change in the economy, 36 percent.
- The economy is getting worse, 34 percent.
- The economy is improving, 30 percent.[3]

If the first two probabilities are added together, this means that 70 percent of respondents believe the economic and financial difficulties will continue even if they fall short of global meltdown. In the latter case, which is scenario "B" in Roubini's classification, the situation becomes disorderly with some Euroland countries defaulting while another bubble is bursting in the United States as well there is hard landing in China while other major emerging markets are stalling.[4]

We are told that there has been soft landing in China. But should we believe it? If yes, how can we explain that there is a big drain of capital from China, part of it heading for Africa, among all places. In addition, big part of this capital drain is made of American and Chinese capital. The answer cannot be found in an aversion to state capitalism, because this has been China's choice since Day 1 and so far it worked alright.

Experts suggest that the rift between Beijing and Shanghai is a more believable reason. If it happens, economic disruption will be akin to the "real perfect storm," at least an order of magnitude bigger than that of Lehman Brothers. Compared to this fear, never ending troubles in Euroland look like a joke, and the tsunami from a rift in China will hit the US economy in full force.

State Street Global Advisors, the world's third biggest funds manager, said 71 percent of investors (in a global survey of 300) globally fear an imminent Lehman-like debacle with Asia the likely epicenter. Participants have included largest pension funds, asset managers, and private banks. Surveyed executives could give 1 or 2 reasons for the tail risk:

- 66 percent answered it would be triggered by the global economy falling into recession,
- 66 percent responded it would be caused by the break-up of the euro, and
- 20 percent said it would be created by big bank insolvency.

Others cited an oil price shock and monetary stimulus creating asset bubbles.[5] The responses identified the prevailing investment market psychology and you cannot successfully fight market psychology. Of those surveyed, only 20 percent were confident they were protected against tail-risks. In 2008 "you would have been better off sticking your money under a mattress," said a senior American assets manager. "Frankly, that could be the best strategy today, too. At least you keep your cash, and inflation is very low."[6]

In contrast to the perfect storm and meddling through scenarios, option "C", which is low probability but optimistic, is based on the hypothesis that Euroland finds its way toward a greater economic, financial, fiscal, and political union. In parallel to this, the US economy is improving, China has a soft landing, and many of the developing countries resume their growth. Also, most importantly, there is no war in the Middle East. All this takes place in what is still a bumpy road.

Scenario "C" is sustained by the hope that after 5 years of a great recession things start looking up. *Not so*, says Jamil Baz in an article he published in the Financial Times. To his opinion, it will take a minimum of 15 years for the economy to reach escape velocity and attain a level consistent with healthy growth. For this to become a reality, the debt overhang will need to come down very sharply.[7]

Baz bases his opinion on historical evidence which suggests that it is impossible to reduce debt by more than 10 percentage points per annum without social and political upheaval. What has happened in 2011 and 2012 in Greece and in 2012 in Spain corroborates Baz' estimate, as well as his suggestion that:

- When we finally start cutting our debt, the economic impact will be massive, and
- Because of negative feedback loops between deficit cuts and growth, each country engaging in servicing debt may lose more than 20 percent of its GDP.

These are well-received points. It is reasonable enough to guess that a big chunk of this 20 percent of downsizing, in GDP terms, relates to "assets" which have been acquired through steady leveraging over 30 years till the debt became unsustainable. Behind this required deleveraging we find the:

- Impact of households repairing balance sheets,
- Persistence of weak labor markets,
- Major cuts in entitlements,
- An effort toward fiscal consolidation, and
- Macroeconomic outlook across the globe surrounded by a high degree of uncertainty.

There is little doubt that the markets will continue focusing on what happens when Spain and/or Italy is (are) forced to ask for bailout and austerity measures have to be taken while the deteriorating macro picture suggest further monetary easing.[8] Spikes in commodity prices may unsettle scenario "A" and tilt it toward scenario "B." In such a situation, the best chiefs of state and central bankers can do is to stay level-headed, without engaging in absurdities by denying the facts.

3.2 "The Worst Is Over" Is a Defeatist Slogan

In an absurd way, emulating the forecast of a Merrill Lynch senior VP who a couple of months prior to the Lehman bankruptcy had said, "The worst is already behind us," and on March 22, 2012 Mario Draghi, ECB's president, declared, "The worst is over!" Is it really? Which is the evidence? Which are the preconditions? Is money thrown at the problem enough to solve it? What is the role of political misconduct in engineering the drift from scenario "A" to scenario "B"? (see Section 3.1).

Here is in a nutshell what I mean by political externalities and associated misconduct: In February 2012 George Papandreou, the former socialist prime minister, found the courage to say to the Greek parliament, "Our political system is collectively responsible for all the bureaucrats we have hired because of favoritism, the privileges we have accorded by law, the scandalous demands we satisfied, the syndicalists (labor unionists) and businessmen we favored and the thieves that we did not bring to prison."[9]

In one well-phrased statement, expressed in lucid and focused terms, the former prime minister and socialist party leader described what is wrong with the current western democracy. All of the reasons Papandreou mentioned converge to create an impossible economic climate and a mountain of debt which will be paid by the same public who elected these second rate politicians—of the left and of the right—which means by all of us.

Forgetting about political meddling and its (sometimes) disastrous effects, and depending only on running faster, the printing presses serves in solving no economic problems whatsoever. Instead, it creates new ones and makes those already in existence even worse. Aside that fact, politicians at the vertex of the stage and governors of central banks should not allow themselves statements such as "the worst is over" because:

- They show short-termism, and
- They reveal a cheap way to cover facts and figures.

In early 2012, when it were made, Draghi's statement contrasted to that of economists who, that same day, declared that Italy and Spain were big economies (the third and fourth in Euroland) and *if* they caved-in *then* the existing firewalls will not be able to contain the fire from spreading. In addition, just a day prior to "the worst is over" declaration, the message by the financial ticker on Bloomberg News was that Spain risks a default now more than ever. As for Italy, the way an article in the Economist had it, there was a near-paralysis in the country's domestic banking system with rickety banks reluctant to lend to local firms.

In addition, timing-wise "the worst is over" came at the worst moment possible. Greece is under band aid with the Troika reluctant to release bailout funds; Portugal is uncertain about asking for second bailout; Ireland demanded delays in reimbursing its loans. Economists characterized the bailout problems, including those of Italy and Spain as intractable, while Club Med's[10] governments find it difficult to get themselves together to embrace necessary changes.

Part of staying level-headed is avoiding excessive printing of money in order to continue being all things to all people, all companies and all other sovereigns—allowing no entity to fail and salvaging even the most derelict. This is a Maginot Line mentality, a basket case of poor leadership because:

- History does not repeat itself in an exact manner, and
- Leaders who cling to past recipes are almost certain to fail.

The message all this conveys is that the future survival of the euro is in doubt while Club Med countries, which are feeling the heat of past profligate follies, are nervous. Neither should it be lost from sight that the global economy, too, is highly leveraged. At the end of 2011, global GDP was estimated to stand at $73 trillion. At that time, equity capitalization, debt instruments, and derivatives were slightly in excess of $591 trillion, with the following weights:

Equity capitalization	$50 trillion
Bonds	$95 trillion
Derivatives	$446 trillion
	$591 trillion

As these numbers document, the gearing of the global virtual economy over the global real economy has reached an unprecedented 822 percent, with derivative financial instruments responsible for roughly three-fourth of that huge sum. This is creating an unbelievably large and risky overhang, documenting that the worst is by no means behind us.

"The system could work as long as there are *no* substantial bankruptcies," said one of the experts, adding that precisely because of such an ultrahigh gearing, a couple of big ticket bankruptcies will precipitate a global catastrophe. To the opinion of other knowledgeable analysts, the global debt is no more manageable and if governments are so bewildered and uncertain about the "way out," it is because the gearings of such a magnitude are unprecedented.

While the buildup of the global bubble took roughly three decades, the worst part has happened over the last dozen years. In 2000, the world's bond market stood at $36 trillion, composed of three main parts: governments $12 trillion, financial entities $ 18 trillion (half the total), and nonfinancial entities $6 trillion. As we have just seen, at the end of 2011, the world's debt instruments reached $95 trillion with the following approximate distribution:

- Sovereigns nearly $40 trillion, a 333-percent increase,
- Financial entities over $45 trillion, practically doubling their debt, and
- Nonfinancial companies $10 trillion, a jump of almost 167 percent.[11]

These are stratospheric levels of indebtedness, and they have the point of being unsustainable. The way an old proverb has it, "When you lose your way go back to the beginning and start again." Let's do that based on the analysis of the Great Depression by Irving Fisher, the economist. Fisher had suggested two basic conditions to escape a debt trap.

- Balance sheets of insolvent households, banks, and sovereigns must be repaired by *letting them default* or by a bailout, doing so as fast as possible without causing new defaults.
- Prices of assets such as bonds and real estate issued by insolvent borrowers must fall as fast as possible to levels that attract buyers and get the economy moving, but not so fast as to trigger a spiral of defaults.

Defaulting without causing new defaults could be achieved through ring-fencing, the way the British Vickers Committee suggested for retail and commercial subsidiaries versus investment banking units of big banks. The purpose of such risk-fencing is to stop contagion which is likely to damage otherwise viable enterprises. Indeed, this is what should have been done in 2008 instead of providing an unprecedented amount of public capital to the self-wounded banking industry.[12]

As for the first bullet's option, given the super-leveraging which now prevails around the world, it would be absurd to contemplate bailouts at global scale because there is no ultrarich *deus ex machina** to do so—like America did it for Europe with the Marshall Plan, after World War II. Both America and Europe can now depend only on their own forces.

The ultimate goal of monetary and fiscal policy in the EU should be to reengage the private sector, says Bill Gross, chief investment officer of PIMCO. Gross adds that the EU needs the private sector as a willing partner in funding its economy—a point which often gets lost in the all too frequent promises, such as the one to defend the euro made by the European Central Bank president.[13] As Gross observes, however, private investors are balking.

Private investors no more accept cold economic policy pronouncements, and IOUs that make for media headlines. Fisher's advice about allowing entities to default is sound. Freedom to enter the market and freedom to fail are, after all, pillars of capitalism. The principle of freedom to fail was broken by the George W. Bush Administration in 2008 when it intervened to "save" self-wounded big banks from bankruptcy. Freedom to fail was further destabilized by the European Union's, ECB's, and IMF's 2010 "bailout" of Greece whose aftereffects threw the country in despair.

There is nothing wrong when borrowers who cannot service and repay their debts declare bankruptcy. It is up to themselves and their creditors to sort it out. Eventually, the bankrupt entity will come out of the tunnel. In the case of Argentina, it took 2 years while Greece is 3 years in the bailout tunnel and nobody can see the end of it. If governments send the fire brigade (usually the central bank) with plenty of money to put down the fire, there will be constant pressure to:

- Enlarge the limits of this firefighting, and
- Soften the bailout rules, which means making the pain longer lasting.

To participate to the common currency game, whose perceived benefits were attractive, but whose challenges proved to be enormous, sovereigns conducted secret negotiations and faked their economic data. In doing so, they were helped by investment banks and their derivatives games. The inadequacy of results being obtained underlines the inadequacy of that rigged system.

One more critical element should be brought to the reader's attention. The western economy will not start moving again by applying cookbook solutions. New

---

* It means "god from a scaffolding", an artifice. In ancient greek tragedy a machine was used to bring actors playing god into the stage.

ideas are necessary, as the story of Apple Computer and other successful companies documents. Coming up from under is a great enterprise, and great enterprises need ideas which are new and vibrant, as well as the will to apply the decisions being made. In Britain, in the nineteenth century, the great idea was the empire. At end of World War II, in America, the great idea was leadership of the free nations. What's the great idea of western countries in 2013?

3.3   The Italian Government's Daisy-Chain

In World War II, victory bonds by the US Treasury were the source of great profits for banks because they made possible daisy-chain exploitation of money created by the Federal Reserve. To assure successful bond sales and stable interest rates, the Fed expanded bank reserves by buying up government securities. Commercial banks lent this expanded money supply to private customers who then lend it to the government by buying new Treasury bonds.

The daisy-chain continued as customers sold their new government securities to commercial banks, who (eventually) sold them back to the Fed when the central bank was again required to expand the money supply to provide the liquidity necessary for war effort. In essence, the US government was borrowing its own money, while paying a fee to the middlemen.

This is roughly what the Italian government has been doing in peace time, during the last few years. Experts say that the Italian government's daisy-chain will become king-size with OMT (Chapter 2) which will significantly expand its present version. To appreciate this argument, the reader should know that Italian public debt is primarily incurred and funded by the central government, which uses several debt issuance venues:

- The largest portion, about 72.5 percent, is issued in the form of long-term bonds (Buoni Poliennali del Tesoro (BTPS)), presently standing at euro 1.79 billion, and
- The Italian Bills program (BOTS) fluctuates in bracket of euro 0.16 to euro 0.25 trillion, with average refinancing cycle of 5 months.

A study by UBS suggests that as far as Italy is concerned, till the end of 2014, total bond redemptions will amount to euro 414 billion while new debt resulting from fiscal deficits and interest paid on debt would be about euro 102 billion—to a total of euro 516 billion ($671 billion).[14] That's a great deal of money.

In 2012, Italy was expected, but only expected, to have a primary (before interest) budget surplus of 2.9 percent GDP. Since about 20 percent of the just mentioned "new debt" was earmarked for interest payments on the country's huge public debt of about euro 2.1 trillion ($2.73 trillion), that amount of money eats up for breakfast the 2.9 percent primary surplus. That's a first class example of how much money costs a high public debt policy.

Excluding any surprises, over the time frame under consideration, that is, till end of 2014, Spain is confronted with bond redemptions of euro 226 billion; interest payments of euro 50 billion (for 2 years); an estimated budget deficit in 2012 of over 5 percent with a GDP of euro 1.16 trillion amounts to over euro 61 billion. For 2013, Spain faces an estimated euro 50 billion budget deficit (probably much more) and some euro 65 billion to recapitalize its banks.[15] The total is nearly euro 447 billion ($581 billion). This is an optimistic estimate of the Spanish torrent of red ink. Let's recapitulate:

Italy	Euro 516 billion ($671 billion)
Spain	Euro 452 billion ($587 billion)
Spain and Italy	Euro 968 billion ($1.26 trillion)

The sum euro 963 billion is large, well above the remaining lending capacity of the EFSF (euro 248 billion) and the ESM (euro 500 billion) which still has to be funded. As the UBS study states, the total amount available in the two Euroland funds "... would be clearly insufficient to cover a full funding support program." The reader should also appreciate that the combined EFSF and ESM capacity would be much lower if Spain and Italy were to become borrowers.

The net result of such a major switch is that the third and fourth Euroland economies will be withdrawing their contribution as guarantors and capital providers to Euroland's support facilities. Spain currently contributes 12 percent of guarantees to the EFSF by Euroland member countries, and it would confront cash and guarantee contributions to the ESM at the level of 11.9 percent. The respective shares for Italy are 19.2 percent and 17.9 percent—to a total of 32 percent to EFSF and 29.8 percent to ESM.

Clearly, it is not Greece and Portugal who will supply the missing funds, Germany is in a state of bailout fatigue and, sometime in the future, France itself may change to become net borrower from net contributor to EFSF/ESM. With the treasury of these two Euroland salvage funds drying up, credit rating agencies will issue negative ratings on the remaining guarantor countries, which will be particularly painful news for (in alphabetic order) Austria, Finland, Germany, Luxembourg, and the Netherlands.

As Euroland core countries fall down the cliff in a deadly embrace with the profligates, the market will be unforgiving. Its reaction may well change Roubini's scenario from "A" to "B" (Section 3.1)—a drift which could not be easily stopped. It would be silly to discount this possibility and its dramatic aftereffects.

As if these likelihoods were not enough, the September 2012 announcement of "unlimited" sovereign bond-buying by ECB through the OMT (Chapter 2) opens the way for obliterating the treasuries of EFSF, ESM, and the whole of Euroland in one go. Table 3.1 presents the stated statistics and estimates in a nutshell to help in keeping them in memory when making financial stability and investment decisions.

None of the figures presented in this section and in Table 3.1 should come as a surprise to people warming armchairs at the European Executive, EU member state governments, and the ECB. Therefore, the recent talk that EFSF and ESM will bailout Spain and Italy is smoke and mirrors. As for the idea of *leveraging* their funds, this is total nonsense.

Table 3.1 Spain, Italy, and Their Use of EFSF and ESM Funds

A. Estimates of Funding Needs to End of 2014

Italy	Bond redemptions	Euro 414 billion
	Interest payments	Euro 102 billion
	Total	Euro 516 billion
Spain	Bond redemptions	Euro 226 billion[a]
	Interest payments	Euro 50 billion
	Deficit 2012-09-28	Euro 56 billion
	Deficit 2013 (Est.)	Euro 50 billion
	Bank restructuring	Euro 65 billion[b]
	Total	Euro 447 billion
	Sum of Italy and Spain	Euro 963 billion[c]

B. Estimate of Available Euroland Funds

	EFSF has	Euro 248 billion
	ESM will have	Euro 500 billion
	Total	Euro 748 billion
However,		
	Spain contributes	12.8% of EFSF funds
	Italy contributes	19.2% of EFSF funds
	Total	32.0%
	Spain contributes	11.9% of ESM funds
	Italy contributes	17.9% of ESM funds
	Total	29.8%

Hence, with Spain and Italy borrowers rather than contributors:

	EFSF will have left	Euro 168.6 billion
	ESM will have left	Euro 251.0 billion
	Total	Euro 519.6 billion

Moreover, Greece, Portugal, and Ireland are already under bailout regime, hence they contribute nothing.
It follows that total EFSF and ESM available funds are well below euro 500 billion. That's roughly half the amount needed (under best conditions) for Spanish and Italian bailouts.
The discussion about leveraging ESM lacks seriousness.
[a]Known as the Greenspan–Guidotti rule (Guidotti P. remarks at G33 seminar in Bonn, Germany, March 11, 1999; Greenspan A. *Currency reserves and debt*, remarks before the World Bank Conference on Recent Trends in Reserves Management, Washington, DC, April 29, 1999; available at http://www.federalreserve.gov).
[b]The results of the Spanish banks' audit, released on September 28, 2012 stated that euro 59.3 billion will be needed for their recapitalization. I added to this a margin of 10 percent which I am sure will prove to be inadequate.
[c]UBS Chief Investment Office. The debt crisis, May 8, 2012. Statistics updated as of September 27, 2012.

The leveraging options most often discussed involve banks and private investors. It should not escape the attention of Euroland's chiefs of state and central bankers that a hit in the treasuries of these entities in the leveraging of EFSF and ESM can have severe consequences. Banks and private investors may buy Spanish and Italian bonds as long as they expect the ECB to play *deus ex machina*. When this hope fades, they would rush to the exit—at the same time and from the same door.

It is not for nothing that on September 27, 2012 the Finnish government said that ESM money should be used only for bank bailouts.[16]

It is as well useful to remember that sovereign bond acquisitions by ECB started already in May 2010 through the SMP,[17] and a quarter trillion euros has been spent under that program. In December 2011 and February 2012, the ECB also pumped more than euro 1 trillion through the LTRO at 1 percent interest. The lion's share was taken up by Spanish and Italian banks that—rather than using that money for lending and rebuilding their balance sheet—employed to buy the debt of their governments. No wonder that, even if the economic situation is morose, in mid-2012 eurozone inflation jumped to 2.7 percent.

All this is leaving the ECB under Draghi hanging on a fork. What is happening is *dereliction of duty* because a central bank's first and foremost duty is to assure that the currency under its watch does not lose its value, and that economic stability dominates. Both goals require conservative policies rather than throwing taxpayers' money to the four winds.

Instead of statements promoting financial stability, what we hear is the noise of the western central banks' money printing presses, as well as an interminable (pseudo) neo-Keynesian/anti-Keynesian debate which has come to dominate much of the economists' time (and that of the media). This is a largely sterile exercise that obscures the real choices we need to examine and discuss. For instance:

• Should a Euroland (or any other) sovereign qualify for economic help if he or she does not balance, at least, its primary budget?[18]
• Should the hat-in-hand sovereign come up with a believable, serious plan on how to repay the debt within a period which could be negotiated but not to exceed 5–7 years, prior to be taken under Euroland's wings?

Answers should be factual and documented, with similar challenges confronted in the past providing the evidence. Marriner Eccles, the Federal Reserve chairman in the Roosevelt years, is a good reference. He has been very careful with monetary policy because he appreciated that money can be easily printed but the productive forces of the economy grow slowly.

The result of turning the central bank's presses overtime is inflationary, Eccles said. This is as true today as it were in the 1930s. Current money is no longer covered through any material assets. Bank notes are printed paper and knowledgeable people appreciate what this means, says Jens Weidmann, president of the Deutsche Bundesbank.

During the war years, roughly 60 percent of the federal government's expenditures were financed through borrowing, not revenue. Eccles continually urged the Roosevelt Administration to borrow less and tax more, to finance the war from the swollen savings of consumers rather than the artificial expansion of money. (From 1940 to 1945 immediate inflation was avoided through wartime controls on wages and prices.)

To make his point that a grossly expanded money supply would become an engine of inflation, on September 18, 2012 Weidmann resorted to Goethe's *Faust*.

Mephistopheles provides an interesting precedence to paper money-based monetary policy as well as the potentially dangerous correlation of:

- Money creation,
- Deficit state financing, and
- Resulting inflation.

Early on in Goethe's play Mephistopheles persuades the heavily leveraged Holy Roman Emperor to print more and more paper money, notionally backed by gold that had not been mined. This, the devil maintains, would help the emperor to solve the economic crisis confronting him. For a short time, the flood of paper money strategy works, but as more and more money is printed:

- Rampant inflation follows,
- The currency is destabilized, and
- Everybody, particularly the economically weak members of society, is worse off.

There are clearly parallels with the performance of the ECB, the Federal Reserve, Bank of England, and Bank of Japan with Goethe's Mephistopheles. In fact, it looks as if Mephistopheles has multiplied like the head of the hydra and each of his clones landed a job with a western central bank, which allows it to destroy the currency under its jurisdiction.

3.4   Banks Did Not Deserve the Bailout

Decided by politicians who are freely spending taxpayer money, and by central bankers who just as freely print it, bank bailouts have been the extravaganza of the casino society. In America and in Europe, taxpayers felt that they were forced to salvage big banks who did not deserve it. "They should be enraged by the broken promises to Main Street and the unending protection of Wall Street," says Neil Barofsky, a former US federal prosecutor and former special inspector general of the TARP.[19]

In his book *Bailout*,[20] Barofsky reviews his argument with Timothy Geithner, the US Treasury secretary, whom he saw as over-sympathetic to Wall Street.[21] Other critics agree. True enough, regulators face conflicts between their dual mandates of disciplining banks and keeping the financial system running. This, however, is no excuse for permanently turning a blind eye on cases of fraud as well as on the high stakes in gambling with derivatives and other poisonous products. Everything considered:

- Barofsky's criticism of the close relationship between the Fed and the Treasury is well founded, and
- He is right when he says that the financial industry is inherently corrupt.

The pros answer that if there are oversights in supervision, they are there to preserve stability;[22] otherwise, life will be too difficult for banks.[23] By so saying, they confuse the banks with the bankers—particularly the wrongdoers. The argument that a regulator has to go soft on credit institutions, particularly during financial upheaval, is biased. Bringing to court those who deserve it, is the regulators' obligation. As for each individual bank, it should have enough people trained to replace the incumbents prosecuted their act.

Neither is the recapitalization of wounded big banks the way to kick-start lending. The credit crunch continues as lending has become practically unavailable to small and medium enterprises (SMEs). This is, quite evidently, which is detrimental to economic growth, but it is nobody's secret that economic growth will return on the heels of confidence.

This is an age-old principle conditioned by other, more recent developments. With globalization we have been experiencing international transmissions of credit supply shocks which impact on both credit and credit spreads. This transmission of credit supply shocks takes place by way of:

- Persistent decline in credit,
- Rise in risk premiums,
- Short to medium term decline in interest rates, and
- A parallel deterioration in the psychology of financial markets.

The noticeable, and often sharp, downsizing of loans activities is amplified by an international financial multiplier which represents the effect of contagion. While the global propagation of financial market shocks has gradually grown stronger over time, it is no less true that bankers and economists do not quite understand the complex national and worldwide effects of financial market disruptions.

True enough, the process of improving capital ratios often includes reduction of risky assets. Except loans, however, banks are not keen to reduce their assets, even those of their "assets" which have only a make-believe value. Instead, they increase them through gambling and risky speculations—games particularly favored by big banks. Ponzi games repeat themselves even if the previous tries have failed. For instance, in the United States, bundled loans are back in play at precrisis level.

- The use of low-rated debt in the funding market has returned to the pre-2007 high water mark, and
- This is fueling fears that the shadow banking system is becoming riskier and riskier.

Several types of securitized loans are prone to sudden pullbacks like the one in 2008, particularly when securitizations employ less liquid longer term "assets." Over and above this comes the fact that in a market crisis, nearly all of the parties to a repurchasing deal would be hit. Those who care about the banking system's stability, point out that underlying connections characterizing financial products played a critical role in the build up to the 2008 financial crisis.

- Banks used toxic assets, such as repackaged subprime loans, to secure trillions of dollars worth of cheap funding, by selling these leveraged instruments to one another.

• But when the American housing bubble burst, the banks' trading partners refused to accept such securities as collateral, with the result that the repo market rapidly contracted.

There are good reasons why many seasoned experts, and bank regulators, are now raising their voice against the mammoth-sized banks whose empire has become uncontrollable. Sandy Weill has been an old hand in Wall Street. He is also considered as the father of the "big bank" concept, after he engineered the merger of Travellers with Citibank to form Citigroup, in the 1990s. Therefore, financial analysts pay attention to his call for breaking up the big banks.[24]

Weill's advice that "small is beautiful" reinforces the ongoing discussion on the regulators proposal calling for separation of investment banking from commercial banking. "What we should probably do is go and split up investment banking from banking, have banks make commercial loans and real estate loans, have banks do something that's not going to risk the taxpayer dollars, that's not too big to fail," Weill told CNBC.[25]

Other senior bankers, too, have made the same suggestion. The list includes the chairman of the Vickers Commission;[26] John Reed, former co-chief executive of Citigroup with Sandy Weill; Phil Purcell, former chief executive of Morgan Stanley; and Tom Hoenig, director of the Federal Deposit Insurance Corporation (FDIC). Correctly, the latter has called for a richer, deeper Glass–Steagall Act.[27]

As boss of FDIC, Hoenig's business is to watch out for banks sliding toward bankruptcy, try to avert it, and pay out if it happens. To his opinion, recent proposals for bank regulation have fallen short of establishing a solid regulatory environment. These include the Volcker rule,[28] which bans banks from trading on their own account but not on behalf of a customer; and the Vickers Commission, in Britain, which suggested forcing banks to ring-fence their retail operations, separating them from their investment banking activities.

To confront adversity, banks also need a solid capital base. Basel III,[29] by the Basel Committee on Banking Supervision, has established higher capital requirements aimed at making financial institutions more resilient. However, as recent demands for capital increase by well-known banks have shown, private investors are unwilling to provide the asked for capital, particularly if the entity is active in investment banking.

This dart of capital has a curious effect which is becoming another hallmark of the casino society: the manipulation of models which are supposed to be objective. Big banks with lots of rocket scientists[30] in their employment, are trying to meet capital requirements by tinkering with their internal models. The aim is to make their holdings appear less risky to satisfy Basel III rules phased-in between now and 2019, but model manipulation is trickery, and therefore, it is pure nonsense.

The attempt to lie through models by downsizing the exposure which they have assumed by means of what is wrongly called "risk-weighted asset (RWA) optimization" lacks ethics. Changing the way risk weights are calculated to cut the amount of necessary capital is cheating, while *optimization* is a misnomer. What lies behind is buying, packaging, and selling toxic assets. Allegedly, banks are playing with the risk weights on various loans, so less capital has to be placed against them. Sometimes, this is done with and in other cases without the agreement of regulator(s).

Still another casino society practice adopted by banks is the massaging of popular indices to their profits. An example is LIBOR, which stands for London Interbank Offered Rates, a widely used benchmark with transactions in billions of dollars worldwide. Allegedly, LIBOR's cousin the Euro Interbank Offered Rate (EIBOR) has also been the subject of tickering. The scandal was revealed in March 2012 and since then it continues to amplify.

The manipulation of LIBOR rates by Barclays, Royal Bank of Scotland, and other big banks can be traced back to the lax system of regulation which prevailed prior to the financial crisis of 2007−2013. The Barclays Bank admitted that in 2008 it was submitting false LIBOR rates and it had as accomplices in doing so other big banks.

At the time, the president of the New York Federal Reserve was Timothy Geithner whose response was to look the other way and let the case be buried. Many other central bankers have allegedly embraced what has been christened as *the Geithner doctrine*: the risk of causing big banks to fail, and hence undo all of the bailout efforts, froze them out of action. No attention has been paid by central bankers and regulators to the fact that:

- Each settlement on favorable terms to the wrongdoers reinforces the perception that *crime pays*.
- The lack prosecution for wrongdoing encourages fraudulent conduct.

The western central bankers and regulators espoused the Geithner doctrine spread the wrong kind of incentives around the world. Punishment for wrongdoing took a leave and personal accountability went alone with it. The lack of accountability for a person's acts further reinforced the wrong incentives.

- Plenty of big banks have been involved in this LIBOR scandal and paid high penalties for it.
- In Britain, the chairman of Barclays and the CEO had to quit, and
- The European Union's financial regulator said he will make the manipulation of benchmark rates *a crime*.

As the investigations continued, Barclays' chairman and deputy governor of the Bank of England were grilled by a parliamentary committee. At the other side of North Atlantic, it emerged that the Federal Reserve of New York was by all likelihood informed of alleged manipulation of LIBOR sometime after 2007, but took no action. Ethics has taken the back seat; precisely the place where the casino society wants it to be.

3.5 Political Backing for Financial Stability Has Declined

On June 26, 2012 Sigmar Gabriel, leader of Germany's Social Democratic Party, said the euro was "born with a congenital defect − it lacked a common budget, financial and economic policy." Gabriel advised that Euroland's members must pursue closer integration toward a "real fiscal union" to underpin the stability of the common currency; adding, "It would be an illusion to believe that we can create a fiscal union very quickly."[31]

This is the right estimate. The surprise in Gabriel's speech came when he threw his weight behind François Hollande, French president, and Mario Monti, Italian prime minister, in their efforts to persuade Angela Merkel to allow further "short-term" measures (read: flooding the market with liquidity) to calm the different operators. To Gabriel's mind, the instrument of choice is the "unlimited" sovereign bond-buying by ECB—which, when it comes in "unlimited" amounts can as well be the instrument of financial destruction (OMT, Chapter 2).

Slowly but surely, however, leftist and populist politicians, who think that the way to placate the electorate is to throw money at the problem, are in the wrong track. Europe's socialist parties are divided down the middle on this issue.

Prior to the mid-September 2012 elections in Holland political analysts suggested that, in large part, support for the Dutch Socialist Party (SP) grew because of its opposition to Euroland's rescue policies and measures. For some time, the Dutch public has feared that they have to pay other peoples' debts, and their country's AAA credit rating is compromised by southern European countries' spending habits. A traditionally Eurosceptic party, the SP had voted against:

- The Greek and Spanish rescue packages,
- The European Stability Mechanism,
- The European budget pact, and
- Euroland's proposed banking union.

In the end, SP lost the election. Political analysts say that had it come to power it would have instituted a change of regime in the Hague applying a "Holland first" policy with several positions not too different than PVV (Freedom Party), the right wing party. It should as well be remembered that the SP was opposed to the euro in 1999, but in the mid-2012 elections, it did not call for Holland to leave the common currency. The Freedom party, which was explicitly advocating an exit of the Euroland, also lost support.

The Dutch centrist parties maintained their dominant positions. No Dutch party stuck its neck out with a message to the electorate that "the euro must be saved at all cost." The one which got more votes capitalized on the discontent of Dutch people about having good money run after bad. On the other hand, with the exception of PVV, no Dutch party revealed to the electorate that there is a deeper reason why so much money is thrown down the drain.

"The real reason for current political action is not to save the euro but to save their jobs and privileges," says Dr. Heinrich Steinmann. The huge EU bureaucracy in Brussels is shaken by the thought that if the euro goes, the EU will fall apart, and they will lose their well-paid positions, expense accounts, and rich pensions. These are personal goals of the Brussels elite, and correlate very badly with the search for financial stability.

The "save the euro to save my job" connection is further reinforced by a financial–political complex which has interests invested in ECB's ability to continue spitting out other people's money. And it is further promoted by the general unwillingness of governments to make tough decisions, even if they know that tough and painful decisions are needed to stop *déclinisme* from gaining the upper ground all over the North Atlantic (Chapter 2).

"Save the euro to save my job" requires short-term action, which explains why many among the present political leaders of Euroland are pushing for more short-term measures while they know that they are ineffectual. In this camp, the ideas on how to spend money have no limits. Monti was the first to suggest the policy of using Euroland's ECM, and its euro 500 billion, to buy bonds of "virtuous" countries (whatever that means). What a miracle! The "other Mario" (Draghi) was precisely of the same opinion.

Lost in the dust of missing political backing for financial stability is the fact that Italy's and Spain's reforms have been approved by the respective parliament only after lots of trimming and abandonment of vital restructuring measures. As a result, a mare's nest of financial, social, and political risks remain, including litigation, social unrest, and a great deal of ineffectiveness hardly covered by rising populist rhetoric.

Spain's economic mess is a combination of ailing banks, nearly bankrupt regions, double-dip recession, 28 percent general unemployment, 57 percent youth unemployment—and other dismal statistics which are getting worse. Regarding Spain's budget, with popular support dropping like a stone Rajoy's government will, has to find further savings, or additional revenue of at least euro 20 billion. This is easier said than done as the Spanish prime minister has promised not to cut pensions, while under pressure by EU/ECB/IMF the Greek government did just that to the tune of 40 percent and even the Italian government moved in the same direction.

Following ECB's giveaway money policy of unlimited purchases of useless government bonds (OMT, Chapter 2), Spain managed to auction some short-term debt at reduced interest rate, but experts said the markets would not tolerate the ongoing uncertainty for long. By all evidence, the window of opportunity for Spain to issue debt at rates relatively mild, as they were in mid-September 2012, is closing. At that time, markets had priced-in an ECB-backed bond-buying program for Spain, but delays had a negative effect in market psychology.

In France, after the victory of the left in the presidential and parliamentary elections, little has been done to reshape French economic policy in a rational and effective way, as contrasted to doing so according to the party's ideology. Hollande is more prone to tax than to cut costs. In his first trimester in office, he also chose the dangerous road of head-on confrontation with Germany,[32] all the way:

- From Eurobonds,
- To ECB's buying the sovereign bonds of Euroland's profligate states, which is a liability, and
- To ECB's oversight of European banks,[33] a job for which the central bank and its boss are singularly *unqualified*.

Draghi's fame as super-banking regulator of Euroland got particularly weakened with the scam of Monte dei Paschi di Siena, Italy's third larger bank, of which he was regulator as president of the Bank of Italy, prior to being appointed to the ECB.

On January 17, 2013 two Bloomberg News reporters Eliza Martinuzzi and Nicholas Dunbar broke the story that in December 2008 Deutsche Bank designed a derivative instrument for Banca Monte dei Paschi. The goal was to hide the Italian bank's losses before it sought a 1.9 billion euro ($2.6 billion) taxpayer bailout in 2009. This is the now famous *Project Santorini*—one of four of its kind under Draghi's watch at Monte dei Paschi alone.

According to the law of the land, the Bank of Italy has the statutory responsibility for regulation, inspection, and control of the Italian banking industry. It does so through a powerful Auditing division (Ispettorato) which employs highly competent personnel and is always on alert. It is virtually impossible that for 5 years since fraud and deceit started till 2013 when it was revealed, the governors of the Bank of Italy were unaware of it.

The fact that a scam is left on its own devices while the Bank of Italy is alerted, is already something suspicious. Still more damaging is the fact that, as governor of Bank of Italy, Mario Draghi, did not make Monte dei Paschi disclose that scam information, neither did he call-in the prosecutors. Only in 2012, under his successor Ignazio Visco, Italian prosecutors opened a criminal investigation—one that includes the Bank of Italy.

As for Monte dei Paschi itself it searched for ways to justify its act. Its thinly veiled excuse has been that the "structured deals" were part of its "carry trade," and were not submitted to its administrative body. Top management knew nothing about multibillion euro deals which turned sour and sank the bank. Evidently, this is a silly excuse, but it seems that it worked as long as Draghi's Bank of Italy conveniently turned a blind eye.

Whether bank regulation should be hard or soft is one of the issues dividing northern from southern Euroland. The north is for real inspection. The south would not bother pushing the scams under the carpet.

A similar deep divide in economic thinking characterized Euroland's forces of financial stability. Attempts to throw more money at struggling banks, or to mutualize debt of 17 countries with varying degrees of profligacy, has been anathema to northern Europeans. Those upholding the value of the currency are promoted *inter alia* by the Bundesbank. The Germans talk with the experience of hyperinflation they went through in 1922, and its devastating aftermath. They are joined by the Finns and the Dutch who also chose financial stability as the best monetary policy.

This dichotomy in economic thinking is the principal reason why Europe's politicians did not commit themselves to a firm solution out of the debt crisis. As Andreas Höfert, the chief economist of UBS, comments, "On paper, certain solutions to the euro crisis may appear rather simple economically, but they look hugely complex from a political perspective. ... Since the beginning of the euro crisis, 12 governments in 10 eurozone countries have already been ousted by general elections or lost confidence votes in their parliaments."[34]

If tough decisions cost political careers,
Then such decisions will not be taken with the result that both the economy and the currency suffer.

It is infantile to pretend that the "European spirit" would carry the day, at the expense of hard-working people and to the benefit of the profligate. Which "European spirit?" Solidarity means reciprocity; it is not a one-way street. As for real European integration, it has proved to be a chimera. An article in the Financial Times put it in this way:

- The envisaged leap into "more Europe" is unlikely to be agreed, and
- If agreed, is likely ultimately to fail.[35]

The featherbedded last two generations of European citizens are unlikely to welcome further austerity till their countries come up from under. This would probably mean a series of crises. Bailouts will reach nowhere as it has already happened with Greece. Profligate countries, mismanaged banks, and people living on debt share as their credo Louis XIV's *après moi le deluge*.

3.6   Reinventing Personal and Collective Irresponsibility

The majority of citizens today believe that the public has little influence on government decisions, and that the days of real democracy are past. This means that we have to reexamine the nature of the state and of its governance. In a democracy, the state exists for the individuals; not the individuals for the state. The latter option characterizes the socialist, fascist, Nazi, and Bolshevik credo which mutilates individual freedoms and reduces each individual into a cog in a big machine, degrading him or her to the level of an appendage of a mass society, where:

- Theoretically everything is for "free," but
- Practically independent human thought and action are forbidden.

Part of the reason for this drift in western democratic values is the wave of materialism which pervades all layers of society. Another major part is the surprising absence of leadership. It looks as if only average men and women are in charge, and everything else has also become average. The breed of politicians in WWI and WWII (the Churchills, Roosevelts, and de Gaulles) is extinct. Today's politicians are indistinguishable from bureaucrats. As Claude Adrien Helvétius (1715−1771) said long ago: Every period has its great men, and if they are lacking it invents them.

Our generation's inventions[36] are the bureaucrats—along with the personal and collective irresponsibility they represent. "Bureaucrats," commented a Swedish executive in the course of our meeting in Stockholm, "don't take risks. Their promotion is based on zero mistakes, and not all initiatives succeed." To the contrary, for an active person failures are great opportunities for learning. When everything works like a clock without any problem, a real leader knows that the time of crisis is approaching.

Successful leaders neither remain inactive nor are they unpredictable when they act.[37] They take calculated risks because they realize that it is much more dangerous to avoid tough decisions than to fail now and then. But they also clearly structure their priorities and carefully follow how risks under their watch develop so that timely corrective action can be taken.

The touch of leadership has been visible with all important issues. Plenty of examples exist from years past but habits, credos, skills, and ethics have changed. How did this change develop? In my research, I have found that recent generations of politicians lack three important ingredients for leadership:

- Self-confidence,
- The ability to tear to pieces the information they are getting to find what lies beneath it, and
- The will to honestly study their strengths and weaknesses, prior to making up their mind on an important decision.

In his book *Dereliction of Duty*, H.R. McMaster points out that President Johnson's lack of self-confidence manifested itself in a reluctance to trust those around him. Reflecting on his service in the Johnson White House, McGeorge Bundy had said, "Johnson was worried about the unknown..."

- "He knew how many unknowns there were,
- "He knew how complicated and uncertain life was,
- "He knew that the only way to avoid failure was to put yourself on guard ...."[38]

Michael Forrestal, a White House special assistant, had this to say about Lyndon Johnson which applies to most present-day politicians: "There was a bad thing in this period. The government was extremely scared of itself. There was tremendous nervousness that if you expressed an opinion it might somehow leak out...and the president would be furious and everyone's head would be cut off...It inhibited an exchange of information and prevented the president from getting a lot of the facts that he should have had."[39]

In violation to sound management practice, people were unable to disagree with what they felt were Johnson's choices.[40] This led to the desire to demonstrate unity by coordinating positions *before* discussing them with the president. This unavoidably leads to serious errors. The last thing a president needs is to be confronted with a unanimous view. He has to hear *disagreement*. Only then can he use his own judgment in examining a range of options.

I had the privilege to work for 16 years as personal consultant to the president and CEO of one of Europe's largest industrial and financial groups. His policy in regard to decision making at the vertex was precisely the opposite to Johnson's. He wanted his immediate assistants, presidents and general managers of his banks and manufacturing companies, to come to board meetings without any prediscussions:

- Everyone had to present and defend his or her thesis on the topic of the meeting.

- Parties with opposing viewpoints had to debate their differences in front of everyone else.
- Even a suspicion of having prearranged positions was a negative to every person who took part in it.

To Carlo Pesenti's opinion, bringing up every issue, including its externalities, was the only way to see clearer in a situation. He was more interested to discover how well thought-out were the decisions of his immediate assistants than wait and see if they turned to be "right" or "wrong." Something can happen turning on their head otherwise well-documented hypotheses, but lightly made business assumptions will always be a loser.

The mind of Alfred Sloan, the legendary boss of General Motors, worked the same way. He wanted to see and hear dissention. Otherwise, he would delay the board decision to the next meeting. By contrast, weak CEOs, like Lyndon Johnson, try to cover their shortcomings by distributing fountain pens, or other highly expensive goodies, such as the twin monsters Medicare and Medicaid, which lack a sense of cost control and threaten to sink the American economy.[41]

The search for unanimous view, which is typically based on compromises, is that of the weak, not of leaders. In the majority of cases, it locks itself up in a one-way street and from there to disaster. That's precisely where we are today with the different European Union "summits." There is a long list of issues on which disagreements exist, but without the appropriate analysis of *pros* and *cons*, which are brought to public attention so that they can be discussed as democratic values require, decisions are taken through power politics.

Jens Weidmann was criticized as lone wolf when he voted against ECB's "unlimited" buying of sovereign bonds. Curiously, very curiously, dissent was muted. *No other member of the central bank's executive board fulfilled his or her duty of examination by asking*:

- Is the ECB turning the monetary union into a debt community with unlimited liability by buying government bonds?
- Where is the factual estimate of the depth of the commitment in money terms and on its effect on financial stability?
- Are we able to reconcile spending big money on profligate states, when we know that all 17 Euroland countries need huge financial resources for an aging population—from retirement to health care?
- *What if* we have it all wrong and the ultimate outcome for Euroland's economy resembles a Japan-like scenario of two decades of stagnation, or worse?

Just as an example, the aging of western populations and rapid rise in health care costs mean that sovereign budget gimmicks which worked in the past cannot work in the future. In fact, a major reason for the deficits which incurred and continue to incur in *Club Med* countries have their origin in the aging of their population and associated to it:

- Early retirement, and
- Generous benefits.

Both are unaffordable. The debt crisis has not gone away because the ECB (incorrectly) decided to buy sovereign bonds. Neither has the bad news run its course. As Section 3.1 brought to the reader's attention with Roubinis' three scenarios, it may well be that the worst is still to come, and this should discourage politicians and central bankers from spending funds reserved for the worst case.

3.7 Conclusions

When governments forget about the growing array of their obligations, and the costs these represent, which have to be weighted against receipts, then funds set to general public will be dissipated at no time. What follows in terms of rush decisions is piling error upon error. When this happens, debt and fiscal policy is far from being an example of political and social strength, and sometimes down the line the rescue mechanism breaks into pieces.

For over 6 years, since July 2007 when the global economic, financial, and banking crisis began with the subprimes, the western world has seen average annual government deficits skyrocket from 1.5 percent to 6.5 percent of GDP.[42] By ballooning the cost of the western countries social safety net while confronted with reduced tax receipts, governments turned the tables on sound management of the economy.

The result has not only been that the rich got richer but also, and most regretfully, that the western middle class has been decimated. As I had the opportunity to explain in previous books, the government-run *State Supermarket*, into which has grown the nanny state, is simultaneously confronted by:

- Rapidly rising health care costs,
- Unfunded pension obligations,
- Upward racing costs for university education "for all," and
- A large public sector characterized by low productivity but high expenditures.

The net result is a decline in sovereign sustenance, and this reflects in an important way upon the western nations' creditworthiness. The vicious cycle of debt piling upon debt and error upon error is sealed by the sovereign's loss of risk-free status, as it has happened with the downgrades of the United States, France, Austria, and other western nations. This is a sort of drift which undermines financial stability and leads to contagion.

From the standpoint of sound management, an independent country must have adequacy of international reserves. The way to judge such adequacy is by comparing its reserves against benchmarks calibrated by the collective experience of countries in past crises, and modeled through a cost-benefit analysis. Adequacy metrics described in an article by the ECB[43] call for coverage by international reserves of at least:

- 3 months of imports,
- 100 percent of short-term debt at remaining maturity,[44]

- The current account balance, and
- 20 percent of the M2 monetary base.

The ECB article notes that IMF has recently proposed still another metric which involves benchmarking international reserves against a *risk-weighted liability stock*. This should capture all potential drains on reserves, weighted against the likelihood of their occurrence derived from a tail-event analysis of past foreign exchange market pressure. I would be inclined adding to that the effect of recent estimates by international agencies. For instance, in January 2012 the World Bank stated that a new oil shock will lead to hard landing.[45]

Each of the options we have considered is likely to have unwanted consequences which cannot be smoothed over by word-of-mouth assurances as substitute to hard facts. False assurances are by no means recent inventions. As Talleyrand said to Napoleon, "The art of diplomacy consists of masking one's plan by verbs."

End Notes

1. Such a slow recovery compares poorly to the average recovery time over the last three decades.
2. Bloomberg BusinessWeek, August 13–26, 2012.
3. CNBC, August 9, 2012.
4. These were the words Roubini used in his Bloomberg Business Week article, mid-August 2012.
5. Financial Times, September 27, 2012.
6. *Idem.*
7. Financial Times, July 12, 2012.
8. Even if bond spreads are zero across Euroland, Britain, and the United States.
9. *Le Canard Enchaîné*, September 19, 2012. As I never tire repeating *"Le Canard"* is not a satirical paper. It's a well-informed political weekly communicating with its readers through both cartoons and hard facts.
10. Spain, Portugal, Italy, Greece, and eventually France.
11. UBS, Wealth Management Research, December 19, 2011.
12. Particularly the big entities which pose systemic risk. In 2011, John Paulson's hedge fund lost more money than JPMorgan's London unit. Regulators didn't worry, because Paulson's private partnership was not too big to fail.
13. Financial Times, August 7, 2012.
14. UBS Chief Investment Office. The debt crisis, May 8, 2012. Statistics updated as of September 27, 2012.
15. Which by all likelihood is also an underestimate.
16. Bloomberg News, September 27, 2012.
17. SMP has been phased out with OMT.
18. Its annual budget without counting the interest paid on past debts.
19. The US financial bailout fund.
20. Barofsky N. *Bailout.* An inside account of how Washington abandoned Main Street while rescuing Wall Street. New York, NY: Free Press; 2012.

21. Particularly when, in the George W. Bush years, Geithner was president of the New York Federal Reserve. Notice that during that time Geithner allegedly approved the manipulation of LIBOR which led to the LIBOR scandal of 2012.
22. Let me laugh.
23. No kidding.
24. With that merger, Weill created a sprawling conglomerate. Commenting on his call to spin off businesses and abolish the financial supermarket concept, Weill said, "I think the earlier model was right for that time."
25. Financial Times, July 26, 2012.
26. Originally the Vickers Commission, in Britain, was proposing breaking up the big banks, but this finding curiously disappeared from its final report—allegedly under the pressure of lobbyists.
27. The Glass—Steagall Act, passed after the Great Depression, forced a separation of commercial and retail banking from investment banking. It was repealed in 1999 by Bill Clinton, in his last year in the White House.
28. Named after Dr. Paul Volcker, former chairman of the Fed.
29. Chorafas DN. Basel III, the devil and global banking. London: Palgrave/Macmillan; 2012.
30. Chorafas DN. Rocket scientists in banking. London and Dublin: Lafferty Publications; 1995.
31. Financial Times, June 27, 2012.
32. Which defeats the very purpose of the European Union.
33. In the context of a very poorly studied banking union. The timetable has been pushed from an original implementation deadline of late 2012 out to early 2014.
34. UBS Investor's Guide, July 6, 2012.
35. Financial Times, June 27, 2012.
36. Or, rather, reinvention since the mighty bureaucracy was invented with the Mandarin culture in China and reinvented by the Byzantines.
37. In his biography of Stalin (*Staline*. Paris: Editions des Syrtes; 2005) Simon Sebag Montefiore says that the Russian dictator misjudged Hitler because he was an admirer of Bismarck and passionate reader of Bismarck's works. Bismarck was predictable and Stalin thought all German political leaders are predictable. Hitler was neither German, nor predictable.
38. McMaster HR. Dereliction of duty. New York, NY: Harper Perennial; 1997.
39. Michael Forestal, Oral History Transcript, November 3, 1969, MBJ Library.
40. To the contrary Alfred Sloan, chairman and CEO of General Motors, would not accept that his assistants or board members had a unanimous opinion. He wanted to see and hear dissent.
41. The same is true with the unaffordable Obamacare, which comes as no surprise as Barack Obama is a sort of Lyndon Johnson "bis."
42. Bank for International Settlements, 82nd Annual Report, Basel, June 24, 2012.
43. ECB Monthly Bulletin, June 2012.
44. Known as the Greenspan—Guidotti rule (Guidotti P, remarks at G33 seminar in Bonn, Germany, March 11, 1999; Greenspan A, Currency reserves and debt, remarks before the World Bank Conference on Recent Trends in Reserves Management, Washington, DC, April 29, 1999; available at http://www.federalreserve.gov).
45. Bloomberg News, January 18, 2012.

Part Two

Destiny in the Land of Homer

4 The Greek Economy Pays the Price of Drift

4.1 "My Lord," Said Demaratus to King Xerxes, "Do You Want Me to Tell You the Truth or Flatteries?"

"My lord," said Demaratus, the former King of Sparta (515–491 BC) exiled in the Court of Xerxes[1] to a question posed by the King of Kings, "Do you want me to tell you the truth of flatteries?" Xerxes answered: "The truth," and assured him that he will not alter his hospitality no matter what his answer was. Demaratus' policy of saying the truth is the one described in this and the next chapters deliberately.

"Greece has been brought up in the school of poverty," Demaratus informed Xerxes. *"Virtue was not born with it. Virtue is the result of temperance and severity of our laws — the very laws which give us the arms to fight poverty and tyranny.*[2] Therefore, I dare say (the Greeks) will not listen to your propositions because they aim to enslave them. In regard to their number, don't ask me how many they must be to resist your army. Even if they are only one thousand, they will fight you."[3]

Demaratus concluded by saying that while the Greeks were free, they were not so in an absolute sense, because "the law is for them an absolute master and they follow its letter much more than Xerxes' subjects follow their King. The supreme authority is the command of the law, and its command is that no matter how numerous the enemy's army may be they have to hold their post at all cost, win or die."

This was true of antiquity, but it is no longer true today. The laws are being interpreted in a lax way, as corrupt politicians make promises they know very well they cannot keep—and common citizens find it convenient and profitable to believe them and therefore they reelect these corrupt, do-nothing politicians. Promises engage only those listening to them, said Charles Pasqua, a French politician. It's a concept worth repeating.

For twentieth and twenty-first century Greece, the result has been a disaster. Countries in which financial competence is better aligned with political responsibility have a lesser need for draconian[4] measures. This is not true for Greece. After three long decades of mismanagement, the need for correction is God size. Public debt in comparison to GDP is an important (negative) barometer, and among western nations (ex-Japan), Greece excels by a margin:

- Greece 160 percent
- Italy 123 percent

Public Debt Dynamics of Europe and the US. DOI: http://dx.doi.org/10.1016/B978-0-12-420021-0.00004-X

- United States 111 percent
- Portugal 110 percent
- Belgium 100 percent
- France 94 percent
- Germany 83 percent
- Austria 70 percent
- Switzerland 36 percent
- Luxembourg 20 percent

Debt-to-GDP ratios—both their absolute value and their trend—are an important measure of economic health. Hiding or massaging the numbers does not improve a bad situation; it is only worsening it. Yves Mersch, governor of Luxembourg's central bank did the wrong thing when he denounced "increasing speculation on the capacity of Greece to honor its debts."[5] In late April 2010, when this statement was made, for any practical purpose Greece was bankrupt.

When Standard & Poor's downgraded Greece long-term debt to junk, the European Commission responded that it expected rating agencies like S&P to be responsible at this difficult and sensitive time.[6] This, too, has been the wrong initiative. As Demaratus would have commented if he lived today, people and countries should never fail to listen when independent critics start saying that they are going downhill.

Debt has to be served and repaid. A great deal of tax money which might have been used for investments to provide the ground for future jobs goes into debt interest and repayment. What is more, the higher is the public debt the lower becomes a debtor's creditworthiness—therefore the higher the interest rate he or she has to pay.

- In 1993, in the years of Andreas Papandreou, the then Greek prime minister was spending money by the bushel, Greece had to pay 25 percent interest on its debt.[7]
- By 1995 the interest fell to 20 percent, still way too high, and slid under 5 percent after Greece joined the euro in 2001.
- A decade later, as economic mismanagement returned in full force, interest rates rose once again to 25 percent (at end of 2011), in spite of the bailout plan.

In a way, it comes as no surprise that the European debt crisis got bone and muscle in Greece. Since Euroland's start, the weak links in euro's chain have been Greece, Italy, Spain, and Portugal—but Greece was also hit by exceptionally bad political mismanagement. Part of it was the derivatives trick to hide a large chunk of the country's debt, done in collaboration with Goldman Sachs and *allegedly* arranged by Mario Draghi, currently president of the ECB. (More on this is described in Section 4.3.)

Contagion from economic mismanagement knows no borders. When the Greek debt crisis flared up in 2009–2010, European Union leaders hoped to contain it at the Greek shore by providing a bailout of euro 110 billion (then $160 billion) over 3 years. Of this, euro 80 billion came from Euroland member countries and euro 30 billion from the IMF.

The European Commission, ECB, and IMF who loaned their money to Greece, Portugal, and Ireland set up a tri-party commission, known as *troika*, to supervise how the money was spent and whether agreed upon measures were taken. The troika's mission has been to find out whether agreements associated to the bailout loan were kept, and document its finding. The IMF has a long experience in that sort of measures and in control.

Lenders want to see that the party borrowing their money works and does not use it for festivities. In Philadelphia, Benjamin Franklin was walking in the night past the shops of artisans who had taken a loan. If the borrower was busy at his shop, he would be patient even if that man was in arrears. But if he saw him drinking in a tavern, he would call in his loan.

The first bailout package for Greece proved to be insufficient. The country needed more money for a longer period of time. As an article in *The Economist* put it: "This sent European policymakers into frenzy. Their attempts to find a solution have sometimes seemed to spring from the pages of an overwrought thriller."[8]

On June 23/24, 2011 Euroland's heads of state met in Brussels to decide on the second rescue package, under condition that the Greek parliament endorses the extra austerity the country had to swallow, along with a program to privatize state assets. Overoptimistic estimates suggested that assets to be privatized could fetch between euro 50 billion and euro 80 billion. These were numbers picked out of a hat.

In their book *Why Nations Fail* Acemoglu and Robinson advance the thesis that nations fail because their leaders are greedy, selfish, and ignorant of history.[9] Drifting is accelerated by accommodating and weak institutions, and when drifting starts, there is little to discourage elected officials (or for that matter dictators) from looting even the little bits and pieces that still remain of public wealth.

Rescue packages can do no miracles. Those authorizing them try to shake up sclerotic economies, but politicians able to undertake sweeping changes and liberalize conditions characterized by conflicts of interest are not on hand. Economies can benefit from bailouts *if*, and only *if*, those who govern push through harsh measures to first stabilize the debt level then start paying it off.

Whether we speak of Club Med (Italy, Spain, Portugal, Greece) or larger economies, a bailout strategy will never work in a vacuum. Somebody has to be in charge and, as first act of faith, correct the wrong impression created by successive governments that citizens and nations can continue living beyond their means. A leader must explain to the citizen that getting loans to pay for excesses is the worst possible policy.[10] Also, that entitlements serviced by loans end up in a disaster. This is precisely the point where the plain talk by Demaratus to Xerxes provides an awakening. Europe has:

- Less than 5 percent of global population,
- Not quite 24 percent of global GDP, a shrinking global share, and
- Nearly 50 percent of global spending on entitlements, in their different forms.

If one doubles these figures, the resulting statistics would include the United States and point to the fact that a shrinking productive capacity coupled with the demands posed by a rising nanny state is the prescription for economic and social catastrophe. This is not just a Greek problem; it's a problem which has infiltrated every corner of the West.

- The engine of growth has been put out of gear, and
- In the absence of a rigorous budgetary discipline governments have relied on debt.

Even if by a magic wand all debts were extinguished, *if* nothing changes in spending more than the nation earns, *then* the current situation will reproduce itself in a few years. In righting the balances, the most important advance of all is not austerity but the understanding by everybody that past conditions should not be allowed to repeat themselves. Even after it wanes, the crisis will come back with a vengeance if spending and spending continues, which means that the nation will never go back to stability.

4.2 The Target Should Be Competitiveness

Until the EU/ECB/IMF bailout came along, the Greek crisis has chiefly been a drifting, with euro's helping hand wearing off and the country feeling pressure from the markets. But sovereign finances, and even more so the economy, are not defined by markets alone. Rather the limits of solvency are tested by people's willingness to accept tax rises, spending cuts, a (hopefully) temporary lower standard of living, and what it takes to bring up competitiveness in a globalized economy. A government, any government, runs out of political capital long before it runs out of money.

Whether center-right or center-left, Greek governments did not spend what scant political capital they had in negotiating with IMF and with Euroland for a break. They did not press the basic fact that above all the economy needs to grow, but globalization has wiped out the medium-sized Greek industries. Neither did they undertake growth-promoting structural reforms, albeit a controversial issue because of internal opposition by entrenched interests (labor unions included).

To promote structural reforms, governments have to explain to the public the need for change in attitude and culture, facing down public-sector unions and enforcing changes which may be painful but are also deadly necessary. They did not even do so after the bailout was decided. George Papandreou and his successor prime ministers took the easy way out. No wonder, therefore, that by March 2013, not quite years after the first bailout:

- General unemployment reached 26 percent, and
- Youth unemployment went beyond 55 percent, which is tragic.[11]

True enough, Euroland and the IMF placed more emphasis on austerity than on structural reforms, aggravating Greece's economic woes. But it is no less true that since Day 1 of the bailout the government did not take the measures it should have taken by instituting a new economic policy centered on *competitiveness* in the globalized market.

Competitiveness is a concept which has often been misinterpreted, and in many cases misused. The better way to define it is in the words of Warren Buffett who once said that: The single most important decision in evaluating a business is pricing power. If you have the power to raise prices without losing business to a competitor, if you have got a very good business. (But) if you have to have a prayer session before raising the price by 10 percent, then you have got a terrible business.[12]

Buffett's definition is equally valid for companies and for a nation's industrial standing. In fact, *pricing power* is particularly important in a low-growth environment like that of Italy, Spain, France, Portugal, and Greece. A nation's companies and its labor force need two things to be ahead of the curve in pricing power:

- High quality[13] of their produce, and
- Low cost of production.

Notice that *innovation* is deliberately not added as a third bullet because, very important, it is an ingredient demanding R&D budgets, research laboratories, and people able and willing to challenge the "obvious" and a sophisticated infrastructure. Each one of these issues enhances competitiveness but is outside the main theme of this discussion.[14]

The Swiss mechanical watch industry provides a good example of what I mean by attention to, and competitive advantage from, high quality. Like jewelry, the watch industry is more cyclical than other sectors, and therefore more vulnerable in a downturn. But the effect on market share is uneven, and quality makes the difference.

Roughly 1.2 billion watches are produced annually in the luxury class, but only 26 million of these are made in Switzerland. However, 95 percent of watches priced above CHF 1000 and sold worldwide are Swiss-made, and the label "Made in Switzerland" is one of distinctive quality, especially appreciated in emerging markets. High quality is not assured just by trying to do a better job:

- The manufacture of mechanical watch movements requires specialist knowledge that cannot be acquired overnight, and
- The Swiss advantage lies in the fact that for more than a century, Switzerland has built a reputation for excellence in precision engineering backed by an effective quality control.

By contrast, the Greek industry has problems in competing both cost-wise and quality-wise. Like quality, costs matter a great deal in competitiveness. A proof of a mismanaged economy is that over the years of the euro, wages grew 30 percent more than corresponding wages in Germany. It needs no explaining that under these conditions, the Greek industry lost its competitiveness in Euroland's market and in the global market.

Governments, and even more so labor unions, have the bad habit of continuing to live in a make-believe world of their own—a world totally detached from current reality. While professing loudly that they want to see more jobs, they do whatever it takes to destroy jobs. Short of a long-term plan which accounts for competitiveness, unemployment has no other way to go but up.

The case of lack of competitiveness is vividly displayed in Italy, where Sergio Marchionne, the chief executive of both Fiat and Chrysler, has been trying to overcome powerful labor union resistance to competitiveness. In 2009, Fiat's five biggest assembly plants in Italy produced 650,000 cars using 22,000 workers. That same year, a single Fiat plant in Tychy, Poland, produced 600,000 cars with 6100 workers each earning about a third of their Italian counterparts. In terms of deliverables:

• Fiat's plants in Poland are 333 percent more productive than in Italy, and
• Evidently, Fiat scheduling favors the Polish plants; hence, Italian assembly plants operate at less than 40 percent of capacity, far below the rest of Europe.

In Greece, too, as a result of loss of competitiveness, plenty of Greek employees and workers lost their jobs. Not only Greek industries, such as textiles, went under when the "low-costs" came along, but other sectors of the economy, too, went into decline. Even agricultural products are now imported. As a recent news item has it, Greece is importing salads and other vegetables from north-western Africa (the Maghreb). This is absolutely inexcusable. Fresh vegetables should be a home-grown industry.

The positive effect of competitiveness is seen not only on jobs but also on current account figures which improve with exports. Greece's improved current account deficit shrank mainly due to collapsing imports. Exports are up, but not much. In the first 2 years after the first bailout, exports rose 2 percent while imports plunged 15 percent. Competitiveness can only be regained the hard way:

• Planning for it,
• Changing working culture,
• Learning how to market Greek produce,
• Swamping domestic costs,
• Betting on quality, and
• Increasing productivity.

That is why structural reforms, including "internal devaluation" (Chapter 13) are so essential not only to Greece but also to Italy, Spain, Portugal, and Cyprus. These are not incidental remarks but basic observations which help in explaining why bailouts don't work. When assessing the practicalities of rescue plans, the reader should familiarize himself or herself with *Gresham's law*. Simply put, it states, "Bad money drives out good." As long as bad money remains in the economy protected by special interests, good money will keep away.

"We have got to a point where we're at a complete standstill," said Constantine Michalos, president of the Athens Chamber of Commerce.[15] The chamber's study revealed that from January 1, 2011 till mid-June 2012 some 68,000 Greek businesses closed and the expectation has been that a further 36,000 were at the edge and could shut down with disastrous effects on the economy.

Even tourism, one of the last remaining going industries in the Greek economy, suffered greatly as strikes drive away tourists, and street demonstrations lead holidaymakers to cancel bookings.[16] Strikers, whose behavior ranged from the irrational to disgraceful, were practically cutting the branch on which they were sitting.

Tourism is a service industry and those who suffered stranded in a port because the sailors went into a wild strike, curse the hour they went there and they never come back. Nothing should have been done putting at risk the tourist industry. There are conditions under which strikes turn into folly as they kill the jobs for whose sake (theoretically) workers and employees are striking.

The scarcity of bank loans has been another big negative. It was therefore good news that on September 13, 2012 the European Investment Bank (EIB) agreed on the immediate disbursement of euro 750 million ($986 million) in loans to SMEs as well as for transport, energy, and education projects. The SMEs are scheduled to absorb about 60 percent of the loans.

This deal, whose execution was somehow delayed, was scheduled to bring real money into the economy at a time when the lack of liquidity is causing problems suffocating the market. The problem is a low timetable. Yannis Stournaras, the finance minister, said that the lender would disburse the loans to Greek SMEs by the end of 2015 through the country's banks. But will this money be used to promote competitiveness or only to pay past debts?

Another commendable effort aimed to create jobs has been that of special economic zones which can attract foreign direct investment. China, a country with experience with special zones, suggested a special economic area should be set up near Athens and the port of Piraeus where Cosco (the state-owned Chinese shipping company) operates a container terminal. China pledged participation by other Chinese companies.

Special economic zones offering tax breaks to attract investors and reinvigorate its economy are in no way set up for the asking. They require accelerating EU-backed infrastructure projects as well as the political decision to reduce bureaucracy and red tape. The irony with the EU is that as far as special zones are concerned, Greece still had to overcome objections by some other member countries on grounds of unfair competition because the creation of such zones would give a comparative advantage. That's the EU.

4.3   Fakelakia and the Wages of Corruption Buy Yachts

According to history books, emperor Zhu Yuanzhang, founder of China's Ming dynasty, skinned corrupt officials, stuffed them with straw and put them on display to discourage others from unethical behavior. In the aftermath, wrongdoers and transgressors took a leave, but when Zhu died corruption returned and contributed to the Ming dynasty's downfall.

Big corruption is not the only game in town. Widespread little corruptions exemplified by the *fakelakia* (envelopes with money) left on the desk of, or passed under the table to, a civil servant, doctor, or any other professional can be just as devastating. Fakelakia have become a culture in Greece, and this bad habit is more difficult to eradicate than big time corruption because it has woven itself into the fabric of society.

I have an aunt who in her 80 years needs a cataract operation for both eyes. She has the right to go to a military hospital and that's what she did. The eye doctor knew her; unwisely in previous visits she had left behind his fakelaki. The doctor confirmed a date for the operation, but given the severe cut in pension for retired senior servants, this time she could not afford his fakelaki.

The eye doctor asked for it; she excused herself for not being able to provide it (which she should not have done). Upon hearing that this time his hand is not greased, the doctor returned to his desk took his appoints book and stroke out her date. No fakelaki, no cataract operation. This is just one example, but rumors have it that the steady flow of fakelakia make many people rich, and professionals who get plenty of fakelakia display their wealth by buying yachts.

The way a feature article in the *Financial Times* had it, the main political parties in Greece are seen as "pillars of a parasitic system, fuelled by political patronage and cronyism."[17] This is a double whammy from which the country has suffered for decades; hence, it comes as no surprise that the popularity of politicians and political parties is at an all-time low. The overwhelming feeling is one of disenchantment with two main parties whose:

- Corruption,
- Nepotism, and
- Incompetence created this terrible mess.

Mid-April 2012 Greek prosecutors revealed money laundering that funded a former defense minister's, Akis Tsochatzopoulos, life of luxury. A 103-page prosecutors' report provided shocking evidence of an extensive money-laundering network. Allegedly, since 1997, the 73-year-old ex-minister pocketed millions of euros in under-the-table payments, with the frequency of illicit transactions peaking between 1999 and 2002.

Illegal activities were concealed with the help of close associates who ran offshore companies to hide the money, some of which was used to buy the ex-minister's array of assets the prosecutors stated. Millions of euros' have been linked to the procurement of Tor M1 missiles. In a related development, it was revealed that George Papandreou Jr., the then prime minister[18] and Tsochatzopoulos' boss, had hired 300 consultants (read: highly paid political appointments, typically loafers) while local authorities hired 60,000 people at the same time.

The irony behind this "60,000" is that, due to bailout provisions, the government fired about the same number of public employees.[19] They went out of the door for the troika to see, and then they came back from the window.

An even greater and more damaging disgrace has been the one engineered by Goldman Sachs, in which *allegedly* Draghi had a role to play.[20] The derivatives product by the investment bank allowed Greece to gain membership to the euro by circumventing Euroland's rules. Mortgaging assets and using creative accounting debt was hidden. The tool has been cross-currency swaps, a sophisticated derivatives instrument. Government debt issued in dollars and yen was swapped for euros, then later exchanged back to original currencies. This is said to have been the top Ponzi game of 2002.

In the words of Stephen Lendman: "Debt entrapment followed. Greece was held hostage to repay it. The country's been raped and pillaged. Paying bankers comes first. Doing it left Greeks impoverished, high and dry. Goldman profited enormously by scamming an entire country and millions in it... Standing armies pale by comparison. Michael Hudson calls finance warfare by other means. Generalissimo bankers run everything... It's up to public rage to change things."[21]

Nevertheless, while Greek voters may be sick of the corruption and clientelism that has flourished under the two traditional parties, Panhellenic Socialist Movement (PASOK) and conservative New Democracy, they still vote for them. The two have alternated in power for about three decades. Both have been discredited. Ironically, in his first EU summit 2009, George Papandreou described his own country as "corrupt to the bone,"[22] but forgot to say that he was part of it.

Greece is by no means an exception. Other examples of corruption and nepotism can be found all over the political constellation from Italy and Slovakia in Euroland to the Philippines in the Pacific Rim. On October 4, 2012 Gloria Arroyo, the former Philippine president, was arrested while undergoing treatment at a military hospital on charges of misusing $8.8 million of state lottery funds during her last year in office.[23]

In Slovakia, Robert Fico, leader of the Social-Democratic party won the election in March 2012 in spite the fact that his first stint in office, from 2006 to 2010, was marked by cronyism. Instrumental in his electoral victory was an intelligence report nick-named "Gorilla" which suggested that center-right politicians in a previous government may have been pocketing commissions from privatization and public procurement deals.[24]

In the Balkans, Bulgaria and Romania, northern neighbors of Greece and Italy in the west have a long tradition in corruption. In Rome, 20 years after the bribesville (*tangentopoli*) scandal that swept away Italy's post-WWII political establishment Paola Severino, the justice minister, says that corruption is as extensive now as it was then. If Severino is right, and probably she is, this is a damning verdict.

The generation of politicians, who came to prominence after *tangentopoli* with promises of change, abused power as much as their predecessors (see also in Chapter 8 the scandals connected to the country's parliamentarians). According to observers of Italian nepotism and other social ills, the torrent of scandals flooding over the country in recent years are in inverse relation to the economic incompetence of professional politicians. Mario Monti is right in:

- Describing these happenings as "unspeakable", and
- Warning of the incalculable damage they inflict on the whole country, even if only a minority is involved in them.

In Greece, too, corruption is alive and well among the lawmakers. On February 25, 2012 the Greek government threatened to name and shame members of parliament accused of funneling huge sums of money abroad in spite of a call to ordinary Greeks to return their savings to the country's cash-strapped banks. Afraid that Greece leaves the euro, Greek citizens have allegedly withdrawn over euro 75 billion in bank savings since the onset of the debt crisis in 2009, hiding it at home or keeping it in safety boxes. Allegedly, some of that money left the country.

Corruption leads to major doubts about the credibility of reform efforts particularly when a country is in the middle of a severe and protracted debt crisis. It also strengthens the critics' argument that parliaments don't really care to pass anticorruption bills unless these are all but stripped of real content.

Neither is corruption limited to the political vertex. It is also widespread among those who benefit from the goodies distributed by the government within the realm of the ever-growing State Supermarket, and its entitlements. In January 2012, the Greek authorities caught a scheme involving 63,600 false pensions. Typically, the money went to nonexisting or no longer living persons, or was calculated according to wrong information at the cost to the taxpayer of about euro 450 million a year.[25]

At end of February 2012, Swiss authorities reportedly froze three bank accounts of the former head of Proton, a private Greek bank. Lavrentis Lavrentiadis has been under investigation by Greek prosecutors for alleged fraud, embezzlement, and corruption involving up to euro 700 million. An audit by the Bank of Greece found that in 2010 more than 40 percent of Proton's commercial loans were made to companies allegedly connected to Lavrentiadis—a flagrant misuse of basic banking principles.

While accusations related to corruption and mismanagement mount, in September 2012, the government of Antonis Samaras called for "zero tolerance" of corruption after reports surfaced of politicians being investigated on suspicion of taking kickbacks and evading taxes while in office. In an interview marking his first 100 days at the head of a coalition, Samaras referred to the publication of a list of 30 names of former and present politicians under investigation by SDOE, the financial police.

The leaked list of politicians under investigation included the leader of a small political party, a former mayor of Athens, a former lawmaker who was responsible while in office for promoting transparency, and a former finance minister. All denied any wrongdoing.[26] On information available until these lines are written the cleanhands campaign's only victim has been Evangelos Meimatakis, speaker of parliament, who stood down after he and two of his former cabinet colleagues were accused in a newspaper article of involvement in a euro 10 billion ($13 billion) money-laundering operation in collusion with two Athens real-estate brokers. They, too, denied the accusations.

Greece has also been criticized by the EU and IMF for not cracking down on tax evasion, including the use of offshore companies and transfers of capital by wealthy individuals to international financial centers. Moreover, SDOE reported that its officers inspected thousands of businesses and found 55.7 percent of them to be in breach of taxation laws for a variety of violations led by failure to issue receipts.[27]

Failure to issue receipts is a globally widespread practice and little can be done about it. In the late 1970s, the Italian government used the financial police and the carabinieri to inspect *if* customers leaving a restaurant and other shops had a receipt. This led to a new profession: *accompagnatori fiscali*. These were typically unemployed people who followed a restaurant's clients till they were out of range of the carabinieri, politely asking to be given the receipts which they swiftly sold to the restaurant's owner so that he or she did not need to report the income which he or she made.

4.4 Coming Up from Under Is a Tough Job

The firebrigade's work known as "bailout" is based on the premise that time is being bought and recovery is given a chance to show up. An economy, however, is not returning to good shape of being asked to do so. It takes time, effort, willingness to come up from under, and luck.

This is true of both Euroland's economy and of the European banking system. To save itself from collapse, and the economy from a second dip, the European banking system needs time to build up its reserves and improve its capital ratio which was severely damaged by the 2007−2011 deep economic and financial crisis.

Time is also needed to try to stem a negative psychology in the market, which significantly worsens when investors, economists, and analysts cannot see a light at the end of the tunnel. Instead, the risk in a bailout is that the psychology may worsen—as it did with the failure of the effort which started in April 2010 aimed to salvage the Greek economy through ill-studied program of throwing money at the problem. Critics say that the same will happen with Spain and Italy which are bigger economies than those of Greece, and when it does it will:

- Break the euro down the middle, and
- Put in reverse gear the whole process of European Union.

This is a pessimistic assessment, but it is not totally unwarranted. Much depends on the efforts the country's citizens put to restructure their economy as the cases of Iceland and Latvia so well document (Chapter 13). Ireland's efforts, too.

In Ireland, the euro 68 billion ($88.4 billion) bailouts by European Commission, ECB, and IMF protected Dublin from free fall in the hands of debt markets and less than 2 years on, things look much better. The Irish banking sector, which at its peak had assets 5 times Ireland's annual GDP is downsized and reasonably recapitalized. Budget improvements, too, are realized.

This did not prevent that unemployment zoomed and thousands of young Irish men and women migrated abroad. There is no recovery from debt, particularly deep debt, without pain. The troika returns periodically to Dublin to make sure things are on track, providing fresh cash only if it is satisfied with its findings:

- Ireland's economy is growing again, and
- Some economists look at it as a good case study on how bailout lending should work.

This is not the case with Greece, because of a number of reasons—with paying scant attention to competitiveness, and associated industrial development, while contesting rather than working is at top of the list. A banking industry at disarray further hit by the so-called Private Sector Involvement (PSI) (Sections 4.5 and 4.6), as well as governments changing like shirts—with limited vision and leadership both because they are ephemeral and run by second-raters.

It does not take the brains of Albert Einstein to understand that interminable strikes, protests down the street, Molotov cocktails, and social strife aggravate the economic problems and make recovery so much more difficult. They also end by aggravating the debt problem. Within a year after the April 2010 first bailout, public debt grew:

• From euro 300 billion
• To between euro 330 and 340 billion

The most likely is that this 10 percent to 13 percent increase in national debt was used to cover the continuing public deficit. Unavoidably, part of it has gone to security. Molotov cocktails and interminable strikes are as powerful as high debt in killing employment opportunities in Greece, and not only in Greece.

Strikes should be a weapon of last resort, not a daily business. The European industry as well as the workers themselves are hurt by the labor unions' policy of too frequent strikes. In this regard, Spain, Italy, and Greece have the worst record. In terms of average number of days lost per year per 100 workers during the first nine years of this century:

• Spain led the list with 13 days (or 13 percent).
• Italy came second with 9 days, or 9 percent.
• By comparison, Britain had "only" 2.8 days,[28] or less than 3 percent, and even this was judged to be high.

Over the same period Germany had less than 0.5 days lost and Switzerland almost half that. What the labor unions don't understand that such statistics have a great impact when companies decide where to invest, not only foreign companies but also the country's own. Strikes are the killers of employment. A good example is Fiat.

According to Fiat, almost one in three Italian car workers is involved in stoppages *every day*.[29] It comes therefore as no surprise that in a last-ditch attempt to fix Fiat's loss-making Italian manufacturing base, Sergio Marchionne, its CEO, promised to invest in the company's Italian factories *if*, and only *if*, Italian workers (who are among the world's most "protected") and their labor unions adopt US-style flexible contracts. Globalization is a tough critic:

• Of costs,
• Of efficiency, and
• Of competitiveness.

Marchionne's challenge to unions also lifts the curtain on a wider debate on how competitiveness can be restored in Western industry, as companies and governments seek to recover from the downturn which followed the 2007−2011 deep economic crisis. Like socialist parties, labor unions still live in nineteenth century style confrontation involving not only social but also political conflicts.

Marchionne's ultimatum to unions to accept the deal or Fiat Auto will downsize and eventually close-out its Italian factories left no ambiguity at the side of the politicking labor unions that the cost of conflict would have been a big block of jobs. Albeit at a smaller scale, this is the challenge confronting a lot of Greek jobs, as well as Spanish, Portuguese, French, you name them.

There has been no divine punishment to explain why the economic and financial situation in Greece continues to deteriorate. This is in part the result of successive strikes by labor unions which paralyze the country, while social strife in the wake of austerity measures applied by the government kills tourism. The most worrying aftereffect is the economy's inability to grow.

* Credit has been scarce,
* Foreign capital stays away,
* Investment stalls, and
* Fiscal tightening forces down wages, and therefore demand, so the economy shrinks.

In turn, a shrinking economy misses its targets, opening the door to eurozone demands for yet more austerity. No wonder therefore that on May 9, 2011—a year and a month after the first rescue package—S&P downgraded again Greek debt. The market felt that there is no way out, as the April 2010 bailout was poorly studied in its premises for longer term impact. It was the result of pressure to arrange a deal rather than that of clear thinking on how to turn around a situation which kept on deteriorating.

(When the first Greek bailout was still in discussion, a French economist had commented that the choice confronting Nicolas Sarkozy, then president of France, was between lending to Greece through the troika and never seeing his money again, and recapitalizing French banks exposed to Greece and never getting back his money. In the end, the chosen course was a double loser (Sections 4.5−4.7).)

Not only foreign banks exposed to Greece but also Greek banks, and Cypriot banks who unwisely helped with loans to the Greek government, were devastated. "Looming election results make savings banks a swansong," said Lucas Papademos, a former prime minister and central bank governor.[30] Wrongly, indeed most wrongly, time and again prior to the rescue, the Greek government raised short-term funds from local banks. That was instrumental in decapitating the banking system.

The government did so again in the week of August 7, 2012 following the bailouts—to the tune of euro 6 billion—after Euroland rejected a request for a bridge loan to repay a bond held by the ECB that matured in that same month. As for the ECB, it rejected a Greek proposal to delay the repayment by a month, highlighting the approach being taken by international lenders as Athens struggled to bring its bailout program back on track. Greek banks were hit by a triple whammy:

* The 73.5 percent heavy haircut of the so-called PSI (Section 4.5),
* The government's heavy hand, asking them to lend it money, and
* A massive exodus of funds by depositors who had good reasons to worry about their savings.

Three months prior to the euro 6 billion loan, on May 14 Karolos Papoulias, the president of the republic said that, as he had been warned by the central bank, depositors had just withdrawn euro 700 million ($890 million). Bankers whispered that over euro 1.2 billion flowed out on that very day and the days immediately after. "Most of the hard money has already left," said one of them. "Now we are seeing a flare-up [of withdrawals] from small depositors who don't know what to make of what is said on the evening news."[31]

The self-reinforcing interaction between public debt and economic downturn adds its weight on debt sustainability, as it has been particularly evident in Greece. It also raises doubts about the effectiveness of troika's role which in Greece has been less successful than in Ireland. The first rescue proved to be insufficient, leading to a second bailout. In retrospect, part of the first package's failure was largely due to:

- The sheer scale of the country's debt,
- Unreliable economic statistics,
- Competitiveness problems (discussed in Section 4.2), and
- Plenty of wishful thinking that every party will play a constructive role.

Both bailouts confronted an iceberg and no one seems to have questioned how much of the iceberg was under water (usually it is the 7/8). Privatization revenues were estimated at over euro 50 billion. The EU, ECB, and IMF unwisely accepted this impossible number even though the IMF's experience suggested it was far too high. There were as well other problems which worked against the bailout.

The agreed upon first Greek bailout of April 2010 included front-loaded cuts and tax hikes worth euro 30 billion, or 13 percent of GDP. These were both deeper and faster implemented than elsewhere, contributing to an ongoing drop in Greek output with GDP in free fall. The failure of the first Greek effort hit the EC/ECB and IMF coffers hard, since the second package ran to euro 130 billion, and also led to the idea that the private sector, too, should feel part of the pain—officially, voluntarily.

4.5   Private Sector Involvement in Downsizing the Greek Debt

The debt crisis of the euro rests on two legs: overleveraged sovereigns and undercapitalized banking industry. Because of the links existing between these two legs, the euro crisis is deeper and more widespread than almost anyone feared at its start. The joke about it has been that both in Europe and in America government bonds have turned from offering a risk-free return to exhibiting a return-free risk.

Since the 2007 subprimes crisis revealed the amount of leveraging by governments in the United States and Europe, the credit of western sovereigns has no more been safe. Debt-to-GDP ratios suggested that it is actually risky. For Greece, Portugal, Spain, and Italy this led to interest rate spikes to compensate for that risk. The effective 73.5 percent write-off of bond values held by private-sector holders of Greek government debt sent ripples through the financial system.

Back in early 2010, the negotiations on the first bailout package of euro 110 billion (then $154 billion) went on for several months while in the meantime the debt position of Greece deteriorated. Part of the delay was due to the fact that not all

Euroland members were in accord with the bailout of Greece. Slovakia said that its GDP per head was half that of Greece. Hence, why should they loan money to Greece? Finland asked for collateral for its loan, and other countries had their reservations. But the wish of Germany, France, and the IMF prevailed.

This first package gave to banks, which had lent big money to the Greek government, the false assurance that their loans and interest derived from them were safe. This proved to be a mistake in judgment. In the wake of the failure of the first bailout, and to bring down at a more affordable level the debt-to-GDP ratio of Greece, EC/ECB/IMF promoted the so-called PSI agreed by EU political leaders in their October 2011 summit (more on this later).

Was this "voluntary" downsizing of loans justified? Was it intense government pressure, or the scare of a *credit event*, such as a Greek bankruptcy, which made the banks compliant? Which events are instrumental in launching a CDS has been a prominent question since early 2010 when Greece found itself at edge of bankruptcy. The fear of a credit event brought up PSI, and the irony is that, in the end, the CDS event was not avoided.

Because so many factors came into play, the answer to the questions posed by the preceding paragraphs is in no way linear. Prominent among them is the vicious cycle of debt-and-recapitalization between the banks and the state. The former's overexposure to international loans, particularly to governments, has become unsustainable. On the other hand, the habit governments acquired to treat some banks as "too big to fail" makes no sense either.

The band aid of more loans, offered by the European Union and the IMF, eased somewhat that stress but it did not really improve the ability of Greece to service the loans and repay the capital. By late 2010 with the reforms agreed upon in April 2010 with the first bailout still to be enacted and Greek foreign indebtedness rising from euro 300 billion (then $420 billion) to 350 billion ($490 billion), it became evident that the Greek loans could not be repaid.

- By the end of 2010, it was a common secret that a haircut will be necessary.
- IMF accepts no haircuts and ECB neither.
- This left exposed the private sector, and a haircut originally estimated at 30 percent to 35 percent grew to more than twice that level.

A recently coined technical term for such haircut is *bail-in*, which contrasts to a bailout. Bail-ins have been undertaken in response to costly government support of banking companies during the recent crisis: certain creditors are forced to take loses before banks benefit from taxpayers' money.[32]

A bail-in requires the statutory power of a resolution authority, which involves the recapitalization of an institution by converting and/or writing down primarily unsecured debt, while preserving other creditors. This procedure can apply both on a *going concern* and on a *gone-concern* basis (liquidation; orderly wind down) when institutions enter into resolution.[33]

In the course of the early 2011 negotiations, only part of the loans taken by Greece could be the subject of a haircut, particularly those originating in private institutions and investors. Loans by the IMF, EU, and ECB were untouchable. This way, up to euro 217 billion ($282 billion) out of euro 350 billion could be subject to the PSI. Table 4.1 presents a bird's eye view of the debt distribution.

By mid-2011, as negotiations dragged on, the haircut had risen to 50 percent, and from there it climbed to 60 percent to reach 73.5 percent by February 2012. (These percentages count both the direct haircut and aftereffect of favorable conditions attached to new bond issues to replace the old ones issued to private sector investors by Greece.)

Though reducing debt by nearly three quarters is a large sum, it became evident that the goal of swamping the sovereign debt of Greece from 160 percent or so of GDP to 120 percent—as Angela Merkel, the German chancellor had wanted—could not be attained only through the PSI. According to Bloomberg News, George Papandreou, then Greek prime minister in 2010 when the PSI discussion started, said that the 50 percent haircut in the bank debt of Greece "buys us time." That statement has shown what was wrong with the Greek side of the debt reduction initiative.

The challenge confronting the government, therefore the Greek society as a whole, was *and is* not just to "buy time" but rather to turn the economy around. This requires much more than a haircut on loans. It calls for a full scale rise in hard work and in competitiveness (Section 4.2). Even a high share in forgiveness in the accumulated huge public debt would not make a great deal of difference. Instead, the priorities should have been to:

- Make the economy competitive at global scale,
- Outlaw fiscal deficits and new debt,
- Keep inflation under lock and key,
- Restructure the labor market, which is anyway "a must,"
- Open-up all professions to new entrants and to talent,
- End the wild strikes and bloody demonstrations, and
- Revive exports, this being key to swamping unemployment and avoiding current account deficits which pile up on debt.

These should have been the Greek government's top priorities, instead of "buying up time" and keeping on with mismanagement, nepotism, and corruption, European policymakers pushed on with restructuring of Greek debt due to their fear that left in its own devices Greece would confront bankruptcy sparking wider contagion. PSI was one of the measures.

The most vocal opponent of PSI has been the ECB. On June 14, 2011 Mario Draghi, the ECB's president-in-waiting, warned that any attempt to impose costs on Greek debt bondholders could lead to its own "chain of contagion."[34] It did not, but neither did the PSI help the Greek economy; the government's main preoccupation continues being kicking the can down the street.

From the Greek economy's viewpoint *internal devaluation* Latvia-style (Chapter 13) was the best solution. The next best to it, back in late 2009 or early 2010, was plain bankruptcy, provided that from then on budget deficits were outlawed and entitlements re-dimensioned to a level affordable by the

Table 4.1 Lenders in the Greek Sovereign Debt[a]

Lender	Euro Billion	Share
Greek and Cyprus banks	52.2	14.96
Domestic Greek creditors	35.5	10.17
European banks and insurers	36.0	10.31
Unidentified bondholders	92.3	26.45
ECB lending against collateral	60.0	17.19
EMU loans	53.0	15.19
IMF loans	20.0	5.73
	349.0	**100.00**

[a]UBS Wealth Management Research, January 31, 2012.

not-so-prosperous Greek economy. The unavoidable companion is, quite evidently, austerity. The problem with austerity measures is that they affect in an uneven way different segments of the population.

There exist similitude between Greek austerity measures during 2010−2013 and the plight of German pensioners and savers during the 1922−1924 hyperinflation. As an ancient Greek proverb advises, avoiding what fortune has decreed is impossible. The drift of the Greek economy should not have reached the point of no return. When this happens, the way back to "normal" is not made of roses. The curious thing is that none of the politicians and other actors of the disaster ever got punished for their malfeasance.

As for the banks which lost with the haircut 73.5 percent of the capital they had loaned to the Greek sovereign, directly or by buying its bonds, it is only evident that they accepted that deal under pressure by their governments. Some foreign banks, particularly the French, lost a small fortune, and their hope has been that this was a one-tantum not to be repeated. Particularly devastated were the Greek and Cypriot banks. Given the amount necessary for their recapitalization, one doubts that PSI made much sense.

Still, many politicians and credit experts criticized the position taken by Draghi who declared himself against imposing costs on Greek debt bondholders, because of a chain of contagion. The critics stated that only normal lenders should be sharing the pain on the Greek debt. Otherwise, the Greek rescue will be a gift to the banks who will lose capital on their bonds but could lose everything if Greece defaulted.

Normally, banks would have looked at the loss of a big chunk of their loan capital as involuntary, but with practically the whole Euroland in a debt crisis credit institutions, hedge funds and other lenders seemed willing to lose money now in order to avoid a tandem of defaults by the euro's peripheral countries later. They did put, however, certain conditions.

The foremost of these conditions has been that even if Greece was allowed a *soft default*, this will not be repeated with Portugal, Spain, Italy, and may be other sovereigns thinking of leaving behind their obligations. In other terms, integral part of the negotiations conducted by Washington-based Institute of International Finance (IIF) on behalf of the banks was that Greece will be a unique soft default situation.

This was more wishful thinking than a realistic condition. Experience demonstrates that once a small window is opened, it rapidly turns into a big door with lots of traffic passing through it. The "unique one-in-a lifetime" small window theory is just smoke and mirrors. International Institute for Finance (IIF) Section 4.6, the banks, IMF, ECB, and EU who did not expect the Greek case to be repeated were willingly deluding themselves.

- Soft defaults can become at no time the way out of financial obligations, and
- No guarantee can be provided *a priori* that a soft default could avert a CDS credit event, which came along short time thereafter.

The second major condition in the negotiation with the lenders centered on the terms of restructured sovereign loans. Practically, every party seemed to agree on 30-year bonds, but at which interest rate? The banks wanted 5 percent or more, the Greek government offered less than 4 percent. This "1-percent plus" made a lot of a difference for both parties given the amount of rescheduled debt and the fact that inflation was expected to raise its head if—after long years of a lousy monetary policy—and when the economy picks up.

4.6 The PSI's 73.5 Percent Writedown Did Not Really Help Greece

One of the opinions often heard as Euroland's debt crisis deepens has been that lawsuits stemming from this crisis may be the silver lining for lawyers, their Ferraris, wives' mink coats, and kids' university educations. The restructuring of Greek sovereign debt in early 2012 has been one of Euroland's biggest tests, but it did not lead to a legal fight. Lawyers are, however, patient; they wait. The PSI talks centered among a limited number of:

- Greek government, advised by Cleary Gottlieb Steen & Hamilton,
- EU authorities including the ECB,
- International Monetary Fund, and
- Private bondholders, including banks, hedge funds, and other investors.

The private bondholders organized themselves into a steering committee, which is a rare event. This had failed to materialize during Argentina's debt restructuring. The strategy was advised by Allen & Overy and White & Case, though the negotiator on behalf of private bondholders was the IIF.

One of the issues that might have led to court is that the majority of previous Greek debt was held in bonds governed by domestic law. This meant the government could insert collective action clauses into the securities, forcing all bondholders to accept a haircut if a majority agreed to a deal's implied conditions.

By March 2012, a deal emerged with around 95 percent of private bondholders agreeing to swap their Greek-law bonds and accepting losses of 73.5 percent. Key part of the negotiation was that new bonds will be governed by English law; therefore, they will not be subject to future collective action clauses by the Greek government.[35]

The jurisdictional issue taught a lesson. Bondholders demanded and obtained that all new Euroland sovereign debt issued after January 2012 will have collective action clauses inserted. Quite likely, this was the most important direct legal consequence of Greek debt restructuring.

On paper, taking off some 62 percent of outstanding public debt, all that related to private bondholders (including banks), provided no minor advantage to the Greek Treasury. It lifted a heavy load off the government's shoulders. There were however four problems still left to deal with:

1. The heavy haircut applied to only part of the Greek debt; precisely this 62 percent.

   The euro 158.76 billion ($206.4 billion) which drained out of the credit institutions' treasury and individual private investors' pockets were a large sum, but at the same time, this debt reduction only affected part of the outstanding public liabilities.
2. The other 38 percent of Greek public debt was held by institutions which would legally accept no slimming down of their assets.

   Already by late 2011 financial experts had said that according to their calculations, to put itself back on a sustainable trend, Greece needed a 70 percent reduction in its euro 350 billion total debt.[36] The achieved euro 158,76 billion reduction represented "only" 45.4 percent of total Greek public debt.

   Many experts question whether the balance of Euroland's EFSF and ESM will be able to bear the lion's share of the next big write-off. The IMF is a preferential creditor and will not accept any losses. However, the ECB, too, cast upon itself the status of untouchable, and (prior to OMT) stated that it will concentrate on the need to recapitalize member states' banks. Neither were Euroland's governments ready to accept a haircut.[37]
3. Several of the banks which bled with the 73.5 percent haircut were Greek and Cypriot. They were weakly capitalized and recapitalizing them took care of a good part of public debt reduction.[38]

   The Greek and Cyprus banks, which were by no means global institutions, have been devastated by the PSI. With good reason, critics said that it was bad judgment to lend to an overleveraged government in the first place. The only excuse for recapitalizing them with public money[39] was that the government had obliged them to buy its bonds—which was plain mismanagement.
4. While the troika insisted and obtained significant reductions in Greek state expenses, as well as tax increases, the government's receipts still did not cover expenditures.

Nobody seems to have paid enough attention to this issue in early 2010, at the time of the first rescue. A bailout makes sense only if public debt stops growing. If it does not, the process is reduced to replacing one set of loans with another, or, more precisely, of supplanting more liberal with much stiffer loan conditions. The banks that bought Greek sovereign bonds had never asked for a troika.

Market operators who speak their mind say that Greek public debt remains unsustainable. Speculators capitalized on this in two ways. First, they sold short the debt restructured through the PSI. Then, as its price fell to the abyss they started buying it, expecting that even a temporary return of confidence will bring the price up. This is indeed what has happened, and hedge funds which bet on it made a fortune (Section 4.7).

Because of the reasons explained in the preceding sections, the Greek public debt remained a menace, and with it the uncertainty on whether the country will gain just enough time to survive until the next recession in Europe. Once this comes, the public debt leaps again, and the same is true in case Greek governments continue accumulating debt:

- Because of mismanagement, and
- Under pressure from the street.

This is not all. When in March 2012 holders of Greek debt exchanged their bonds for longer term paper with lower yields, international institutions labeled the swap "a success" and decreed that the second bailout for Greece was on the rails. But as we have just discussed, the value of new supposedly safe Greek bonds plummeted to a level roughly equivalent to where pre-exchange debt had traded.

According to expert opinions, the market's response reflected the view that Greece's financial position was no more sustainable than earlier on. Some analysts also said that the plummeting was a direct rebuke to the IMF, reminiscent of the Fund's overlending to several African countries in the 1980s (so far, this African lending was the most important sustained failure in the fund's long history).

Then and now not everything was IMF's failure. In the 1980s, the fund was prodded by the United States and other Western donors to provide a significant amount of loans to countries ignoring the foundation of its credibility: its financial objectivity. Only if there is a sustainable path is the IMF supposed to make refinancing available. Moreover, progress must be assured by regular on the spot reviews —which is essentially what the troika is supposed to be doing.

In the case of Portugal, Ireland, and Greece, the foundations of credibility were not necessarily present. This time under pressure by Euroland governments, the IMF stepped into uncharted territory which explains its reluctance to do it again in 2013. The curious nature of PSI has not improved things.

4.7   Credit Events and Bonanzas for Speculators

Literally speaking, it mattered little if the PSI was "voluntary" or "involuntary." This, however, was no academic issue because it's the prevailing ambiguity that weighted heavily on the fate of CDSs.

In a first time, on March 1, 2012, New York-based International Securities Dealers Association (ISDA) ruled that the PSI is not a credit event even if it applied 73.5 percent haircut on lenders. This was a unanimous decision, and it evidently raised eyebrows. In one stroke, it:

- Liberated the writers of CDSs from their obligations,
- Penalized the CDS protection buyers, and
- Made irrelevant the list of conditions and clauses in credit default swaps.

The fear that CDS protection proves worthless led to unintended consequences in the real world. At one major Wall Street company, the chief risk officer said his firm concluded that the contracts are too risky, and it is either tearing them up or trying to trade out of them. This institution was also shorting sovereign bond issues, which drove down their value and contributed to Euroland jitters.

In addition, because bonds protected through CDS are used as collateral in the interbank market, the ruling that CDS is not triggered in the "voluntary" restructuring engineered by PSI made that collateral less valuable (for a broader discussion, see Chapter 5). The aftermath of a noncredit event ISDA opinion led to:

- Falling liquidity, and
- Pressures in the funding market.

Critics said that the "noncredit event" decision by ISDA has been a nice present to those American banks which had provided, in aggregate, guarantees of more than $500 billion on all sorts of debts in Euroland's peripheral countries: Greece, Portugal, Spain, Italy, and Ireland. There were also big losers from that curious decision and, evidently, they did not remain idle.

No surprise therefore that on March 8, 2012, a week after its first decision, the ISDA reversed itself. It issued a statement saying that the debt swap engineered by PSI indeed constituted a *credit event*. As such, it had two consequences:

- It prompted payouts on CDSs, and
- It confirmed that Greece defaulted on its bonds.

All told, few people came out of the PSI negotiations and associated debate looking good. At early stage, it seemed that banks would be getting away with it lightly. Reportedly, hedge funds even bought Greek bonds in the hope of freeriding their way to full repayment. Depending on their price of entry to the market, many of those who did so got burned.

Germany and France had pushed ahead with PSI despite warnings from the ECB about the contagion it could unleash. At the end, the ECB protected itself from the heavy haircut and the EIB did the same in spite of the request by the boss of IMF, Christine Lagarde, who asked that to solve the Greek crisis all lenders should take losses.

Opponents of the "voluntary" private initiative argued that it came to be seen as a central cause of contagion in Euroland. For many investors, the precedent set by PSI has spooked the markets leading to widespread fear that the structure could be replicated in countries such as Italy and Spain, with a list of legal hurdles. "There has been an increasing realization in many quarters that this is a core evil," said a bondholder, "It has been a transmission device of contagion into other sovereigns."[40]

The acceptance rate of the PSI, too, caused concerns because it has been a crucial condition imposed on both parties to the legalities underpinning this transaction. First, a statement was made about targeting a 90 percent or better acceptance. Then, when it became clear that the market showed no particular enthusiasm for this deal, the targeted rate of acceptance was reduced to between 70 and 75 percent—while Greece had to impose losses on private bondholders by passing a new law affecting all bonds:

- Issued under Greek law, and
- Held by private investors.

That law was voted by the Greek parliament on February 27, 2012, but its wisdom is debatable at best. Strictly speaking, a retroactive law is not illegal; however, the fact that retroactivity is anathema to the markets sees to it that it can take long years for a country adopting such measure to tap again international capital. In addition, the structure of its public debt has been such that Greek entities were the first in line to be wounded by the PSI as given in Table 4.1 (Section 4.5).

Those who bought restructured Greek debt at very low price had reasons to celebrate. One of the hedge funds was Third Point headed by Dan Loeb. He tendered the majority of $1 billion (euro 770 million) position in Greek government bonds, built up a few months earlier at 17 cents to the euro. Third Point doubled its capital as it sold at 34 cents to the euro.

This windfall of profits came on December 18, 2012; it was a legally correct trade. Loeb took a big risk and reaped king-size reward. He bet on the likelihood that, with OMT on the air, the ECB would make a fool of itself if it left Greek bonds value drop to zero. Indeed, the market turned around, though not necessarily for long.

CDSs and market bets should not be confused. Notionally speaking, they overlap only a little, while they contrast to each other at broader range. CDC buyers seek protection. The buyers of widely downgraded debt seek exposure. Audacious bets on heavily discounted bonds are made only by a handful of risk takers who either get huge amounts or get broken. Ironically, in 2012 such successful bets have been a rare exception to the hedge funds industry record, as many players got burned.

Third Point manages assets of $10 billion and made its investors a 20 percent return in 2012 compared with an unimpressive 4.9 percent for the average hedge fund. Down to basics, the bet behind the $500 million (euro 385 million) profit Third Point made was that Greece would not be forced to leave Euroland. This was contrarian to the prevailing trend, and 2012 was in a difficult year for guessing what comes next.

George Soros, who bet against the British pound and, so to speak, "broke the Bank of England" in 1992 had a hard time to find a profits engine in 2012, after 2 years of lackluster returns. Even worse, John Paulson, the hedge fund manager who called the 2007 US housing crash which landed his fund $2.5 billion, was among those wrong-footed in 2012. He saw both his bets on a US economic recovery and a deterioration in the health of German bonds unravel.

End Notes

1. Demaratus, who accompanied the Persian king on his invasion of Greece in 480 BC, was a former co-king of Sparta with Cleomenes. The latter had many personal ambitions. The two co-kings were not in good terms. In an intrigue, in which the oracle of Delphi played a rather sinister role, Cleomenes declared Demaratus' birth illegitimate, deprived him of his kingship and put in his place Leotychidas. Worried about an assassination, Demaratus fled to the Persian court. (Ehrenberg V. From Solon to Socrates. Abington, Britain: Routledge; 2011.)
2. Emphasis added.
3. D'Andrezel L. Extraits des Auteurs Grecs. Paris: Imprimerie et Librairie Classiques; 1836.
4. Dracon, the first lawgiver of ancient Athens, found himself obliged to apply the most severe rules to redress the drift which characterized the early decades of democracy.
5. The Economist, May 1, 2010.
6. *Idem.*
7. ECB. Financial integration in Europe, April 2012.
8. The Economist, June 18, 2011.
9. Acemoglu D, Robinson J. Why nations fail: the origins of power, prosperity and poverty. New York, NY: Crown; 2012.
10. Overemployment by the public sector has the same disastrous results.
11. These are, as well, the statistics characterizing Spanish unemployment.
12. UBS Investor's Guide, August 10, 2012.
13. Chorafas DN. Quality control applications. London: Springer Verlag; 2013.
14. Chorafas DN. Business, marketing and management principles for IT and engineering. New York, NY: Taylor & Francis/CRC/Auerbach; 2011.
15. Financial Times, June 20, 2012.
16. A silly anti-German campaign made matters worse, since many Germans used to take their vacation in the Greek islands.
17. Financial Times, May 9, 2012.
18. Who resigned in 2011.
19. Bloomberg News, June 25, 2012.
20. Prior to his nomination to the presidency of the European Central Bank, Draghi was asked by the wise men of Euroland if he was involved in that scam. He answered "No"—but there has been no public investigation to establish the truth one way or another, and find out who was really responsible.
21. http://www.progressiveradionetworkl.com/the-progressive-news-hour/, March 17, 2012.
22. Financial Times, May 9, 2012.
23. Financial Times, October 5, 2012.
24. The Economist, March 27, 2012.
25. This information comes from a report which the Greek Labor Ministry published in the Greek press. It affected 37,500 main and 26,000 smaller additional pensions.
26. Greek newspapers carried details of MPs allegedly enjoying high-rolling lifestyles in suburban Athens villas equipped with indoor swimming pools and luxury holiday homes.
27. Copyright: http://www.ekathimerini.com, August 21, 2012.

28. The Economist, April 24, 2010.
29. For many years, Fiat's autos division made most of its profit in Brazil, where it is the market leader, but lost money in Europe. In 2011, Fiat Auto lost $400 million in Italy while Chrysler (largely owned by Fiat) had a profit of $1.2 billion, and this has helped Fiat to escape bankruptcy.
30. Bloomberg News, April 18, 2012.
31. The Economist, May 19, 2012.
32. A global policy of bail-ins is under consideration by regulators and the Financial Stability Board (FSB).
33. The power to bail-in creditors in failing financial entities is listed as one of the key attributes of effective bank resolution regimes in an October 2011 paper from the FSB, for both banks and nonbanks. The resolution regime will come into force in 2015, whereas the proposed implementation date for the bail-in tool is January 1, 2018, both on newly issued securities as well as on outstanding ones. The tool allows resolution authorities to write down existing liabilities or convert them into shares (Crédit Suisse, Research Monthly Switzerland, June 26, 2012).
34. It is indeed very interesting to compare this mid-2011 Draghi position with his mid-2012 decision to buy unlimited sovereign bonds through OMT. These have been contradictory opinions coming out of two different Draghis.
35. Of total privately held debt, euro 177 billion was issued under Greek law and euro 18 billion under foreign law. Another euro 7 billion related to bonds was issued under Greek law by public enterprises (DEKOs) and euro 3 billion to DEKO bonds that were issued under foreign law. The latter classes were guaranteed by the Greek government.
36. UBS Investor's Guide, October 28, 2011.
37. After all, that was the money of *their* taxpayers.
38. It also made the Greek banks highly subservient to the state.
39. The Greek but not the Cyprus banks which, unwisely, had also lent heavily to the Greek government.
40. Financial Times, January 9, 2012.

5 Impact of Bailouts on the Economy of a Sovereign

5.1 Bailout Fatigue

To describe the array of ultra-leftist and ultra-traditionalist forces bent on blocking reform Alexis Papahelas, editor of *Kathimerini*, easily Greece's best newspaper, has coined the term "coalition of the unwilling." He also noted that the number of citizens suspicious of all change may increase, as middle-class Greeks see their hard-earned prosperity go up in smoke.[1]

That's Euroland of the bailouts but is the alternative any better? By all likelihood, if Greece were to break with Euroland and launch a new drachma, local banks would be besieged by panicked depositors. "...The shops will empty and some people will jump out of windows," Theodoros Pangalos, deputy prime minister, told the Spanish daily *El Mundo*.[2]

Pangalos impressed some of his compatriots (and annoyed others) by saying that common citizens in Greece, as well as the political elite, wasted loans and subsidies and brought the country to the edge of chaos. His explanation of the debt crisis has been: "We ate it up together," and in this he is right. The bill came due and the Greek Treasury did not have the reserves to pay it.

Instead, in April 2010 Euroland and the IMF offered a bailout but by mid-2011, when the statements by Papahelas and Pangalos were made, it had proved to be insufficient (if not outright inefficient). A few months later, on February 21, 2012, Euroland's finance ministers sealed a second bailout for Greece, to the tune of euro 130 billion ($170 billion) in new financing.

Theoretically, the Eurogroup (finance minister 17 nations that use the euro) gave Greece the funding it needed to avoid a potential default. This was a marathon session and Olli Rehn, vice president of the European Commission, said that the previous night he learned that marathon is indeed a Greek word.[3] Practically, however, the die was far from being cast.

Rehn pressed the point that the Greek economy cannot rely anymore on a large public administration financed by cheap debt, but rather needs to lean on investment—both Greek and foreign. According to Rehn, another goal Greece has to honor for the second rescue is to reduce to 120 percent, by 2020, the ratio of

Public Debt Dynamics of Europe and the US. DOI: http://dx.doi.org/10.1016/B978-0-12-420021-0.00005-1

public debt to GDP. (This stood at 160 percent at time of first bailout.) Instead, 10 months later, as 2012 came to a close:

- The Greek debt-to-GDP ratio stood at an unhealthy 179.8 percent, and
- Nobody can really answer the question how it happens that rather than going down with the PSI, it has gone up.

Bailout fatigue starts being felt when objectives are not met and hopes evaporate, but it is not easy to say "to hell with it" because of the *funding gap* which will leave the Greek Treasury empty of money for the essentials. Economists calculate that until 2016 (three years away) this funding gap will stand at about euro 43 billion, while they don't see that (under current conditions) Greece will be able to restart financing in the capital markets till 2015−2016 even for modest amounts.

Moreover, interest costs will be higher due to a greater usage of short-term treasury bills while, because the PSI wounded Greek banks, bank recapitalization is pressing (some analysts believe that eventually this would require about euro 50 billion, instead of the much lower figure I gave in Chapter 4). With all this in mind Table 5.1 presents the major chapters of the current Greek sovereign debt toward the EU (really the EFSF), European Central Bank, and IMF.

Prior to Bailout I and of the PSI haircut Greek public debt stood at the euro 350 billion level ($455 billion). Some Bailout I money was used to repay ECB. Other has been employed to confront demand for cash to pay for maturities (interest and capital). PSI has saved euro 158.76 billion[4]; but at the other side of the balance sheet there has been the guarantee by Athens for new sovereign bonds and Greek bank recapitalization.

Some economists argue that the TARGET II imbalance (which is a Bank of Greece liability) should not be added to this account, because it is relevant only if Greece leaves the euro. While this remains a possibility (Chapter 6) even if Greece stays in euro, the negative balance of euro 106 billion in TARGET2 is due. As far as clearing accounts are concerned there should be only a small and temporary payments balance which is sometimes positive and sometimes negative.

Table 5.1 Greek Public Debt Toward the "Untouchables": EU, ECB, IMF

	Euro
Bailout I	110 billion
Bailout II	130 billion
Bailouts I + II (some of this money is still to be paid)	**240 billion**
ECB is owed by Greece (because of bonds used as collateral with SMP (Chapter 4))	40 billion
In TARGET2[a] Bank of Greece owes	106 billion
Total current exposure in public debt	**386 billion**

[a]TARGET2 is ECB's payment system, and member states are supposed to pay their accounts.

All accounts made, however, with "pluses" and "minuses" rapidly changing (hence difficult to track), the fact remains that even without the huge TARGET2 negative balance as 2012 came to a close the Greek debt-to-GDP ratio stood at nearly 180 percent and was projected to reach 190 percent in 2013. This is a significant increase over 160 percent when Bailout I started—despite the debt reduction brought by PSI.

Evidently there exist hypotheses about why this is so, and one of them is that the assumptions which were made about the positive effects of Euroland's rescues were wrong. The second bailout was supposed to give Greece enough space to improve its competitiveness. At least that's what Christine Lagarde, IMF's CEO said. But is it really documented by facts?

Theoretically, the conditions attached to the second Greek bailout were to be executed by the next government, to emerge from the April 2012 elections. Practically, this was not at all sure because in February 2012 nobody could tell what kind of government will come out of elections two months later. Predictions were precarious, given:

- The ongoing reaction of the population against austerity measures, and
- The possibility left parties might gain a majority of sorts in the new parliament, form a government and call for renegotiation of all conditions.

On paper, most of what came out of the marathon 13-hour session at EU headquarters, in Brussels, might have made sense, but there existed notable risks in its implementation reflected in widespread concern among economists and analysts. Details which started to be released brought these risks in perspective. While the second package seemed to be more realistic than the first (launched in April 2010) it still contained unrealistic hypotheses.

The implementation of tougher austerity measures and other requirements was hanging on the new government's resolve and popular support for the measures. But by large majority the Greek public doubted any money will filter down to common citizen, as most was supposed to be in a blocked account earmarked for paying past obligations. New debt is accumulating to pay down old debt.

For instance, more than half of the payments scheduled for late March 2012 were supposed to go to the ECB to cover a maturing position. This was partly a reflection of the fact that the Greek public debt has been staggering. Exposure to Greek bonds by the ECB consumed the lion's share of its reserves. (Over and above that came ECB's exposure to Portugal, Ireland, Spain, Italy, and so on.)

The common citizen's worries and uncertainty about the future contrasted to the optimistic scenario at EU headquarters which assumed that even if eventually Greece exits the euro this will happen only after policymakers have erected a credible firewall. Furthermore, in real life the hypothesis that Spain, Italy, and other member states will not be greatly affected by the economic earthquake in Greece made no sense.

Decisions made in an ivory tower by EU chiefs of state and confirmations by parliaments are not enough, all by themselves, to carry the day. The strength of a commitment rests squarely on the ability of those who have accepted it to continue to deliver. Open-end compromises, as for instance the likelihood of not keeping the implied deadlines for:

- Restructuring the labor market
- Selling assets (Port of Piraeus, government land), and
- Implementing the new and tougher set of cost control measures[5]

work against the results expected from bailout packages. This is counterproductive. In addition, independent estimates pointed out that Greek budget figures slipped during the first bailout and the euro 130 billion of the second rescue was no longer enough to fill the financing hole faced by the government over the next three years.

"There is clearly the need for everybody to carefully look into their contributions," said one of the senior officials involved in the negotiations. "The pieces are not yet in place to support a more aggressive strategy," commented Mutjaba Rahman of the Eurasia Group, a risk analysis firm, "While Greece is unequivocally insolvent, Portugal is not, but it will be the next victim absent a credible firewall."[6]

5.2   Aristophanes, Euroland, and Greece Today

Two bailouts are already one-too-many, and we are not yet at the end of the rescues. Is this a comedy or a tragedy? Tragedy and comedy are the same thing and they should be written by the same author, Socrates once said. But laughing is an unfamiliar concept to people who take life more seriously than it is which does not mean that there exist no human tragedies in economic crises.

A master of satiric laugh has been Aristophanes, the ancient Athenian poet and dramaturge. His approach was the laugh that cuts to pieces the stupidities of those who reign, as well as the absurdities which multiplied in the course of the 30-year Greek patricide war, at the end of the fifth century BC (incorrectly known as Peloponnesian war).

Ancient Athens had tried and failed to put together the pieces of its empire using as glue the blood of repressions. In the course of the last quarter of the fifth century BC at the theater of Dionyssos, Athenians would listen to the thunder of the laugh of Aristophanes. Tragedy was in the air, but the poet made fun of it, and the Athenian public laughed.

The satirist dramatic author denounced the contradictions into which the Athenian democracy had cornered itself, the way the silkworm does when it locks itself up in its cocoon. He spoke against the disasters of ancient Greece's civil war, the resulting misery of the people, the blood spilled for nothing, the acts of demagogues and whereabouts of profiteers who exploited other people's misery, the stupidities of sovereigns, and unhappiness of common citizen abused by those it (s)elected to run its fortunes.

This laugh was *against* the sort of things to which the Athenian public had offered itself as hostage. It was not the lyrical laugh of pleasure which springs out of love, be it that of other people, of landscapes, bees, trees, and flowers. The lyrical laugh is spontaneous, the satirical one has long roots often expressed in cartoons and mapped into comic or terrifying masks like those used in ancient Greek theaters.

It is quite interesting to note that satiric authors and cartoon designers confine their art to thoughts, matters, and actions involving their own people, not foreigners, because in their own people they find both the source of satire and the way the cure should be administered. In 2011 and 2012, however, what has been seen in the daily press of Athens is not Aristophanian satire but a low grade, unfunny criticism which has neither base nor salutary aftereffects.

In the wilder fringes of the Greek press Angela Merkel has been compared to Adolf Hitler. This is not only is highly inaccurate but as well total absurdity. In Spain, too, she is damned for being the inventor of austerity, and the picture emerging from the media is of a stubborn individual whose actions threaten the world— *as if* it is not Merkel who provided the bigger part of fresh money to pull up from under Greece, Portugal, Ireland, Spain, and Italy.

The hanging tree is not satire, it is simply ridiculous. An aberration engineered by the empty headed and politicians who do not dare to express themselves publicly but only in a circle of intimates.[7] Pierre-Antoine Delhommais, of the French news magazine *Le Point*, is much more objective than many politicians when he asks: "Is Angela Merkel responsible:"

- "If the Spanish banking system imploded?"

Delhommais answers his question by saying: "No! The party responsible is the delirious model of growth based on debt and massive real estate construction."

- "If France registers a commercial deficit of euro 70 billion, and if its companies make products which cannot be exported?"

To the opinion of the French journalist in no way can Merkel be held responsible if manufacturing costs in France, and most particularly social costs, are way too high making French products uncompetitive in the global market. (The same is true in Greece.)

- "If Euroland is not moving toward federalism?"

"No!" says Delhommais; "Merkel is favorable to European federalism but François Hollande, the French president, does not want to hear about transferring budgetary sovereignty."[8] And this, of course, for evident reasons.

In quite a similar way one can ask if Merkel is responsible for what has happened and continues happening with the implosion of the Greek economy. The answer has been given by Theodoros Pangalos (Section 5.1). Let me add that there is no evidence Merkel was part of the Andreas Papandreou, Costas Karamanlis Jr., and George Papandreou Jr. governments—the gang of three who brought Greece to the abyss—or that she acted as their advisor. Yet, these were the governments which ruined the Greek economy.

- Like Pericles, who launched the destructive Peloponnesian war, they were chosen by free citizens, and

• They bought votes by way of granting unsustainable entitlements, which brought Greece from one disaster to the next.

Neither is there any evidence that Merkel invented the bailout, and austerity which went with it. The talk in France is that Nicolas Sarkozy was the first to press for a rescue because of the high exposure to Greece of the French banks, and asked Christine Lagarde (then French finance minister and currently president of the IMF) to come up with a solution—which she did.[9] The bailout had to involve the IMF because it contributed money as well as for its long decades of experience with rescue loans and restructuring.

Euroland probably took the wrong decision. Economists doubted that bailout funds will provide Greece with *financial stability*. Independent credit rating agencies have been unimpressed. On February 28, 2012 a week after the second Greek rescue package was approved, Standard & Poor's downgraded Greece from CCC, the lowest level in its creditworthiness scale, to SD—which stands for "selective default." That same day the ECB suspended Greek bonds from being used as collateral. Both were bad omens for the continuing bailout package.

The irony is that the second rescue package and PSI were celebrated in Brussels as milestones, with EU top brass professing that Greek default was avoided. To the contrary, critics pointed out that part of that arrangement was nothing else than new austerity measures, including higher direct and indirect taxes, such as a beefed up flat value added tax (VAT) which essentially penalized the financially weaker members of society. In addition, the new burdens were coming in a period when:

• Greek households were finding it increasingly difficult to serve their obligations to tax authorities, and
• Finance ministry officials conceded that there has been an increase in outstanding debts because of the financial crisis.

Clearer heads than those in the celebrating EU Commission made the point that the situation in Greece is a precursor of what will happen in Spain and Italy; and, later on, also in France. It is quite significant that these worries were expressed a whole year prior to February 2013 when it became evident that Italy and Spain were not far from asking for rescue via the European Stability Mechanism (ESM), through ECB's expedient of OMT mandating purchases of useless sovereign bonds of self-wounded countries.[10]

Greece, Spain, and Italy have been expecting too much of the German taxpayer in terms of handouts. This is irrational because, as history shows, the citizens of each country are always inclined to first protect their own standard of living and their own future income. (Of the euro 385 billion of Greek Bailout I and Bailout II (Table 5.1), the German share will probably reach about 30 percent of this amount or over two years Germany's intake in household taxes.[11])

The way a Financial Times/Harris Poll had it, only a quarter of Germans think Greece should stay in Euroland or get more help from other countries in the currency union. Such a public verdict highlights Merkel's domestic dilemma as she comes under pressure to agree for more time and more money for Greece to get the second bailout back on track.[12] As for seeing again their money, only 26 percent of Germans believe Greece will ever repay its bailout loans.

In a democracy, public opinion weights on decisions taken by governments and the aforementioned statistics are bleak. The Financial Times/Harris Poll also found that in France opinions are mixed: 32 percent of French respondents thought Greece should leave Euroland (compared with 54 percent of Germans), but the French were as reluctant as their German counterparts to provide Athens with extra money.

In an article he published in Nice Matin, the French Daily, Philippe Bouvard, the journalist, used Aristophanes' satire to describe what the French feel: "The Greeks are not easy-going cousins, since they refuse to satisfy the imperatives of modern democracy: The payment of taxes... industrial activity...and even affable tourist services. By tradition and culture the Greeks work only a little. No doubt they find the example in Venus of Milo, the divine protector of broken arms."

The public mood in France is captured, in a more crude but realistic way, by a blogger on Internet who put it this way: "Euro 110 billion in 2010! What did they do with that money? Now we must loan them euro 130 billion!! If we must assist these people at 100 percent my children and grandchildren will not ever pardon me for that!!!" The exclamation marks are not the end of the blog. Its author continued his criticism in a way that would have given Aristophanes food for his satire:

> ... And if we were asking these demonstrators what they really want? Europe does not want to pay for these cheaters, and they know it. They can no more live on the back of it. Then what? It reminds me the attitude of pedalodreou; he knows how to criticize, but as proposing something intelligent we always wait for it.

Aristophanes would have loved this "*pedalodreou.*" From Papandreou Jr. to pedalodreou changes only one syllable, but there is also realism in it. The way the Junior of the political family (and president of Socialist International) talks and acts is like going in a pedalo.

5.3   State of Politics and of Sovereign Debt

In its research, the Financial Times/Harris Poll contacted 1000 adults in Britain, Germany, France, Italy, and Spain. Their opinion demonstrated that there are disagreements between northern and southern Europe over important aspects of Euroland's management. But at the same time there is a common ground. A consensus has started to develop that things are not going the way hope had it.

The reader will probably say that what is happening in Greece, Portugal, Spain, and Italy is tragic; it is not for laughs. That's true, but neither the highly destructive Peloponnesian war was a joke. The great merit of Aristophanes is that he has shown the absurdity of the patricide war without using words which led to another quarrel.

Satire has been the best way to wake up the public to the fact that among the elected representatives of the people are egoists and incapables. Through their lack of public conscience, they take a self-centered holiday from social reality. Pericles started a brushfire of local repressions among Athenian colonies which turned into a five ring alarm and burned to ashes the social edifice of ancient Greece.

Centuries upon centuries passed since then, and the alarm bells are now ringing for another event which has disastrous social, economic, and financial aftereffects at the same time. Living on debt has been insanity. Doing the same thing over and over but expecting different results is the act of people who have lost any sense of judgment and of government.

This is as true of strikes, rallies, and Molotov cocktails as it is of guessing progress toward competitiveness. In early September 2012 officials in Brussels estimated that the Greek Bailout II program already slipped by up to euro 20 billion since, it was agreed in February of that same year. A decision on how to fill that gap had to be made before an already-overdue euro 31 billion was distributed (finally approved at the end of October as the Greek government said that by November it will run out of money).

What is happening with the Greek bailouts which led to a long list of consequences, should serve the EU, Euroland, and ECB to wake up to the fallacy that Italy, Spain, and eventually France can be rescued. Estimates published on the cost of an uncertain bailout of these bigger economies are not reliable because they only focus on what has been so far committed in Euroland funds, which is nothing more than an entry price.

If the billions and billions of Greece's mismanaged bailouts are taken as a basis for calculating the cost of salvaging the other self-wounded sovereigns,
Then we reach a level of roughly euro 5 trillion ($6.5 trillion) which turns the euro into dust.

That's a worst-case scenario, but from time to time worst cases have the nasty habit of turning into real life. Some estimates, very approximate ones, made by those who would like to see a blank check signed by Germany, suggest that altogether euro 1 trillion without France, and no more than euro 1.5 trillion with France, will be enough. I look at that number as an intentional miscalculation.

A more realistic, though also approximate, estimate of rescue costs should take into account the total debt of the aforementioned countries, plus bank recapitalization. In rounded-up figures, the total debt of Italy, France, Spain, Greece, Portugal, Cyprus and Slovenia[13] stands at:

Italy	euro 2.10 trillion
France	euro 1.80 trillion
Spain	euro 0.85 trillion
Greece, Portugal, Cyprus, Slovenia	euro 0.75 trillion
	euro 5.50 trillion

This does not include bank bailouts for which could be taken as proxy the LTROs by ECB to the tune of euro 1 trillion.[14] The lion's share of all this money, which in large part will be thrown to the four winds, will be eaten up by unsuccessfully trying to sustain the status quo in standard of living in profligate economies. In addition, the large majority is contributed by Germany since the second, third, and fourth economies in Euroland find themselves at the receiving end.

- Euro 5.50 trillion plus euro 1.0 trillion (for all banks) are 340 percent of German GDP, and
- Euroland's sovereigns who look at German money as *deus ex machina* prepare for themselves the deception of their life.

Theoretically, but only theoretically. Germany has been condemned to pay and pay and pay. Current thinking is best expressed by paraphrasing what Stalin said to Chou En-Lai about the North Koreans: "The Germans can indefinitely continue to finance Euroland. After all they are losing nothing but their money."[15] Practically, the probability this happens is zero-point-zero. No German government can ever propose it and survive public anger.

Compared to losses by Euroland's sovereigns in the case Greece runs out of rescue money and stop debt payments, the numbers brought to the reader's attention are astronomical. In May 2012 François Baroin, the former French finance minister, estimated that a Greek bankruptcy will cost the French Treasury euro 50 billion. This roughly corresponds to two years of tax intake by the French Treasury. Think about bailouts and associated bankruptcies of the magnitude we are talking about.

Always using the two Greek bailouts as a proxy, the distribution of losses changes by altering the reference made to Euroland funds, particularly those connected to guarantees by the ECB. An example is the massive withdrawal of funds from Greek banks by depositors which shows up in the TARGET2 central bank balances. By all likelihood, massive withdrawals by common citizen will spill over to Spanish and Italian central banks, making the situation of the two Club Med countries even more unattainable.

As far as overall effect of a Greek bankruptcy is concerned, Pierre Moscovici, the French finance minister, put it in this way: "Greece will provoke a contagion of the crisis whose amplitude cannot be foreseen and most likely it cannot be put under control. Think about Greece plus Spain, Italy, and France. The effects will be at least an order and a half greater than those of Greece alone.

Not only are headline costs unaffordable and unsustainable, but also costs have the nasty habit to keep on increasing leading to unpleasant surprises. When the Swiss were persuaded to join the Schengen agreement[16], they were told by the EU that the annual cost will be Swiss francs 11.4 million. This was the case in the first year, but six years down the line, by 2013, the Schengen cost reached Swiss francs 114 million —an order of magnitude increase. The same is going to happen with the hugely undercapitalized banks of Euroland, and most particularly with the derelict Spanish banks.

Using LTRO as proxy, my estimate for recapitalizing Euroland's self-wounded banks has been euro 1 trillion. This may well come short. Conservative estimates talk of a euro 400 billion to recapitalize banks—evidently including German banks—and pay deposit insurance. This is totally inadequate. Without reliable statistics which, if they exist, are kept close to the banks' chest and the vaults of their governments, it is difficult to make realistic analysis of recapitalization requirements.

Take the Spanish banks as an example. Available numbers indicating shortage of capital are totally unreliable. They are pulled out of a hat and then massaged. The October 2012 number for recapitalization has been euro 60 billion, so said a study by a consultancy. Market players however commented that needed capital is at or beyond euro 300 billion, and even that may be an underestimate. The euro 60 billion is just the bait to catch the big fish.

Totally unclear has as well been the issue of recapitalizing foreign banks for their losses in Spain, if worse comes to worse. No numbers have been provided, but an idea of likely red ink can be obtained from reference to bank losses in Greece. The French banks losses are estimated at over euro 19.8 billion, with Crédit Agricole leading the list. Compared to this amount German banks will be losing "only" euro 4.5 billion; still a hefty amount. There are moreover the banks' losses associated to loans to private Greek companies to the amount of euro 21 billion; and so on and so forth.

Some economists are comparing the choices facing Euroland and the IMF to those confronting the American Treasury and Federal Reserve in the days before Lehman Brothers collapsed in September 2008. The fourth largest US investment bank was at the center of tens of thousands of interconnected trades, the large majority hidden from view and difficult to value. Lehman's balance sheet was $613 billion, before its failure. But with panic following the collapse other players had no way of knowing:

- Who were the counterparties to its risky trades, and
- Whether Lehman owed them so much money that they too might fail.

Reliable information about a sovereign's assets and liabilities prior to even proposing a bailout is very important, particularly when a common currency area is already in the middle of debt restructuring some of its members. Mistakes in estimates jeopardize the continued provision of assistance, and all of a currency union's members will bear the consequences of such a scenario.

The same is true of overextending the ESM and EFSF budget by way of leveraging. A significant dilution of assumed agreements would damage confidence in Euroland policies and treaties, strongly weakening incentives for national reform and consolidation measures. It will also call in question the institutional *status* comprising:

- Euroland-wide liability, and
- Individual responsibility of member states.

Aristophanes would have enjoyed writing an act about the October 2012 dispute centered on highly pessimistic views taken by the IMF on whether the (then) new Greek government can succeed where its predecessors failed. Could it truly implement economic reforms to return the country to economic growth in a rapid and thorough way? IMF's pessimism caused friction within the Troika: The European Central Bank and European Commission believed the new Greek team of prime minister Antonis Samaras has shown a credible willingness to tackle the most intractable problems.

A month later, mid-November 2012, Euroland's ministers of finance found it difficult to decide on authorizing the euro 31.2 billion tranche of Greek bailout. The save the day, the Bank of Greece borrowed euro 5 billion from ECB to pay euro 6.5 billion in bond's due at that time.[17]

At stake was not only the euro 31.2 billion aid payment, already more than two months overdue, but the whole issue of what may happen if Spain and Italy joined the hat-in-hand folk. At stake was as well IMF's willingness to sign off on a revised bailout extending the program two more years into 2016. EU officials said that the extension was likely to add euro 30 billion to Greece's bailout cost, and not the least of questions asked was: Who pays?

Another critical query was and remains: What all this tells us about bailouts in Euroland at large? Martin Wolf, Financial Times' chief economist, compared Greece to the canary in the mine: "Its plight shows that the euro zone still seeks a workable mixture of flexibility, discipline and solidarity." The eurozone is in a form of limbo:

- "It is neither so deeply integrated that break-up is inconceivable,
- Nor so lightly integrated that break-up is tolerable."

To Wolf's opinion, the most powerful guarantee of Euroland survival is the costs of breaking it up: "Maybe that will prove sufficient. Yet, if the Eurozone is to be more than a grim marriage sustained by the frightening costs of dividing up assets and liabilities, it has to be built on something vastly more positive than that."[18] We will return to "something" in Chapter 6.

5.4 Restructuring Efforts Don't Necessarily Provide Expected Results

In an environment of risk-off trades, the name of the game is capital preservation. Investors look at both the history and the prospects of a country, prior to proceed with direct investments. Debt crises scare them off, whether these investors are big corporations, insurance companies, private individuals, or pension funds on whose results tens of thousands of families depend for their living.

We must base our asset allocation not on the probabilities of choosing the right allocation, but on the consequences of choosing the wrong one, said in a 2009 speech Jack Bogle, founder and retired CEO of The Vanguard Group. As far as Greece, Portugal, Spain, and Italy are concerned, investors look at their past status and prospects, coming up with the conclusion that investing there would be the wrong allocation.

For Greece this is dramatized in Figure 5.1 through the spread of 10-year Greek government bonds against German Bunds, in 2010 and 2011 the years of the first bailout. Note that in the very beginning of 2010 the spread was not greater than 300 basis points. With the bailout discussions hitting the news, the market woke up and by April 2010 the spread zoomed past 1000 basis points. Subsequently, 2011

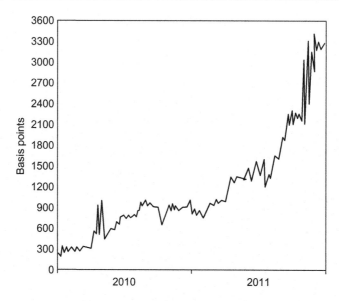

Figure 5.1 Spread of 10-year Greek government bonds against bunds.

was a disaster as the spread past 3200 basis points. Yet Greece was already laboring under the first bailout.

That's what the French call "the tyranny of the market," but in this they are wrong. Nowadays the global market is composed of millions of individuals who watch over creditworthiness and market risk. Though sometimes the market may be wrong, when there is a pronounced trend, as in Figure 5.1, the way to bet is that the market is right.[19] It is not easy to fool millions of individual, independent players. As Abraham Lincoln once said: "You can lie to all of the people some of the time, or some of the people all of the time, but you cannot lie to all of the people all of the time."

So what is to be done? The answer is change in course, by living on assets not on debt, and through restructuring. To have a chance, restructuring must be done in earnest. Theoretically, since 2010 Greece had adopted extensive consolidation measures. Practically, these consisted of taxes and more taxes. There has been no restructuring of the labor market and no relaunching of the economy. Quite to the contrary, plenty of companies closed down.

Also theoretically, Greece recorded a 1.2 percent point decline in its deficit ratio in 2011. Practically, following the exceptionally sharp deficit increase in the preceding years, the budgetary deficit still stood at 9.1 percent. Greece missed the original target of 7.6 percent agreed when the bailout program was drawn up. These is no evidence that this "7.6 percent" is anything else than a random number, but 9.1 percent greatly increased the debt-to-GDP ratio.

While it is true that 2010 and 2011 were generally difficult years because of a worse-than-expected global economic environment, it is proper also to account for repeated failure by successive Greek governments to implement consolidation and reform measures. The market watched these developments and responded with ultrahigh interest rates for Greek debt postponing the country's return to the capital markets (originally scheduled for 2012).

In the coming years, economists will be debating whether it was right or wrong that the requirements for fiscal consolidation have been relaxed discernably—by EU, ECB, and IMF—compared with the original agreements. When one goes through a bad period, and feels plenty of pain, it is wise not to relax the rules which (hopefully) lead out of the tunnel. *If* he does so, *then* the light at the end of the tunnel becomes dimmer.

Over and above the relaxation which extended the time scales, came the uncertainty about the euro's future, and the role of Greece in it (Sections 5.5 and 5.6). John Thanassoulis, an Oxford economist who led a study of European corporate finance during the crisis, sees signs of companies positioning themselves for a break-up of the euro.[20] He is not alone in this projection.[21] As for the role of Greece in Euroland (debated in Chapter 6), at best it is uncertain. As long as it were still the proprietor Crédit Agricole, one of the major three French banks:

- Emptied the tills of Emporiki, its Greek subsidiary, every evening,
- Shipped the balances electronically to Paris, and
- Returned them in the morning to Emporiki, so that it is ready for business.

Crédit Agricole sold Emporiki to a Greek bank for one symbolic euro. Carrefour, the big French supermarket, sold stores in Greece also for a single euro. Other companies, too, gave up their operations in Greece, while very few increased their exposure. Alfa Beta, the supermarket, is an example. The story behind these references is disinvestment, while Greece urgently needs foreign direct investment (FDI).

As one misfortune: lack of confidence, never comes alone, inflation is present in parallel with deflation. According to Thanassoulis since banks are short of capital and their ability to lend is impaired, companies are holding prices up to preserve profit margins and have collateral for future borrowing. At the same time, companies shed full-time staff and turn to outsourcing. No wonder that Greek unemployment zoomed past 25 percent.

Some of the advice the Greek government receives looks funny. In their early September 2012 descent to Athens, the representatives of the EU, ECB, and IMF asked that the country's citizens work six days per week,[22] but left aside the issue of rising unemployment. Labor market flexibility is very important, but thought has also to be given to the fact that unemployment in Greece is now so high that there is not enough work going around for being busy three or four days per week, let alone six.

Even more dramatic is the fact that this free advice which sounds like apple pie and motherhood does not account for the base scenario that Europe and the United States are entering decades of Japanese-style economic stagnation. And there is another similitude with present-day Japan: dysfunctional politics leading to stop-gap decisions which later on corner their decision makers.

This is more or less true for every country in the old continent and constitutes one (but only one) of the reasons why the Troika does not find what it is searching for, when it reads the books of the Ministry of Finance, in Athens. The position taken by EU/ECB/IMF expressed only in too broad terms, that:

- Greece is provided with a large amount of liquidity, AND
- The agreed upon programs should be implemented.

But do they bring tangible results? On February 9, 2012 Mohamed El Erian, the CEO of PIMCO, the largest bond investor world-wide, was interviewed by Richard Quest of CNN about the present and next scenes in the Greek drama. His opinion worths recording because it shows impartiality and focuses on the real problem.

"There is no common analysis, let alone understanding of what is going on," El Erian said. "Therefore each party (the EU/ECB/IMF and Greece) has its own agenda." The interview then turned to what a country confronted with a deep economic and financial crisis needs. El Erian's and Quest's opinion was that it needs not only loans but also:

- Growth,
- Stability, and
- Ways to attract new capital.

Quest asked if the EU is cutting Greece off. El Erian answered that they push it to political fragmentation, pointing out that in the previous days (February 8, 2012) the meeting of Euroland's finance ministers humiliated Greece.

To the opinion of PIMCO's CEO there has been a shift in strategy at the vertex of Euroland, which explains the statement that the deep Greek cuts in salaries and pensions are insufficient in spite of the high unemployment which reaches 55 percent for the young (in the 16- to 25-years bracket). This new Euroland strategy can be summarized in two bullets:

- Refund the core, and
- Let the peripherals go.

It is quite likely that such a shift is taking shape. At the same time, it is no less true that Greece has a euro 250 billion economy and it is crashed by euro 350 billion in debt. When these foreign loans were made by totally incapable populist and socialist governments, the public did not react; neither did it afterward bring the wrong-doers to justice. It simply re-elected them.

"Greece is ring-fenced," said one of the economists who participate to the research leading to this book, "This is far different than being helped to recover. Its problems are not being solved." The position taken by the Eurogroup is different: "You have not done enough. Further work is necessary. Follow the Troika's advice." The Greek government's response tells still another story: "Whatever could be done is done."

These reactions diverge and up to a point explains the fact that the debt-to-GDP ratio continues to worsen. The EU/ECB/IMF want the Greek government to produce a primary budget surplus[23] by 2013/2014. Even a blonde with dark glasses can see that this is a chimera. Neither is the two-year extension asked by the coalition government solving anything because:

- It has been no upside, and
- It is a self-delusion; pure politics.

Restructuring efforts don't necessarily provide expected results, and this is particularly true when politics take the upper ground. With prices continuing going up, the common citizen is squeezed between reduction in income and inflation. The social fabric is under stress, leading many to believe that a full scale bankruptcy could have been the better alternative—from the start (Chapter 6).

5.5 Rescue Funds Can Turn into Monkey Money

If Greece achieved a primary surplus, the result the second bailout's providers wanted to see, *then* this would have improved its chances to start in a path of recovery. It should not be forgotten, however, that the euro 240 billion of the first and second rescues have been *loans not gifts*. Even at relatively reduced interest rates, the servicing of these loans is bound to weigh heavily on the Greek government's budget.

Therefore, it is not unlikely that Bailouts I and II will not reach their goal; and they may or may not be followed by Bailout III. Wolfgang Schäuble, the German finance minister, admitted as much when in early March 2012 said that a third package of about euro 50 billion (then $66 billion) might be necessary sometime in the future if the situation in Greece became critical.

There is no reason to believe that the same less-than expected result of bailouts will not characterize the rescues of Spain and Italy (if ever undertaken). The only difference is that the bailouts of Italy and Spain will run dry the ESM fund and explode the European Central Bank's balance sheet. They will also change the central theme of Euroland's debt crisis which has been that no player has been willing to:

- Recognize that trillions rather than billions of euro are needed to diffuse the debt bubble which keeps on building up, and
- Risk bankruptcy after having bled trillions.

To start with, it is nobody's secret that no Euroland member country, including Germany, has available the needed trillions. Along with this comes the fact that, admittedly, bailout money is unsecured money. Nobody ever said that Greece, Portugal, Spain, Italy will be able to reimburse the funds they received through rescue packages. The same is evidently true of any other country which gets into unpayable debt blues. So far in recent times in Europe only tiny Iceland and Latvia were able to redress their situation (Chapter 13), which they did:

- Without rescue packages, and
- By betting their economy's future on hard work and an internal devaluation.

Ireland, too, is in its way of doing so, but all three are northern economies. Club Med has different standards. There is no secret about that and therefore already some of Euroland's players have hedged their bets. The European Central Bank provides an example. While agreeing (under pressure from Euroland's finance ministers) to forgo euro 5 billion in potential profits on its Greek bonds:

- It has protected itself against forced losses imposed on its bond holdings, and
- Will not make direct payments to the Greek sovereign whose bonds are no more accepted.[24]

When the Eurozone debt crisis first threatened to go out of control, the ECB ruled out taking losses on its portfolio of an estimated euro 40 billion under a Securities Markets Program" launched in May 2010 by Jean-Claude Trichet, its then governor. Subsequently, at PSI's time, the ECB sought special protection for its Greek bond holdings by swapping them for new bonds, to be excluded from collective action clauses (see Chapter 4 on PSI). By contrast, pension funds which had (unwisely) invested in Greek government bonds lost their money.

One cannot really blame the different Euroland players (specifically those with liquid funds) for being prudent. According to many economists, even in the best case what has taken place in Euroland in terms of rescue operations could solve only part of the problem. The likelihood of a more holistic solution to Italian, Spanish, Portuguese, and Greek debilitated public finances is handicapped by:

- The lack of money, and
- Absence of a do-it-yourself plan.

Moreover, while western central banks flooded the market with liquidity, and big banks profited handsomely from it, loans to companies are not forthcoming. An ECB survey, published in February 2012, has shown that banks continued to tighten credit standards to readings last seen in April 2009 in the wake of Lehman's bankruptcy. This has prevailed throughout 2012 with a rising default rate promoted by the deteriorating economic environment.

Tighter bank lending in the microeconomy is matched by concern at the marcoeconomy that temporary relief through bailouts will turn those funds to monkey money because of domestic insolvency. In a nutshell, this describes the evolving scenario in Spain and, by all evidence (given political instability) in Italy.

Self-wounded Euroland countries asking for rescues tend to forget that these funds come out of other Euroland citizens' pockets, and the latter don't like the idea of a transfer union. They also look at the absence of positive results given the fact that, in spite of spending billions, the debt crisis has not been averted. German, Dutch, Finnish, and other Euroland citizens believe it is not too much to ask that each of the wounded economies searches and finds its own way out of the economic chaos into which it has descended, rather than exporting:

- Financial uncertainty,
- Economic contraction, and
- Political as well as social turmoil.

In addition, the depth of the crisis is making structural reforms needed for long-term growth harder to agree upon. It also becomes more difficult to define and implement corrective steps, particularly as the EU tries to do it without a firm plan and a hope from getting out of the debt abyss at a predefined date. The worst-off governments say that they find it politically impossible to ask for needed structural changes, but on the other hand they fail to explain to the citizen that without a plan for recovery, and changes that go along with it, the misery years will continue.

"Summits" come and go, but they are largely love affairs and change nothing to the dismal situation. Sacred cows lead to lack of a plan and therefore of hope to get the country and the economy moving again. This is the first major concern, while the absence of truthful accounting spreadsheets mapping *cost* and *return* of rescue packages are the second. Without generally agreed solutions to both issues, there is the risk of:

- Deeper recessions, and
- Further increases in debt-to-GDP ratios.

In an article in the Financial Times, Professor Grezgorz Kolodko, of Poland's Kozminski University, put it this way: We now stand at a crossroads. I think it is time to face the truth. If there is still a chance to avoid the train crash, it is not by ignoring reality and believing that the Greeks will fast as much as it takes to pay the mounting debt... Nor is it by lying and sweeping part of the challenge under the carpet, as Eurozone finance ministers and certain European Union leaders are tempted to do again and again.

But getting the whole of Euroland and each individual country, as well as its economy, moving again requires leadership, and leadership is in very short supply all over the West. If proof is needed, the difficulty to reach comprehensive decisions—and outline their consequences—is proof enough. On February 14, 2012 Rehn, the European Commission's top economics official,

- Warned that there would be "devastating consequences" if Greece defaulted, and
- Pleaded for Eurozone governments to approve the bailout quickly.

This has been Rehn's opinion. Precisely that same day a group of Euroland governments, particularly those which retain AAA credit ratings, made it clear that they lost faith that Greece will ever deliver its end of the bargain. "We are getting closer to default," stated a senior Euroland official. "Germany, Finland and the Netherlands are losing patience."[25] "Until we have it all definitely on paper, with really solid guarantees from Greece as well, and legislation, we can't make any decisions," said Jan Kees de Jager, Dutch finance minister.[26]

What rattles the Euroland member states providing the funds is that a bankruptcy by recipient countries would turn their money into monkey money—admittedly not a good prospect. Neither is the drain of funds for nation-state bailouts the only game in town. As Chapter 4 brought to the reader's attention mismanaged financial institutions, too, have an insatiable appetite for rescue money.

A sound principle in financial management, as well as in good neighborly relations, is that every country takes care of its own sick banks, who gambled and lost in the derivatives markets or kept too close to the unhealthy deadly embrace of banks and sovereigns. The United States, Britain, Germany, and Holland rescued and/or recapitalized their own banks. By contrast Spain, already at the edge of bankruptcy, wants its banks to be financed and recapitalized by Euroland—no questions asked.[27]

This is permanent free lunch, at its best. As John Major, the former British prime minister, had it in an article he published in the Financial Times, "The ease of (Greek) entry exemplifies the follies of the founders. France insisted: "You cannot say no to the country of Plato." Maybe not, but every European is now paying the price..."[28] The same is practically true of all other Club Med countries' membership to the single currency.

To Major's mind, Euroland's Club Med member states should devalue to become competitive, but they cannot because they are locked in a single currency. And because they cannot devalue their currency, they must devalue their living standards. Promoting reforms to enhance efficiency will take years. Meanwhile, as Major has it: "Wages must fall, unemployment will rise and social unrest will increase." And, of course, bankruptcies, too, will rise.

This is the right diagnosis, but the prescription is much more complex because it involves not only economics and finance but also (and primarily so) plenty of social issues. The global economy is not at the best of health, and Euroland is no exception to it by any means. In fact, the forecast for 2014 is that Euroland's economy, as a whole, will grow by less than 1 percent dragged by economic problems in Southern Europe.

5.6 Using CDSs as Predictors

The concept of CDSs has been introduced in Chapter 4 in connection with credit events associated to PSI. A concise way of looking at them is as insurance policies aiming to protect their buyer against credit risk associated to the likelihood that the issuer of debt, or other financial instruments, defaults. At the same time, however, while paying for this protection the buyer assumes two new risks:

• Creditworthiness; the writer of a CDS may not be able to face its obligation, and
• The possibility that a default may be masqueraded, so that a *credit event* is not being declared triggering the protection payment, as it has nearly happened with PSI.

CDSs are characterized by *spreads* conveying to buyers and prospects a message on creditworthiness. Not all entities in the same class (sovereigns, companies) have the same quality of credit. Spreads vary as a function of time for the same entity as its financial position (hence, its chances) strengthens or wanes. *If* one instrument is taken as benchmark for instance German Bunds, *then* watching the spread of other sovereign bonds against this benchmark provides an interesting measurement.

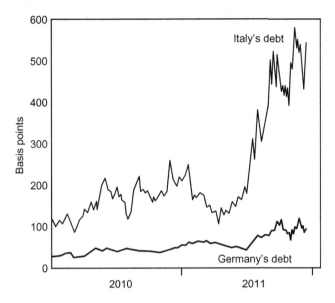

Figure 5.2 Twenty-four months CDS spreads of Italian sovereign bonds against German bunds (in basis points; 100 P = 1%).

CDSs *spreads* in Figure 5.2 measure the likelihood of Italy's inability to honor its debt obligations; for instance, to repay its bonds. The benchmark is German Bunds and the difference is expressed in basis points (100 basis points = 1 percent). Because CDSs are tradable, they act as real-time market signals for financial anxiety associated to sovereigns, companies, or any other debtor.

The volatility of CDSs increases significantly at times of stress. Even for well-known governments (or companies) CDS spreads can easily double and then halve again within a few months. Bankers, investors, and traders look at these spreads as a warning. Even if they are not necessarily the best measurement of an entity's intrinsic value, they are:

- Easily available,
- Dynamic, and
- Show market restiveness.

Investors behave like voters and CDS spreads are a vote. At end of April 2012, less than two months after the PSI and second bailout negotiations, Greek two-year bond yields (which move inversely to bond prices) jumped 133 percent—as a news item revealed that the country's budget deficit for 2010 was 10.5 percent.[29] This jump reflected market uncertainty about the Greek economy's future.

With market uncertainty at an all-time high, the spread between Greek 10-year bonds and German Bunds of similar maturity widened to 1208 basis points, the most since data was first collected in 1998. The cost of borrowing for Portugal also reached Euroland highs, because of rising concerns that peripheral economies will be forced to restructure their debts. Many investors were keen to hedge their risks using either of the principal ways of positioning one's portfolio against default:

- Shorting government bonds,[30]
- Buying CDSs, or
- Buying new recovery swaps.[31]

The first alternative is more classical, but shorting becomes problematic with complex debt instruments. There has been, as well, a scarcity of bonds available for investors to borrow on the heels of PSI (Chapter 4). In part, this is also due to a ban in Greece on naked shorting of stocks (where investors do not own the underlying equity), leading to increasing use of CDSs.

CDSs and recovery swaps, said an expert, give banks and investors more ways and more scope to hedge their risks. At end of April 2012 outstanding gross CDS contracts of Greek, Portuguese, Spanish, and Irish debt totaled about $330 billion. The recovery swaps market also grew. Remember, however, that CDSs and recovery swaps are only activated in case of a credit event; *if* an issuer:

- Fails to meet coupon payments,
- Alters the terms of a bond to longer maturity,
- Changes the currency the debt is denominated in, or
- Proceeds with restructuring or reprofiling involuntary to investors.

While corporate defaults that lead to payment of CDS protection are routine, the case of sovereign credit event associated to PSI was a novelty. Traders rushed to calculate exposures. The notional value of Greek sovereign bonds insured by CDSs was between $70 and $74 billion, according to DTCC, a data repository. But banks and hedge funds have offsetting exposures, having issued some CDS insurance contracts and bought others. This saw to it that the net exposure to a Greek default was "only" $3.3 billion. Not so deadly.

Both gross and net CDS figures (the $70 to $74 billion and $3.3 billion) are important and necessary; all by themselves CDSs net figures are not transparent enough. Net figures help in calculating capital requirements, while gross figures provide the dimension as well as the basis for estimating credit risk assumed by Bank A which bought protection from Banks B, C, and D. They help to judge if anyone of them might not be able to face its obligations.

In addition, the aforementioned 1 to 22 difference between gross and net has its own risks. Largely contracted over the counter, the CDS market is opaque. Netting is done on initial values which may significantly change as events unfold. The bought-and-sold algorithm used for netting does not account for the price of these contracts. A bank which offered CDSs for Greece when the credit gap to German Bunds was 300 basis points, would pay an exorbitant price to net when the rating of Greece dropped to "CCC" and the credit gap is 1208 basis points.

As Chapter 4 brought to the reader's attention, on March 1, 2012 the first time around the International Securities Dealers Association (ISDA) ruled that the 73.5 percent haircut on lenders by PSI (in the Greek debt), was not a credit event. But a week later, on March 9, ISDA declared a "credit event had occurred" and billions of euro of credit default insurance had to be paid out. Still, there was no market panic even if risk tends to show up where least expected. That sum seemed reasonable and manageable, it did not keep protection sellers sleepless at night.

Greece was declared to have technically defaulted, as a total of 85.8 percent of Greece's international creditors approved the restructuring deal which reduced the value of their investments by 73.5 percent. Lucas Papademos, then Greek prime minister[32], stated this was the largest restructuring even made, adding that:

- He understood the significant damage unleashed on investors, and
- The country had no right to squander the debt it had been forgiven.

Papademos promised to "modernize the country, make our economy competitive, and tidy up the state," his government however fell afterward and all that proved to be just words. Politicians will do well to desist from promising any more than they are sure they can deliver.

In retrospect, this first experience with a risk event associated to sovereign credit event was orderly, though painful to the banks who lost nearly three-fourth of their bonds' face value and to those who had to pay the $3.3 billion protection money. By being orderly:

- It has not created major disruptions in financial markets, and
- The settlement of CDS contracts went smoothly, thereby creating precedence.

At the same time it provided an example for a possible orchestrated sovereign restructuring. Most market participants had anticipated the default event, and plenty of contracts were unwound ahead of the largest losses for government bond investors in history.

It would, however, be wrong to conclude that all future sovereign defaults (which will definitely occur), can be organized in an orderly manner. For instance, the Spanish sovereign, a candidate for the next in line sovereign credit event, has so far kept the status of its Treasury (and that of its banks) close to its chest. Because of prevailing opaqueness, several financial analysts believe that an eventual default by the Kingdom of Spain is unlikely to be isolated and orderly.

End Notes

1. The Economist, July 11, 2011.
2. *Idem.*
3. This particular Eurogroup meeting had taken 13 hours.
4. The four parts of PSI published by an investment bank analysis are euro 52.2; 35.5; 36 and 92.3 billion. Of the total of euro 216 billion was taken a haircut of 73.5 percent = euro 158.76 billion.
5. Their nature has been explained in Chapter 4.
6. Financial Times, February 7, 2012.

7. As reported in the *Canard Enchainé*, François Hollande, the French president, said in a meeting with his ministers that Merkel is "a very selfish person", because she did not agree to his demand to mutualize the bottomless pit of French public debt.

8. *Le Point*, July 5, 2012.

9. See also Section 5.4.

10. In fact, the heated late January 2013 argument between Wolfgang Schäuble, German finance minister, and Mario Draghi, ECB's boss, about Cyprus had little to do with Cyprus which found itself in the crossfire. The targets were Spain and Italy.

11. Not counting VAT and corporate taxation.

12. Financial Times, September 3, 2012.

13. As we have already seen, Cyprus and Slovenia are also in the sick list.

14. The LTROs took place in December 2011 and February 2012. At end of January 2013 the better off banks returned to the ECB euro 148 billion.

15. What Stalin said to Chou En-Lai in plain Korean War has been: "The North Koreans can indefinitely continue fighting because they lose nothing else but their men." Simon Sebag Montefiore "*Staline*", Editions des Syrtes, Paris, 2005.

16. Of free circulation of people among subscribing nations.

17. November 12, 2012.

18. Financial Times, February 15, 2012.

19. Yield spread of Greek sovereign bonds reached 4000 basis points in early 2012, collapsing to 1600 and returning to 3000 basis points.

20. The Economist, October 6, 2012

21. Chorafas DN. Breaking up the euro. The end of a common currency, New York, NY: Palgrave/Macmillan; 2013.

22. *Le Monde*, September 7, 2012.

23. A budgetary surplus prior to calculating the interest to be paid for outstanding public loans.

24. Later on, this decision was reversed.

25. Financial Times, February 15, 2012.

26. *Idem*.

27. Unwisely, Euroland's finance ministers approved a euro 100 billion ($130 billion) rescue package for self-wounded Spanish banks.

28. Financial Times, October 27, 2011.

29. The deficit was above the government's estimate of 9.4 percent, although below the 2009 shortfall of 15.4 percent of GDP.

30. Which involves borrowing a security and selling it with an agreement to buy it back at a later date.

31. With recovery swaps investors bet on the haircut level in any restructuring.

32. Papademos is a central banker turned politician.

6 Drachmageddon: Exit from Euroland and Bankruptcy? Or Bankruptcy Within Euroland?

6.1 Drachmageddon

At the time these lines are written, Greece is still in Euroland, but its economic and financial situation has not been stabilized; nor is the broader euro crisis solved. As Chapter 5 documented, Greece did not capitalize on an austerity program to bring itself back to a stable debt trajectory. With Bailouts I and II its debt-to-GDP ratio increased, which means that another default is brewing up.

Chiefs of state, economists, and financial analysts foresee that within 18 months either of two events will happen: Greece quits Euroland, reintroduces the drachma, probably defaults, prunes its balance sheets and, in an unlikely but not impossible move, rejoins Euroland. Or, it defaults within Euroland (Section 6.6), obliging the other member states to ring-fence its economy to avoid contagion. (Though contagion may also come from Spain and Italy, neither of them being in an economic situation much better than Greece.)

The pattern described in the preceding two paragraphs may sound strange but it is not so unexpected given the euro's twists. In early July 2012, David Cameron expressed his frustration about the lack of progress in putting Euroland's finances on track, after more than 2 years devoted to the euro debt crisis. A little earlier on Robert Zoellick, who was at the time World Bank's president, put his finger right where it hurts: "European politicians always act a day late and promise one euro too little. Then, when it gets tight, they add new liquidity."

The problems confronting Euroland remain daunting and Greece is just one cog in a chain of challenges. The bigger and more general are the salient problems, the less the likelihood of solving them without assuming risks. One of Euroland's big goals is building up the foundations of a fiscal union; a daunting task. If I remain skeptical about the euro and Euroland it is precisely because what needs to be done to get the fiscal union on the right foot, is not among the EU politicians' priorities.

Quite to the contrary, the majority of Euroland's sovereigns have adopted a policy leading off the tracks. "No" to fiscal discipline, "no" to a harmonization of taxes and duties, "no" to a biting form of banking supervision, but "yes" to keeping

Public Debt Dynamics of Europe and the US. DOI: http://dx.doi.org/10.1016/B978-0-12-420021-0.00006-3

the banking system afloat at great cost to the taxpayer. Yet, practically everybody knows that a sound policy requires:

- Euro-wide capital measures to address bank solvency issues,
- Strong controls to stop with derivatives gambling and start lending, and
- Rebuilding of confidence to avoid the drainage of deposits by Euroland's citizens.

The discipline necessary to redress the balance sheet of European banks is just as important for sovereigns. By majority, Euroland's sovereign Treasuries have to be recapitalized but, given the astronomical sums being involved, this cannot be done by way of presents. Iceland, Latvia, and Ireland (Chapter 13) have shown the way. They have demonstrated that in the absence of political union it cannot be "all in one," and therefore decided that since it is each on his own they have to do their best.

These three countries did not need to apply Euroland's *Fiscal Compact* (which entered into force on January 1, 2013) requiring signatory countries[1] to incorporate into their national legislation a structurally close-to-balance general government budget—as well as debt brakes[2] which trigger an automatic correction mechanism if targets are missed.

They did so on their own initiative, and labored to put in order their national fiscal policy. Neither did they spend their time in celebrating that the EU won Oslo's 2012 Nobel Peace Prize[3] which makes it a sort of colleague to Barack Obama; a prize which neither in the one nor in the other case was deserved, or for that matter it means anything. Instead, they tightened their belts and worked hard to regain economic independence. (See also Chapter 1 about debt leading to slavery.)

These three small countries did not listen to the trickery song of some economists that "the best way to insure government debts is to follow the example of Alexander Hamilton." True enough, in 1790, Alexander Hamilton decided to mutualize the debts of the American states in a single US debt. But in 1790, the United States was *one nation*, and the different states having formed *a political union* (not just a fiscal union). This is *not* the case of Euroland, let alone of the EU. Moreover,

- Alexander Hamilton was a federalist and mutualization was a good way to tie the states of the union together,
- But looking into the future and knowing that there may be surprises with profligate states, he did *not* make mutualization the law of the land.

Since then each state in the United States looks after its own budget. Washington no more pays the states' debt (or the municipalities'). Therefore, the Hamilton argument of big spenders (mainly French, Italian, and Spanish) is a fake and it is as well ridiculous.

If by a majestic wand all debts of Euroland's member states were zeroed out, these would rise again at no time because the Club Med's (and others) big spending habits have not changed. Only nations[4] able to confront and solve their financial problems on their own appreciate money's worth. "Rescue" packages perpetuate slavery, not independence.

An argument one hears about the exit of Greece from Euroland is that the country failed to reduce its budget deficit despite the bailouts. This can be turned around: It failed because manna from heaven saw to it that the deficit remains high. People are not taking their future in their hands, neither do they appreciate that the bailouts are loans not presents.

That's what *Drachmageddon* is all about. As with everything else in life, there is a *cost* associated to it and a *will*. Some chiefs of state and their economists argue that Greece is unlikely to be better off outside Euroland than in it. They give as examples:

- The support provided by Euroland's institutions
- The cost of getting out of the Euroland (more on this later in Sections 6.2 and 6.3), and
- The risk that once Greece opts out of the euro other countries, too, will start quitting the common currency.

Part of the cost of going back to the drachma will be the forced conversion of bank deposits, and strict capital controls. The latter are required to prevent massive capital flight at two critical times: just prior a *new drachma* is introduced and immediately afterward. Proper planning and costing, too, is part of drachmageddon.

Forced conversion will present several problems. While Greek government debt might be redenominated with few legal hiccups, private sector debt owed to non-Greek financial institutions would remain liable in euros, dollars, pounds, or whatever the currency of the original obligation. With the new drachma depreciating in the currency markets (why else issue it?), the Greek private sector would experience rolling defaults.

In paper money terms, after decades of current account deficits, Greece, its companies and its residents, owe the rest of the world a lot. Particularly since the euro was introduced, Greece has added up external liabilities well in excess of its GDP. This was highly unwise. A bankruptcy could take care of that, but "exit the euro" and bankruptcy are not the same things even if they might happen simultaneously.

By opting out of the euro Greece (or any other country) needs to redenominate all contracts made under its laws into the resurrected national currency. To avoid legal fights, which last many years and enrich only the lawyers, it should continue to meet its nonnational law obligations or at least try to do so.

For its part, the Bank of Greece needs to assure that all foreign branches of Greek banks balance their foreign exchange positions. As for the government, as briefly mentioned, it will have to impose temporary capital controls necessary because the drachma would immediately fall against the euro—possibly losing 50 percent or more of its value within a rather brief period of time.

The government will have to redenominate domestic bank assets and liabilities into drachma and insist that domestic contracts, such as pay and prices, be set in new drachmas. All this suggests the need for minute preparation. A precipitous exit without studying and planning every detail would leave the country not only without notes and coin but as well without the financial links necessary for the new drachma.

As long as external debts remain at their current or, even worse, higher levels, both the Greek financial sector and the nonfinancial would confront the risk of collapse. Credit may well evaporate, with a deep recession following on its heels. Moreover, given an economy open to trade, drachma weakness will result in rising import prices, eroding domestic purchasing power and (up to a point) undermining the hoped-for competitiveness from depreciation of the currency.

Sound financial management will require that prior to the opt-out announcement, the government deposits its portion of foreign exchange reserves held by the ECB with the Bank for International Settlements. While the new currency is minted and till it is supplied to bank branch offices, it should also declare a temporary bank holiday.

The EU and Euroland, too, will be confronted with a mare of organizational problems. There are good enough reasons to believe that once Greece opts out of the euro other countries using the common currency will adopt the same policy. The same will happen if Germany leaves the euro, followed in the exit by Holland, Finland, and more—except that in the latter case Euroland member states opting out will be those economically stronger. By contrast, in the case of Greece, Italy, and Spain the opt-outs will come from southern Europe and their finances will be weak.

6.2   Exit from Euroland?

Jens Weidmann, Bundesbank's president, believes that Euroland's current framework for bailing out distressed member states will weaken the common currency's stronger economies. Germany has pledged a lot more than euro 300 billion ($400 billion) in loans and guarantees to bailout Greece, Ireland, and Portugal—not even counting ECB's OMT. With ECB's "unlimited" buying of distressed nations' sovereign bonds, Euroland's taxpayers will be financing mismanaged states like Spain and Italy till bankruptcy dawns upon the EU. This is not what the single European currency was meant to be.

For his part, in mid-October 2012, Adair Turner, chairman of the Financial Services Authority, argued in a London speech that Britain has an enormous national self-interest in Euroland either taking the steps required to succeed or, if that is politically unattainable, dissolving in a controlled rather than chaotic fashion. This will help to avoid a catastrophic outcome and it's what a controlled bankruptcy is all about.

Decades down the line, economic historians will debate how did happen that since the common currency came into existence in 2001 a debt virus spread through southern European governments. Politicians have been struck by that *virus of spending* well beyond their country's means, by amassing unpayable liabilities.

- It used to be "tax-and-spend."
- But for the last dozen years it has become "get in debt-and-spend."

This reflects a deeper malaise which seems to accompany the euro, and is fed rather than cured through bailouts. As *The Economist* put it: "The euro is a troubled child, a single currency without a single state that is questioned by the markets."[5] Weidmann is right when he says that, if things stay as they are, the consequences of unsound policies (by some member states) will be passed on to others. Instead of putting their house in order, the profligate states depend on Germany to be both:

- The "no-questions-asked" financier, and
- The country which will economically wound itself, igniting a homemade inflation by allowing wages to rise too quickly.

To the twisted mind of profligate politicians and pseudo-Keynesian economists, a German inflation will be instrumental in rebalancing competitiveness within Euroland. That argument is silly, and Weidmann is right when he says that an increase in wages of even 5 percent would damage Germany but have no impact on resurgence of profligate countries. The latter might, only might, become more competitive versus Germany, but not against states outside the euro.

One does not come up from under by damaging others. He does so by exercising cost control and self-discipline necessary for cleaning up public finances. If a Euroland country which is under bailout is unable to put itself together again, or finds it too difficult to regain competitiveness within the currency union, exit is the remaining option. This can be achieved under either of three conditions:

- As a managed process,
- By way of an uncontrolled exit, and
- By way of default within Euroland (examined in Section 6.7).

A managed process will be, first and foremost, based on the other member states' agreement. Conditions will most likely include rules of disengagement; haircut on debt which includes the so far "untouchable funds"[6]: surely ECB and probably IMF, and conversion of all remaining debt into a new currency, for instance, the drachma.

It is quite probable, but not sure, that a managed process would require that the IMF acts as advisor and controller, particularly, controller of conditions aiming to avoid, or at least limit, contagion to other member countries.

Some of these conditions will probably involve ESM and ECB, including support to other at-risk member countries who, otherwise, might plausibly conclude they are the next to go. This effort will be more effective if it addresses the worries of both the sovereign and the citizens. Short of that, after a run on their domestic banks common citizens will be sending their wealth abroad, precipitating a collapse of the financial sector and, by extension, of the economy.

As the issues associated to a Greek exit intensify, the rest of Euroland must make preparations for the case other peripheral countries want to exit. Even if no other Euroland member state actively contemplates quitting the common currency, the way to bet is that market pressure may force it to do so, soon after Greece leaves.

The cost to European banks and insurance companies will, as well, have to be accounted for. An orderly exit process must pay attention to the expected and unexpected effects on the banking industry. Credit institutions will have important treasury problems to attend, and the stock market may see a major correction.

Economists believe that an uncontrolled exit of Greece from Euroland would lead to a selloff in financial markets, particularly hurting the most risky asset classes even calling into question the stability of the European financial system. Even if the credit market does not freeze (which is a remote possibility) there will be deep recession causing default rates to substantially rise in Euroland.

The way to bet is that the credit market will demand higher yields from the sovereign of the exit country as well as from the country's banks (resulting in structurally lower profitability). Other Euroland member states leaning toward exit will also be affected. In terms of credit, the exiting country's ability to market its bonds, a managed approach will probably be characterized by a two-phase reaction:

- Starting with an initial selloff, and
- Followed by a subsequent recovery in the not-too-distant future.

Even if the exit is properly managed, the turnaround will come only after uncertainty about its aftereffects subsides, there is evidence that contagion to other peripheral countries has been prevented, and there is no pickup in default rates. To enhance the capital market's willingness to buy the country's debt, the government will have to:

- Significantly, increase the retirement age,
- Reduce or eliminate cost-of-living increases in pensions,
- Institute a pensionable salary cap, and
- Use a sharp knife to cut health care expenses, including those for medicaments.

Clearly enough, the beneficiaries will oppose any attempt to water down pension and health care entitlement, arguing that "the constitution guarantees that the benefits of pensions and other state spending cannot be diminished or impaired." If I am not wrong, however, former state employees currently receive free health care benefits while in retirement, and there is no constitutional right assuming unstoppable benefits from unaffordable and unsustainable sovereign expenditures.

Always under caution of a managed exit process, not only the new drachma but also the euro might lose market value. "How much" will depend on whether Germany and other core countries maintain their safe-haven status relative to the highly indebted Euroland members, and on whether short-term liquidity needs of the global financial system prop up the euro.

As Section 6.3 will document, unfavorable economic and financial aftereffects will increase with an uncontrolled exit which will see further pressure on the sovereign's and banks' ability to buy money. The quality of their collateral will evidently be affected, and will as well experience significant deposit outflows in the other countries in a way that has already happened with Greek and Spanish bank deposits.

The outflow of bank deposits from Greece and Spain in 2011 and 2012 are just a glimpse of what can be expected for weaker countries in case of uncontrolled exit. Its aftereffects will, by all evidence, last longer and put under severe test the politicians' ability to limit contagion, not only in Euroland but in the global market.

An uncontrolled exit will increase by so much the tail risk scenario with a very negative impact on markets because of sharply rising uncertainty about the medium-term future. The general opinion is that markets will question the function of the ECB as lender of last resort, while European and international investors will search for protection in the dollar, pound, other hard currencies and gold.

Globally stock markets would correct heavily, the conversion risk premium on Club Med bonds will surge, and investors will demand greater compensation for the risk that a country may leave Euroland.

"Only at a later stage, once the fate of the "leftover euro" becomes clearer could a gradual buildup of European assets again become attractive," said one of the analysts participating to this study. When and by how much will exposed entities: sovereigns, banks, institutional, and other investors as well as common citizen recuperate a good part of their losses will depend on so many factors that at present time it is impossible to predict. In 11 years the cost of Afghanistan has been $1.5 trillion. Who would have predicted that at the beginning?

6.3   Cost of an Uncontrolled Exit

One of the major banks looked into the cost that may entail an uncontrolled Greek exit from Euroland, over a 7-year time frame: 2013−2020.[7] Its estimate is that this would stand at more than 30 percent of the 2011 *global* GDP, with Euroland countries footing much of the bill followed by America and China.

- Most costs will be incurred upfront,
- Severe recessions will follow given the impact on international trade,
- The global economy will experience recession because of sharp drop in demand for imports, as well as market selloffs.

For Greece alone, economists have estimated that the cost of an uncontrollable exit might amount to between 40 and 50 percent of GDP in the first year.[8] This is an approximate figure which assumes that Greece would have to leave both the euro and the EU, which most likely would not happen at the same time. But nobody can be sure, either.

Even if approximate, the stated GDP figure suggests that for the exiting country itself, the cost of drachmageddon[9] is an important, indeed a crucial issue. This is true not only of Greece but of all Euroland's cash-short Club Med member states contemplating exit. They simply may not have the funds to pay for it and nobody is likely to lend them *that* money in view of the opt-out's debilitating costs, which were in no way known or even guessed at time of entry into Euroland.

It is most likely that the ECB will make it a matter of principle not to lend, or permit the Bank of Greece to lend to the country's banks against collateral consisting of bonds and guarantees from a government going out of the monetary union. This, in turn will cut Greece off funding, with serious consequences because (by late 2012) Greek banks relied upon some euro 130 billion of central bank money. Without ECB's cash the entire banking system might collapse.

- *If* the flow of liquidity was reduced, and settlements conditions became strained the sovereign might start to issue "I owe you" (IOU) to its workers to make up the shortfall.
- *If* the flow stopped, leaving the banks no euros to pay out, *then* speculators will play their hand against the new currency which (at that time) will timidly start to get in action.

It might sound exaggerated but Greece, Spain, and Italy may find themselves obliged to live with the euro because they lack the liquidity (and the capital) to do otherwise. An important issue for the sovereign is to have enough hard currency reserves to pay for the essentials which have to be imported. This is far from being self-evident; Euroland's bailout comes drop by drop, leaving no chance to build reserves.

In June 2012, DEPA, the Greek state gas utility, battled to raise euro 120 million to pay Russia's Gazprom for natural gas supplies,[10] as the country's public finances come under strain in the run-up of a general election.[11] The state gas utility was seeking an emergency loan from banks to keep supplies flowing while it tried to collect debts owed by the loss-making Greek electricity grid operator. The utility's last-minute borrowing illustrates the pressures on public sector corporations as:

- A cash crunch cuts off access to bank funding, and
- Revenues are hit by delayed payments by households and by business failures.

As the knock-on effects of DEPA's financing problems were felt PPC, the Greek state electricity utility, stated that it had shut down all its gas-fired power stations as a protective measure. To compensate, it boosted production at units fueled by locally mined brown coal. (Environmentalists may object to this, but whether they like it or not coal is rebecoming a major source of electric power.)

For state enterprises, liquidity is a problem even under the bailout. In the words of a PPC official: The liquidity squeeze is getting worse, we don't know what the situation will be next month, so we took action. This highlights the cost of political and economic uncertainty. Think about the case of creating a new currency and implementing the changes required by drachmageddon (briefly reviewed in Section 6.1), and of being controlled by the fallout of exit (Section 6.2).

Another example on liquidity woes is provided by inability to meet health care costs, because of the cash crunch damaging effect. The Greek state's health system cannot pay arrears owed to pharmacists and medical suppliers. Pharmacists and pharmaceutical companies have appealed to the head of the EU's taskforce, assisting Greece with reform, for emergency assistance of euro 1.5 billion to rescue the health care system.

"That would keep the system working for the next three months," said Andreas Galanopoulos, president of the pharmacists' association. He added that his association's members were owed a total of euro 70 million, adding: "That's euro 100,000 for each of us."[12] These are the collateral costs of a situation which is not even drachmageddon. The way to bet is that:

- The real event will be more costly and unsettling, and

- Estimates of total cost have to account for a period of time featuring a nearly paralyzed economic activity.

A different way looking at this problem is that no cost estimates will really worth their effort unless political risks and social costs are taken into full account. Many social costs revolve around adverse reactions to redimensioning of endowments.[13] Collateral damage, too, must be paid due attention. As long as political uncertainties put in doubt Greece's next loan tranche from the EU and IMF, there exists the risk of bankruptcy by default.

Resetting health care and pensions at sustainable level is one of the limits in search for compromises. Today without the EU and IMF money, Greece will be unable to meet even the trimmed pensions, salaries, and health costs— let alone debt commitments. As a financial analyst put it: If income from taxes is not enough to pay pensions and wages, this would speed up the day of truth.

What Brussels and some of Euroland's sovereigns particularly fear is that the first forcible exit of a country from the common currency would create profound uncertainty and difficulties for the entire Euroland. It will provide both pressure and an excuse for other peripheral sovereigns who contemplate leaving the single currency but are afraid to take that path all alone.

There exists a contrarian view to this argument. It states that the markets gave up on Greece some time ago, and it does not really matter what happens next. It is all down to politics now, and *if* the politicians or public opinion are not prepared to accept wide-ranging cuts on government expenses, *then* they have little choice but to leave Euroland.

It would be unwise to discard a contrarian opinion; still I do not subscribe to this argument. For reasons explained in this and the preceding two chapters the amount of preparation put into an "exit" strategy matters a great deal. Several of senior international bankers I met in the course of my research, now think that they may be able to cope with the fallout of a Greek departure—which they see as highly likely.

The better-managed big banks have what they call a Plan A for orderly departure with advance notice, Plan B for uncontrollable exit, and Plan C for surprises involving adverse events. Their planning depends a great deal on the dynamics of Greek exit. Therefore, subjects that used to be taboos are now openly being discussed. Government officials of different Euroland states have started to talk in public about Greece leaving the euro. Many corporations have analyzed the consequences creating emergency plans.

Reportedly the ECB is establishing support measures like bond purchases to mitigate the impact. While this is not enough to turn a Greek euro exit into a "nonevent," it could create conditions which are (at least) manageable enough to be considered an option.

According to one of the bankers I was talking to, this change in perception about future course of events came with the realization of an awkward truth: That when it received its first bailout the Greek state was broke. Even after a default that more than halved the face value of private bond holdings and reduced their net present value by 73.5 percent (Chapter 4), the IMF expects Greek government debt in 2013 to be over 160 percent of GDP where it stood in early 2010. (The way to bet is that it will be in excess of 190 percent.)

There is still another issue to consider in respect to the prevailing situation dynamics. The rising likelihood of bailing out Italy and Spain has most reduced the core countries' interest in saving Greece. One of the many arguments being heard is that for Spain and Italy, a Greek exit will be even positive, since it would lead to increased readiness on the part of core countries to support them. This does not really make sense. An uncontrollable Greek exit would, most likely, have dismal and dangerous consequences for Italy and Spain, as well as for the ECB and the rest of Euroland.

6.4 Parallel Currencies

Belatedly economists have come to recognize that the world in which we live is nonlinear. Linear thinking doesn't work in a nonlinear world. As Section 6.2 has shown, a Greek exit is likely to produce quite a set of higher order outcomes making it nearly impossible to guestimate with a certain degree of accuracy economic and social costs—even more so to decide about the "right" asset allocation in the event of Euroland's breakup.

The reason for such complexity is that a breakup runs the risk of becoming one wretched scenario where everyone is on his or her own. The fear of dismantling a huge (though shaky) edifice may lead to alternatives which necessarily lead to compromise(s), and compromises have their own downside.

Greece may eventually find a compromise with the EU authorities, but it is wise to know in advance that this will (quite likely) mean more muddling through, the way it has worked over the last 3 years. As with all compromises many questions will remain unclear for the Greek citizen, while investors will be tempted to avoid Greece because there may be bank runs and other problems brought to the reader's attention in the preceding sections.

One of the compromises that has been discussed as a rather remote possibility is that of *parallel currencies*. Greece could keep the euro, but also get the drachma. This is a major change from the current approach of bailouts which appears to have reached the end of the road. The concept of a dual currency was not invented last night. In the seventeenth and eighteenth centuries, under Louis XIV, France had a dual currency. In the second half of the twentieth-century France and Belgium had a "franc commerciale" and a "franc financier."

The challenge for sovereigns, central bankers, and economists is to find a dynamic balance between the two currencies. Over time, any solution which systematically gives an advantage to the one over the other, or to particular participants, will harm both currencies' relative position. Theoretically,

- The euro which may be used for payments and settlements of international transactions, including debt repayment, and

- The drachma will act as national currency, on which Athens may impose restrictions regarding the amount in circulation as well as the amounts which may be taken in and out of the country.

The drachma will be subject to upward and downward changes in rates of exchange against the euro, with a high probability of devaluation at issuance. When in September 1931 Britain came off the gold standard, sterling depreciated immediately from $4.86 to $3.97, and continued depreciating till November 1932 by which time it had fallen 30 percent. A successful dual currency solution will account for the fact that:

- Money is not just printed paper; it is a social institution, and
- Precisely this social and economic role provides it with public acceptance which gives money its worth.

In addition, a dual currency solution will have a chance when the public and the market have confidence in it. *If* the drachma becomes subject to speculative frenzy, *then* the only possible outcome will be failure. To avoid it will require great care in the planning phase identifying in advance all possible Ponzi games and making them subject to criminal prosecution. When asked whether the stock of the South Sea Company will continue rising, Isaac Newton, who was Master of the Mint[14], answered that "he could not calculate the madness of the crowd."[15]

It needs no explaining that a thorough examination of "pluses" and "minuses" of a dual currency for Greece may provide useful scenarios for Italy, Spain, and Portugal. It will as well respond to current Euroland worries that *if* Greece falls out of the euro *then* a chain reaction may follow. By contrast, with a dual currency, which has to be clearly defined in its details, it might be possible to avoid:

- Banking collapse,
- Disintegration of the new currency, and
- Fierce pursuit of narrow national self-interest through the proliferation of opt-outs from Euroland.

Furthermore, the ECB would not need to print tons of paper money—the 300 wagons of Weimar Republic—to make good its promise of "unlimited firepower" to support Italy and Spain, whose bonds already holds as collateral on loans to banks.

In a way this would mean being in and out of the euro at the same time. *If* Greece stays in the euro without an alternative currency, *then* the country's depression, now in its 5th year, will never end; this is by no means a pleasant prospect, says Thomas Krümmel, a UBS analyst, in his short paper on the dual currency option.[16]

A variation of this option is the real-time OUT/IN switch. According to this theory, there should be a weekend exit where Greece leaves the Euroland, devalues, and rejoins, all by breakfast on a Sunday. The idea is not stupid, but I don't think it is practical. Since there exists no such precedence, at least to my knowledge, it is hard to know where to begin with the critical analysis of instantaneous exit and reentry.

In addition, a fast switch may raise legal and other challenges, including Lisbon Treaty changes and the need to re-denominate private sector assets in one go—a task which is tough though not impossible. The reason for bringing these issues up is to provide out-of-the box ideas. *If* they are properly analyzed, *then* they may suggest ways to:

- Handle conversion challenges, and
- Study their further out aftermath.

If a dual currency, or a snap OUT/IN, presents challenges and risks which are still unknown, so does ECB's (and the Fed's) unstoppable money printing policy which leads to currency debasement. This is treason to their statutes which specify currency stability as topmost goal.[17]

The first irony with this sort of currency debasing is that the United States and Euroland, respectively, pursue a secret aim at dollar and euro devaluation not versus one another but versus emerging currencies—to support United States and European exports. The second irony is that both the American and European monetary authorities failed in their devaluation objective. The wanted currency depreciation proved to be a nonevent; a road which went from nowhere to nowhere.

Along a similar vein, Greece's fiscal austerity measures are also offtrack because of similar reasons. The dynamics of a situation cannot be properly studied only by looking at numbers and in the books. Major errors can be made when the bookkeeping entries (which are often massaged) are taken as God-given, while capital analysis (and judgment derived from it) takes the back seat.

Frequent risk-on/risk-off changes in the global market see to it that uncertainty becomes the status quo, obliging those in charge of countries, banks, and other entities to account for Euroland's breakup distracting them from other duties. Stories appear in the press about foreign exchange brokers and treasurers of multinational firms mobilizing teams to figure out how to:

- Deal with new currencies to be born,
- Recalibrate cross-border accounting and invoicing systems, and
- Estimate the cost and likely advantages/disadvantages from Euroland's breakup.

Contingency planning is, of course, a prudent and necessary move. But what sort of contingency are we planning for without having analyzed the dynamics of different scenarios? For instance, which new currencies are more likely to be introduced? Which may trade freely? Will capital controls accompany them? Is there a risk of not getting paid at all in one or more of the postbreakup new currencies? Will forwards, futures, swaps, options and other currency derivative contracts materialize? Which will be the most likely constraints in current account transactions?

Another critical issue which may radically change the dynamics of the situation is whether the IMF ends its involvement with Euroland. (Already in mid-October 2012 it gave a signal that it will not participate in new Euroland bailouts.) Still another is: Which core European countries, possibly including Germany, would most likely end their support for bailouts? Will parallel currency solutions relieve some of the aforementioned constraints?

6.5   Myths and Realities About Sovereign Bailouts

If the institution of parallel currencies seems to be far-fetched, so is the decision to salvage countries which cannot pay back their debt through rescue packages. Let me put this statement in a little stronger term: The rescue of sovereigns with long histories of devalued currencies by way of loading them with more debt is a myth.

Since the end of World War II, Italy has been making ends meet through steady, soft devaluations. As the lira floated, the first question asked at top-level banking meetings was: "How the market treated our currency today?" For the government in Rome this was a nice way to avoid hard decisions, but the sovereign's public debt continued to mount.

This is precisely what happens with Euroland's bailouts. With the first rescue package of April 2010 Greece got an envelope with euro 110 billion in loans. The second bailout contained even more cash: euro 130 billion. So the handout was roughly euro 24,000 ($32,000) for every Greek man, woman, or child. True? False!

First of all, these are *loans* not handouts. Hence, they have to be repaid. Second, and equally important, while the price tag attached to the two "rescue plans" is euro 240 billion, the average Greek, who just experienced a sharp income reduction, would not see a cent of it:

- What remains of the first rescue package is a debt of euro 110 billion, to be served and paid back.
- Of the second bailout of euro 130 billion, 30 billion have been used in buying collateral to secure the new Greek bonds, euro 50 billion will be employed to stabilize Greek banks, and another euro 50 billion went into an escrow account to pay interest on Greek debt.

Another fiction associated to these rescue packages is that because of them and of the 73.5 percent haircut connected to PSI (private sector involvement, Chapter 4) Greece is no longer headed for default. This is absolutely nonsense. Greece defaulted the moment ISDA decided that the PSI has been a credit event.

In the last analysis what has happened with PSI's big haircut was the result of an ill-studied, forced agreement which replaced one creditor group (the banks) with another (EU/ECB/IMF). The haircut did not take Greece out of its ongoing depression; neither have the bailouts done that miracle.

That much about rescues. Another myth is associated to Euroland's ability to pull the Greek economy up from under as (supposedly) by 2020 public liabilities will shrink to 120.5 percent of GDP from the 160 percent at bailout time. The fact that at end of 2012 Greek public debt-to-GDP rose to 179.8 percent speaks otherwise. It proves that such claim is plain smoke and mirrors, no matter how many economists subscribed to it.

The dismal science of economics, John Maynard Keynes used to say, finds it pretty difficult to forecast the next 3 months. Adds "ifs" and "buts" in forecasts and what you find is that many of them are an exercise in futility; a way to lie with numbers. Forecasting what will be happening 7 years later with the public debt: from 2013 to 2020, is not the stuff serious people deal with.

This leads us to the conclusion that, with so many unknowns in the recovery equation, there is practically no chance that the second salvage plan is the last one. At best the rescues allow Greece to buy time up to 2014, or so. No virtuous economist will stick out his head to prognosticate what might happen then. The main two variables influencing the sovereign's future are:

- The ability of the government to implement a thoroughly studied course toward sustainable public expenditures, and
- The attitude of the common citizens in accepting labor restructuring, restraining entitlements, and establishing a restarting plan.

Unavoidably, this will be painful. Restructuring and restraining must be watched carefully over the medium to longer term as their effect will rest on the ability of successive governments. Those governments' performance must be far better than that of their predecessors which run Greece after the end of World War II, and brought the country in the mess it finds itself at this moment.

Equally important to the success of any sovereign plan is the attitude of common people—particularly if these were corrupted by unstoppable entitlements. Let me take a brief example to illustrate this point.

My 80-year-old aunt, who lives in Athens, was telling me on the phone that the medicines she needs to take are no more "free." I reminded her that in the 1940s, when we were young, the medicines were not "free" either. We had to pay for them and yet we survived better than what people manage to do now. She answered: "Yes, but the government took upon itself the responsibility to provide free medicine for all."

True enough the sovereign did so, and it went bankrupt. What many people don't appreciate is that the government has no money of its own. It gets its money through taxes and by means of the central bank's printing presses, which contribute to inflation. *If* the list of "free" goodies increases *then* taxes also must increase to a level which crashes personal initiative. In some Scandinavian countries personal taxation is up to 80 percent, and (contrary to the Club Med countries) the people pay their taxes.

The government, any government, has no major wand to make ends meet when expenses increase but its income shrinks—anymore than a household can perform that miraculous act. *If* weak governments have allowed endowments to skyrocket, *then* the political leadership must have the courage to cut them down to affordable size, defined by the standing of the economy not by politics.

This downsizing is resented by the public and is exploited by the media as sensational news. Even serious people fall into the trap of thinking that unsustainable endowments can be preserved. Here is how Nikos Xydakis, chief editor of Kathimerini, looks at the future of endowments in Greece: "Abiding by the terms of the new bailout agreement ... will inevitably lead to the shrinking of the Greek welfare state and sweeping changes in social structures."[18]

It would have been better if Greek governments had downsized the unsustainable entitlements (which have become a second income) and cut down other unsupportable expenses—but it did not happen that way. As in all Western countries the State Supermarket[19] kept on increasing the public debt, which led to the current depression (or, if you prefer, major recession). Therefore, it's good news that by the force of things the nanny state will be slimming down. Xydakis makes two points:

- There will be an unavoidable reduction in social services and privileges offered to the weaker members of society, and
- This will eventually have profound consequences on everybody's life.

True enough, redimensioning entitlements is neither a popular nor an easy job. There will always be people who say that "downsizing the access to publicly paid medical care runs against the concept of "equality" (whatever that may mean). But it is no less true that prior to WWII and immediately thereafter there was no publicly paid, medical care—yet people lived nicely. What's more at that time there were plenty of jobs (see also in Chapter 10 the trend toward high cost in abused health care).

What is described by these two bullets can be said of every western nation which has espoused the policy of living beyond its means. It is not only the Greek, as Xydakis says, but every welfare state that is too expensive, corrupt, and ineffective at the same time. Every State Supermarket is characterized by:

- Abuse of power,
- Inept management,
- Lots of nepotism, and
- Plenty of fraud.

Here is an example. Four female employees of Greek Social Security (IKA) in Kalithea, an Athens suburb, and two of the women's husbands faced an Athens prosecutor in connection to a benefit scam believed to have cost the public institution as much as euro 20 million ($26 million). An arrest warrant was also issued for a seventh suspect, a woman who had been employed at an IKA branch in the Peloponnesus.

Allegedly, the suspects had illegally assigned benefits to people not insured with IKA, taking a cut of that windfall money. The police found in a diaper box of one of the accused euro 960,000 in cash. Its owners and accomplices now face multiple charges of fraud, embezzlement, and money laundering. That's far from being the only case of fraud in social net benefits.

State Supermarket and fraud are nearly synonymous. If one thinks that he can stamp out corruption, and squeeze out of the health care system, or any other endowment, profiteers and crooks, then he or she is living in a cloud. Profiteers got their schooling in the snake pit of politics and are protected by politicians elected by the people.

The talk that public health care is an "inalienable right" is made by those who profit from it, and it is patently false. Life has never been a "right," let alone an inalienable one. We know nothing about why we are on this planet, or where we go afterward (if anywhere). As for the argument that "the only survivors will be those who have money," is still another myth.

The healthier people are those who know how to regulate their life, their body, their mind, and their assets. After all, it has been the ancient Greeks who have said: "A healthy mind can be only found in a healthy body."[20] Reading obesity statistics I doubt whether the majority of people heard of it.

6.6   Bankruptcy Is No More a Dirty Word

The view taken in this section is contrarian to the one Section 6.2 has presented; it is based on the opinion of people who maintain that early on a Greek bankruptcy would have been manageable, if approached by way of a thoroughly studied and coordinated program. The public debt problems of Greece were magnified as the terrible *ifs* accumulated and guts to take bold decisions were as scarce as chicken teeth.

The IMF executive made no reference to Greek bankruptcy if restart and recovery were not on call, but in the back of his mind he did not stay fenced-in. He got out and interacted with the problem. When this statement was made, 2 full years had passed since Bailout I and nearly 2½ years from the time the budgetary deficit of Greece stood at a stratospheric 12.5 percent of GDP.

According to an article published in *The Financial Times*, on October 19, 2009, George Papaconstantinou, then Greek finance minister, informed his Euroland colleagues that (in that year) his country's *public deficit* would be *12.5 percent* of GDP. This was more than 300 percent higher than what the government in Athens had estimated for 2009.

Behind the scenes Papaconstantinou's admission set off alarm bells. Still it took from October 2009 to April 2010 till Euroland leaders presented an ineffective crisis response. The latter included the bailout fund's launch. In Euroland, chiefs of state and their advisors knew that by that time the Greek sovereign was bankrupt, but nobody dared to say this aloud.

"They are all irresponsible, none of them is capable of ending this crisis," said Aristomenes Antonopoulos, a lawyer,[21] expressing in a dozen words what the majority of Greeks thought about the government(s) and their role in the crisis. We live at a time when even the meaning of the word: *bankruptcy* is no more what used to be.

- Personal bankruptcies have become common currency and a matter of abuse, particularly in the United States.
- In the financial industry, bankruptcy and receivership have been transformed from a way to liquidate insolvent banks to a mere stratagem to keep them alive with taxpayer money.

In America and in Britain this transformation of bankruptcy's concept and meaning has been a political maneuver to advance the private agenda of speculating big bank managers and that of their lobbyists and political friends. Though some bankruptcies such as Lehman's might have rocked the global financial system, in the end the results were attenuated as the US Treasury saved from the ropes everybody else than Lehman.

Some sovereigns, for instance Argentina, capitalized on this change of attitude toward what bankruptcy means, and used the new definition (legalizing theft) to their advantage (see Chapter 13). In October 2009, Greece too could have done the same if Papandreou Junior had the guts to do it. Argentina recovered from bankruptcy in a mere 2 years rather than going for 4 more years through the tunnel without seeing an exit. Several economists say that for Greece things were not that simple, because:

• Argentina was in better condition than Greece when in 2001 it declared bankruptcy.

This is questionable because, after the multiyear absurdity of the currency board, Argentina's economy was in very bad shape indeed.

• If Greece declared bankruptcy, it would not have been able to access capital markets for 10 years.

This argument forgets how eager bankers are to put their institution's money to work, incorrectly discounting the risks they are assuming. According to several opinions, in the case of Greece the failure to declare bankruptcy in October 2009 has been a lost opportunity. It was much better to do so and then use the EU/ECB/IMF money to restructure and to invest in industry and jobs.

Such a contrarian move had chances to succeed provided that it was accompanied by fiscal discipline and zero new debt; also, that a new Heracles showed up in Athens to clean out fraud and scams. In his letter to *The Economist*, Greece, A. Manthos suggests that Greece has a corrupt political class, people who:

• Featherbed benefits for themselves and their preferred trade unions,
• Operate state-owned enterprises as vehicles for employing cronies, and
• Obstruct the functioning of the private sector to neutralize potential competition.[22]

Bankruptcy or no bankruptcy, as long as these ills persist neither the economy nor Greek society will recover. The change must come from within. Foreign pressure for clean-up will not work because those who profit from the status quo and the State Supermarket's goodies will be quick to cry against "foreign intervention" and "the way to slavery"—while the real slaves are the majority of Greek people and the masters those Manthos calls *volevomenoi*—loosely meaning those "made comfortable" as recipients of state favors and patronage by the politicians.

The *volevomenoi* are by no means only in high places. They support their political friends and cronies all the way down the social ladder. Another letter to *The Economist* looked at this issue: "It must surely seem "austere" to cut by 30 percent the pension of a Greek civil servant who was undoubtedly counting on that income to live out the next 25 years ... But when the pension is a monthly euro 1800 ($2300) paid to a retired assistant garbage truck driver in the Peloponnesus (I kid you not), perhaps some other term would be more appropriate."[23]

In Italy and in Spain, too, the young are counting on grandfather's pension so that they don't need to work. It does not take a genius to understand that compared to the might of some emerging countries (like China) which are in their way to conquer the global market, Mediterranean economies are weak. They simply cannot afford excesses and survive.

If Greece had defaulted (which it may still do; Section 6.7), it would have been the first developed country to default for 60 years. A bankruptcy would have cost the EU/ECB/IMF much less to ring-fence (to avoid contagion) than the euro 240 billion, with plenty of money left to help in restructuring of the Greek economy, provided the aforementioned cultural change became entrenched and well-documented.

An article in *The Economist* has pointed out that, as hard numbers "suggest a Greek default would do little lasting harm to the rest of Europe's financial system ... What is more worrying for Europe's policymakers is the thought that Greece's afflic-tion would spread not just to foreign banks but to foreign governments. Just as Lehman's collapse told investors that a Wall Street bank could fail, a Greek default would tell them that a Western government could renege on its debts."[24]

This point is well-made. Fear rather than facts led to the tandem of bailouts and from there to bailout fatigue (Chapter 5). One of the opinions heard in the course of my research is that those who engineered these bailouts will live to regret them. Not only for Greece but also for Spain, Italy and other countries in trouble, bailouts will not avoid sovereign bankruptcies.

In itself the fact that progress toward the economy's ability to stand on its own feet is being watched is a positive act. The downside is that it adds to the risk that a protracted liquidity crisis turns into a solvency crisis. On October 18, 2012 the evening bulletin of Euronews pointed out that in a month's time (mid-November 2012) the Greek government will be short of liquidity and that's the fourth liquidity crisis since January 1, 2012. *If* bankruptcy came as a result of such successive liquidity crises, where is the positive effect of the bailouts?[25]

If the purpose of a bailout program is to redress the economy and win back the citizens' confidence, *then* the Greek bailouts were a failure. Capital markets are still afraid of Greek debt and economic recovery—in real life sense—is nowhere to be seen. The goal of a rescue program should never be to leave the economy in a condition that it is not capable of reviving through its own forces in the foreseeable future.

6.7   The Difficulties Greece Encounters Are Extreme, Not Unique

Sovereign leveraging was invented 25 centuries ago by Pericles, as an instrument to assure his re-election year-after-year by the demos of ancient Athens. What he spent was public money and when the wealth of the city-state of Athens could not afford anymore his handouts, Pericles paid for them with the wealth of the Alliance carefully kept in the Parthenon.

As it should have been expected, the other city-states objected to this cavalier use of *their* money, and some quit the Alliance. Pericles started military expeditions to subdue them and with this he ignited the Peloponnesian 30-year civil war which signaled the end of ancient Greece and opened the road to Roman conquest. Let's make sure not to repeat the same mistake.

Nowadays, like practically all other western countries, modern Greece has suffered from spending beyond its means, a direct result of total lack of political leadership. Nikos Xydakis, of Kathimerini, is right when he writes in an article that "Greece has been in a state of emergency for some time now, and it must be addressed. The people have a duty to themselves to reevaluate their priorities with a view to the future, without, however, compromising democracy or breaking society into so many pieces that it can no longer be put back together."[26]

There is plenty of work to do to come up from under. "The reason Greece has caused such difficulty is that the country's failings are extreme, not unique. Its plight shows that the Eurozone still seeks a workable mixture of flexibility, discipline and solidarity," wrote mid-February 2012 Martin Wolf, the economist, in *The Financial Times*.[27] Wolf's words have been tough but prophetic.

By early October 2012, not quite a semester after the PSI, Greece's official unemployment rate rose to 24.4 percent, the EU's second-highest after Spain. The jobless rate among young Greeks hit a depressing 55.4 percent, overtaking Spain's by a fraction. A lot of private-sector workers, among them teachers and nurses, complained of not being paid regularly by the sovereign (who allegedly used some of bailout money to pay salaries and pensions).

A decision on disbursing the new bailout funds for Greece has been time and again delayed until the Troika, and then Euroland's finance ministers, approve— and they approve only if they believe the Greek government has lived up to its promises. These are the bailout's conditions which include deep wage cuts and plenty of layoffs in the outsized public sector.

The difficulty to make ends meet at national budget level led to renewed uncertainty over whether Athens will default or will not, even if debt restructuring theoretically cut the amount due on public loans. The Greek finance minister believed that cuts of almost euro 5 billion in pensions and public-sector salaries, included in the draft budget for 2013, were deep enough to achieve a primary budget surplus of 1.4 percent of GDP.[28] The Troika was concerned that because of the economic situation:

- Tax revenues will be lower than forecast, and
- The budget would still leave space for spending overruns.

To the opinion of some observers, the government shied away from reducing the bloated number of civil servants, despite a commitment to cut public-sector payroll by 150,000, with civil servants taking early retirement after a year on 75 percent of their previous salary. A not-so-satisfactory solution reached to accommodate the government's coalition partners.

The multiplying budgetary difficulties brought under question the wisdom behind the chosen course of rescue packages, which did not assure that Greece was not going to default or leave Euroland. On these two subjects the economists' opinion was and remains divided.

Several experts think that Greece will default on its debt following an insufficient overall debt reduction and the fact that there is no economic resurgence. Moreover, the second aid package left the country in an unsustainable debt situation. There is a difference between accepting 12th-hour financing conditions and returning to growth potential.

If the management of the Greek economy when it was still growing left so much to be wanted, the management of the austerity program, imposed since the first bailout, has been worse. The way an article in *The Economist* had it: "The biggest blows have fallen on small family businesses (with 50 employees or fewer), which make up 99 percent of enterprises and employ three-quarters of the private-sector workforce. Many have closed (and) sacked most of their staff ... the entire private sector is hemorrhaging workers."[29]

If Greece had its own currency it would have needed to devalue by at least 40 percent to get itself into a growth path, provided that other clauses like restructuring the labor market and promoting competitiveness are fulfilled. Of course, what is written about Greece is equally valid for Spain, Italy, Portugal, Slovenia, and Cyprus. With Ireland that makes 7 out of 17 Euroland member states. That's contagion and the trouble with high debt is that it tends to remain excessive.

- Simply paying the interest requires new indebtedness, and
- Taxpayer's money keeps on being used just to keep the country from defaulting.

According to economists and financial analysts, even if a Greek exit from Euroland did not materialize, it would not be the end of the European debt crisis. Negotiations will have to be undertaken with Spain and Italy. Both are over the cliff—but ask for conditions better than those provided to Greece.

"Better terms" is what Spain's Mariano Rajoy is asking—which is an expression of a hope rather than a vase backed by solid argument, and "hope" is not a strategy for sovereigns. What the case of Greece, Portugal, Italy, and Spain has demonstrated is that politicians can become a destabilizing force on the country's prospects. The public knows that a survey by Edelman, a public relations firm, found that only 13 percent of the people trust political leaders to tell the truth.[30] Lying to the public and spending beyond the state's means:

- Weakens democracy by making the ballot subject to favors,
- Perverts the responsibility of each citizen to look after himself and his family, and
- Leads to overleveraging of society by consuming so much more than the country produces and importing the difference by paying through debt.

A mistrust of politicians is representative of the postwar spirit in Europe where democracy, wealth, and prosperity have been used as being synonymous—which they are not. Spending way beyond the state's means eventually leads to bankruptcy.

The social net and its entitlements have nothing to do with democracy. They saw the light under an autocratic regime. Pensions have been first established in the nineteenth century under Otto von Bismarck. Prussia was no democracy. The entitle-ment Bismarck instituted at his time was affordable by the state, because retired peo-ple would live another 2 or 3 years, not 20 or 30 years as they live today.

6.8 Conclusion: Oedipus at Colonus?

In ancient Athens, the role tragedy cast upon itself was one of knowledge and explanation of the human psyche. Dramatic authors made an analysis of a mortal's soul and of the role of destiny. Usually, though not always, their thesis contrasted to the role played by science and philosophy. Science searches into the physical unknown while philosophy's contribution is speculation and examination of alter-natives in ways of life, in an effort to provide an integrative approach and more comprehensive course.

As a dramatic author, Sophocles is a believer in the role of the divine and at the same time an analyst of the ambiguities of destiny. The myth of Oedipus has accompanied the dramatic author's long career way into old age. At 75, Sophocles wrote *Oedipus Rex* with the hero falling from the pinnacle of power to the trough of misery. Fifteen years later, at the age of 90, he produced *Oedipus at Colonus.*[31]

In this second Oedipus, Sophocles' aim is to meditate, and then explain, whether or not the Gods can punish an innocent; to clarify what may become of the human soul (and of the body it inhabits) in a world governed by deities who define the destiny. To do so in a way leaving few doubts about the forces behind the outcome, events develop slowly along Oedipus' life till the blessed death of the tormented sufferer whose place of disappearance from Earth (the sacred precinct of Eumenides) will bring blessings to the country and people who received him—Colonus and (ancient) Athens in particular.

- The old men of the chorus know what old age means, and
- Appreciate that he is a fool who craves for more than normal length of life.

In a way emulating what has happened in Greece after World War II and prior to Euroland's bailouts, in *Oedipus Rex* events go to the hero's head, sometimes with sorrow and in other times with joy. Nothing informs in advance about the divine's next move and the spectator's mind moves between three stages which fol-low one another. The one is *revolt* against a diabolical trap into which an honest man has fallen. *If* Oedipus is innocent *then* who is to blame? The Gods?

The second stage is *fear*. The main player in this is Iocaste, who does not believe in oracles. She thinks of herself as being a woman of experience and of sound advice: What's the use of being scared when the hazard is the sovereign master? The best is to show no resistance she counsels Oedipus, who now feels that he has been abandoned by the Gods.

The third state is *catharsis*. "Apollo, where is Apollo the only author of my mis-eries," Oedipus asks. He knows that other Gods, too, hate him. His tragedy is that of the human race, it's not that of a single individual. In searching for what may lie in the human soul, no ancient tragedy is more penetrating than this one.

"Apollo dedicated me to misery," Oedipus says. "But it is myself, and by my own hands, who punctured my eyes." No other ancient Greek tragedy can describe in a more eloquent and pragmatic way the status of modern Greece. Globalization made life difficult for the Greek industry which was not so secure of its standing, but there was a textile, chemical, and mechanical industry offering; they were wiped clean by the developing countries' competition.

As the chances of the Greek economy standing on its own feet in a globalized market waned and incapable governments were unable to redress the situation, the public pressed on with its demands for "more and more" goodies provided free of cost by the nanny state. That's what Theodoros Pangalos called "We ate it up together" (Chapter 5). Getting deeper into debt succeeded in puncturing the Greek economy's eyes.

"Guilt" or "innocence" was not touched upon in *Oedipus Rex*, but in *Oedipus at Colonus* he assures that his frightful sins were not his fault. Literary critics say that, in this, Sophocles was dealing with an important theme widely discussed at his time and, as matter of fact, ever since. Guilt or innocence is a question always present, and the chorus of the economic drama offers divided advice.

Argentineans visiting Athens suggested that Greece should default the big way, like their own country did in 2001. This argument forgets that in 2011 Argentina's condition was singular because of strong export prices and sustainable external surpluses. By contrast, today's Greece cannot rely on favorable external conditions in case it opts out of the euro and at the same time declares bankruptcy. Moreover, it is already in a deep, fiscally induced recession.

Other voices are contrarian to "the big way" bankruptcy. To the opinion of Mario Blejer, former governor of the Central Bank of Argentina, and Guillermo Ortiz, former governor of Mexico's reserve institution, exiting the euro at present time would require the compulsory redenomination of:

- Banks' assets and liabilities, and
- Practically all contracts, prices, and wages.

In Argentina, where dollars were widely used as a unit of account, redenomination took the opposite road of "pesification." This had quite significant redistributive consequences. Argentina's experience also demonstrates that exiting a long-term peg[32]—which might be compared euro membership—tends to sink large private corporations with access to international financial markets, because their foreign currency liabilities cannot be redenominated.

As far as redenomination in a drachmageddon is concerned, the condition of Greek companies may be even worse because Greece would have to deal with a universe of covenants since every contract is in euro. By contrast, Argentinean contracts had continued to be denominated in pesos, since the currency board did not eliminate the local legal tender.

Ernst Juerg Weber, Professor of economics at the University of Western Australia, suggests that leaving Euroland is no option for Greece. The new drachma would be valueless, as there would be no demand for it, and it would stay in circulation only if the Greeks were denied access to foreign exchange, preventing the informal use of the euro. That would require draconian exchange controls.

It is always rewarding to examine alternative courses of action because the scenarios can become eye-openers. With an early bankruptcy, the crucial question would have been how to regain competitiveness as early as possible. Whenever this is being asked *costs* and *benefits* pop up, as well as drastic measures. The head of the IMF mission to Greece said that even after 5 years of recession, Greece needed another 15 percent cut in labor costs, adding that this could best be done by attacking the rigidities imposed by vested interests. *If* that proved politically impossible, *then* it had to come from real wage cuts.[33]

Larry Summers, former US Treasury secretary and former president of Harvard University, told the 2012 Aspen Ideas festival that the different rescue plans only bought Euroland a bit more time to sort out its longer-term structural woes. Summers is right. More doubtful is whether the time being bought served in correcting Euroland's woes, and the answer is not positive.

On July 6, 2012, Jens Weidmann, Germany's top central banker, criticized the decisions of the preceding June 28/29 Brussels summit to help debt-laden Euroland members, warning that the bloc was constantly mutualizing risks and weakening the agreed rules. "Fiscal aid should be the last resort of crisis management," the president of the Bundesbank said. "This position has by now been recognizably weakened."[34]

Less than 3 weeks later, on July 25, 2012 José Manuel Barroso, EC president, arrived in Athens to face a 1-month-old government that had yet to agree on a plan to fill the euro 11.5 billion budget hole identified in 2011, plus an additional shortfall estimated at euro 20 billion which EU officials believed Greece will confront during the next couple of years. That meeting also brought in perspective that, till that date, Greece had completed only one-third of some 300 benchmarks for fiscal and structural reforms detailed in the second bailout.

The Oedipus story in search of a psyche[35] is being widely repeated in the West: from neighboring Italy to Spain, France and all the way to the United States.[36] Western societies have reached the state of inability to decide what they want to achieve, a situation reminiscent of an answer Stalin gave to Mao during their interminable negotiations in Moscow. Mao suggested to send for Chou En-Lai. Stalin answered: "If we cannot define what we want to achieve, why to call Chou?"[37]

That is, indeed, the question. What do we *really* want to achieve? A political and economic resurgence of the West? Another "do good" and "be good" nanny state society, like the one just descended to the abyss? A way to enter immortality so that 1000 years from now, *if* Homo sapiens are still in charge, people will talk of Greece in 2113?

Oedipus King and *Oedipus at Colonus* don't have the same ending because the second time around Sophocles searched behind Oedipus psyche and on the role of destiny, with the result that the scenario has taken a different road. With hindsight in *Oedipus at Colonus* the ancient dramatic author looked for clues about what constitutes the change in his main actor's psyche, and its opposite a thinly veiled fallacy.

Oedipus is no more cursed for crimes committed in his youth, but neither is he the mighty king of Thebes. In his new status he has become a fragile person who lives a curious life in the land of Attica. Between these endings, Oedipus' death comes in the middle of two currents: That of combat (*Oedipus King*) and the alternative of fulfilling a long but peaceful time (*Oedipus at Colonus*). For mortals and for nations that choice is always present. The latter, however, requires a much greater strength of the soul than the former and a great deal of more patience.

End Notes

1. All EU member states except the United Kingdom and the Czech Republic.
2. Introducing a ban on borrowing.
3. !!!
4. As well as people and companies.
5. *The Economist*, January 26, 2013
6. Surely ECB and probably IMF.
7. UBS, CIO WM Research, December 11, 2012
8. *The Economist*, May 26, 2012
9. Or lirageddon and pesetageddon, if you prefer.
10. DEPA imports 80 percent of its gas from Russia.
11. *Financial Times*, June 16, 2012
12. *Idem.*
13. D.N. Chorafas "*Household Finance, Adrift in a Sea of Red Ink*," Palgrave/Macmillan, London, 2013.
14. In early eighteenth-century Britain, Master of the Mint was a job comparable to governor of the Bank of England. Isaac Newton spent more years of his life as Warden and Master of the Mint than as physicist at Cambridge University.
15. Stephen Zarlenga "*The Lost Science of Money*," American Monetary Institute, Valatie, NY 2002.
16. UBS Investor's Guide, June 8, 2012
17. The Fed's dual goal of currency stability (the original mission when the US central bank was created) and employment, is bad political ploy. The incompatible second goal dates back to the 1960s and makes the central bank's key mission of financial stability next to impossible.
18. http://www.ekatherimerini.com, March 2, 2012.
19. *Kratos bakalis*, in Greek.
20. And vice versa.
21. *The Economist*, May 19, 2012.
22. *The Economist*, February 11, 2012.
23. *The Economist*, May 26, 2012.
24. *The Economist*, June 25, 2011.
25. The same Euronews bulletin stated that Greek public debt stands at 179.8 percent and no more at 160 percent prior to the PSI. *If* this is really the case, *then* one has some understanding that the citizens of Greece—and eventually the citizens of Portugal, Spain, and Italy—bring their money somewhere else, in a safe place.
26. http://www.ekathimerini.com, Friday March 9, 2012.

27. *Financial Times*, February 15, 2012.
28. The difference between a *real* surplus and a *primary* surplus is that the latter does not account for the servicing of public debt.
29. *The Economist*, January 14, 2012.
30. *The Economist*, January 26, 2013.
31. The village where Sophocles was born and grew up.
32. After defaulting Argentina had no choice but to ditch its peg since the currency board was a unilateral arrangement that did not envisage counterparty support or institutional safety nets (*The Economist*, February 18, 2012).
33. *Financial Times*, April 16, 2012.
34. *Financial Times*, July 7, 2012.
35. A country's psyche in the present case.
36. Total US government debt has risen 42 percent over 3 years (*Financial Times*, March 13, 2012). That's not too different from the way Greece accumulated its huge public debt.
37. Simon Sebag Montefiore "*Staline*," Editions des Syrtes, Paris, 2005.

Part Three

Case Studies with Teetering Sovereigns

7 Spain in Free Fall

7.1 Spain Is in the Danger Zone

A look at Euroland shows that the debt crisis, particularly in the so-called "peripheral states," or "Club Med," is anything but solved. All of them, including France, are in recession, an additional obstacle to easing austerity measures and for stabilizing their mounting debt. The ECB may be trying to put up firewalls around Spain[1] and Italy (for whom it designed OMT) to prevent further escalation of the crisis along the Greek scenario, but:

- The associated financial pain is high, and
- There are no takers.

Everybody knows that debt sustainability requires fiscal discipline and tightening for several years. Whether we talk of Spain, Italy, or Greece, the country's leadership must explain to all citizens that austerity is not a punishment. It is the correction of severe imbalances, over many years, between the sovereign's income and its expenditures which led to near bankruptcy. Statistics help in studying the trend, and as Table 7.1 shows Spain has not yet learned its lesson.

It does not come as a surprise that southern European countries are under close scrutiny from financial markets, not least with respect to their spending habits and fiscal policies. Spain clearly missed its deficit targets for 2011 and 2012 and Brussels eased those of 2013 to avoid another deception. It serves nothing to initially announce a target deficit, then having it revised upward again and again.

While a deviation from target may be due to lower-than-expected revenues, the repetition of the same spending policies from one year to the next is budgetary mismanagement. The government is not really in charge. According to the European Commission's forecast, Spain will miss the 2013 deadline for correcting its excessive deficit by a long way unless significant measures are taken—which are not likely.

Worse yet, considerable uncertainty has arisen regarding the state of the Spanish financial system, placing additional strain on Spanish public finances. Having obtained some euro 40 billion ($52 billion) out of a pledged euro 100 billion to beef up the treasuries of its badly wounded banks, Spain is hesitating to apply for support from the ESM, and therefore from ECB's OMT program. Yet, continuous fiscal slippage will lead to rising costs of funding, pushing Spain into that program by default.

Financial analysts are of the opinion that even with OMT support longer Spanish bond yields would stay elevated as bondholders remain concerned about

Public Debt Dynamics of Europe and the US. DOI: http://dx.doi.org/10.1016/B978-0-12-420021-0.00007-5

Table 7.1 Spain's Negative Trend in Budget Deficit Is Here to Stay

	2011	2012	2013 Est	2014 Est
GDP growth	0.4%	−1.5%	−1.7%	−0.5%
Budget deficit (as of GDP)	−9.8%	−10.6%	−6.3%	−5.5%[a]
Budget primary balance	−7.0%	−7.6%	−3.0%	−2.0%
Gross debt to GDP	69%	84%	99%	110%

[a]Very unlikely. Probably above 6 percent.

the country's ability and willingness to implement necessary reforms over many more years; also about Spain's *de facto* subordination to European Union guidelines. Neither is it sure whether:

- A fiscal union will be decided and established (in Euroland).
- A banking union would come once a fiscal union is established,
- Effective banking supervision at the ECB would be operational by 2014, and
- Euroland's fiscal union will hold or fall apart over the next few years.

The message conveyed by these bullets is negative for Spain, Italy, France, and Euroland as a whole. Many risks are weighting on Euroland's fortunes. The Spanish economy is about twice the size of Greece's, Ireland's, and Portugal's put together. The ECB's OMT rescue program would put a large dent in ESM's coffers.

Theoretically, the common currency area has enough resources to finance a bailout, but the failure of the Greek rescue saw Euroland's ability to influence economic policy weakened. The ECB might stand ready to intervene in secondary bond markets, pushing prices up and yields down. But if Spain falls behind in its economic reforms, as it looks like happening, it would give the ECB a black eye and at the same time damage the creditworthiness of other Euroland member countries.

Spanish slippages started showing up shortly after (in early April 2012) the new Popular Party's government presented to the Spanish parliament a budget with euro 27 billion ($36 billion) of spending cuts and tax increases. These budget cuts hit Spain's muscles rather than its fat. Instead of cutting the state wage bill and removing layers of bureaucracy, the budget cut spending on research and development. In addition, it was nobody's secret that the central government had to rein in Spain's 17 autonomous regions, responsible for most of:

- Budget overspend, and
- Rapid increase in borrowing in 2011.

Misfiring had an evident effect on investor confidence. At the April 4, 2012 bond auction, the Spanish government raised only euro 2.6 billion, shy of its euro 3.5 billion target. The yield on 10-year bonds rose to 5.7 percent while Spanish banks equities fell, as the ongoing sovereign-banking industry feedback loop added to investor doubts about the lenders' asset quality.

Let's face it. Not only because of economic but also due to political reasons Spain is at the abyss' edge. Even after the hundreds of millions of euros made available by

Mario Draghi to Spanish banks through the LTRO program their balance sheet did not improve. Instead, they used the ECB money to buy government bonds and bring down their interest rate. Critics said that Spain continues absorbing money like blot paper and still continues confronting the risk of default.

Other Club Med countries, too, live with the same illusions, but it is wrong to believe that ECB has bottomless pockets. Theoretically, it might print money at will; practically there is a limit. These funds come out if German, Dutch, Finnish, and other citizens' pockets and only serve to mask Spain's fiscal weakness. Moreover, suspicion exists that Spain's (and Portugal's and Italy's) official debt numbers are questionable —a fact that the Spanish prime minister unofficially confirmed in March 2012 by canceling his still wet signature on Euroland's Spanish budget deficit plan.

This unilateral act raised plenty of questions. The announcement that the country will not be able to fulfill its 2012 deficit target was a knife in the heart of its credibility. It has also provided another piece of evidence, if one was needed, that the euro crisis is far from being over.

Economists whose opinions contrast to those heralded after the different European Union "summits" and by the ECB, have said that Euroland's current remedies doctor the symptoms of the common currency's fundamental problems—not the illness. The illness results from the peripheral countries'

- Lack of competitiveness, and
- Mare of social costs related to the nanny state.

Sovereign balance sheet and valuation fundamentals are so much in disarray that even heads of neighboring countries find it necessary to speak out. In late March 2012, Mario Monti, the then Italian prime minister, said that Spain could reignite the euro risk.[2] This is also true of the other Club Med member states. Southern European nations are not only overloaded with debt, they are as well uncompetitive both within the European Union and in the global market. If they wish to come up from under they have to:

- Work hard, very hard like the Icelanders did (Chapter 14).
- Swamp their weaknesses by restructuring their labor market and avoiding dilapidating strikes.
- Bet on their strengths to gain market prominence, and
- Do away with the habit of indebtedness as a "solution" to their social and economic troubles.

This requires leadership and cultural change which have not yet taken place. Those who hoped Spain will be able to put its worst problems behind it, have been disappointed. After some calming down as the ECB threw money to the problem, the country's sovereign debt crisis has been gaining force again. Market volatility increases as the soothing effect of the ECB's flood of funding for self-wounded member countries, and their banks, wanes.

Mariano Rajoy, Spain's prime minister, may claim that he has been the victim of mistakes made by his predecessor socialist government. The uncontrollable rise in wages under José Rodriguez Zapatero, is an example. In the earlier years of the euro, Spanish labor wages rose significantly while German wages almost stagnated. German labor productivity moved ahead much faster than the Spanish (as well as the Italian, Greek, and French) productivity—with the result of leaving southern European economies in the dust.

Over the years of the common currency no Club Med politician, of the right or of the left, has cared to bend the curve of his country's decline. Instead, business continued "as usual." Yet the Club Med governments, the Spanish being one of them, have been well aware that an economy which is overextended, leveraged and weak in natural resources cannot afford to keep on carrying more and more debt.

Neither did the Spanish socialist government of the first decade of this century pay attention to the sorry state of Spanish banks (Sections 7.5, 7.6, and 7.7). Only on February 2, 2012, Spanish banks were told by the Rajoy government that they must find euro 50 billion ($65 billion) from profits and capital to finance a cleanup of their balance sheets, or those in weak position must agree to merge with another bank.

Luis De Guindos, Spain's finance minister said that for the time being no public money was being used. This was only partly true. Spanish banks that needed state help had to apply for high-interest loans from the Fund for Orderly Bank Restructuring (FOBR), which reportedly planned to charge 8 percent interest. It did not happen that way as Euroland's finance ministers after a couple of telephone conversations (unwisely) decided to throw euro 100 billion ($130 billion) to "solve" the Spanish bank's treasury problems.

As it should have been expected not only was this money thrown down the drain but it also left the markets unconvinced. On June 19, 2012, LCH.Clearnet, the bonds clearing and settlements company, raised the margin (or extra deposit) it required from clients to hold Spanish government debt. The move had implications for the cost of funding for the country's banks. Past margin increases on Ireland and Portugal were blamed for:

- Unnerving bond markets,
- Adding to problems at sovereign level, and
- Eventually pushing both countries toward a Euroland rescue.

Raising the margin to secure short-term funding to repurchase (repo) deals is a widely followed more stringent policy to dealing with heightened risk on debt. This was no arbitrary move by the clearer. LCH had on previous occasions imposed an additional margin requirement of 15 percent based on a number of factors, including when the yield spread between 10-year government bonds and a basket of euro AAA government-rated bonds rises above 450 basis points. Spanish debt was trading above that level.

7.2 Internal Devaluation Would Have Been the Better Solution

A preoccupation of any government confronted with the problems Spain has should be to shake up the supply side of its economy which is typically hamstrung by an inflexible labor market. The Spanish labor market's ossification and exclusion of those who have no job[3] hardly serves the interests either of companies or of the majority of workers—particularly the young who find no employment. In Spain (like in Greece) youth unemployment hit the rate of 53 percent.

When it came to power the Rajoy government signaled that it is committed to restructure the labor market and liberalize it, but so far nothing has really been done as labor unions oppose any talk of restructuring. People familiar with the EU's bailout programs are of the opinion that:

- *If* the government does not have the force to enact changes which can filter through to the real economy
- *Then* the bailout's chances of success will be nonexistent, no matter how much money is thrown to the problem.

Like the rest of southern Europe, Spain is saddled with a sclerotic service sector and inefficient manufacturing outfits whose high cost drags down exporters. The currency union was supposed to drive all of Euroland toward greater efficiency and lower costs, but no rules were set *a priori* on labor restructure and therefore the common currency contained the seeds of its own downfall.

- Spanish prices began to rise to uncompetitive levels after the euro was introduced, and
- Without an independent central bank, which could raise rates to chill inflation and without the will to take drastic measures the Spanish government fell into inertia.

Spain and the other higher-cost countries of Euroland lost their competitiveness, began running trade deficits and resorted to borrowing as their way out. Up to a point, surplus nations such as Germany, the Netherlands and Finland were willing to underwrite those deficits, but as the fiscal imbalances of Club Med continued the old Continent's crisis began.

The Spanish government had the option of an *internal devaluation*, but it also had weak leadership and shock therapy was not popular (to say the least). Except for the traditional policy of devaluation the trade gap could not be closed. There was no way of putting the country's goods on drastic markdown making at the same time imports impossibly expensive—as Solon had done in ancient Athens, besides cutting down on imports.

Yet Spain, like Italy, Portugal, Greece (and eventually France) had no other option than putting its house in order. It had to close the yawning competitiveness gap that caused its problems in the first place. As the Latvian experience has demonstrated (Chapter 13) internal devaluation may be a grinding process of cutting workers and employees' pay while trying to improve their productivity, but it is also effective. Through it Latvia succeeded in:

- Correcting its budgetary imbalances, and
- Reducing the cost of living.[4]

However, internal devaluation is not conceivable without austerity, and "austerity" has been anathema to the Spaniards, though not to more disciplined northern European nations. From 2008 to 2012, not only Latvia but also Iceland as well as

Ireland have been able to cut their unit labor costs, because there was a political will to do so and the common citizen cooperated.

This is not common among Mediterranean countries. True enough, among European countries Hungary topped the lot of sovereigns who confronted their problems with a unit labor cost decline of nearly 12 percent, due largely to a big currency devaluation which, as already explained, Spain could not do. As for Germany, it cut costs mercilessly for the first decade of the euro by applying an iron discipline, a concept totally alien to Spain.

The "solution" suggested by some economists regarding a southern European devaluation and northern revaluation within the euro framework has been impractical or, more precisely, impossible. There was talk of a northern euro (neuro) and a southern euro (seuro), but this was just that talk.

Spain had to cope with the fact that in the less competitive nations, costs are falling only because high unemployment takes away the workers' bargaining power. There is as well the fact that if companies cut wages too much, employees can't pay their car loans, mortgages, and other debts they have contracted. Household indebtedness sees to it that deep cuts create a vicious cycle.

Neither are short-term solutions a real fix. When China offered to buy Spanish bonds, financial analysts commented that the market recognized China's intervention could bring only short-term relief. If anything, Chinese bond buying allowed to procrastinate over the radical reform required by the Spanish economy, which alone could give hope of a longer-term future.

By contrast, ECB's intervention of August 8, 2010 in buying Spanish bonds was essentially perceived as a longer-term commitment. With this, the market sentiment changed and the yield on 10-year Spanish government bonds went from 6.3 percent down to 5 percent, though a month later it rebounded to 5.4 percent.

The macroeconomic and fiscal assumption underlying the Spanish economy, however, was not altered. Real GDP growth was nearly 0.7 in 2011, fell to -1.7 percent in 2012 and is forecast at between -1.0 percent and -2.0 percent for 2013 (the economists' projections for 2013 originally ranged from -0.5 percent to -1.4 percent). The public debt has been projected to rise to 91 percent in 2013. What happens afterward is uncertain since the amount ultimately drawn by the Spanish government from ESM and ECB is not known.[5]

Several economists suggest that it could help if Spain requested an ESM bailout to trigger the "Unlimited" bond-buying plan announced by the ECB. Mario Draghi would be delighted to spend plenty of money. According to some accounts Spain's gross financing need for 2013 will probably be a cool euro 250 billion ($325 billion)[6]—while according to other accounts Spain plans to borrow even more money in 2013.

In August 2012, Spain has been downgraded by independent credit rating agencies to BBB, while the increase in its debt ratio and funding stress may trigger further negative rating, taking Spain to junk levels. Indeed, on October 11, Spain was downgraded to a notch above junk. There is as well an elevated risk that the current mild, fiscal adjustment program falters as neither the government nor the public had their heart in it.

To the opinion of financial analysts, the large structural deficits of both the central government and Spanish regions (which also feature significant public debt), plus a weak banking sector, were quite likely to trigger a further increase in the debt-to-GDP ratio, pushing it toward 100 percent over the next couple of years and leading to another downgrade. Voices are raised that Spain requires:

• Debt reduction measures, and
• Policies able to assure the debt would be sustainable in the longer run.

As of the end of August 2012, the Spanish government had issued bonds at the level of euro 700 billion, but over and above that came the regions' debt of about euro 150 billion; a large sum escaping central government control but obliging Madrid to come to the rescue. Therefore, debt reduction policies are urgently required at all levels even if the Spanish economy is squeezed by the deflating housing bubble, credit crunch, budget slippages, and government bond market stress.

The weak economy is hurting company profits, while banks continue piling up debt. All these factors see to it that the ongoing negative economic momentum is strong, while in the Spanish banking industry nonperforming loans are back to levels not seen since the first half of the 1990s. Spanish banks have become wholly dependent on Euroland and the ECB rather than laboring to improve their performance.

The Spanish banks are also facing another whammy. A Draconian mortgage law[7] voted by parliament to protect the banks' solvency forces families to go to extreme lengths to avoid succumbing to a default, but there are still many foreclosures. By November 2012, some 350,000 Spaniards had been evicted from their properties[8] (over the past 4 years), a number which had much to do with the country's 26 percent joblessness rate, and the way to bet is that this is going to worsen. Back in late April 2012, a Fitch report said repossessed homes were selling for just over half their initial valuations.

In conclusion, without an internal devaluation aimed at righting the balances, and labor restructuring to regain competitiveness, Spain will continue to weight on Euroland's debt crisis. Due to the reasons which have been explained, no immediate solution can be expected. A vague reference to austerity aside, the government has not put forward any crucial measures to resolve the crisis at home, and this means that the effects of the Spanish debt crisis will continue being exported.

7.3   The Spanish Government Is Not in Charge

Critics say that it is not only the Socialist former prime minister, José Luis Rodriguez Zapatero who during his tenure dispensed public money left, right, and center (particularly during his last 2 years in office). It is as well the whole system which has been tuned to excessive deficits and therefore requires additional measures as well as the policy of living within one's means.

Precisely because spending beyond the sovereign's income has become a fad, considerable uncertainty has arisen regarding the state of the Spanish financial system and its ability to pay back its debts. Optimists say that the bulk of Spain's troubles stems not from Madrid's excessive budget deficits, but from the

- Undercapitalized banks,
- Construction and property market bubble, and
- Steady current account deficits, aggravated by declining business competitiveness.

While the message conveyed by these three bullets is correct, among them they don't tell the full picture. Another key factor is Spanish politics. The country's politicians have been consistently exploiting their country's Euroland membership for national, regional, and other political ends, spending an awful lot of effort in largely symbolic gestures while avoiding hard decisions.

No wonder therefore that the Spanish debt still makes the news, with the country remaining at the receiving end of Euroland's funds. As an example of avoiding urgently needed restructuring, Spanish retirement benefits have so far been untouchable while in Greece the Troika demanded that they are reduced by 40 percent, and this heavy haircut was voted into law by the Greek government.

Spain's weak economy and the worsening of its public finances have refocused markets' attention on the European debt problem and, more generally, on investment risks. Even if the current situation is far from being stellar, things would become less comfortable if economic disappointments were to coincide with a rise in social and political agitation reinforcing economic woes.

Investment risks have grown fed by years of easygoing and ill-studied credits, way beyond the fallen real estate. While the Spanish banks are in the frontline and they will take the first hit, behind them hides a "who is who" list of international banks. Figures published in April 2012 (latest available statistics) by the Bank for International Settlements show that at the end of 2011 German banks had $146 billion of exposure to Spain, more than the banks of any other country—with over a third of this exposure to Spanish banks and the balance to the private sector.

Deutsche Bank has been one of the largest foreign banks in the Spanish retail banking market (behind Barclays of Britain) with 250 branches and a euro 14 billion[9] (nearly $18.7 billion) residential mortgage book. Other German banks too were big commercial property lenders at a time when most property values were so much higher, even if the Deutsche Bundesbank had identified property lending in countries such as Spain as a potential problem for the banks it supervises.

Commercial bankers should have listened to the central bank's advice. They also should have known through their own studies that Spain's financial industry was woefully undercapitalized, and they should have abstained from Spanish real estate lending.

Because of overexpansion and imprudent lending the weakness of the Spanish financial industry has been so pronounced that experts said at least a fraction of the real estate writedowns will have to be borne by the government, as the wounded Spanish banks had to confront the economic recession. Otherwise they were at risk of losing credibility with their clients, correspondent banks, and investors. The more the market's focus shifted to the Spanish banks the more the sovereign felt the market's heat.

While the market's pressure softened with the early September 2012 announcement of OMT, that would allow the ECB to intervene massively in Spain's debt market, Mariano Rajoy, the Spanish prime minister, has yet to give any firm signal that he is prepared to accept the main condition of such aid:

- The official request to ESM for bailout, and
- An economic reform drawn up by the EU authorities.

ECB's announcement initially triggered a rally which removed some pressure off the Spanish government. But markets are unlikely to give the benefit of doubt for long; and investors are concerned by a statement in late September 2012—from the finance ministers of Germany, Holland, and Finland—who said plans to move bad assets off government books would not apply to *legacy assets*.

While swimming in red ink, the Spanish government also has to cope with angry street protests at home against fiscal austerity. These underline the existing political tension between northern and southern Europe. Part of the cost of shoring up the Club Med economies and pulling up from under self-wounded banks is the austerity they should adopt to rebuild their balance sheets. Euroland's crisis will continue haunting financial markets.

With the Spanish government undecided on what to do next, by the end of September 2012, the cost of insuring against Spanish default by means of CDSs rose to a 3-week high of 400 basis points. Analysts said that even with LTRO and OMT Euroland failed to break out of the "complacency crisis" merry-go-round which characterized the past 3 years.

"The eurozone crisis has long been two steps forward, one step back," says William Davies, head of global equities at Threadneedle, the investment manager. "The prospects of the ECB buying bonds and bank recapitalizations led to a period of euphoria, but now we're taking a step back again."[10] Yet the Spanish government was offered good money (running after bad money) to fix its creaky finances before it was shut off from financial markets.

Relief in the markets is typically short-lived unless decisive measures are taken of handouts continue at rapid pace. The reason for continuing market pressure has been that Spain's fiscal deficit, current account deficit, property and bank bust is compounded by a massive loss of investor confidence. Capital has drained from Spain at an accelerating pace for three reasons:

- Investors are worried by the vicious spiral of a weakening economy, worsening government finances, and banks at brink of bankruptcy.
- Economists were losing confidence in Spain's place within the common currency, and
- Politicians have started to doubt that the poisonous links between the banks and the sovereign could be severed before it was too late.

A state of general nervousness was attested by the fact that rather than injecting the funds straight into the Spanish banking system, rescuers were lending them to the sovereign, which raised the public debt level. It could also see to it that Spain's borrowing costs rise further as investors start questioning the government's solvency.

To alleviate such fears, talks between the Spanish government and the European Union were focusing on measures that would be demanded by international lenders as part of a new rescue program, aiming to assure that they are in place before a bailout is formally requested. What Rajoy particularly feared is that the Commission would request more austerity measures to meet existing EU budget targets, which Madrid has repeatedly missed.

High in the Spanish prime minister's mind has probably been the fact that ECB's OMT sovereign bond buying would be triggered only after the government requests help from the ESM and there is an agreed reform plans. At the same time, bond buying by the ECB would lower Spanish borrowing costs somehow easing Madrid's debt burden while increasing its level of debt.

A concept which, by all likelihood, is missing from Spanish government's reasoning is the fact that fiscal discipline can be as effective in lowering borrowing costs as money from heaven. CDS risk premiums for Spain dropped drastically after the first LTRO (of December 2011), rose again and then sunk when the *Fiscal Compact*[11] was announced and Spain let it be known that will go along. (Relatively speaking, the second LTRO of February 2012 had a rather minor effect on Spain's CDS risk premium).

Investor confidence was further shaken by the fact that the recession in Spain deepened, driven by an accelerated decline in domestic demand; and various regions, including Catalonia, Valencia, and Murcia needed financial support from the central government, raising further concerns about the viability of the sovereign's fiscal targets. The fact that Euroland's Stability and Growth Pact put a limit at 3 percent for budget deficit and 60 percent for public debt ceilings made a sort of negative contribution because such ceilings have been breached chronically by member states, including Spain.

7.4   Investors Fear Spain Will Battle Against Austerity

Mid-April 2012 Spanish government bond yields broke above the critical 6 percent mark, and continued standing north of where they were before the ECB's LTRO operations of December 2011 and February 2012. Traders' eyes turned squarely back toward Euroland's central bank, the only institution with the inclination to drive Spanish bond yields lower.

Critics nevertheless pointed out that while the LTRO cost was big—over $1 trillion—the rescues of Spanish and Italian credit institutions did not provide the expected results. The banks which got the LTRO funds at a mere 1 percent interest rate used them to buy their government's bonds rather than rebuild their balance sheet. Moreover the central bank's governing council was divided over this operation's wisdom.

Neither have the public debt and the banks' undercapitalization been the only problems. Parts of the nonbanking private sector's debt became a burden for

Spain's public sector accounts, worsening the fiscal debt crisis. The country's manufacturing industry was in poor shape because, as the reader is already aware, after the adoption of the euro rapid wage growth (and an influx of low-skilled immigrants) has caused a drop in

- Competitiveness, and
- Productivity across large sections of the economy.

As if to make matters worse, while the Spanish labor market has long been plagued by rigidities, neither the Rajoy government nor the Socialist which preceded it had taken the initiative to right the balances. Critics said that this was not just a show of the government's lack of guts but also, if not mainly, a Machiavellian calculation that Spain was simply "too big to fail." Hence, if market pressures intensified support would be forthcoming from Euroland's funds and the IMF.

Not all investors looked at this "too big to fail" argument as undisputable. Many have been worried by the fact that, according to estimates, an estimated euro 100 billion ($130 billion) of capital left Spain in 2011, and euro 160 billion ($205 billion) left Italy that same year—partly from each country's citizens and partly as foreigners withdraw bank deposits or sold government bonds.

Neither were investors fooled by the calls in Paris and other Euroland capitals about "growth through more debt." François Hollande, the French president, called for more spending and more taxes. In June 2012, Hollande, Mario Monti of Italy, and Mariano Rajoy of Spain teamed up to trap Angela Merkel, the German chancellor, into financing a silly spending-and-spending program, but their game fell flat.[12]

Economists who respect themselves and care for the opinion they are expressing, said that *if* high deficits were the answer, *then* Spain, Italy, Greece, and Portugal should be economies in upswing. This, however, they are not and they have no choice but austerity in their effort to pull themselves together, calm bond markets and avoid outright bankruptcy. Integral part of this opinion has been an undisputable fact of life. The debt of western economies has reached levels exceeded only during World War II and the evidence is that high debt stifles long-term growth.

- The first condition for reigniting the economy, therefore growth, is to rid oneself from the current mountain of debt, and
- The second condition is to remove uncertainty and its disastrous effect on most western economies, bringing back confidence.

How much sizable government deficits weight on the economy can be easily seen from the lack of trust investors have shown to the Spanish equity market—a proxy of the economy. Companies operating in Spain confront a shrinking market for their products and see their profits melting. Spanish equities excelled in volatility, which was generally low in 2012, as well as in negative values.

Mid-June 2012, Danone, the French food company, said Spain more than any other country was behind its steadily declining profit performance in southern Europe and that would shave half of 1 percent of its projected 2012 operating margins (Danone has been expanding into emerging markets for a decade to compensate for the uncertainty characterizing western markets).

Restoring investor confidence requires strong medicine. But are the measures being taken up to standard? On July 11, 2012, the Spanish government unveiled a euro 65 billion worth of tax increases and public spending cuts as part of a deal to secure European aid for the country's banking system.[13] As if to contradict Madrid's action, that same day, thousands of miners marched on the center of the Spanish capital to protest against austerity measures which hit the coal's industry's subsidies.

In response to a tandem of demonstrations in Madrid and provincial capitals, Mariano Rajoy issued stark warnings about the risk to Spain's future. What the Spanish prime minister did not say, but should have said is that while euro 65 billion looks like lots of money it is only a quarter of the funds the Spanish government is expected to need in 2013 to make ends meet—which, according to an estimate, stand at euro 250 billion (Section 7.3). And there is as well the massive euro 380 billion ($494 billion) property and construction overhang equivalent to 35 percent of Spanish GDP.

When it comes to antigovernment rallies, the Spanish are learning a great deal from the French and Greeks. When spending cuts are announced thousands of protesters demonstrated outside the Spanish parliament. However, analysts note that unlike protests held in 2011 when tens of thousands occupied the central squares of Madrid, Barcelona, and other cities, several 2012 demonstrations were isolated though violent clashes took place with police.

There is, as well, folklore. While Spain dearly depends on Euroland's aid to avoid bankruptcy, animosity about largely political issues also has a field day. In early July 2012, Luxembourg and Spain have been at loggerheads over a board seat at the ECB which had to be filled. At a first time it was supposed to go to a Spanish banking official; but most Euroland governments backed Luxembourg's candidate for the job. In retaliation Spain blocked his appointment until it gets another senior post for one of its bureaucrats.[14]

In addition, economists say that the money Spain gets from the EU is far from being optimally used because investments are not properly studied in terms of services and profitability. An example is the Ciudad Real airport, a euro 1.1 billion ($1.43 billion) white elephant. The last commercial flights ceased at the end of October 2011 (though the airport remains open to private planes). This is one of many examples of poorly planned spending in the past decade, during *el boom*. As money poured in, it was deviated to political pork barrels.

Most of Spain's 17 regional governments channeled cash into trophy schemes with little or no concern for whether they would pay their way. The Ciudad Real's airport, though private, was backed by the Castile La-Mancha region's Socialist government in part funded by Euroland money and in part by a savings bank (*caja*) that went bust. At the end, the unnecessary airport filed for bankruptcy.

Other costs, too, have run out of control. Health care is an example and in this case Spain is in good company. All western countries are confronted by outsized public health care budgets. Health spending makes up between 30 percent and 40 percent of Spain's regional governments' budgets.

Like other westerners under a nanny state socialist regime, Spaniards enjoy free health care from cradle to grave. But an aging population, soaring drug bills, poor cost controls, and reduced tax revenues make this system unaffordable and unsustainable. Year-in, year-out, health budgets are allegedly overrun by over 15 percent. When tax revenues were steady, that could be handled up to a point. Now health care debt adds itself to the other public debt, worsening an already bad situation.

Aside other aftereffects, runaway health care costs add to the friction between the central government and the regions. The financial pressures on Madrid have been intensified by a constitutional crisis brewing over Catalonia. "Spain is increasingly slipping from his (Rajoy's) hands," said Alfredo Pérez Rubalcaba, leader of the socialist party. "There are very clear fractures in Spain, and the one I am most worried about is social fracture."[15]

Catalonia, Spain's largest region by output, is also its most indebted; it is euro 42 billion in the red. End of August 2012, it got a euro 5 billion mini-bailout from the central government. Other regions followed the same policy of asking Madrid for funds. Economic vows fuel the secessionist mood, and regional governments blame their troubles on a national tax system which, in their view, obliges them to make disproportionate contribution to the rest of Spain.

Catalonia is by no means the only Spanish region in deep red. With half Catalonia's GDP Valencia is also heavily indebted. The same is true of Andalusia, Spain's most populous region, which requested a bailout from the central government. Along with Estremadura, Andalusia has a GDP per capita of euro 17,000 versus euro 30,000 for Madrid.

Catalonia's money shortfall has led an increasing number of its citizens to conclude that their prospects for recovery would be enhanced by loosening or breaking ties with the rest of Spain. For the time being this is on hold, as the pro-independence center-right party did not benefit from recent elections to promote its program for independence. But for how long?

7.5 Spanish Banks and Euroland's Taxpayers

For the virtually bankrupt Spanish banks, a challenging problem in search of a solution is that nobody really knows—including the Spanish government and the banks themselves—how deeply exposed they are, and whether their equity is positive or negative, as is the case of Bankia. This makes the search for way out from the Spanish banking crisis so much more complex, while the results expected from "this" or "that" fire-brigade action become more uncertain.

In mid-2012, when Euroland's finance ministers started to have doubts about the Spanish government's ability to recapitalize its banks, was advanced an estimate of euro 40 billion as being more or less enough for the recapitalization job. Shortly thereafter, however, it was said that this far from being enough, and filling the bottomless hole of Spanish credit institutions will require euro 90 billion ($117 billion), or more.

One of the key problems confronting both the central government and the Spanish banks is that no inflection point has shown up in credit quality. Bad news continue coming in. Good news is needed for provisions and subsidies to make a real difference. Spain has practically nationalized Bankia[16] which in 2011 received euro 30 billion of state aid and in May 2012 required at least euro 10 billion more to survive; but all that money was used for fire-brigade operations—it was not employed to create a war chest.

It needs no explaining that depositors did not appreciate Bankia's travails and part nationalization. Mid-May 2012, *El Mundio*, the daily newspaper, reported customers had withdrawn euro 1 billion of deposits since the government's move.[17] There has also been continued uncertainty over the final costs that Madrid will have to pay to clean up the partly nationalized lender.

Analysts noted that Madrid converted a euro 4.5 billion convertible bond into common equity in Bankia's parent company,[18] but it did not inject fresh cash nor did it decide on the final amount it will have to put into the lender. The move was primarily intended to stem a "run" at the wounded credit institution, which suggests that the Spanish government's cash injections left much to be wanted in salvage terms.

For its part, the ECB was reluctant to come forward, as Maria Draghi waited for results of the then forthcoming Spanish elections, and kept some dry power to eventually negotiate a bailout. The EU Commission, too, has been holding back in spite of verbal (but only verbal) comments made by its top brass that "the time for Spain is running out."

As friendly but empty of substance verbal exchange continued, soaring losses of Spanish banks cast doubt on the estimated public cost of propping them up. The crucial question among Euroland bureaucrats, politicians, and Spanish bank observers was "What would be enough?" Some estimates suggested Spanish banks would need as much as euro 60 billion; others spoke of euro 100 billion; still others of euro 300 billion ($390 billion).

According to other accounts the loans books of 14 Spanish banks showed that more than half of them did not have enough capital. The two major banks: Santander and BBVA as well as Caixabank seem to have been able to meet Basel IIIs 9 percent core Tier 1 target—but not the other banks, which included Sabadell, Bankinter, Unicaja, Banco Mare Nostrum, Banco de Valencia, Catalunya Bank, Bankia, and many more.

In power since December 2011, Mariano Rajoy's government was at once confronted by central government deficits, regional government deficits and the big red ink holes in the treasuries of Spanish banks. Rajoy seemed to think he can perform feats that his Socialist predecessor could not. He set the regions new targets and asked the banks to recapitalize themselves with private money. Neither of these targets worked out.

As direct consequence of slow-motion recognition of the Spanish banking industry's financial problems, the central government found itself in an impasse. Critics said that the contemplated banking industry recapitalization did not address the basic issue coming from the fact that Spanish banks are highly reliant on wholesale funding. To make matters worse, the relative scarcity of deposits also increased as a consequence of deposit outflows. There was therefore no alternative than to reduce the risk-weighted assets (RWAs) which the Spanish banks registered.

The Spanish banks' RWAs are a conglomeration of credit risk (by far the large share), market risk, and operational risk. In late 2012, RWAs at Santander stood at euro 560 billion; at BBVA, euro 340 billion; Caixa, euro 195 billion; Bankia, euro 165 billion; Popular, euro 100 billion; and Sabatel, euro 80 billion. Among themselves the next 10 in line Spanish banks featured euro 325 billion in RWAs.[19] The total is an astronomical euro 1765 billion (nearly $2.3 trillion).

Indeed, conditions set by the European Commission required that Spanish banks reduce their loans-to-deposits ratios from a prevailing 150–160 percent level toward 110–120 percent (the way it happened in Portugal and Ireland). The Spanish banks however answered they cannot rapidly reduce their mortgage portfolios, which represent about 40 percent of loans, and what the EU demanded would require a sharp reduction of company loans, representing another 40 percent.

In fact, the downsizing of company loans creates another vicious cycle by bringing in evidence the nonperforming loans which, along with bad real estate loans, continued to depress the banks' balance sheets. This further complicates the other problem confronting Spanish banking: their covered bond issuance. Spanish banks have extensively issued covered bonds with a total outstanding amount estimated at euro 350 billion ($455 billion), using large parts of their mortgage book as collateral.

While these numbers are big and pose many challenges, the worst of all is that by all likelihood they will continue to increase. On December 18, 2012, just prior to the end of the year, it was announced that Spain's bad loans ratio has grown to an all-time high.[20] Experts say that the Spanish banks' bad loans ratio will continue going north as the worst-case scenario turns real.

There is plenty of evidence, therefore, as to why Spanish banks heavily depend on the ECB for liquidity. They have borrowed a record amount of money estimated at 25–30 percent of Euroland's total. Even so they are struggling to increase provisions and capital during a recession. Needless to say that they will need a huge amount of extra funds if the economy deteriorates more than predicted. How much more?

Nobody can answer this query in a sure way. The Spanish government depended on a "bottom-up" review of 115,000 loans,[21] conducted by two consulting companies with close international supervision from authorities, including the IMF and ECB. Rajoy's hope was that the results will dispel doubts over the true extent of losses in the Spanish banking industry. This has been largely wishful thinking.

Overall, the total shortfall computed by the Oliver Wyman study dropped to euro 53.7 billion after including deferred tax assets and ongoing mergers, according to the reports. But several Spanish bankers have been critical of the process, attacking it for "weakening" banks and adding "confusion." While to the opinion of financial analysts, neither of the two aforementioned studies dispelled the uncertainty about the depth of the red ink hole in Spanish banks' capital.

The analysts argued that with the banks having suffered a sharp fall in share price, and the capital markets all but closed to most Spanish lenders, it will be a grueling process for them to borrow money let alone sell new shares. Even if this were possible, it would have been highly dilutive for existing investors.

Back in October 2011, Luis Faricano of the London School of Economics had estimated that the capital required could total up to euro 100 billion, around

10 percent of Spanish GDP. To his opinion, the banks would not be able to raise that much money in a hurry, and Spain would have to seek help from Euroland.[22] Many months later Euroland's ministers of finance worked around this euro 100 billion estimate, in the understanding that:

• It will target the problem of large amounts of nonperforming assets held by Spanish banks,
• But it should not reduce the incentive for the banks to deleverage their balance sheets.

Several analysts and economists expressed the opinion that something is wrong with the logic behind these two bullets. Too little money would not solve the Spanish banks' problems; but too much will exacerbate the vicious cycle linking government and bank finances. It will as well inhibit the banking sector from cleaning up its balance sheet.

Experts believe Spain must follow the example of other countries that have been through similar banking crises, setting up one or more *bad banks* (Section 7.7) to work through the maze of nonperforming loans and eventually dispose them. This policy would force the banks to mark assets down to realistic levels, but with the banking crisis in full swing realism has been the most vital missing ingredient.

Reducing their balance sheet's leverage would be the best policy, but Spanish banks say that at this very moment cash is king and since mid-2011 they had few opportunities to attract unsecured funds. They therefore stick to the priority of finding capital even if most of their liquidity is drawn from collateralized funding offered by the Bank of Spain and the ECB (which takes its money straight out of the pockets of Euroland's taxpayers).

7.6   In Financial Terms Spanish Banks Wounded Their Clients[23]

Spain is in the danger zone both because of fiscal reasons and due to the fact its banking industry is in shambles. The central government does not have the hundreds of billions of euros needed to recapitalize the country's credit institutions, finance the regions and pull itself up from under. This problem of very shaky finances has been known for years by Zapatero's socialist government, but the former prime minister has shown no rush to fix it. He cared more to block the takeover of Endesa, the Spanish energy company, by Germany's EON, than to fix his country's leaky roof.

All this is typically socialist government doing and it has been quite superficial. A few years later, in 2012, superficiality characterized the "unanimous decisions" by Euroland's finance ministers (who were spending "only" taxpayer money) to recapitalize the Spanish banks without any questions asked. A short time thereafter, at the end of July 2012, Euroland allocated to this vague and poorly documented financing an approximate figure of euro 30 billion, raised on November 29, 2012 to euro 37 billion ($48 billion). The money was supposed to come out of EFSF till ESM is operating.

Critics said that so much money thrown at the problem was an unwarranted spoilage. Moreover, the euro 100 billion might calm down for a few weeks the markets confronting Spanish economic and financial problems, but they will not be a cure—the more so as the Spanish banks themselves estimated the needed capital injection at the level of euro 300 billion ($390 billion).[24]

The problem of pulling Spain and its banking industry up from its descent to the abyss is complex, as evidenced by the fact that the Spanish government tries to separate the banking crisis from the sovereign debt crisis, and it does not even succeed to go halfway in this direction. There is as well the fact that both the banks and Madrid are suspected of not being truthful with their statistics. "The EU smiled as Spanish banks cooked the books," said one of the critics.[25]

Many European Union countries which have had, and still have, banking problems of their own have found out that the sovereign debt and banking debt are so closely connected that they cannot be split in a neat way. Neither is it rational to spend a big chunk of a loan the Spanish government will probably contract with Euroland on the banking industry. In principle, the money going to beef up banking capital should come from the banks themselves by liquidating some of their assets.

Quite likely, Madrid knew some secrets when it wanted the money in a hurry but it would accept neither accountability nor responsibility on how it will be used. The Spanish government was angry that the package came with a clause requiring to write down investors who had bought hybrid debt from the country's financial institutions to be bailed out through Euroland money. This preferred treatment of its retail investors added insult to injury already suffered by Euroland's taxpayers, who were forced to foot this very poorly studied "salvage."

Spanish bankers had sold risky instruments to unsuspecting common citizens who did not know that there is money to be lost with derivative financial products linked to preference shares. Nobody ever assumed responsibility for mis-investments sold to unaware customers who subsequently feared that their lifetime savings will be wiped out. Several cases of mis-selling were so blatant that:

- Writedowns are likely to cause a backlash against both the government and the banks, and
- Infuriated depositors started pulling their money out of the Spanish banks involved in this scam, aggravating their precarious situation.

In the casino society of ours Spanish and other banks have acquired the habit of loaning their retail depositors with preference shares which, technically speaking, are bonds not equity. They are senior to ordinary shares, but subordinate to bonds. Even in a casino society, however, preferred share issuers and investors cannot have it both ways. Regulators should abide by—and enforce—the gold standard of pure, loss-absorbing pecking order:

- First ordinary equity,
- Then preferred shares, and
- At the following level of shock-absorbers bonds.

Banks should be punished for selling their customers complex products which they don't understand, and one day they will blow up and sink their savings. Take as an example the use of a derivative instrument designed around euro/US dollar currency exchange. The offered structure is known as *one touch*. The bank's client effectively enters in a forward contract on euro/dollar rate with a barrier. If at any time before maturity the spot rate breaches the barrier the client would receive leverage return of his or her initial investment. If not (which is likely) the capital being bet is lost.

Plenty of economists and financial analysts said that Brussels should resist the investor reimbursement plan which Madrid pressed on Euroland to mollify savers. Critics stated that using EFSF funds for repaying investors goes against the principle that creditors should take a hit before taxpayer money is injected into a bank in difficulty.

- Euroland money should not be used to refund private interests, and
- Banks and bankers who by words or acts cheated savers should be punished.

Integral part of the *moral hazard* we are talking about is the compensating of sophisticated savers who consciously sought high returns when buying the Spanish banks' hybrid debt. Critics added that Madrid should also assure that acts of mis-selling are not being repeated, amending the Spanish law to prevent such practices from reoccurring, as well as making Spanish banks and their accounts totally transparent.

While this has been a sound advice, it did not find its way to Spanish legislation probably because of conflicts of interest. Delays also characterized the so-called *bad bank* (Section 7.7), to be instituted and financed by the government, with the mission to purchase at heavy discount the Spanish banks' nonperforming loans allowing them to:

- Get rid of their toxic waste, and
- Rebuild their balance sheet.

The presence of moral hazard should not be ignored even in an emergency, by letting mismanaged banks (and their tricky instruments) escape unscathed. When rules are drawn up for bailouts it is hard to justify the turning of a blind eye to the scams. A cleanup will lead to better resource allocation in the economy and moral risk should not be permitted to persist. After all, the ECB/ESM money comes out of the pocket of German, Dutch, Finnish, and other taxpayers who will be badly cheated if the cleanup is half-baked.

This is only one of several cases with which should be directly confronted the new bank regulator for Euroland, under the ECB. Already the question of when this authority will be created, and what powers it will have, has caused a storm in some Euroland capitals. The ambiguities which persist are forcing several sovereigns to backtrack on soft commitments others thought had been finalized.

To be successful the new supervisory framework will be required to provide firm solutions to many tricky issues. For example, there are clear signs of clashing views about the amount of debt Spain would be saddled with once the bank rescue system is complete and operating. Officials from several Euroland countries insist that, in the end, Madrid must still guarantee at least some of the losses the ESM would face if rescued banks defaulted—which by all likelihood they will do.

Therefore, a critical question has been how strong should the rescue link between derelict Spanish banks and their indebted sovereign. This is a question which concerns all of Euroland's sovereigns as well as all of the banks. In Spain's case part of the difficulty has been associated to the fact that the Spanish banks' bad debt rose to the stars.

The sovereign will be confronted with plenty of losses to carry on its balance sheet if several of the country's banks default. With OMT Mario Monti has already positioned himself to come to the rescue by buying Spanish bonds. This however does not mean that the Spaniards get a free lunch. Germany has already clearly stated that outside inspectors will supervise the euro 100 billion emergency loans for Spanish banks, just like other financial bailouts over the past 2 years—even if Madrid insists that it should escape the onerous conditions imposed on Portugal, Ireland, and Greece (a request which evidently makes no sense).

7.7 Bad Banks and Wanting Spanish Fiscal Policies

Bad banks is a term used to describe financial entities set up and backed by management's own initiative or (more often) by governments to facilitate the removal of "bad assets" from a going entity's balance sheet. This is supposed to give a lease of life to wounded credit institutions. "Bad assets" are loosely defined as those that:

- Are at risk of severe impairment, and/or
- Are difficult to value or, when valued, worth very little in comparison to their book value.

Bad banks are created to assist in the resolution of a financial crisis; permit refloating the wounded bank by relieving it of its worst "assets" (including holdings and nonperforming loans); and try to recover the most of what may be seen as lost money, by avoiding a fire sale of those wounded "assets."

The first case of a bad bank arose in 1988 when the Mellon Bank spun off its energy and property loans, which had turned sour, into Grant Street National Bank. The latter was financed with junk bonds and private equity. A successful example of a government-sponsored bad bank has been Sweden's *Securum*, engineered in the early 1990s to relieve Nordbanken of its mountain of bad loans and private equity holdings.

As these examples demonstrate, the bad bank idea is flexible and it can be given different interpretations at different times by different people. But success is in no way guaranteed. Much depends on the nature of the "bad assets," market conditions and how well the disposal operation is being managed. Josef Stiglitz, the economist, criticizes the bad bank idea as "swapping cash for trash," but the pros say such an approach has advantages:

- An independent entity can focus on the job of recovering the fair value of wounded assets, and

• Taking toxic assets off the balance sheet of a bank teetering on bankruptcy leaves behind a cleaner credit institution, which should find it easier to raise capital or attract a buyer.

Finding a buyer at fair value price, however, may well be a pipe dream. In addition, the real problem with *bad banks* is that, as usually, the taxpayer will be asked to foot the bill. Someone has to pay for the assets transferred by the wounded bank to the new equity, or to a buyer, at deep discount.

The transfer of big chunks of a loan portfolio, specifically nonperforming loans and similar "assets," from a credit institution to a specially set up vehicle will take the form of the former selling them to (which may be the government, or its agent) at large discount. Superficially, this is similar to a securitization transaction but in reality it is not as it raises the questions of:

• Case-by-case classification,
• Reasonable valuation, and
• Right treatment of transferred assets.

If, and only *if*, this operation is properly done and conflicts of interest are avoided, transfer of nonperforming loans to a bad bank buys breathing space since (presumably) the new entity is under no pressure to go ahead with sale of wounded assets. Theoretically at least, it can wait till market conditions improve to get its money back or even make a profit.

In the 1990s Sweden's *Securum* was able to dispose Nordbanken's nonperforming assets it was entrusted with at 75 to 80 cents to the kroner—while they would have fetched much less than 50 percent in a fire sale. Securum however was very well managed and acted in full independence from Nordbanken. This is not the general case with bad banks.

Neither are all assets in a portfolio of dubious securities able to fetch 80 cents to the dollar, and this is true of both commercial banks and central banks. Many economists and financial analysts worry that that's the case with what can be found in the vaults of the Federal Reserve, Bank of England, and ECB. An Italian banker characterized these positions as garbage worse than in the streets of Naples. No doubt the Bank of Spain has plenty of them, even if the real mountains are to be found in the Spanish commercial banks and savings banks.

Confronted with a rapid escalation in the amount of funds necessary to buy the Spanish banks bad loans and other useless "assets," even at big discount, Madrid does not want to put up any money. In theory, moving bad property loans off Spanish banks' balance sheets looks attractive. In practice, this makes sense only if someone acquires them. This "someone" must:

• Crystallize valuations, and
• Put on the table the required funds.

Early on, the Spanish government's hypothesis on who will be the acquirer was vague envisaging a corporate entity financed either by local deposit guarantees, by the domestic banking sector collectively, or by unspecified "private" investors.

Anecdotal evidence suggests that little attention is paid to the fact that a basic requirement connected to the bad bank concept is to limit as much as possible the risk of spreading toxic waste to even more banks or other entities.

For a bad bank project to be effective, reliance on public funding is a "must," but the Spanish government is short of funds. To make matters more complex, as many analysts noted, valuing bad property loans and properly reflecting their remaining worth (if any), is no easy business either.

Even if the "right price" is guestimated, this will remain exposed to further price declines—an issue particularly true of Spanish real estate where there is a huge amount of surplus property in an ailing economy. Worse yet, the overhang of bad bank-owned assets can turn into a factor preventing stabilization of Spain's property market.

Nobody can tell in advance how many cents to the euro the Spanish bad bank will recover. The rumored 70−80 cents is a pipedream. Even half that may be too much. The difference between what is recovered and the face value of the bad loans being taken over will be paid by somebody, and the way to bet is that that's the Spanish taxpayer.

Madrid has to review its fiscal policies (which are currently wanting) to account for that load. This brings into the picture the Troika to supervise the eventual euro 100 billion Euroland loan for the Spanish banks as well as all other Euroland money flowing into Spain for the bailout, including the Spanish bonds bought by ECB under OMT.

The Spanish government is caught in a dilemma. Economists say the country's real estate crisis is so dire that weak banks risk falling by the wayside without a chance to clean up their balance sheets. According to political commentators, Mariano Rajoy sidetracked the issue when he said that Spain needs, and needs urgently, deep structural changes. Without lots of capital to buy up the bad assets, the bad bank will be a sort of window dressing.

In addition, several Spanish ministers have been against the bad bank idea, as first reaction, though by October 2012, the government was poised to set up a *Banco Malo*. This has been counterproductive because confidence in Spain and its banks has been further shaken by the procrastination on:

- Banking reform, and
- Balance sheet restructuring.

Investors still question banks' asset valuations, and whether bad loans will be transferred at their right price. According to some opinions nearly all property loans, good and bad, including property developer exposure with a face value of between euro 1.3 and euro 1.5 *trillion*, could end up in the bad bank.[26] This is a huge amount of money even with a brutal haircut, raising *inter alia* the question: Will the bad bank really work?[27]

As if to make matters even more obscure, on December 18, 2012, the ticker at Bloomberg News carried the message that, according to Madrid, private investors already subscribed to 55 percent of Spanish bad bank's capital. No information was given as to who are these private investors, to make such a news item believable.

Forcing investors in some of the banks' debt to take losses was a condition imposed by Euroland's contributors to the bailout funds, to minimize the burden on taxpayers (Section 7.6). But a bad bank is a separate, independent entity and this radically changes the answer to the query: "Who is responsible for its losses?" The answer is its owner, and *if* the owner happens to be the government, *then* so be it.

Neither is the bad bank the only elephant in Madrid's financial glass house. Several of the Spanish banks who, after shedding some of their bad loans, optimistically hope to return to profitability, may still go under since their financial staying power is questionable. All the bad bank will do it to take on dud loans. There is no guarantee that Spanish banks will be able to regain the market's confidence as Madrid hopes.

All counted, the picture for Spain is not that pretty. In 2013, the country confronts "a further fiscal contraction equivalent to 4 percent of GDP to set its finances on a sustainable path, and a loan-to-deposit ratio of nearly 180 percent leaves its banking sector vulnerable of funding crises," states a study by UBS.[28] As in the case of Portugal and Greece, how and how well Euroland's and IMF's money is employed in Spain, and whether Madrid sticks to its obligations for a bailout, will be controlled by a Troika (consisting of Euroland's, ECB's, and IMF's representatives).

The money will come from ESM which in OMT terms Spain must approach with a request for financial help, and the loans will carry preferred status to Madrid's existing sovereign debt. The ESM is senior to other creditors, assuring that Spain's debts to other Euroland members would take precedence over private lenders in the event of a default.

This is not money to be spent at will even if Mariano Rajoy called his decision to seek as much as euro 100 billion in funds "the opening of a line of credit" for the country's banks, rather than a bailout with strict external monitoring of its economy. Rajoy also said owners of existing sovereign bonds would not be affected—which is patently false if the money comes from ESM.

In the first quarter of 2011, the yield of Spanish 5-year government bonds stood at 4.5 percent. It peaked to about 6 percent in December 2011 but with Mario Draghi's LTRO (of which Spanish banks benefited handsomely, using the borrowed billions at 1 percent interest rate to buy government bonds) the 5-year bonds yield dropped to 3.5 percent. Then it rose again to nearly 7 percent.

To help Spain and Italy the ECB announced OMT and made the commitment "...to do what it takes..." The market liked this announcement because "it saw euros now."[29] The interest rate on Spanish 5-year bonds dropped to about 4.5 percent (where it was earlier on, even if neither Spain nor Italy joined the OMT saga. Critics say that in spite of LTRO and OMT the ECB has failed in altering the market's perception and therefore lost some of its credibility.

It therefore comes as no surprise that policy makers in Brussels and Euroland worry that privileging emergency loans over existing sovereign debt, through the use of ESM, would spook the bond markets. Facing more risk of losing their investment in the case of a default, investors would demand higher premiums from Spain. In turn, this will drive interest rates up instead of down. (It did not happen yet.)

Precisely the same will take place if "most favorable" conditions are awarded to Italy which, due to 4 months without government and prevailing political uncertainty, was in its way of undoing whatever prudent fiscal measures were put in place by Mario Monti's administration. Economic history shows that weaknesses are provocative, but at the same time the Spanish, Italians, French, Greeks, Cypriots, and Euroland at large know that there is no chance for wholesale change in European Union policies.

End Notes

1. In Euroland, Spain and Greece share the worst possible statistics. In Spain, general unemployment is 26.5 percent and youth unemployment 56.6 percent. In Greece, unemployment statistics stand just below these numbers.
2. Bloomberg News, March 25, 2012.
3. Which also exists in all other Club Med countries.
4. Latvia chose to keep the peg of its currency unaltered, though it could have devalued. Because of this peg, Latvia's can be taken as proxy to that of a country which cannot devalue having adopted the common currency.
5. Much depended on whether Spain asks for bailout. The only known red ink was the euro 100 billion ($130 billion) earmarked to recapitalize Spanish banks.
6. *The Economist*, November 17, 2012.
7. Under a 100-year-old law, returning the keys of ones' property to the bank does not rid him of his debt. A bank can seize a home for 60 percent of its appraised value, and then pursue the owner for the outstanding difference including interest and legal fees.
8. This is softened by a new law.
9. Deutsche's first quarter 2012 report showed euro 29 billion of gross exposure to Spain but the bank said collateral and other hedging brings net exposure at about euro 14 billion.
10. *Financial Times*, September 27, 2012.
11. Chorafas DN. Breaking up the euro: the end of a common currency. New York, NY: Palgrave/Macmillan; 2013.
12. *Idem.*
13. Cuts include a rolling back of unemployment benefits, an increase in value added tax (from 18 to 21 percent) and a reduction to local government subsidies.
14. *Financial Times*, July 10, 2012.
15. *Financial Times*, September 27, 2012.
16. Bankia has been the result of wider merger of Spanish savings banks primarily, but not exclusively, wounded by their real estate loans. By the third quarter of 2012 Bankia was deemed to need euro 25 billion up from euro 19 billion capital gap identified only a few months earlier. Then, mid-December 2012, came the news that Bankia had a negative net worth of euro 4.1 billion. Banco Popular was another listed bank in deep troubles, Spain's sixth biggest lender.
17. *Financial Times*, May 18, 2012.
18. Banco Financiero y de Ahorros (BFA).
19. Statistics from *Financial Times*, October 1, 2011.
20. Bloomberg News, December 18, 2012.

21. These 115,000 individual loans were picked at random and individually examined by a team of auditors. Critics attacked the narrow focus of this exercise, echoing the 2011 Europe-wide stress test of Euroland sovereign debt which failed to extrapolate the risk of sovereign default to other related risks like funding costs.
22. *The Economist*, October 8, 2011.
23. Italian banks did something similar when, a short time prior to Argentina's bankruptcy, sold Argentinean government bonds to their clients.
24. Euronews, June 14, 2012.
25. Bloomberg News, June 15, 2012.
26. Officials in Brussels said some euro 45 billion in Spanish banking assets would be transferred to it.
27. Other things equal, its chances for success will be greater if it has a life cycle of 7 or 8 years rather than being allowed to become another permanent bureaucracy.
28. UBS, CIO Year Ahead, December 2012.
29. At the end it proved to be only an illusion.

8 Italy Tries a U-Turn on the Road to Nowhere

8.1 Public Debt Is Mounting, Growth Is Elusive, and the Country Has Been 124 Days Without a Government

Italy's debt is "most unsustainable" said professor Johnson of MIT.[1] Italy's fiscal deficits are much smaller than Spain but its rollover problem is bigger, commented another expert. Both are the right opinions. With a public debt at 127 percent of GDP, Italy has loaded itself with red ink, but at least under the Monti government its annual deficit has been more contained.[2]

According to the International Monetary Fund's Fiscal Monitor, in 2012 Italy needed new financing equal to 28.7 percent of GDP to roll over maturing debt and pay the interest. This has been well above Spain's 20.9 percent of GDP which is also high. King size financial figures like those of Spain and Italy do not bode well for either country or for Euroland's future.

The large and growing public debt aside, Italy also suffers from a political instability which fell over the country like thick fog and it is not about to lift. Critics say that the people of Italy have decided to avoid reality. They are wrong. The problem is much deeper than that. While it is true that Italian voters have been spoiled by unsustainable promises made by populist politicians, Italy desperately needs

- Serious structural reforms in the labor market,
- Liberalization of professions and sectors of the economy, and
- A tough control of government expenditures specifically including the pension and health care system (see also Chapter 10).

Both the politicians and the public must understand the challenges confronting them. Since 1994, Italy's average growth in yearly GDP has been substantially below that of the Euroland (1.1 percent versus 1.9 percent). Italy's labor costs continue rising due to old and rigid labor laws. Also, since 1994 Italy's labor productivity has grown +0.4 percent per annum versus 1.4 percent in the Euroland.

As if all this was not enough, Italy's demographics look bad. People aged above 65 years represent 21 percent of the overall population (almost as high as in Japan). Still, the country is confronted with a high rate of unemployment. Unless these salient problems are fixed any government's (coalition or no coalition) political program will be a jump to the unknown. "Only an insane person can have the eagerness

Public Debt Dynamics of Europe and the US. DOI: http://dx.doi.org/10.1016/B978-0-12-420021-0.00008-7

to form a government in this moment," said Pierluigi Bersani, PD's leader, after he tried to form a government following the late March 2013 elections.[3]

After the Monti government fell in December 2012, the country was without a government for 124 days. Its 66th administration after the end of WWII, under Enrico Letta of the Partito Democratico (PD) is a coalition. Letta succeeded in forming it with the support of PD, Popolo della Liberta (PdL), and Monti's centrist Scelta Civica (SC). Italy today needs more reform than austerity, but "reform" is a word with many enemies, particularly in a coalition.

PD is a rally of center-left and different leftist groups with wide differences of opinion on how society should be structured and who should pay for what. It contains both old and young politicians but critics say that the majority of the Italian left finds it impossible to distance itself from nineteenth century socialist ideas.

PdL is an amalgamation of right-leaning populist elements frantically opposed to change. Their leader gives the example of low ethical standards: Affairisme, good living, no taxes, troubles with Italian justice, and obstruction to any measure which might remotely upset the status quo.

SC is a new party by Mario Monti. As head of the technocratic government which lasted a little over a year, Monti planned a new center-right political party with serious objectives and untainted leaders. But he miscalculated the resistance of the old political establishment which saw him as an apostate from a pure right-wing stance.

The new element in the vote of late March 2013 did not participate in the government, yet it was the favorite of about 25 percent of the Italian public: 1 out of 4 Italians voted for Beppe Grillo and his Five Star Movement (M5S). Political analysts compared Grillo to Robespierre, but without the Guillotine. He seeks to

- Sweep away Italy's old politicians, "those who have destroyed the country," and
- Put in their place a web-based direct democracy, a trend also rising in other European countries.

Beppe Grillo's movement seems to be solid based. But nothing is sure in politics. At the end of March 2013 a poll for *Corriere della Sera*, the foremost Milan newspaper, found that 77 percent of M5S voters were against supporting a government that included the traditional parties and for good reason.[4] One of the outstanding risks is the absence of assurance that old politicians who in the past fought one another tooth and nail will not show restraint. Most likely there will be political instability and different economic policies the subject of political quarrels.

The critics were right in their opinion. Instead of attacking the country's salient problems, the coalition government's program is full of compromises which include: repeal of the real estate tax (MUX) at the demand of PdL; tax credits for hiring companies to do government jobs, for which there is no money; complaints that the PD's social program is downplayed; and new rules for the reform of the tax system, for which there is no general agreement. All these issues are contentious and financing will prove difficult to find.

Ask Paris-based Organization for Economic Cooperation and Development (OECD, former Marshall Plan and now the club of supposedly "rich states") its opinion about all this and it will tell you that it is negative. In its latest survey of Italy, released the first days of May 2013, OECD warned that "Italy remains exposed to sudden changes in financial market sentiment." Therefore, it urges the new Italian government to make its priority:

- Large and sustained reductions in public debt, and
- Consolidate "gains" from structural reforms initiated by Mario Monti.

Sound advice, but are the politicians listening? and are they decided to act? The market thinks that Italy might fail on both scores as anger at austerity meets reform fatigue. In an article in the *Financial Times*, Wolfgang Munchau points out that under the *fiscal compact*

- Italy will be required to pay back debt worth more than 2 percent of GDP each year, and
- (To do so) Italy will need to run very large structural surpluses for almost a generation.[5]

Munchau aptly suggests that this is not going to happen; treaties are not going to be renegotiated and austerity is here to stay. Neither is it a positive fact that the coalition partners have other priorities in mind. A battle royal will take place around judicial reform. It will provoke debate but will not necessarily reach a conclusion. The PD maintains the judiciary functions are well balanced while the PdL intends to weaken the current status. They will fight it out.

Any analysis of the Italian political situation must account for the fact that, like Greece, Italy has far too many protected economic interests, from pharmacists to notaries and from energy suppliers to taxis. There are as well too many protected layers of government: provincial, regional, and local administrations. Most often than not, these duplicate rather than support and complement each other's activity.

All this is bad news indeed because Italy is third largest sovereign borrower in the world. When political uncertainty is raising its head, this is not made to provide comfort. If Greece needed nearly euro 300 billion for bailouts, Italy will require a couple of trillion, as the Italian economy is more than six times that of Greece. Here are the statistics:

- Greece, Ireland, and Portugal combined represent 6 percent of Euroland GDP.
- Italy alone stands at 17 percent of Euroland's GDP or over 26 percent together with Spain.

There is simply no money in Euroland's coffers, including ESM and EFSF, and the phantom of OMT, to pull the Italian economy out of the abyss. Officially its debt stands at euro 2.0 trillion, unofficially it is past euro 2.2 trillion including interest.[6] (The euro 2.0 trillion debt was made official in mid-December 2012; this is an understatement.)

8.2 Italian Premium and Spanish Premium

In 2011, while the Berlusconi government was in power, the ECB began buying Italian bonds only to have the then Italian prime minister abandon reform commitments within days. Though the Monti government held the line in its commitments, it could not do miracles. Berlusconi's unreliability (as well as that of other Club Med politicians) saw to it that Germany, Holland, and Finland are back-tracking on some promises for financial assistance, because they can see that they are confronted by a bottomless pit.

It is only normal that northern European governments, which use their taxpayers' money to help self-wounded southern European member states, want to see that their money is not thrown to the four winds by the profligates. And they expect their effort to be appreciated rather than damned by those receiving bailouts, which is by no means self-evident.

On August 24, 2012, the *Financial Times* published a letter signed by two professors at the Department of Economics of the University of Rome, stating that "The abnormal interest rate differentials between the Bund and long-term Italian and Spanish debt are unrelated to economic fundamentals."[7] This statement is undocumented, nationalistic, and highly biased: the professors are awfully wrong.

The pricing of 10-year Italian and Spanish bonds correlates with the two countries dismal economic fundamentals. Both are living beyond their means as evidenced by Italy's public debt which stands at over 123 percent of GDP, and by Spain's real estate boom and bust which left a huge black hole in the balance sheet of Spanish banks and of the Spanish sovereign.

Precisely because the Italian and Spanish fundamentals are so negative the market asks for an *Italian premium* and *Spanish premium* to buy their bonds. Towards the end of 2011, Italy had to pay nearly 8 percent interest to sell its 10-year sovereign bonds and Spain over 6 percent. The ECB's LTROs eased their plight (at the expense of German, Dutch, and other northern European taxpayers) and for both countries interest rates fell slightly below 4 percent—but not for long.

As for the objections raised by the Bundesbank in regard to ECB's extra curricula interventions (and not only by the Bundesbank) that the buying of government bonds by the ECB violates the no-bailout clause of the Lisbon Treaty as well as of its constitution and ultimately its independence—this is a fact. It is ridiculous to say that keeping within one's remit of responsibilities and of authority is: "unfounded, anachronistic, and fuels speculation." It would have been much better to think of the consequences of unsustainable debt before getting so deeply into it.

Even after the lavish LTRO of December 2011, a sort of present by Mario Draghi, as Italian and Spanish fundamentals did not improve (or, more precisely, they continued to deteriorate), the interest rate of their 20-year bond rose again to over 7 percent for Spain and over 6 percent for Italy. The second LTRO of February 2012 had a mild effect, but ECB's "unlimited" bond buying promised with OMT brought Italian and Spanish 10-year bond interest rates down to between 4 and 5 percent.

Instead of the ECB doing "what it takes" to flood the market with liquidity, it would have been much better if the Italian and Spanish governments were doing "what it takes" to improve their economic fundamentals. And if they were watching out to assure that CDS spreads don't hit nearly 550 for Italy and almost 500 for Spain (between July and September 2012).

In the stressed time in which we live, it is only normal that uncontrollable sovereign debts and other frivolities account for a great deal on the way investors evaluate a country's creditworthiness. As for the half-baked structural reforms done by the Monti government—because they have been watered down by labor unions and the public resistance to change—they invited speculators rather than being able to deter them.

True enough, before the financial crisis the spread between the Bunds in one side and the public debt of Italy, Spain, Portugal, and Greece in the other was small. But as subsequent events have demonstrated in the most dramatic way, the resilience of the euro was a chimera, though it did provide a window of opportunity for Mediterranean countries to redress their balance sheet. This, however, was not done. No surprise, therefore, that with the Monti government's measures Italian GDP contraction has been greater than forecast.

Made by well-known investment houses, fiscal sustainability analysis of the Italian economy shows that the country has problems that are different in nature but similar in magnitude to those of Spain. Therefore, mild commitments to consolidation can immediately translate into a pronounced increase of bond yields. Neither is a more rigorous change in economic policies producing instantaneous positive results.

Even if Rome succeeded in fully implementing significant fiscal reforms, a formerly profligate country is likely to remain for some time an unfavorable mix of high debt levels and low economic growth. Prudent governance requires that a person, a company, or a nation is not living on debt. Once this happens, getting out of the hole is not done (much less served) by denying realities.

Let's face it. Profligate habits change very slowly and there is as well a time lead to healing. As for "stringent fiscal policies" to which the two professors make reference, they are a mirage. Even with the right fiscal policies Italy barely, if at all, can have in the immediate future anything else than a small primary deficit. To the state budget, however, must be added the interest it has to pay for euro 2 trillion of public debt. May be the two professors would like to explain

- How this colossal sum of liabilities accumulated in the Italian economy, and
- By what sort of miracle it is going to disappear, other than a consistent and painful effort by the government and the citizen.

For their part, financial analysts recommend avoiding medium- to long-term Italian government bonds as well as those of Italian banks. According to Brussels-based European Banking Authority (EBA), the most exposed Italian credit institutions are Intesa San Paolo, owing euro 71 billion; Unicredit euro 49 billion; Monte dei Paschi euro 30 billion; UBI Unione di Banche Italiane euro 18 billion, and Banco Popolare euro 15 billion. Still Italian banks seem to fare better than the Spanish in terms of likely bankruptcies without massive bailout by Euroland money.

Last but not least, regarding the European integration process to which the two professors make reference it is not only "seriously at risk," it is in shambles. Be what may, European integration does not mean that people in so-called surplus countries would put at risk their savings and their pensions to pay the debts of profligates.

Last but not least, this perilous Italian economic situation cannot be handled by a government expected to be weaker than that of Monti who quit on December 22, 2012 right after the new stability pact and 2013 budget were voted by parliament. Economists are divided as to whether recent developments affect mainly Italian assets or have a Euroland-wide impact by way of lack of confidence.

8.3 The Public Debt Will Not Be Paid by Santa Klaus

Debt crises put extraordinary pressure on economies and big spenders eventually discover that there is a great difference between what they thought that is in their treasuries and what they find. For Euroland's peripheral countries cheap money, or at least access to it, has been one of the initial attractions of euro membership. This is no longer the case. And if Euroland provides rescue packages these are directed to sovereigns and banks rather than to the local citizen, except that the latter are invariably asked to honor the loans.

Spending more money than one has is irresponsible because it leads to stress and eventually to bankruptcy (if one is unable or unwilling to honor his debts). Sovereigns and their politicians have to be honest to themselves and to the common citizen. They need to figure out how to balance their budget, be truthful to the public when they make promises, and transparent about the reasons which lead to overspending and deficits.

To say the least, this is not the most common policy. "I just find it astonishing," said Paul O'Neil, the former US secretary of the Treasury, "that people find it unusual that I tell the truth."[8] Daniel Patrick Moynihan had told O'Neil about what 20 years on the US Senate Select Committee on Intelligence had taught him. This could be summed up in a single, sterling lesson: the threat to (US) national security is not from secrets revealed; it's from bad analysis—which is as well true with the management of finance and the economy.

"Where, Mr. Chairman, do you find a surplus?" US South Dakota Senator Ernest Hollings asked Alan Greenspan, then chairman of the Federal Reserve, "I find a deficit."[9] Asked in Italy, Greece, Portugal, Spain, and France the same question will receive precisely the same answer. In all countries the money governments spend comes from taxation and high spending means high taxes or debt to be paid by their citizens. Public debt is not automatically rolled over. Hence, it is a crucial subject to keep an eye on. Many economists believe that

- *If* Italy cannot rollover its debt,
- *Then* something big will happen to the euro.

According to some opinions this has been quite likely in the background of Mario Draghi's LTRO[10] which injected into the market a liquidity of over euro 1 trillion ($1.3 trillion), and greatly expanded the ECB's balance sheet. As a saying in Italy goes: "Every tramway conductor in Milan knows that one Mario made a present to the other Mario—and what a present."

The favored beneficiaries with LTRO have been, as expected, Italian and Spanish banks with French coming third. Beyond that, as sovereign debt exposures in ECB's books show, Italy has been the central bank's favored baby with bond purchases equal to the sum of the next three debtors. Published by the *Financial Times* in the wake of the second LTRO, ECB sovereign bond holdings are as follows:

• Italy, euro 100 billion
• Spain, euro 40 billion
• Greece, euro 40 billion
• Portugal, euro 20 billion
• Ireland, euro 20 billion.[11]

Periodic gifts to Italy through direct lending, LTRO and eventually OMT are a wrong-way policy, resulting in debt balances stagnating in ECB's books, have created a favorable but volatile environment for Italian debt. Favoritism has short legs when judged by the reaction to it by the global financial market, and its effect on the interest rate sovereigns must pay to sell their bonds.

The worst spike in Italian government bonds came in July 2011, under Silvio Berlusconi as the interest rate on 10-year Italian debt instruments demanded by the market jumped from 4.8 percent to over 6 percent (then slightly fell to 5.8 percent). This rise in bond yields had wider implications than those for the Italian treasury. An economy with

• High public debt,
• Moderate growth, and
• Light public finances

can fall off the cliff at no time. If yields could rise so quickly, threatening Italy's solvency within a week, then Spain and France may be in for rude surprises of their own. The German Santa Klaus should not be expected to behave as everybody's firefighter, in an environment where booming public debts are game changers which can lead to systemic crisis overnight.

Economists look at the uncontrollable rise in public debt and the market's reaction to it as existential for Euroland. Analysts say that countries with labor markets sclerotic and saddled with public sector debt well in excess of national income are the target of bond vigilantes. This is an answer to those who superficially believe that Italy shares none of the problems of other peripheral Euroland economies:

• Unlike Spain, it had no residential construction boom and bust.
• Unlike Greece, its government had not concealed its debts.[12]
• Unlike Ireland, its banks had not engaged in a wave of uncontrollable lending.

According to other opinions, it is Berlusconi's extravaganzas that focused attention on the actor and on the country, making it difficult to hide from view the financial precipice. But with the public debt burden of 127 percent of national income and with euro 900 billion ($1200 billion) of debt maturing over the next 5 years,[13]

Italy is vulnerable to a change in market sentiment and political risk could become the country's undoing.

A sudden anxiety was caused in early July 2012, in part by a quarrel between Silvio Berlusconi, the prime minister, and Giulio Tremonti, the finance minister who preached for an austerity budget. Berlusconi's verbal assault on Tremonti created much greater uncertainty than the usual one in Italian politics, as the government in Rome was split down the middle.

It may be that Berlusconi was waiting for a mid-year Santa Klaus to appear but, as this did not happen banks, who had lent big money to the Italian government got cold feet. French banks held almost $100 billion of Italian sovereign debt and had total exposures to Italy that were about four times larger. "If the crisis reaches Italy, then France will probably be part of the hurricane," said a senior Italian banker. American money market funds, a big source of short-term funding for European banks, were said to be trimming their exposures to French banks.[14]

Even so, Italian banks were confronted with a bigger problem than the French because, as part of the unholy sovereign bank togetherness and vicious cycle, they held more Italian government debt as a percentage of their assets than any other country's banks do of their domestic debt. That, too, caused investors to fret that by being already overloaded with Rome's bonds Italian banks drop out of future bond auctions.

Governments in dire straits like this resort to taxation, but Italian parliamentarians rejected raising top income tax rates and the introduction of a wealth tax.[15] It looked as if not only the Italian prime minister but also the parliamentarians were waiting for the Santa Klaus, while failing to understand that once the government loses credibility it can be difficult to regain it.

By mid-November 2011, Mario Monti and his technocrats were set to take office riding on the hopes of Italians that the new premier will pull the country out of the abyss. This prospect of an emergency government brought Italy's 10-year bond yields just below the 7 percent level, and also mellowed adverse reaction to some sort of mirror austerity. Even the CGIL, Italy's leftist and largest trade union federation, gave its cautious backing due to the emergency situation. But Susanna Camusso, CGIL secretary general, stated "We don't give blank checks to anybody."[16] The markets were not thrilled.

On December 28, 2011, Italy sold 6-month bonds at an interest rate just below 4 percent. But a day after its 10-year bonds sold at a 6.98 percent rate and, worst of all, the demand for them was thin. They were not covered. On January 5, 2012, Italian 10-year bond yields jumped back above the key 7 percent (to 7.06 percent) despite some relatively successful auctions by other Euroland members. Spanish 10-year yields also rose (to 5.64 percent) in a sign of continuing nervousness over the Club Med bond markets.

Another problem Italian and Spanish government bonds have been facing is that their average maturity is too short. It stands at 7.1 years for Italy (the same is true for France) and 6.2 years for Spain. By contrast the average maturity of British government debt is nearly double at 13.9 years.[17]

Critics suggest that there is nothing really unique in the Italian economic drama. Governments end up over borrowing, particularly when the money is cheap as was the case in the euro's first decade. Unwarranted borrowing is helped by the fact that living beyond one's means has become a western culture and new loans are "needed" to pay the bureaucrats and MPs as well as deliver the public goods people regard as their "endowments" for which they fight with

- Their ballot,
- Their rallies, and
- Their other antigovernment demonstrations.

In an article he published in the *Financial Times*, John Plender asks the question: "Has Italy finally turned the corner? Or could it go the way of Japan, with two lost decades in prospect?"[18] This question is most relevant because Japan has been the epitome of a formerly vibrant economy which fell in doldrums then drifted toward an eclipse. Chances are it will not be lonely in that road. This, however, is not inhibiting Italian parliamentarians from having their fun.

8.4 Italian Parliamentarians Could Ask: "Austerity? Which Austerity?"

Ancient Athens was a democracy small enough to assure that the participation of all free citizens in her political life was a reality, not merely a question of voting for a political representative, a deputy or middleman in the governance of the state. Indeed, practically every Athenian citizen could feel he had a good chance of playing an active part in conducting the city-state's affairs.

For a very large part of the population this is no truer today, under any stretch of the imagination, even of the regimes under which we live (at least in the West) are called "democracies." But neither are the frivolities of parliamentarians (and not only those of Silvio Berlusconi) made to inspire confidence in democratic processes and their ethical impact.

The deputies, parliamentarians, MPs, middlemen, call them as you please, have highjacked the state. They use its goodies and its levers to further their interests and profits. They may vote laws promoting austerity and a balanced budget, but these laws by no means put a break to *their* spending of public money. Democracy has turned into a regime of decadence, Roman decadence in the particular case we examine.

"Austerity? Which Austerity?" That's the way an October 5, 2012 article in the Neue Zürcher Zeitung (NZZ) described the world in which live Roman parliamentarians, as opposed to that of common citizen. Oysters, champagne, parties in historical costumes, luxury cars, and holidays on the Costa Smeralda—all at the cost of the taxpayer.

According to this article, what the September 2012 investigation of the Italian capital region Latium has shown is a decadence reminding on that in old Rome, which deeply shocked even those Italians used to scandals. Nick-named "Laziogate" this decadence brings to the reader's attention has become a shameful example of the greediness of a corrupt political caste.[19] More investigations are under way in Campania, Lombardy, Sicily, and other regions.

Moral risk of Costa Smeralda variety comes over and above (lesser) scandals justified by national interest, like weighting export tax reduction in a bid to help Fiat. Or for political interest, like the reduction of taxes announced on October 10, 2012 "because the Italian economy has improved,"[20] when everyone knows this is a hyperbole, and a purely political decision.[21]

Royally compensated members of parliament earning thousands of euros per month are adding to their gains through allegedly faked travel, other vouchers and party money. These funds are finding their way onto private accounts while the deputies have a high time, even if Italy is in the midst of a depression and common citizens suffer under steadily increasing taxes and growing unemployment.

After years of excesses and embarrassment under Silvio Berlusconi, the Italians seem to expect no more well-behaved politicians. It therefore comes as no surprise that the popular movement under Beppe Grillo, the comedian, has a high approval rate in polls. The way NZZ looks at it, Grillo and his Five Stars party present themselves as "antipolitician," though without offering solutions for Italy's problems other than jokes and laughs.

While the social responsibility of elected representatives has become questionable, that of some businessmen has not been much better. In early July 2011 Cesare Geronzi, one of Italy's most powerful financiers—former president of Banca di Roma, former chairman of Mediobanca, Italy's prime investment bank, and acting chairman of Assicurazioni Generali, Italy's largest insurer—was given a 4-year prison term in relation to the bankruptcy in 2012 of Cirio, a food company.[22]

A problem by no means native in Italy but widespread in the West is that leadership is in short supply both in politics and in business. Post mortem it can be said that while in office Mario Monti has tried to change that decadent culture, as he knows the issues, but this is a Herculian task, and making the parliamentarians vote against their interests is next to impossible. Hence he often had to give in to political pressures, even if he wanted to reform the country.

By the end of November 2012, political interests from Berlusconi's side saw to it that Monti's time run out, and who knows who will be the next politicians chosen to "lead" Italy or how stable the government(s) will be. This comes at the worst possible time as the country's growth outlook has worsened significantly while a thorough sovereign debt restructuring remains unlikely.

Experts say that the most likely scenario in Italy (as in Spain) is that government bond yields and CDS spreads will rise significantly and bank stocks will suffer renewed sell-offs unless the ECB uses its deep pockets—which means inorderly expanding the money supply and its own balance sheet. This will be negative for the euro. Market fears should not primarily be taken lightly because they are part of the worsening growth outlook for 2013.

Even if under Mario Draghi[23] the ECB has become an "easy money" central bank, Draghi has no dictatorial powers. In addition, 2013 is expected to be a volatility year; the American economy is unsettled with the delaying of entitlement cuts and debt ceiling negotiations; and the general political climate is expected to be more unstable—while the euro crisis will reignite if Spain and/or Italy apply for ESM/ECB/OMT bailout.

Finland and the Netherlands, not only Germany, have voiced strong opposition to using Euroland's bailout funds to buy Italian debt under current conditions. A Finnish official reiterated that eurozone purchases of Italian debt in the open market were like "shooting in the dark."[24] By contrast, Helsiniki was willing to consider a surgical operation of targeted interventions on the primary market when Italy auctions its bonds.

Moreover, to gain access to OMT funds Italy (like Spain) will have to ask ESM for support, and this means opening its front door to the Troika, as Greece and Portugal have done. The way to bet is that the center-left government which will take over in Rome will avoid doing so (dissuaded by the results of Troika's whereabouts in Greece) and instead choose bickering. It is not evident that a center-left government in Rome will be more austerity oriented than Rajoy's center-right government in Madrid.

Still another factor providing food for thought is that because Italy is a relatively major economy, and at the same time one of the most indebted in the world, its economic and financial problems are of totally different order than those of Greece and Portugal—hence more difficult. It has to raise euro 160 billion ($210 billion) in 2013, excluding treasury bills. Even a fully ratified and operational ESM would not be able to cope with both Spain and Italy if both are shut out of the markets.

The reader should as well notice that ECB/ESM money does not come as a gift, neither is it offered free of cost. Italy's 10-year borrowing costs remain below the 7 percent mark reached in 2011. By contrast, there has been a spike in short-term borrowing costs, which is important because when an economy is in trouble short-term borrowing is the gateway to the capital market. While in Rome parliamentarians seem to have a *dolce vita*, Italy's borrowing costs are all but unsustainable given the country's wilting economy.

Worse yet, Italy's average maturity of debts, like that of Spain, has fallen to a decade's low. This is partly due to the fact that given prevailing uncertainties the market would buy short durations, not long ones. Another adversity comes from the strategy of selling shorter dated bonds to cap interest payments. Such a strategy does not work when the short-term borrowing costs are moving north.

No matter which government has the reigns in Rome, it must develop alternative options. By end of July 2012, the Monti administration was issuing almost daily denials of an "emergency plan B" which included *inter alia* elimination of the December "13-month" payment to civil servants and pensioners. (This 13th month is still being paid in Spain, but not in Greece as the Troika pressed for its elimination.)

Critics have said that the best policy for Italians (and evidently for Spaniards) is to get their house in order prior to a Troika's intervention, and try to get by themselves their economy functioning again. Continuing to ask for help by other Euroland countries which have also their own problems to solve, is both ineffectual and a moral hazard.

Countries finding themselves in peril because of long-term mismanagement should have the courage to revert course and take the responsibility for ending their vicious cycle. Mario Monti has made some changes along that line. A pension reform which was part of the "Save Italy" program assists by extending working years. It also discourages early retirement and, quite importantly, it switches all workers into the contribution-based state pension (first introduced in 1995) which induces people to work longer.

Less successful has been the liberalization of hire-and-fire. Italian companies are reluctant to hire because obsolete labor laws see to it that workers are hard to fire. Employers face heavy penalties, reinstatement of sacked workers, and lengthy legal procedures under cases brought to labor courts. In early 2012, Monti's government tried to alter this regime but had to concede that judges could after all reinstate staff if they found that the economic grounds for dismissal were lacking— which practically means no easy firing, hence less hiring.[25]

A different way of looking at this issue is that while Monti's reforms have been in the right direction, they have encountered significant resistance and several of their provisions were altered or edited out. The status quo in Italy is made worse by the fact that between 2000 and 2012 labor costs increased by over 35 percent. The overall business climate is reflected in a ranking published at end of 2012 by the World Bank for the ease of doing business. This put Italy among the worst in Europe[26]—which does not discourage the Italian parliamentarians from having a ball.

8.5 Italy's Balancing Act and The Labor Unions' Rearguard Action

As in Greece, Spain, and Portugal, successive Italian governments gave a semblance of a balancing act between expenditures and receipts, but in reality they turned a blind eye every time the scales tipped towards more public debt. Critics say that this became a policy and over nearly three decades the mismanagement of the Italian economy has been a legion.

Politicians are masters in hiding the economic facts from the eyes of common citizens, placating social unrest with more entitlements. The sad fact is that central bankers helped them in doing so. Former ECB Board member Bini-Smaghi recently remarked that the crisis in Europe has shown that the political authorities and the markets find it difficult to understand each other. That's true and to a large measure it is due to opacity.

The markets have a good understanding of politics in Italy and more generally in Europe. They appreciate that fiscal action, even a mild one, comes only after a crisis; a fact demonstrated by the pressure on Italian bond yields. When this happened, Rome responded by amending its multi-year budget plans and pressuring the parliament to approve it.

According to anecdotal evidence in November 2011, after the Monti government was formed, it searched for an unorthodox way out of the huge public debt, though economists suggested that short of *deus ex machina* an orthodox way out of trillions of debt is chimera. From some quarters came the suggestion that the only effective solution would be taxing Italy's wealth (not just the wealthy). This wealth consisted of

- Euro 4.0 trillion in Real Estate,[27] and
- Euro 4.8 trillion in all other assets.

This total of euro 8.8 trillion is impressive. Those who looked at a policy of widespread wealth taxation as being the country's salvation added that *if* the sovereign collects between 20 and 25 percent of this wealth the catchment would free the Italian government of nearly all public debt. In effect, it would make Italy one of the richest among high indebted European sovereigns.

It needs no explaining that even the thought about this kind of wide-ranging tax on "patrimonio" raised ferocious opposition. There was as well a mare's nest of technical obstacles. For banks, there was no serious problem to find or at least estimate data on their wealth. Nonbanking companies might have had a harder time. But for private individuals nothing is updated in Italian government registers regarding their wealth.

Technical issues aside, there is no evidence (to my knowledge) that the Monti government bought or even seriously considered that idea. Instead, it worked on a euro 30 billion package of tax increases and spending cuts projected to cost each Italian household an average euro 1130 a year for the next 3 years. Labeled as a "sacrifice" the need for such a measure appeared to be understood but not accepted by the public. As opinion polls showed, in the eyes of most Italians the most effective cuts would be a reduction in the cost of politics. Nevertheless:

- *If* nothing was done to bring the huge Italian public debt under control,
- *Then* the prospect of a financial crisis in Euroland's third largest economy would have been a sword of Damocles.

This focused minds at the euro level of politics. In Italy, the Monti government took some measures, but not enough to force a pruning of the stable from waste and nepotism. In July 2012, the *New York Times* reported that "the island of Sicily employs 26,000 auxiliary forest rangers, while in the vast forest lands of British Columbia there are fewer than 1500."[28]

By contrast, tax evasion became a priority. Mid-November 2011, shortly after he took power, in a quest to stamp out tax evasion the Monti government had a new message: a tax-cheat self test. This came in form of web software enabling citizens to gauge whether their declared income is in line with what they spend yearly on housing, transport, education, vacations, and other pleasures.

This multiple-choice income test asks individuals to input their salaries and other earnings, then specify whether they own a house, car, or boat; live in a villa or studio; and spend money on a range of items from antiques to electrical appliances (among other queries). The tests' output is a green light if information on spending adds up with their income and a red light if it does not. Many Italians, however, have been skeptical about the web's contribution to swamp tax evasion, as allegedly more than 200,000 citizens who are declaring less than euro 20,000 a year own large boats, luxury cars or helicopters. (The total number of Italians declaring less than euro 20,000 per year income is estimated to be in the millions, according to data released in 2011 by Sogei, a company which provides IT systems support for the Italian Treasury).

Aside the close watch on income from taxation, in its balancing act Rome must use a sharp knife to cut down expenses. Entitlements and costs from soft labor laws is the name of the game, as defined by the Italian labor movement which wants "more nanny state."

In Italy, labor unions raised their head in the 1960s following in the steps of what has been known as "the Italian miracle." As the war damages were cleaned away and the economy improved, labor unions grew a voracious appetite for concessions by company managements and the government. And they got them.

A short while prior to the Monti government, Diego Della Valle, chief executive of Tod's, a luxury Italian leatherwear brand, blasted Italian politicians in the country's main newspapers. He called them incompetent and ill-prepared to deal with the crisis.[29] This is a widespread feeling among many people who want Italy to survive and get back on its feet.

Labor laws are so stiff and different labor benefits so out of line with a globalized economy that Sergio Marchionne, chief executive of Fiat, Italy's biggest private company, has several times threatened to make fewer cars in Italy and focus Fiat's investments in other countries. Inflexible labor laws make Italian produce uncompetitive. Fiat, Marchionne implied, cannot afford to operate in Italy in an environment of uncertainty that is so incongruous with the conditions that exist elsewhere.

Since he took office in November 2011 as Italy's prime minister, Mario Monti has been hailed as the savior of his country's economy. By mid-May 2012, however, half-way the Monti's tenure and after having thrust upon himself the responsibility for Italian economic resurgence, the die was not yet cast. The lukewarm support of political parties was one reason; the stranglehold on the Italian economy by labor unions, the other.

A widely accepted opinion by financial analysts has been that despite months of trying Mario Monti had still a mountain to climb. His challenge was to restart growth in spite of an economy which has been almost stagnant for more than the past decade, and in this effort he was supported neither by the old political establishment nor by the labor unions. The latter particularly objected to the crucial steps needed to reform Italy's two-tier labor market.

Contrary to the labor unions' obstination and to Berlusconi (himself a businessman) who wanted to bring down the government in the hope to re-become prime minister, Italian industry was favorable of Monti's measures. On May 24, 2012, Giorgio Squinzi, the president of Confindustria, the industrialists' federation, said that his members could not understand "why the state cannot save and make cuts the way businesses do and the way households do."[30] By that time, however, Monti was confronting three powerful opponents:

- The labor movement,[31]
- Populist big spending politicians, and
- An ambiguous stand by Italian public opinion.

To help the Italian industry become competitive in the global economy Monti tried to appease employers' fury about the difficulties of offloading a dud worker, as well as the threat of court action. He toyed with the right policy that firms should be able to sack staff without cause, so long as they give notice and a payoff linked to salary and service, but this was unpopular among featherbedding union leaders.

Monti did not ask as much as the preceding paragraph implies, but even what he asked was in large part refused by the labor unions which have a hold on Italy's Democratic Party (former socialists and communists who gave themselves a new name). The failure to see through a meaningful labor reform was followed by another, as by May 2012 Italy joined Spain in delaying its deficit reduction. This was a mistake betraying worries that the government was losing momentum.

As if populist politicians, regional bosses and labor unions were not enough, Italy's sprawling bureaucracy also worked against Mario Monti and his reforms. In a way quite similar to the challenge in Athens, the number of government bureaucrats in Rome is significant and they would fight tooth and nail to save their pay and pension from hefty haircut. Apart of holding the keys of government, bureaucrats are voters and the parties supporting Monti fell nervous, when the bureaucracy said "stop."[32]

It did not take so long for that reaction. Already in November 2011, a short time after the new government was in place, rumor had it that it was seeking some unorthodox way to confront the country's mammoth public debt and cuts were in the air. Then, when by April–May 2012 Italy needed to roll over some euro 300 billion ($390 billion) public resistance increased and Berlusconi's mouthpiece said on his master's behalf: "Basta! Italians cannot pay more" (for the debt). To which Monti rightfully answered that nobody else can be asked to pay, because it is not other people or nations who created the Italian public debt.

The way an article in the *Financial Times* had it, noting media reports that in theory a parliamentary stenographer could earn euro 250,000 a year—more than the king of Spain—James Waiston, political scientist at the American University of Rome, said the majority of Italians used to tolerate "legalized theft" because they hoped to benefit from it as well; adding that this is no longer true.[33]

8.6 It's Time to Stop Gambling and Deliver on Economic Change

If the Monti government wanted to cut the fat, and *if* it could do so without ferocious resistance by those benefiting from the status quo, *then* it should have started with the grossly overpaid politicians and parliamentarians.[34] While all politicians get much more money than what they contribute to the nation, individually and collectively, Italian MPs are the highest paid in Europe. Their *monthly* gross salaries of euro 11,300 reach euro 20,000 (!) ($26,000) when generous expenses and allowances for secretarial support are included. This compares badly with the less than euro 2000, in the average, for Italian citizens.

While such huge discrepancies were not corrected by downsizing the parliamentarians' pay, the good news associated to the Monti government has been that debt sustainability and solvency finally came center stage (where it should have been from the outset). The bad news was that, for evident reasons, the privileges of nonproductive parties like labor unions and plenty of others remained a sacred cow.

Analysts said that the government's Plan A involved a rather mild austerity until such time as the recipient economy miraculously recovers, and banks can safely write off their loans to sovereigns. But the fact Italian bond yields rose in an almost uninterrupted fashion during the first months of the Monti government called for an inevitable restructuring of the country's enormous and unsustainable debt burden—as well as for ECB support. Mario Draghi was ready to oblige.

Nothing has been learned from the lesson of the mid-1990s when Russian banks made their profits by buying high interest Russian government bonds till in August 1998 the Russian government, its bonds and the banks went bust. Entering in such a vicious cycle does nothing to improve the prospects of growth. To the contrary, it contributes to bigger deficits as more and more spending followed by more and more debt set in.

- The issue of national solvency goes beyond what governments owe, and
- Even worse, once a country enters the internal mill of high debt it will sweat a great deal to get out of it a whole.

In the general case, even the mild austerity measures coupled with an increase in taxation did not go down well with the Italian public. Critics said that waste and political nepotism is where the big cuts in Italian government expenditures should have started. While the outrageous Italian MPs' wages escaped unscathed (and minor adjustments have been "postponed") which is a scandal, the cuts fell on the common citizens who least could afford them.

Other critics were of the opinion that instead of focusing on well-rounded spending cuts, the Monti government put its emphasis on new taxes on "essentials," like an added *tax on gasoline*. Some 80 percent of Italy rolls on wheels. The special tax on gasoline was supposed to bring-in plenty of money, but it led to widespread strikes, from truckers in auto routes to Roman taxis.

There have been as well measures along the usual battle-cry of the left "Sac the Rich" (which were expected) and some unexpected stakes in high gambling. No fault of Monti *per se*, to ease budgetary constraints in their fiefs bureaucrats gambled on derivative financial instruments. They lost the big way and left the taxpayer to pay for the damages.

Emulating what has happened in the United States, Italian schools and municipalities let themselves being taken to the cleaners by investment banks. Some are biting back. An example is the City of Milan which went to court. On April 18, 2012 it settled with a group of banks, which had sold it toxic waste associated to derivative products, for the sum of $623 million (euro 480 million). City authorities congratulated themselves but refused to give details.

The City of Milan won against JPMorgan, Deutsche Bank, UBS, and Depfa, but a month earlier Italy Inc. had to pay 550 percent as much money as Milan recovered to Morgan Stanley, the investment bank: $3.4 billion (euro 2.6 billion) for the privilege to exit derivative contracts. It is not clear who were the bureaucrats, and politicians covering them, who signed such disastrous derivative contracts, but that sort of losses don't come out of the blue. (On March 16, 2012 Bloomberg News announced the $3.4 billion settlement.)

This is not the first time that sovereigns have been speculating with highly risky derivative financial instruments, and Italy has a long tradition in derivatives-related losses. Bureaucrats should stop paying financial wizards which they are not. If they do so, then *they*—not the taxpayer—should be condemned to pay the damages.

Lotteries might make a very few people rich, but gambling is not an admissible behavior for sovereigns. Italy has enough woes with red ink from budgetary deficits. On a percentage basis of outstanding government debt securities in Euroland, Italy stands way ahead with over 27 percent of the total, followed by Germany (a much bigger economy) with 23 percent and France (with an economy roughly comparable to Italy) with 21 percent. There is simply no reason to bet the remaining furniture in the house with risky derivatives.

Still, the real down-to-earth dilemma confronting the Monti government, in its 13 months in power, has been whether to accept a compromise in labor reform. A much watered down "reform" left those who already have a job nearly unchallenged with their privileges. By consequence it perpetuated the frustration of young people out of school who find great difficulty in carving out a job.

In a way quite similar to what has happened in Athens with the taxi drivers who obliged George Papandreou Jr. (the then prime minister) to move backwards, the taxi drivers of Rome had their way. The government backed down and some of its proposed reforms were put in the time closet to wait for better times, or for the next and bigger crisis.

Both in Greece and in Italy, the decision on whether reform should move forward or backward was left to the taxi drivers. Yet this is an issue which can make or break a government, and the national economy with it. The damage which has been done is nicely expressed by an internaut who asked the question: "What's the difference between the Italian economy and the stricken cruiser?" He answered it by saying: "None. The bottoms dropped out of both."

When the bottom drops out, the government's authority wanes. This is documented by the concessions Mario Monti made on April 4, 2012 to the center-left Democratic party[35] and labor unions. Monti needed the Democratic party's support for a parliamentary majority, but financial analysts said markets would react badly to signs of waning government resolve to deal with Italy's deep-rooted economic problems. As for Silvio Berlusconi he did his best to contribute to political instability.

Moreover, despite concessions by the Monti government remained doubtful whether the watering down of reforms will be sufficient to persuade the more militant unions, led by CGIL, to accept what was finally decided as *fait accompli* rather than betting on the next Italian government to cancel the deal. To a growing body of opinion, the revised restructuring plan demonstrated

- The government's readiness to compromise, and
- The prime minister's recognition that he cannot risk losing the support of the Democratic party.

Neither were all adverse reactions to the government's initiatives of an economic and financial nature. One of them concerned a new electoral law which both Mario Monti and Giorgio Napolitano, the head of state, have urged the parties to approve. The law projected an electoral system that would give a new government the legitimacy and strength it needs to keep Italy's reform agenda on track.

Many Italians saw the old electoral law as incubating and preserving a self-serving parliamentary system based on cronyism by denying the citizens the right to vote for individual candidates on party lists. Even Silvio Berlusconi, under whose center-right government the law was passed in 2005, admitted it was "pig-shit."[36]

Cronyism, however, had not become obsolete and the main Italian parties wrangled for months over the shape of a new law. Tensions also rose as a Senate committee prepared to start the formal legislative process. This is typical of politicians. The issue on which most of them agree is to disagree.

Mario Monti and his government quit shortly before Christmas 2012. Public opinion polls have shown that his 13 months record was not appreciated by the Italian electorate. This is totally unfair. Monti contemplated leading a coalition of small center-right parties in the February 2013 elections (liberals, republicans, and remnants of Christian democrats) and the polls have shown that he could expect less than 15 percent of the public vote.

Worse yet, if the opinion polls are to be trusted, 60 percent of Italians did not want him to lead the next government. By all evidence the main reasons were higher taxes and the mild austerity. Critics as well said that at the end of the day there were no reasons why after raising taxes and reducing social services the Monti government should be popular with the electorate.

To say the least, this is high handed. Monti did what he had to do, given Italy's desperate debt situation, albeit in a mild way. Though in a little over a year he could not, and did not, revolutionize the system, he pulled Italy back from the precipice and gave it a little more time. On the other hand, with the huge public debt overhang he did not improve the debt to GDP ratio—which will haunt the next government and bring Italy to bankruptcy if it is left unattended.

8.7 Wrong-Way Policies Lead to Beleaguered Governments

If the ratio of a country's public debt-to-gross domestic product continues to rise, the debt dynamics becomes unsustainable. Debt and the monetary base cannot increase forever. This is the philosophy of the cancer cell. The bubble will explode and when this happens the country is insolvent. The debt ratio is essentially defined by four variables:

- Public debt to GDP ratio (123 percent for Italy),
- Interest costs of the piling up debt,

- Primary fiscal balance, excluding interest payments, and
- Nominal economic growth of the country.

These four variables plus information on political development (particularly political stability) are used by bankers and speculators to make up their mind about exposure to a country's economy. Estimates and assumptions are typically tuned towards providing foresight to the most vital question: *What is next*—because when the system defined by these variables turns negative, everybody tries to get out from the same door.

Anecdotal evidence suggests that in the second quarter of 2012 Goldman Sachs reduced exposure to Italy by 92 percent. Other investment banks followed a similar course, even if they retained a higher level than Goldman. The way analysts saw the four variables develop there is, so to speak, an inverse "Italian miracle" created by an aggregation of problems. No Italian government led to a new renaissance. Instead, the new reality has been renewed economic pressures on Italy, including

- A move away from a consolidation and restructuring program,
- Political contesting of unstable governments, which are losing power, and
- The specter of a possible Greek exit from the euro, which could well lead to massive deposit flight in Italy.

Monti's relatively modest austerity plan has encountered too much resistance, and absence of true structural changes led several experts to the belief that Italy will eventually revert to its pre-euro model—which involves acceptance of higher inflation, stronger progression of unit labor costs, and low but steady devaluation of its own currency. This is the scenario to be expected, even if the current priority still is that of getting taxpayers money from other countries in Euroland via the ECB, EFSF, and ESM (the Santa Klaus connection).

The world has also seen the prime minister of a country of 55 million people going hat-in-hand to the capital of a country of 4.5 million people (Finland) to ask for money, or at least smooth Finnish opposition to the voracious appetite of Italy (as well as of Spain) for Euroland funds. Helsinki was one of three Euroland capitals Mario Monti visited in July 2012 to lobby support for his country. Not unexpectedly, he did not get what he wanted.

The visit to Helsinki was ill-timed because during the June 28/29, 2012 Brussels "summit" Mario Monti, François Hollande, and Mariano Rajoy had trapped a tired, lonely fighter, Angela Merkel, into concessions.[37] The Finns evidently knew of it and they were increasingly worried about bailing out other countries. Bailout fatigue has finally set in Euroland. A July 2012 poll by a Finnish national broadcaster indicated 66 percent of Finns want their country to avoid shouldering more financial responsibility, even if "it would save the euro."

As far as the sorry state of the Italian economy is concerned, this is not the Finns', Dutch', or Germans' doing. Every Italian government and labor union leadership helped make the mess, and it was the Italians' responsibility to fix it. Of course, an economy under fiscal adjustment is expected to contract. It did so by about −1.8 percent in 2012, and 2013 is not likely to see even modest growth given the global economy's doldrums, remnants of fiscal austerity, and weak exports—even if Italy still has strengths:

- Lack of a deflating housing bubble, and
- A strong private sector balance sheet.

Both bullets are good news, but the bad news is overwhelming. The *fiscal reform* has been contested by those who like to live in the status quo, because it focused on a spending review aimed at introducing national standards for governmental services, questioned the numbers of successive administration levels and tried to curve excessive spending. As for privatizations, primarily projected on the municipal level, they have been minor and protracted.

Moreover, there is the risk of contagion from Greece and from Spain while essentially funding markets are more or less closed for Italian banks. Like the Spanish financial institutions, Italian banks are largely dependent on central bank liquidity and eased repo collateral standards, but this patched-up "solution" may be for an emergency but not as longer term policy.

Some Italian friends told that the ECB will do what it takes to support Italy "because the Germans like the euro." Those who think the common currency will make it are mostly relying on the ECB eventually stepping in to wipe out the debts of Italy and Spain. This is fantasy rather than real life. A country chronically supported by others is one which has already fallen by the wayside.

That's pity for Italy, and while the country's politicians are responsible for what has been happening the attitude of the Italian public towards the EU is also changing. In early August 2012, a poll by Pew Research Center found that just 59 percent favored European unity, against 68 percent in Germany. The single currency was backed by just 30 percent in Italy, far below the 46 percent in Greece.[38]

Going back for a moment to the euro's preliminaries, the Prodi government was wrong in its rush to join the euro against the advice of the then governor of the Bank of Italy that the country was not ready for it. Like Athens, Rome lost an opportunity to establish for itself and its banks the needed financial discipline. Among them, Italian banks have borrowed euro 255 billion,[39] and used the lion's share of it to buy the Italian government's bonds.

The events which followed the fall of the Monti government prove that Jim O'Neil, a senior executive of Goldman Sachs, was right when he said in an interview by CBB, on October 7, 2011, that: "It is time to ring-fence Italy and Spain. With their failure banks everywhere will be at risk"; adding that: "The Italian economy is more than 6 times bigger than the Greek," hence measures taken by the Troika in Athens will not work in Rome. (The measures taken by the Troika in Athens did not work either).

Both the size of the Italian economy and stratospheric level of its debt underline the enormous scale of the problem. According to funding experts, there is no experience in dealing with an amount of debt as large as Italy. Therefore the idea of using the ESM and EFSF to offer even partial insurance against the default of Italy looks superficial at least.

So is another concept used as trial balloon: creating a two-tier market for government debt. Either and both approaches introduce the possibility of default by sovereigns without eliminating it. There is a second irony, this one connected to the announced eventual "unlimited" sovereign bond purchases by the ECB through OMT. This kind of supposedly "unlimited" intervention will ruin ESM and enrich the speculators. From a funding perspective, the ECB can do little to help Italy directly because it is legally forbidden from buying in primary markets at auctions.

This leaves only one solution that Italy itself—and by this I mean both the Italian public and the politicians—decide that enough is enough, and take their own future in their hands. This means to show courage, discipline, competence, and leadership to help rebuild confidence to the Italian economy. They should start by fixing the Italian economy and follow up by mending the broken relationship between electors and politicians.

In economic terms, the priority must be to implement growth-promoting structural reforms, which means reforming the Italian labor market, eliminating the elements of both excessive protection and extreme insecurity. This would require everyone's cooperation, the labor unions included. As this chapter has documented, Italy is a basket case of European labor relations. It is saddled with

- Not-so-efficient manufacturers,
- Unyielding labor bosses, and
- A sclerotic service sector whose high costs make Italian exports uncompetitive.

Furthermore, *internal devaluation*, as in Latvia, could improve competitiveness. To the contrary, should the reform process and austerity measures initiated by the Monti government be abandoned public debt will surely zoom to even more unsustainable levels.

This is precisely what has taken place. On July 16, 2013, it was officially announced that Italy's public debt hit $2,720,000,000,000 (euro 2.09 trillion). This compares very badly with the official debt level of euro 2.0 trillion when the latest (mis)government took office. Notice that the Enrico Letta administration, a right-to-left wing unlikely symbiosis, was running the Italian Republic for about a month before these numbers were revealed—and in that month it seems to have squandered (or at least contabilized) a new public deficit of euro 92.3 billion.[40]

Let's face it. Like those of France, Spain, Portugal, Greece, and plenty of others, Italy's budget deficits are not under control. By consequence the public debt burden continues to rise, past the 130 percent of GDP[41]—while the GDP stubbornly refuses to grow. In 2013, in real terms Italian GDP will be barely above the level of 1999, the year when (by using the trickery of derivatives) Italy joined the euro. Over 13 years of euro membership:

- Labor productivity has hardly shown an improvement, and
- Competitiveness has steadily deteriorated against other countries, particularly Germany.[42]

While constitutional reform is indeed necessary, the amount of politicking associated to it distracts attention from the urgent need to restructure Italy's distressed and stagnant economy—evidently including broad liberalization and truly competitive labor market reforms beyond what the Monti technocrat government was able to pass (due to political opposition). But

- Professional liberalization would upset the right wing's PdL[43] and its middle-class electorate, and
- Labor market restructuring is fiercely resisted by the trade unions; therefore by the center-left PD.

This curious alliance of embedded left-right interests against change has given the government its split personality. The big spenders who dominated Italian politics since the 1960s are still in key positions, inefficiency is all over the place, and the public debt continues its rise to the starts. That's not all.

Critics say that prior to the Letta government, the Italian public debt was euro 2.5 trillion, well above the official version of euro 2.0 trillion. The difference was hidden (and continues being hidden) through derivative financial instruments—a policy which started in 1998 and, as briefly stated, aimed to qualify Italy for joining the euro (see the Case Study and Conclusions and Ineptocracy, Trickery and Politics: Euroland and the Italian Way). It will be a mistake to think that the finances of other countries, for instance France, are much better. Mountains of public and of private debt have been the (sad) destiny western societies worked out for themselves—to their sorrow.

End Notes

1. Bloomberg News, September 9, 2012.
2. The primary budget (before debt interest is counted) has shown a small positive balance, but the national budget turned negative adding to the public debt once the interest on public debt was added.
3. *Financial Times*, March 28, 2013.
4. *The Economist*, March 23, 2013.
5. *Financial Times*, May 6, 2013.
6. As of September 2012.
7. Leonardo Becchetti and Giancarlo Marini.
8. Suskind R. The price of loyalty. New York: Simon & Schuster; 2004.
9. *Idem*.
10. Chorafas DN. Breaking up the euro. The end of a common currency. New York: Palgrave/Macmillan; 2013.
11. *Financial Times*, February 22, 2012.
12. Which, according to other sources, is a doubtful statement.
13. The amount due by Italy rises to euro 1200 billion ($1575 billion) if interest was added.
14. *The Economist*, July 16, 2011.
15. Finally, amid scuffles between police and protesters, Rome's parliament passed a much-amended austerity budget worth euro 54 billion ($74 billion). It also emerged that, allegedly, Silvio Berlusconi's government was peddling its debt to Chinese sovereign-wealth funds.
16. *Financial Times*, November 14, 2011.

17. *Financial Times*, February 15, 2012.
18. *Financial Times*, March 14, 2012.
19. Which is by no means an exclusively Italian case. It can be found in many states; Rome is only taken as an example.
20. Bloomberg News, October 24, 2012.
21. It would be interesting to see if sometime in 2013 Italy asks ECB for OMT's life saver funds.
22. Geronzi was convicted of fraud in a separate case in 2006, but won an appeal.
23. On November 2, 2011, his first day in office, Draghi bought Italian government bonds, then engaged in QE under a variety of names: LTRO I, LTRO II, and OMT.
24. *Financial Times*, July 26, 2012.
25. To appreciate the impact of this change, the reader should know that by large majority Italian judges are left-leaning—a legacy from the time when Palmiro Togliati, boss of the Communist Party, was Minister of Justice in the immediate post-WWII Italian government.
26. Among 185 countries, it came 73. In enforcing contracts, it ranked an astonishing 160. *The Economist*, December 8, 2012.
27. This is an estimate because the Italian cadaster is neither updated nor precise.
28. Bloomberg Businessweek, September 24–30, 2012.
29. *The Economist*, October 8, 2011.
30. *The Economist*, June 2, 2012.
31. Which acted against its best interest, particularly those of unemployed young workers.
32. Italian trade unions are especially strong in the public sector.
33. *Financial Times*, January 6, 2012.
34. See also in Section 8.4 the reference to overpaid parliamentary secretaries.
35. As already mentioned, this label is a misnomer because the party has been the result of the merger of Italy's Communist Party and Socialist Party.
36. *Financial Times*, August 29, 2012.
37. Chorafas DN. Breaking up the euro. The end of a common currency. New York: Palgrave/Macmillan; 2013.
38. *The Economist*, August 11, 2012.
39. *Le Canard Enchaine*, April 11, 2012.
40. Of this amount, euro 40 billion was a loan taken just before Letta took office to pay Italian SMEs which worked for the government but did not receive the money due to them. Half of that loan was dated for 2013 and the other half was written as a loan for 2014—which is creative accounting.
41. By the end of 2013.
42. *The Economist*, July 20, 2013.
43. The Berlusconi clan.

9 France Is Not Italy. True or False?

9.1 The French Balancing Act

Like other Western European countries, after the end of World War II, France experienced nearly 30 years of growth and low unemployment. These so-called *trente glorieuse* approached an end with the oil shocks of the 1970s and the reversal started with the election of François Mitterrand in 1980.[1] Since then, France has spent 33 years moving backward or sideways.

During the first half-dozen years of the 1980s, the French economic model has been characterized by a rather high inflation and of currency devaluation,[2] while growth stalled and unemployment increased. This came as a result of Mitterrand's effort to reignite the economy through an expansive (and expensive) fiscal and monetary policy. With the socialist experiment's failure:

- French companies relocated,
- Unemployment rose, and
- The trade balance (current account) deteriorated.

Another false step was that of renationalizations[3] at the cost of a lot of public money. Then the Mitterrand government made a U-turn. It adopted the German model of a strong currency. France emulated its eastern neighbor trying to keep steady the exchange rate of the franc to the German mark, thereby laying a foundation of the euro a decade and a half down the line.

The economic disasters which accompanied the first years of his presidency taught Mitterrand that a debt-ridden France is in no position to dictate to Germany. At best it can influence, but only if his government gains credibility by pushing ahead with badly needed reforms. Reforms however were not forthcoming. Mitterrand and his socialists remained deliberately vague over how they will prune the country's public accounts while at the same time increasing the entitlements to keep alive the French model of an ever-expanding nanny state.

The current account balance also suffered as imports continued being in excess of exports. The 12 years of the Jacques Chirac presidency, which followed Mitterrand's 14, were just as dull; a do-nothing epoch. The next 5 years of Nicolas Sarkozy presidency were better, albeit not too different, while the public debt reached for the stars.

With the socialists back to power in 2012, François Hollande, the new president, confronted the accumulation of more than three decades of mistakes—reflected in a mountain of public debt and fiscal imbalance—while trying to defer his own reforms. He also attempted to kill two birds with one stone. On the one side, his

Public Debt Dynamics of Europe and the US. DOI: http://dx.doi.org/10.1016/B978-0-12-420021-0.00009-9

first words on taking office were that "public debt is an enemy of the country," and on the other he assured his electorate that there would be no cuts to family allowances, health care, pensions, and social services.

These have been political promises, and promises oblige only those listening to them, according to Charles Pasqua, another French politician. The budgetary deficits remained, and La Cour des Comptes (the French government's state auditor) said that the Hollande administration needed to find an extra euro 20 billion ($26 billion) in savings each year just to stick to deficit targets. That was before adding on the spending pledges Hollande made on the campaign trail which were not negligible.

Centuries ago France had ministers of finance renown for budgetary discipline and measures taken to promote the country's economy. Under the reign of Louis XIII, Colbert has left a long record of successful economic and budgetary policies, followed up by Cardinal Mazarin, his successor. These prudent fiscal policies changed, and the debt culture took over as a result of financing the never ending wars of Louis XIV. By the time his long reign ended, the French government was on the brink of its third bankruptcy in less than a century.

History provides valuable insight. Louis XIV, the sun king of France whose famous dictum was "L'Etat c'est moi" (I am the state), died in 1715. Hardly was he in his grave that it was revealed the finances of the country were in a state of utmost disorder. He was criticized as a profuse and corrupt monarch who brought the country to the verge of ruin, his profusion and corruption imitated by almost every functionary. The national debt amounted to 3 billion livres, a high multiple of the kingdom's GDP.

The state revenues, at that time, amounted to 145 million livres and the government expenses to 142 million, leaving nearly nothing to pay the interest upon the 3 billion livres public debt. Asked by the Duke d'Orlean, the Regent, for his advice the Duke de St. Simon was of the opinion to declare national bankruptcy,[4] but other notables opposed this solution. In the middle of the chaos stepped John Law, later on of Mississippi Bubble fame, who offered two memorials to the regent setting forth the evils that had befallen France, owing to an insufficient currency at different time depreciated.

May be, but only may be, we are witnessing a repetition of that epoch. Balancing the books is becoming harder as growth disappoints and another of Hollande's campaign pledges, to twist Angela Merkel's hands and revise the *fiscal compact* to his favors, fell in a vacuum. Merkel, who had backed Sarkozy's campaign, said she will welcome Hollande "with open arms" but also pointed out to this French president and everyone else that a renegotiation of the European Unions' *fiscal compact* "is not up for discussion."

Together with Mario Monti of Italy and Mariano Rajoy of Spain, Hollande attempted the trick of the June 28/29, 2012 Brussels "Summit",[5] but the trick of overwhelming Merkel failed. Supporting Italy and Spain in their call for more taxpayers money coupled with rather lousy fiscal consolidation targets was a long shot, and it proved to be a nonstarter. Hollande was left with the classical approach of putting the government's hand in the French retirees' pockets and cutting their pensions by 10 percent—as a start.

In fact, there is no reason to believe that *even if* France, Italy, and Spain were ever getting all the money they wanted from Germany and the rest of Euroland, this would have provided anything more than temporary relief. A weak credit and export environment coupled with inordinate public spending, an imports over exports policy and subdued public confidence, are keeping economic growth at low level and negatively affects employment.

A lesser known irony of Euroland's debt crisis is that even if their fiscal deficits have a ball and growth is sluggish, the Lisbon Treaty obliges France, Italy, and Spain to keep on financing Euroland. This is also true of any other of its member states including Ireland, Portugal, and Greece which are on bailouts. Taking as an example the initial guarantors of EFSF, the top member countries' shares of guarantees are:

- 27.1 percent for Germany
- 20.4 percent for France
- 17.9 percent for Italy
- 11.9 percent for Spain

But *if* Spain and Italy request financial support, *then* the share of EFSF guarantees for each one of the other members significantly increases with the lion's share of contributions falling on Germany and France:

- 42.9 percent for Germany
- 32.2 percent for France

Correspondingly, the share of Hollande goes to 9.0 percent from an initial guarantee of 5.7 percent; of Belgium to 5.5 percent from 3.5 percent; of Austria to 4.4 percent from 2.8 percent; and of Finland to 2.8 percent from 1.8 percent. No wonder that countries such as the Netherlands and Finland are so careful about both their commitments and the use being done of their money. Now think what would be happening in contributions if France was asking Euroland for financial support.

If one studies the statistics, one might come to the conclusion that this may not be so unthinkable. From 2000 to 2012, unit labor costs in France increased nearly 30 percent.[6] The unemployment rate fluctuated, and in 2012, it crossed the 10 percent level from slightly over 8 percent in 2000. Government spending as percent of GDP is over 56 percent. The budget deficit has been nearly 5 percent in 2012 (it was over 7 percent in 2009). The current account balance steadily moved south, from +2.5 percent of GDP in 2000 to −2.5 percent in 2012. And GDP growth while somewhat positive in 2012 is projected at −0.5 percent in 2013.

Worse yet, France has been among the more reluctant and slower Euroland countries to reform its labor market, pension, social security, and welfare. It largely failed to undertake the radical shake-ups that happened in Holland, Scandinavia, and Britain during the 1980s and 1990s and in Germany in the 2000s. In addition, as the IMF pointed out, it is still being left behind even by the mild reformers in Italy and Spain.

An evident consequence is a pronounced erosion of competitiveness particularly compared to Germany. The French economy has been deteriorating for many years, and this became fully obvious with the euro which precludes the usual policy of devaluation. Ever since the beginning of the Mitterrand presidency, France came to rely heavily on public spending for growth.

Critics say that French citizens reap too many benefits from the nanny state which are unaffordable and unsustainable. Furthermore, France has 90 civil servants for every 1000 inhabitants, compared with just 50 in Germany,[7] a number which adds up to a large and growing 22 percent of the workforce. France also showers its immigrant population from its former colonies with way too many free services and goodies negatively affecting its budget.

9.2 Creative Destruction and the Limits of Socialist Policies

Like Britain, France is still dominated by the mindset of a world power with neither the reach nor the means of being one. But unlike the British, the French political system tends to produce politicians who are all of a type. The fable of the difference between "home de gauche" and "homme de droite" is just that a fable, while few French political leaders have business or international experience, or speak foreign languages.

Many French political leaders have been graduates of one of the *grandes ecoles*,[8] though Nicolas Sarkozy was an exception. Others, like Hollande, are *énarques* which simply means that they attended ENA (Ecole National d'Administration[9]), which is widely regarded as the high temple of bureaucracy.

A basic characteristic shared by all bureaucrats is that they take no initiative for fear of making mistakes. This is hardly what France needs at this moment. Maurice Levy, the CEO of Publicis, a large public relations firm, argues that a leader who wants to reform France needs two things, a real sense of crisis and balls, and implies that Hollande lacks both.[10]

"Man's character is his daemon, his destiny," wrote Heraclite, the ancient Greek philosopher, who searched for knowledge and believed in a world of "becoming," or eternal change.[11] Change through creative destruction has been the real power of the West, and of capitalism. But after WWII, the process of creative destruction in the West has ebbed, because political leaders supposed to promote it have not been up to the standard it requires.

Economists say that France's fragility directly affects the euro crisis. Moreover, France is no more in position to provide a counterweight to other big nations in the EU. Not only it has one of the largest debt and deficit ratios among Europe's higher credit rated countries, but also its banks are dangerously exposed to Club Med countries. Mid-October 2011 in a summit in Berlin, a journalist from *Le Monde*, the Paris newspaper, asked Angela Merkel whether she was in a partnership of equals with Nicolas Sarkozy, "given that France and its banks have been attacked by the markets." There was no reply.[12]

The name of the French president has changed, but the problems are roughly the same. If anything they have grown worse, as documented by the pitiful request to be excused for the colonization of Algeria by the French. Hollande made this plea to be excused on December 19, 2012 in his address to the Algerian parliament. Colonization, the French president said, was unjust and led to plenty of suffering for Algerians.

If this mea culpa was so important for good behavior in politics, I would like to see Recep Tayyib Erdogan present his excuses to the Greeks for nearly 400 years of colonization; David Cameron to the Indians; Mariano Rajoy to the Mexicans, Columbians, Peruvians, and so on—a list without end. By all likelihood, none of them will admit that his country has been the author of a mischief.

Hollande's unfortunate (and bad taste) expression of sorrow and his asking the Algerians for redemption of French "sins" was just an admission of weakness. Let's face it; unless France restores its economic strength and its self-esteem (the former is prerequisite to the latter), it will be an enfeebled partner for Germany at a time when the two countries should urgently seek to work through their (many) disagreements. If France and Germany cannot settle on a well-rounded deal for the euro, it will be useless to talk about:

- Stability for the common currency, and
- Need to focus on new innovating companies, which in Euroland are rather rare.

The rebirth of economic strength, like that of self-esteem, has prerequisites. Neither will come out of apologies and of the status quo, even if politicians feel more comfortable by keeping things as usual and hiding the facts under the carpet. Living with crumbling structures is, however, dangerous. Once authority falls in ruins, raising it again is a Herculean task.

One of the most daunting decisions confronting Hollande and his socialists is to decide whether France will continue being the waste basket for *illegals*. On May 2, 2012, just prior to the presidential elections, during the televised Sarkozy—Hollande debate it was revealed that 180,000 *legal* immigrants come to France every year, the lion's share from North Africa and Sub-Saharan Africa. Anecdotal evidence suggests that the *illegals* are probably double that number. By contrast, what France needs to promote its economy is well-educated immigrants, and of them only 5000 came to live in the country during the last decade.

Another daunting question for Hollande and his team is how to bend the curve of ever-growing *entitlements* (Section 9.4); still another is the two-edged sword of employment and the financial support the French government (like all sovereigns) gives to selected industries. The latter two issues correlate among themselves and with the popularity of the country's chief executive in the polls.

With growth stalled and unemployment rising to nearly 11 percent of the workforce, by January 2013 Hollande's approval ratings languish at about 35 percent versus the 55 percent he had in May 2012 when elected president. Critics say that this was unavoidable because he lacks credibility and is leading France toward a dead end in economic and industrial development.

Hollande answers his critics by saying that thanks to him Euroland had been "safeguarded" by action taken since he came to power, and now he is set at a single goal: inverting the unemployment curve within a year. That is unlikely even if he abandons his pledge for a balanced budget and starts hiring hundreds of thousands of bureaucrats.

Apart from radically reforming the French labor market, cutting social net costs and introducing flexibility in business, the French socialist president needs to decide behind which industries will thrust the power of the state in economic and financial terms. France is not Spain, where in January 2013 general unemployment hit 26.5 percent and youth unemployment a dramatic 56.6 percent. Still some of the decisions to be made resemble those of Spain and Italy. Should the government give preference to:

- The old dying smokestack industries?
- Or, the new ones which are the future?

Neither France nor any other western nation has the money to do everything at the same time. Choices are necessary, and they are both hard and urgent. No excuses should be found for delaying decisions and actions. Hollande's socialists hold power at all levels, from the Senate and National Assembly down to the Regions and other local government. As of January 2013 he has little to lose, as he is already unpopular. But as he is at the start of a 5-year term, there is enough lead time to earn him an electoral payback.

In terms of choices regarding which French industries to nurture, if Hollande does not do the right thing now, he probably never will. Anecdotal evidence suggests that between the quiet salvaging of self-wounded banks and pulling up from under Peugeot, the weaker of the two French automobile makers, the government has spent an estimated euro 60 billion ($78 billion).

The Peugeot case dramatizes the choice between old and new industries. In July 2012, a couple of months after Hollande took office, Peugeot came at the center of a political storm, at home, after it announced a restructuring plan leading to a net reduction of 6100 French jobs and the closure of its plant in Aulnay, near Paris. To verse gear, at the end of October 2012, Peugeot got from the French Treasury euro 7 billion ($9.1 billion) in exchange for more government clout and preservation of jobs.

In a first time, not knowing exactly how to react, the French government unveiled a recovery plan for the car industry including incentives to buy hybrid and electric cars, but its magnitude and scope was restricted by the country's need to cut debt. Both the market and the automakers were unimpressed. Three months later came the euro 7 billion subsidy.[13]

Then in September 2012 Sanofi-Aventis, France's leading pharmaceutical group, downsized its redundancy program after being paid a visit by Arnaud Montebourg, the socialist minister for "industrial resurgence" considered by many to be the bruiser *en chef*. This was no courtesy call. In the minister's words: "I explained that the lay-off plan was abusive and needed to be reduced."[14]

Forgotten in his exercise of "save the jobs at any price" has been the fact that in France research and development has become a chronic weakness. To "save jobs" at all cost not enough money is spent on R&D, with the result that no truly outstanding new products are coming out of labs. The job cuts at which Montebourg aimed his fire were part of Sanofi's effort to reposition its resources and address the new products issue.

Worse has been the November/December 2012 case of a real smokestack industry: the ArcelorMittal steel plant at Florange. The president of the Republic, the prime minister and minister for "industrial resurgence" aired three different opinions on how to handle the rights of the steel plant's owner and the fact that labor unions were in revolt.

The socialist minister for "industrial resurgence" wanted to throw ArcelorMittal out of France. His first problem was that in France, Mittal employs some 20,000 people and these are jobs which would be gone if the company "was thrown out of France"—while in Florange are employed 1800 and of these only some 800 jobs were in peril.

Montebourg's second problem was that the nationalization of the Florange steel plan, contemplated after no credible party had shown up to purchase it, would have costed euro 1 billion according to some sources, and the French Treasury was short of money. To this was added the fact that ArcelorMittal itself is not in the best of health.

Lakshmi Mittal, chairman, chief executive, and main owner of the world's biggest steel company, said the international economy remained fragile, with evident aftermath on selling conditions for steel. Mittal added that his firm was particularly affected by Euroland's crisis, with the severity of the resulting economic weakness triggering an operating loss for ArcelorMittal's main European plants.[15] That was not the best time to push the steel maker toward the cliff, and the affair ended in a stalemate.

9.3 When the Government Tries to Be Everything to Everybody, Public Debt Is King

There is an interesting parallel between the deep economic crisis in France of Louis XV, in 1720, and the present-day situation in America, Britain, France, and Euroland's Club Med, nearly three centuries later. The seeds for the crisis in early eighteenth century were planted in 1716 when John Law created his bank in Paris. Within a year he set up another bubbly institution, the Compagnie d'Occident to exploit Senegal, the Antilles, Canada, and Louisiana.

With the Regent's patronage, money was created out of thin air. In January 1718 Law won a fight with French politicians scared of leveraged finance. His bank prospered through the introduction of paper money, and by end of that year it was rechristened the Royal Bank. In 1719, a royal decree made him the Kingdom's tax collector. In January 1720, after being named controller general, he took charge of all public financial matters of the French kingdom and put the printing presses of the Royal Bank to work full speed at the request of the royal authorities.

Sounds familiar? Then as now speculation carried the day, then as now the practical day-to-day problems were brushed away, and the spirit of society is identified by the slogan "Let it Be Money." All attention concentrated on creating money for money's sake, and for the benefit of insiders, as enormous amount of liquidity could not be absorbed by commerce.

The mass of money served to feed the fires of an ever higher degree of speculation, while the real assets' counterpart to the increase in money supply, was little or nothing. Then as now there has been no comparable growth in real goods such as merchandize, factories, or gold and silver to back up the newly minted paper "wealth." All there was (and is today) has been more paper money to balance the books and confront the public debt by rolling it over.

Little attention was paid to the fact that imaginary assets, the wealth made of paper money, don't last forever. The bubble grows and grows and eventually it bursts. In Law's time that was the Mississippi Bubble which as long as it grew it made fortunes and by bursting it ruined them. In our time, the new name for "Mississippi" is *public debt for the social net*.

After the end of WWII, from 1945 till 2007, France accumulated a public deficit of euro 1250 billion. First, the deficits were relatively small but with time they grew up, with the interest due contributing to their increase. Then, public debt started to grow exponentially. Between 2007 and 2012 more than euro 500 billion were added to the public deficit, at an average rate of euro 100 billion per year.

True enough, France did not have a balanced budget since 1974, but the rapid rise in public and private deficits started in the early 1980s with the Mitterrand governments, the rapid rise in entitlements, an all out effort to spend money on new immigrants (legal and illegal), and the government's desire to avoid another student revolution like the one of May 1968. The French say that, as far as the young are concerned, this has been a lost generation. Both the state and their parents gave them everything to shut up their mouth. It has not been too different in other western countries.

French teenagers of the generations which followed the 1980s have been called *enfants minute* (minute kids). The "minute" is the time it takes to satisfy their desires. When they want something they don't even ask for it. They buy it with a credit card on the internet, simply adding to household debt which is in competition to the public debt on who will do the most damage to the economy.

While the western central banks' zero interest rates, and resulting very low longer term cost of money, reduced the French government's near-term sensitivity to pressures from bond markets, persistent structural deficits and low growth led to an unsustainable increase in public debt. In France, this is now in excess of 90 percent of GDP, and after having lost its AAA rating, the country is likely to face further credit rating cuts.

Interest rates are important as big time borrowing has become a way of life. On November 25, 2010, for example, the finance commission of the French senate approved an urgent credit of euro 930 million to assure that employees of eight ministries, including Defense, Education, Interior, and Budget will be paid at end of

December 2010. This euro 930 million was part of a bigger account of 1.39 billion with the difference going to other public expense chapters which had overrun *their* budget.

Non-statisticians sometimes say that statistics[16] are nothing more than dry numbers. But when on November 20, 2012 it was officially stated that French public debt stands at euro 1832 billion ($2380 billion), which represents 21 percent of total public debt in Euroland, this was by no means something to be brushed away as "dry number." Interest paid on such a mountain of public debt is a weight around the neck of the real economy, and this is not only true of France but as well as of all other sovereigns: Britain and America included.

This euro 1832 billion in debt also means that sea of red ink approaches 100 percent of GDP; it does not stand at the more modest level of 93 percent of GDP as it is generally believed.[17] The interest paid for this euro 1832 billion is estimated at euro 65 billion, which means that it represents 144 percent the taxes paid by households.[18]

As the public debt is king, expenses continue rising including those unnecessary or fancy. The cost to the French Treasury of the intervention in Libya, in 2011 (along with the British and American forces), has been euro 300 million—evidently paid by increasing the public deficit. Other expenses have been structural. The cost of social security (including health care) is well in excess of contributions to it. Year in and year out health care and pensions provided by the State Supermarket are in the red.

Many economists are worried about the French state's finances. Critics say that when one is deeply in debt, he does not try to play good Samaritan to everybody. France forgave the debt to Ivory Coast, to the tune of euro 2 billion; Republic of Congo, euro 700 million; Morocco, euro 625 million; Madagascar, euro 375 million; Mexico, euro 300 million; and a number of other countries, each for a sum of 125 million or less—but altogether adding up to euro 5 billion.

Another unwarranted expense has been Hollande's pension-age rollback from an inadequate 62 years to an even more profligate 60 years.[19] This was not made to inspire confidence that France faces its economic problems head-on. His 75 percent tax rate for people earning over euro 1 million per year applied only to a tiny minority yet, according to critics, this 75 percent policy indicated hostility to entrepreneurship and wealth creation. (The 75 percent taxation has been struck down by the Constitutional Court's decision, but most likely it will be reborn under different form, as a nineteenth century socialist relic.)

As 2012 came to a close, the forecast has been that by 2016 the French public pensions system will have a deficit of euro 20 billion. The public pensions' black hole is not included in the euro 1832 billion of current public debt—and the same is true of the public health care's deficit where the torrent of red ink is much stronger than in pensions, estimate at another euro 140 billion.

Day-to-day expenses are also running out of control. On January 2, 2013 came the news that the French budget deficit projected for 2013 is euro 61.2 billion[20] (over $80 billion). Just 3 months earlier, the talk was of a euro 30 billion 2013 deficit. The role played in this increase by the (probably temporary) cancellation of the 75 percent tax is minor, as the receipts were estimated to be at the euro 400 million level.

Since public debt is rapidly rising, the fundamentals are grim. Public spending, at 56 percent of GDP, eats up a bigger chunk of output than in any other EU country. Exports are stagnating. The banks are undercapitalized. French banks are geographically diversified across Europe, but this also means sizable operations in peripheral countries: Italy, Greece, Spain—and therefore current and potential losses.

French banks have to increase their capitalization, continue to deleverage their balance sheets, and become fully Basel III compliant. By being itself highly indebted, the government is not in a position to come to their help, though it will undoubtedly do so by further increasing its own debt if one of the bigger banks risks bankruptcy.[21]

One of the more accurate problems confronted by French banks is that they have been losing lots of money because of their sovereign loans: the cost of the Greek crisis to the big French credit institutions has been euro 3 billion, and this is a trifle compared to their exposure to Spain and Italy which is estimated to stand at euro 105 billion.

Statistics on the French current account talk of another gapping hole. From January 1 to July 31, 2012 the deficit reached euro 33 billion versus euro 29 billion a year earlier. While this primarily reflects the lack of competitiveness of the French industry, it also has a direct economic impact. Budget deficit and current account deficit are a double whammy. As the Court des Comptes, the French government's auditor, has pointed out, in 2013 it would not be possible to make ends meet.

9.4 The French Dilemma: Cutting Entitlements or Going Bust

Both geographically and economically, France sits between the profligate Club Med countries of southern Euroland and the northern hard-working ones. Since the end of World War II, the French economy has never been truly strong. Persistent budget deficits have left their footprint, but everything counted, it is the runaway *entitlements* which offered to speculators their next victim.

Health care for all, nearly free medicaments and other goodies provided by the State Supermarket, became a second income for practically everyone—and this created the so-called *French way* which nowadays is an untouchable. To preserve it, every consecutive French president tended to be an even bigger money spender than his predecessor, leaving up to the electorate to answer the question "What's next?"

Even conservative members of society say "Don't touch my entitlements;" the more radical cry is: "We want more;" the greens and so-called extreme-left like to see the entitlements extended to all illegal immigrants making "the rich" pay for them. Nine points will help the reader appreciate how far this chorus goes:

- Still living in the nineteenth century, the "socialos" believe that entitlements are everybody's "rights"—including jobs, pensions, housing, health care.[22]

- The common citizen refuses the redimensioning of entitlements, even though they see that the ongoing bill will be paid by their children and grandchildren.
- The different fellow travelers are always ready to rally for the "good cause" and look at cradle-to-grave publicly paid health care as sacrosanct.
- Those who supposedly fight for the French society's multiculture and diversity, but send their kids to elite schools, where multidiversity is an unknown gospel.
- The bearded fundamentalists and other Islamists who burn down Christian churches in the French countryside and want to build mosques all over Europe.
- The angry students taking to the streets, choose for their studies easy subjects which are not in demand, and think of their pensions even before they have started working.
- Those who have landed a job in public service or state enterprises, and fight to preserve their privileges granted in late nineteenth century, like train conductors who retire at 55 years of age.
- The featherbedders of the labor unions who overpay themselves for doing nothing and call the strikes to immobilize the nation, even if they now represent a mere 7 percent of workers.[23]
- Those who thought that they got a deal with the 35 hours work week, while in reality they were taken for a ride by a socialist government who placated their audience with the slogan: "Less work, more leisure."

Scared of noisy street demonstrations and the aftereffect of trimmed entitlements in the polls, the majority of politicians (both in France and abroad) look at the nanny state as taboo. Yet, it would have been wise to phrase the question on entitlements in a way opposite to the one in which it is typically asked. Not "do you want more of them," but:

- Do you like to pay less taxes and receive less "social benefits"? or
- Do you pay more taxes and preserve the status quo?

What the electorate perceives as austerity measures becomes more palatable when everyone appreciates that those who benefit from wide-spreading "social services" are those who at the end of the day pay for them through new taxes and wider unemployment induced and sustained by the mountains of debt. The public does not know this, because the large majority of politicians would not dare even to tell the truth. But there are exceptions.

In early November 2012 when the French public debt stood at euro 1835 billion, this represented euro 63,000 ($84,000) for every French family, René Doscière, a socialist member of parliament, said clear and loud that it was necessary to reduce this unsustainable figure by retiring some debt or, alternatively, to suspend lots of public services.[24] The point of no return Doscière suggested is not far away. It is typically reached when:

- Public debt snowballs and augments on its own momentum, and
- Thereby it escapes government control.

According to the same parliamentarian, the trend is toward this inflection point because *every hour* France increases its debt by euro 22 million ($29 million), and also every hour the nation pays euro 6 million (nearly $8 million) of interest on the public debt. (Over and above that comes the social security's outstanding deficit of euro 140 billion ($182 billion), including health care and pensions.)

Economists say that no matter how you look at this issue of ever-growing entitlements and public debt, France is showing itself to be a country in denial about its economic challenges. The same can however be stated of the United States, Britain, and many other most countries in Europe—surely of the Club Med.

Just prior to the early 2012 presidential elections, Nicolas Sarkozy had said that the current situation in Spain and Greece reminds of the prevailing economic realities. He also went on to imply that left-wing politics is to blame for the Spain's economic faltering. At the same time, however, his remarks embodied the typical French belief that the government is responsible for everything that happens to a country, no matter what.

By taking Spain and Greece as examples of socialist mismanagement, and there was plenty of it in both cases, Sarkozy avoided to mention the fact that between 1999 and 2007 France failed to meet the Maastricht public deficit criteria 4 years in a row, from 2002 to 2005; and it did not maintain its public debt-to-GDP ratio at 50 percent level. Instead, successive governments tried to reduce the ranks of unemployment by adding workers and employees to the public payroll.[25]

It is not surprising, therefore, that the country's public finances have been permanently in deficit for decades, as fiscal discipline is a rare quality while oversized "social benefits" continue to grow. Since August 2011 (still the Sarkozy years), the government introduced two emergency savings programs but it found it difficult to stay on fiscal track. A steady threat to the deficit and debt targets has been posed by flagging growth, even if higher borrowing costs did not follow the February 2012 downgrade of the country's creditworthiness from AAA to AA+ by Standard and Poor's.[26]

The job of an independent credit rating agency is to estimate, to the best of its knowledge, the creditworthiness of sovereigns, companies, and debt instruments. For highly indebted western governments, however, AAA and AA+ credit rating is a bit like those outposts of empires that still dot the globe, but are nothing more than an accident of history. Let's face it. For the majority of western governments:

- Budgets, current accounts, and income versus expenditures do not add up, and
- Rising health care and other costs make a bad situation worse, even if each sovereign tries to defend his rating.

Prestige aside, one of the advantages of high credit rating is that it helps keep borrowing costs down. Other things equal, downgrades bring the cost of debt up and may well turn away investors trying to find a home for their money. There is a global shortage of assets regarded as "safe." This however does not mean that there are no dangers associated to dollar, yen, pound, and euro investments.

9.5   The French State Spends Too Much. Its Debt Is a Timebomb

The title of the feature article in *The Economist* of November 17, 2012 has been "The timebomb at the heart of Europe," and the subtitle "Why France could become the biggest danger to Europe's single currency." In mid-November 2012, anecdotal evidence suggested that Merkel had asked a committee of six wise men to tell her what Germany could do to pull France out of the abyss, in case it fell in. (Later on, it was stated that this was not an ad hoc committee, but the German chancellor's team of economic advisors.)

At the core of the Economist's article was the statement that while France still has many strengths, its weaknesses have come to the fore with the euro crisis. France spends too much and without the option of currency devaluation, public expenditures add to an already top-heavy public debt. One cannot defy economic fundamentals for long, this article suggested, and if sentiment in the markets shifts quickly to the negative side, the crisis could hit as early as 2013.

At face value, these arguments are right. As the Economist article stated, the business climate in France has worsened—but so did all over Europe. The European governments, like Britain, that have undertaken big reforms have done so because they felt a deep sense of crisis, but they are the exception.

Indeed, the bad news for Europe is not that France is not alone in its travails with public debt. Instead, it is the model. Nineteenth century socialist thinking is widespread (thought it retreated in Sweden). And it has been good to see that the still new in office socialist government of France has been forced into retreat by an online revolt by entrepreneurs and investors, against its plans to raise capital gains taxes.

The strength of the protest by the so-called *pigeons*, French slang for suckers, caught Hollande and his boys and girls off-guard. The finance minister met leaders of the online protest and said changes would be made in favor of entrepreneurs who started their own business. Still the French president knows that scaling back public spending will be painful for a country accustomed to an omnipresent and generous State Supermarket.

Many observers nowadays question how serious Hollande is in meeting his target for a balanced budget by 2017—which is anyway 4 years away and a nebulous statement: a similar question is raised on his determination to go ahead with not-so-popular and difficult reforms giving them a chance of success.[27] On new year's eve 2013, his statement to increase employment opportunities was widely interpreted as a decision to hire even more public workers.

Other issues, too, seem to be already decided on the negative side. An example is the French reaction to political union in Euroland, which ranges between mute and outright hostile. *Le Monde*, the Paris newspaper, called it *a strategy of silence* designed not to stir up divisions. But other sources say that the French government's aim is the so-called *integration solidaire* (integration with solidarity) whose philosophy rests on two pillars:

- Sharing Euroland's money, but

• Rejecting the political integration's obligations.

If a referendum was done today, 64 percent of French voters will reject Maastricht[28] said a pollster in a meeting. The common currency is not the only subject Hollande's voters don't like. They also object to his government's not-so-left economic policies. In the left of the French president, Jean-Luc Mélenchon and his Left Front excite the citizens with promises of social insurrection sweeping away the country's recent pledges of austerity and providing:

• 500,000 new jobs in public nurseries,
• 200,000 new low-rent apartments per year,
• Total reimbursement of all individual health expenditures, and
• Tenured status for 800,000 public service workers now without permanent contracts.

While it is far from clear how the Left Front would handle the costs (the health bill alone is estimated at an extra euro 76 billion yearly), Mélenchon has given a hint: confiscation of annual individual income above euro 360,000. Little or no thought has been given to the fact that this would lead to massive exit of capital from France as well as a drain of the brains creating wealth.

The Left Front seems to have discovered the wheel for perpetual motion, as its program for debt bubbles and mere cheats includes a monthly minimum handout of euro 800 to everybody "to do away with insecurity;" a SMIG[29] of euro 1700 monthly (at the cost of euro 30 billion); general retirement at 60 (which adds euro 35 billion per year to the budget deficit); vast expansion of research and teaching; the nationalization of EDF, GDF/Suez, Areva, Total, and others (estimated at over euro 150 billion); and so on and so forth.

Mélenchon's world view matches his economic policies. He describes the United States as "the world's primary problem" and wants the US Sixth Fleet out of the Mediterranean. While this is simply big-headed thinking, the big question remains whether he and the other fire eaters of the extreme left appreciate that all the sclerosis of the French economy, labor inflexibility, and spend-and-spend policies make the economic situation so much worse than it is.

Mélenchon's Left Front is not part of the government (at least not yet), and the budgetary fraud implied by its political program is not the order of the day. But when it comes to wild spending of not-yet-earned money, neither the left nor the right are opposed, even if they know that it would prove fatal in its consequences— ruining the French economy. The timebomb, however, is not hidden only in the European shore of North Atlantic (see Chapters 10 and 11).

The feature article in the January 5, 2013 issue of *The Economist* put it in this way: "For the past three years America's leaders have looked on Europe's management of the euro crisis with disguised contempt ... Those criticisms were all valid, but now those who made them should take the planks from their own eyes ... the temporary fix[30] ignored America's underlying fiscal problems. It did nothing to control the unsustainable path of "entitlement" spending ... and virtually nothing to close America's big structural budget deficit."

The core message of the Economist's feature article is that while François Hollande and Angela Merkel avoided coming forward to explain to the French and Germans what it will take to fix the euro. Barack Obama, too, does not come clear. He did not tell the American people what is really needed to fix the fiscal mess. High public debt timebombs have been planted at both shores of the North Atlantic, and they might (just might) blow up almost simultaneously.

Prospects of imaginary wealth created by the printing presses of the Federal Reserve and the ECB are an evil of first-rate magnitude. The political leaders as well as the central bankers know it but they play the "I hear nothing, see nothing" game. Both the European and American political top brass is desperately looking for other issues which could divert the public's attention from the economic time-bomb ticking away in their country.

In other times, the threat of a war, supposedly to protect vital national interests, would have been the smoke screen to help the politicians in saving face in a retreat. Soon after he took office Hollande tried to start and lead a cold war in Euroland, against Germany, by way to extravagant demands and a personal attack against Angela Merkel. But it did not work. Instead it is he who adopted Merkel's fiscal compact as a bible.

Therefore, in a second effort to show strength while continuing his determination to preserve the French nanny state model at all costs, and his resistance to change, focused his wrath on Britain. He said that euro transactions should not be done in London, since Britain is not a member of Euroland, but in reality attacking London as global financial center. The same day Boris Johnson, London's mayor, answered: "The euro is a calamitous project."

London is the global financial center, and it is not Hollande's wrath which will change that (apart from the fact that because of socialist high taxation many of the better French forex traders have relocated to the British capital). Of all forex transactions done in the world, the greatest concentration is indeed in London. Statistics are an eye opener:

- 38 percent of forex deals are done in London,
- 18 percent in New York,
- 3 percent in Paris, and
- 2 percent in Frankfurt.

Not only financial transactions but also financial direct investments and capital management activities have deserted the French capital since the socialists took over. Of the 2012 euro 158 billion invested in Europe, more than euro 90 billion have gone to Luxembourg-based wealth management companies and another euro 50 billion to Dublin. For Paris, the catchment is nearly zero.[31]

The value of some continental stock exchanges, too, has fallen like a stone. The week prior to Christmas 2012, Intercontinental Exchange (ICE)—an electronic exchange based in Atlanta, GA—announced that it was near the end of negotiations to buy NYSE Euronext (the company resulting from the merger of New York Stock Exchange and of the holding of four European stock exchanges: Paris,

Brussels, Amsterdam, and London). The agreed upon price is $8.2 billion[32] and ICE let it be known, however, that when the deal is confirmed it will sell Euronext.

The indicative price put on the holding of four continental stock exchanges was a mere euro 1.5 billion, while Frankfurt-based Deutsche Börse masters by itself euro 9 billion.[33] The stock exchanges of Paris, Brussels, Amsterdam, and Lisbon seem to be priced at a mere 16.7 percent of the Deutsche Börse's worth. This is a measure of how low the Paris exchange has gone. On an average, the number of daily transactions in the Paris stock exchange is equal to those for only Apple and Google at NYSE.[34]

*   *   *

In a report that underscored the fiscal task facing François Hollande's socialist administration *La Cour des Comptes*, the French government's auditor, said: "France is hardly halfway towards budgetary consolidation which begun in 2011 and the easing of the timetable, justified by economic slowdown, does not allow for any relaxation." The EU's executive demand for keeping the agreed upon reform timetable angered Paris, with socialist ministers attacking Manuel Barroso, the commission president.

Barroso hit back in Les Echos of June 27, 2013 defending the reforms and saying it was a "complete error" to blame the commission for the rise of populism. "We are worried about France's loss of competitiveness over several decades. If France has too big a gap with Germany we all have a problem in Europe."[35]

9.6 The French Banks' Fragility as Lenders

Both in the United States and in Europe, the majority of banks have been using above-average levels of leverage to run their operations. After the 2007 subprimes crisis hit, this became counterproductive, and in response to equity market pressure, the banks' management announced large-scale deleveraging. Balance sheet restructuring programs have been undertaken and plans were made to reduce their combined risk-weighted assets by billions.

What the French as well as the other European and American banks have found the hard way is that deleveraging after a credit bubble is a painful exercise, as well as a long process. But it is also necessary. Many economists now agree that the deleveraging process gripping the western world will likely continue for several years and remain a drag on growth. But there is no alternative because high leveraging in an economy which is in crisis can be the kiss of death to a financial institution.

In many cases, retrenchment amounts to a scale-down of roughly 12 percent to 15 percent, with banks attempting to downsize assets with the highest regulatory risk weights. Loans to sovereigns have been a case in point. By the end of 2011, the biggest French banks had already reduced considerable amounts of Euroland's peripheral sovereign debt, and wrote down Greek government bonds to 40 percent of par value in preparation for the PSI[36] action.

In early 2012 with the so-called *voluntary* private sector loans writedowns, this 40 percent proved to be inadequate. At the same time, while a 60-percent haircut of other loans in distress strengthened their balance sheets, it simultaneously reduced their profitability. French credit institutions were penalized by the fact that they built up strong franchises in several countries over the preceding decades, and they lent heavily to foreign sovereigns.

Some of the banks sought to deflect ongoing concerns of lending too much to governments. Since late 2011, BNP Paribas reportedly cut in half the amount of Italian government bonds it owned, saying it would be able to maintain an adequate capital cushion by selling assets and reducing the amounts of loans it makes.

Several French bankers, however, blamed the US Federal reserve for their predicament as, worried about the escalating sovereign debt crisis, in the summer of 2011 the Fed asked US money managers to reduce their dollar funding to European banks. (This was allegedly stated by a senior French banker who spoke on condition of anonymity, citing the sensitivity of the situation.) True or false, that caused French financial institutions to pull back on the big business of lending to aircraft companies and other companies to whom they regularly made loans in dollars.

Given the fact that roughly half of global banking assets are European, other markets including the United States and emerging markets faced some funding pressures in the interbank market. According to estimates by their peers, French banks have combined capital needs of euro 30 to euro 36 billion, and at the same time they are holding large positions in Italian and Belgian bonds.

As 2011 came to a close, BNP Paribas reportedly had loans to debtors in peripheral Euroland countries of about euro 135 billion; and Crédit Agricole had euro 101 billion. In late 2011, French banks were downgraded by Moody's due to the pressure they faced on liquidity and in funding markets. Among their challenges in 2011 were the Greek PSI, political upheaval in Egypt, and the downgrade of French government bonds. Available statistics indicate that the French banks exposure to sovereigns divided between:

- Euro 84 billion to France,
- Euro 31 billion to Italy,
- Euro 30 billion to Belgium,
- Nearly euro 10 billion to Holland,
- Euro 7 billion to Greece (prior to the PSI),
- Euro 5.6 billion to Spain, and
- More billions to other countries including Britain, Czech Republic, Poland, more Portugal.

The policies followed by Euroland's sovereigns and banks landed them in a deadly embrace, particularly in the peripheral countries. As their heavy public debt led southern European governments into the danger zone, their lenders have suffered and investors are loath to risk more money on banking stocks.

There is an undeniable toxic relationship between banks and overly indebted governments, which economists call "death spiral" and French banks are part of it. "The French banking system is extremely fragile," said an analyst. "Whether it will result in spectacular events is difficult to say." French credit institutions have as well expanded into business sectors such as:

• Commodities financing,
• Trade financing, and
• Shipping and aircraft financing,

where they held market shares of up to 30 percent. But as the majority of these businesses are dollar-based and French banks had (and are having) difficulty funding themselves in money markets, they have been obliged to reduce their exposure to these operations which were otherwise lucrative.

Retrenchment is a defensive policy appropriate in an economic environment which is teetering. This principle of survival is just as valid of sovereigns as it is of financial institutions. Back in August 2011, Nicolas Sarkozy, the then French president, summoned his key ministers back from holiday for an emergency meeting as concern mounted over prospects for growth and the country's ability to meet its debt targets. In an effort to reassure nervous markets, Sarkozy said his "pledges will be kept whatever the evolution of the economic situation."

In fact, that meeting came as rumors circulated about French credit rating downgrade, with Société Générale plunging by as much as 23 percent on August 10, 2011. It closed down 15 percent, after it denied rumors over its financial stability, while Crédit Agricole was off 12 percent and BNP Paribas down 9 percent. Other European banks slumped too.

Given their sizeable assets in peripheral countries French banks have become nervous as concerns about Euroland's breakup mounted. They could see that recovery of Club Med countries is not for tomorrow, and elevated credit spreads reflected a fading trust. Financial analysts recommended to their clients to avoid new positions in senior and subordinated bonds of BNP Paribas, Crédit Agricole, and Société Générale.

One of the financial analysts said in the course of our meeting that a euro breakup would be particularly disastrous to French banks; over and above the likelihood, it will lead to financial tsunami in Europe, a double-dip in the US economy and severe repercussions in Asian economies. Already Euroland's crisis took a toll on Asian export activity as China became more dependent on demand from Europe than from the United States.

To restore faith in their financial health and regain access to money markets, European financial institutions, not only the French banks, must increase the cash they hold in reserve against losses. But bank executives complain that under present conditions the only way for them to raise more capital is to sell assets and curtail lending. The problem is that:

• In the current environment, assets sales can be only done at rock bottom prices, and
• Curtailing lending amplifies an economic crisis already under way in Euroland.

This leads to tough choices. Further weakening of the economy is evidently unwanted, but *if* the capitalization level of large banks is too low, *then* banks have to be recapitalized to restore market confidence. This in turn means that governments will have to step in if institutions cannot get money in capital markets, but the sovereigns themselves are short of capital. Cash from the ECB does not count as capital for regulatory purposes, though it addresses the problem that credit institutions face in raising money to lend to customers. Commercial banks typically:

- Borrow from the central bank when they cannot get money at a reasonable price in the open market, and
- Deposit money at the central bank when they are worried about the risk of lending to other banks.

In conclusion, the troubles Euroland's economy has been going through are evidently reflected in the financial health of credit institutions. Big European banks have seen the average 5-year CDS spreads rise from just north of zero in 2007 to 450 basis points in 2012. (Though the average has fallen to 230 basis points later on, but rose again to 350 basis points.)

It is not without reason that near the end of June 2012 Moody's Investors Service downgraded the credit ratings of 15 big banks. Economists said that the financial crisis exposed three decades of hubris. Banks that were powered by leverage expanded heavily onto trading, capital markets became very difficult to manage, and the big banks lost a lot of their freedom of action and credibility.

9.7 Efforts to Stabilize the French Banking Industry

In an interview he gave to CNN on June 6, 2012 Jeffrey Sachs, of Columbia University, said that the European debt crisis can be solved only after the banks have been stabilized. Sachs, and all other economists supporting a similar opinion, are only half right because they don't account for the policies and effects of the big unholy connection between banks and governments which we discussed in Section 9.6. As ECB's LTRO experience documents:

- Given the way the banks-and-sovereign complex works, stabilizing the banks is nearly synonymous to stabilizing profligate governments.
- Once the big banks get the money, they buy government bonds which are eventually worth less than their purchase price.
- In the aftermath, their capital ratios turn on their head, so that the banks need again recapitalizing.

The irony with the ECB's LTRO which loaned the banks more than euro 1 trillion ($1.3 trillion) is that they pay ECB a trivial 1 percent per year for 3 years, while the Spanish and Italian government bonds gave them 4 percent to 5 percent.

In part, this wrong way risk was assumed because of greed. Another part, however, was plain pressure by sovereigns on banks domiciled in their real estate.

• Theoretically, the banks made good profits.
• Practically, in different cases they lost money as, for instance, in Greece.

Speculation and stabilization are most evidently opposing concepts. Euroland's banks with the biggest capital shortfalls are those from Spain, Italy, and Greece; but both Crédit Agricole and Société Générale faced serious problems. Some bailouts are a tragedy. On December 27 was announced that Bankia, Spain's fourth largest bank, had benefited from a tandem of multibillion euro rescues—again had a *negative* equity of euro 4.1 billion.

Among French banks, Dexia is the competitor to Bankia in terms of bad loans and poor management. It has been the subject of three highly costly salvage operations by the French and Belgian governments within a few years. The euro 2.5 billion in public money dates December 31, 2012.

Four months earlier, on September 1, 2012, the French government rescued a distressed domestic mortgage lender. It had to seek approval from the European Commission for its bailout of Crédit Immobilier de France (CIF). Just to explain what can be a zombie bank, CIF had liabilities of about euro 40 billion and equity of euro 2.4 billion. In October 2012, it also faced the repayment of euro 1.75 billion in covered bonds. Moodys' had:

• Cut sharply CIF credit rating,
• Stated that it no longer had access to capital markets, and
• Implied that the mortgage lender could not repay the bond without central bank assistance.

Crédit Agricole, the third biggest bank in France by market value, is one of the French institutions which took a hit with the troubles in Greece, as well as with the derivatives gambles of its subsidiary Crédit Lynonnais (LCL). The cost of its withdrawal from Emporiki (Commercial) Bank, its Greek subsidiary, is estimated to exceed euro 6 billion.

Analysts said that back in 2006 the initial Crédit Agricole venture of euro 2.6 billion in Emporiki, and what followed it, would make an excellent case study on what "not to do" in banking. The formerly French farmers' bank thought that it could make a fortune of Emporiki's units in Romania, Bulgaria, and Albania. Altogether Crédit Agricole lost billions and suffered goodwill impairment. The story ended by selling Emporiki to Greek investors for 1 symbolic euro.

Italy, where its main arm is retail lender Cariparma, is Crédit Agricole's largest market after France. The formerly agricultural bank also has stakes in banks in Spain and Portugal though it said it had reduced its stake in Spanish Bankinter to less than 20 percent and was open for its remaining holdings to all potential outcomes.[37]

Critics say that Crédit Agricole's foreign forays look set to haunt it long after it has retreated from foreign ventures. Apart the Emporiki debacle, it has suffered a euro 430 million impairment on its stake in Italian bank Intesa, and profit at its own subscale corporate and investment bank fell almost 60 percent.

Like its French peers, BNP Paribas and Société Générale, Crédit Agricole is retrenching to reduce risk and boost its capital, and it is also downsizing its corporate and investment banking operations. Part of the reason for the French banks' retrenchment is fear of increased supervisory intervention, with legislators given power to limit what the banks can earn from the market as opposed to their clients. This is likely to eat into margins while, at the same time, French banks fear being put to a competitive disadvantage to peers in the United States, where the implementation of Basel III capital rules is likely to be delayed.

On the other hand, American banks have to work within the framework of the Dodd–Frank Act,[38] whose rules are much more severe than any regulation so far existing in Europe. They must also comply with the Volcker rule which bars banks from trading securities on their own account (Although the Volcker rule has yet to be formally implemented in law, American banks have already closed down their proprietary trading desks.).

British banking policy in the coming years has been outlined by the Vickers Commission report of 2011, which is currently on its way through the legislative process. Its basic concept centers on ringfencing to isolate the retail side of the bank, safeguarding its activities.

In Euroland, and the EU at large (probably with the exception of Britain), the basic concept on which will be based bank supervision and the stability of financial institutions is the report by the Likanen Commission, of September 2012. Its implementation will force groups with a universal banking model (comprising investment and retail banking) to ringfence almost all of their trading operations within separately capitalized and funded subsidiaries.[39] French banks have vigorously lobbied in Brussels to stop this plan from being implemented. But the EU Commission is pressing ahead, having concluded that nothing will be gained from reforms which are modest.

Two important themes have not been addressed by the Dodd–Frank Act, Vickers Commission, and Liikanen Commission. The one is how to break the vicious cycle created by the bank–sovereign deadly embrace, which is largely a political subject. The second is more technical than political, and it concerns first of all the wisdom of the policy and then, if this is proven, the criteria for salvaging badly damaged and self-wounded big banks.

Economists say that this too is a largely political issue and its impact is largely cross-border. Euroland's ministers of finance who approved up to euro 100 billion ($130 billion) for recapitalizing (read: salvaging Spanish banks falling off the cliff) were not rushing to do so for philanthropic reasons. They have fallen to the same political fallacy which prevailed in the first months of 2010 when they rushed to "save Greece."

Among them, the French and German big banks have an exposure of nearly $200 billion to Spain, while taken together the exposure of British and American banks exceeds $100 billion. But "saving Spain and the Spanish banks" in no way guarantees that the creditors will get back their money. If the Greek experience is any reference, the German, French, British, and American banks may well be in for losing 75 percent of their wrongly loaned capital.

Christine Lagarde, boss of the International Monetary Fund, was right when, on June 8, 2012 in a CNN interview, she made the point that serious deals don't work that way. Asked if she would consider an IMF contribution in salvaging the Spanish banks, she answered that there are three prerequisites which, among themselves, constitute the golden rule of stabilizing the banking industry.

- The need for a reliable assessment of each bank's assets and liabilities,
- The requirement of a dependable estimate, to assure the banks will not come back again asking for more money, and
- If these conditions are met, the importance to recapitalize rapidly and avoid new capital losses.

This, of course, presupposes first class management at European Union, the governments' and the banks' level. Unfortunately for everybody, first class management is in short supply and the same is true of strong leadership. Successful stabilization requires the breaking of the unholy banks−government alliance which has been a policy for decades. Short of that no solution is going to worth the money which will be thrown at it.

The slogan of May 1968 student revolution in Paris was "imagination in power." In the four and a half decades which elapsed since then, two generations have come to power at both sides of the North Atlantic, but imagination did not accompany them. Life is organized around the old oak, and after the oak is cut down, the hard realities are emerging.

De Gaulle had seen coming the time of mediocrity. "The French," he said to André Malraux (his minister of culture), "I have amused them with flags... (but) the country chose the cancer."[40] This is true all over the West.

End Notes

1. After the presidential election of 1965, de Gaulle said to a confident, "No doubt I would not have been a candidate if the left was represented by a honorable person. (But) I could not let France run the risk of being governed by Mitterrand!" (Alexandre P. Execution of a political person. Paris: Grasset; 1973.)
2. Between 1981 and 1984 the franc devalued by over 20 percent against the Deutschmark.
3. In his early years in power, Mitterrand nationalized 38 banks and 11 important industrial companies.
4. Mackay C. Extraordinary popular delusions and the madness of crowds. An eighteenth century book reprinted in Britain by Amazon.co.uk.; 2011.
5. Chorafas DN. Breaking up the euro. The end of a common currency. New York, NY: Palgrave/Macmillan; 2013.
6. When Europe's single currency came into being in 1999, French labor costs were below Germany's.

7. The Economist, November 17, 2012.
8. Polytechnique (instituted by Napoléon), Ecole des Mines and others.
9. Instituted right after World War II.
10. The Economist, November 17, 2012.
11. Ehrenberg V. From Solon to Socrates. Abingdon: Routledge; 2011.
12. The Economist, October 15, 2011.
13. Peugeot was not alone in these woes. The European operation of both General Motors and Ford also suffered.
14. Financial Times, October 5, 2012.
15. ArcelorMittal's net income in the 6 months to the end of June 2012 was $970 million compared with $2.6 billion in the equivalent period in 2011.
16. Noun, plural.
17. Correspondingly, in Switzerland it is below 40 percent of GDP.
18. In 2010 (latest available statistics) French citizens paid euro 47.6 billion in taxes (Nice Matin, November 16, 2012). Of this, euro 2.1 billion was reverted and redistributed to the economically weak leaving euro 45.5 to the Ministry of Finance to pay interest on the debt.
19. Sarkozy probably knew that retirement at 62 years was not enough, but also appreciated that he could not get anything higher than that.
20. Le Canard Enchainé, January 2, 2013.
21. On December 31, 2012 it was announced that France and Belgium will inject another euro 2.5 billion into Dexia (the third in a few years) and dismantle it afterward.
22. Precisely, the "solution" that led the Soviet Union to the abyss.
23. A French statistic.
24. Nice Matin, November 11, 2012.
25. In a dozen years, January 2000 to January 2012, an estimated 111,000 jobs were created at different levels of government above the communal level; plus another 128,000 in the different municipalities.
26. If S&P was the first of the three major rating agencies to go ahead with a downgrade, Moody's Investor Services followed suite in late November 2012. Paris shrugged off Moody's cut of one notch to its AAA on French sovereign debt. The market in French government bonds also took little notice.
27. The Economist, October 6, 2012.
28. The agreements made in Maastricht which established the common currency.
29. Minimum monthly salary.
30. Through an agreement between Republican senators and the White House on New Year's 2013 eve.
31. Le Figaro, December 20, 2012.
32. The Economist, January 5, 2013.
33. Les Echos, December 21, 2012.
34. Le Canard Enchainé, December 26, 2012.
35. Financial Times, June 28, 2013.
36. Private sector involvement. See Chapter 4.
37. Financial Times, August 29, 2012.
38. Chorafas DN. Basel III, the devil and global banking. London: Palgrave/Macmillan; 2012.
39. This is precisely the opposite ringfencing than the one the Vickers Commission has suggested.
40. Alexandre P. Execution d'Un Homme Politique. Paris: Grasset; 1973.

Part Four

Who Killed the Golden Eagle?

10 Public Health Care Is the No. 1 Suspect

10.1 Sequester

"The president got his tax hikes on 1st January. The issue here is spending. Spending is out of control," said John Boehner, Speaker of the US House of Representatives.[1] By end of February 2013 everybody in Washington was aware of the fact there was no resolution at hand to stop the $85 billion in automatic spending cuts. These were mandated by the *sequester*[2] which targeted a total of $1.2 trillion of reductions on federal budget expenditures over 9 years.

"I don't think anyone quite understands how it gets resolved," Boehner told NBC's *Meet the Press* on March 3, 2013, repeatedly rejecting the White House's call for new tax increases to end the impasse, and questioning some of Barack Obama's most dire warnings about the impact of sequestration. To Boehner's opinion, such claims were exaggerated.

Budgetary deficits are nothing really unusual. What attracts attention is their huge size and tendency to grow by leaps and bounds every year (see also Chapter 11). When the pace of growth is overwhelming and the reasons for it have to be brought to public attention with a clear statement by the White House on whether the US debt can be repaid or has to be written off. (The same is true of Britain, France, Italy, Spain, and Greece.)

Like most of the western European countries, America urgently needs a way to deal with its long-term spending problems as well as its self-delusion to say that the search for a solution can be limited to tax reform. No nation can cut its way to prosperity by being a big spender. To be effective any solution has to lead to real economic growth and this is not done just by

- Taxing "the rich,"
- Closing loopholes,
- Bringing interest rates down on a permanent basis, and
- Flooding the market with liquidity (Chapter 12).

The irony is that sequestration will practically touch only lightly the heavy chapters of expenditures, because in their origin is a swarm of public health care sacred cows. Curiously, without anybody really paying attention to it, the United States joined France and Italy in the art of surviving its big budgetary deficits through a cocktail of inflation and devaluation—but in the case of the United States neither of them has worked (see Section 10.6).

Devaluation of the dollar and "controllable" inflation have been Ben Bernanke's not-so-secret goals with QE 1, 2, 3, and 3.5 (Chapter 12). But after years of trying he failed in reaching his goals. While other "strong" currencies devalued against the international monetary system, such as the British pound and the Japanese yen, the United States cannot do so because the dollar *is* the international monetary system. (More on this in Section 10.6.)

So it is if you like it and so it is if you don't. The Fed engaged in plenty of extra curricula activities to help White House and Congress with their huge budget deficits, but at the end of the day these extra curricula did not deliver. The sequester became unavoidable, given the extremely large buildup of debt, which is undoing the American economy single-handed. Nobody should expect that sequestration will produce miracles. Official statistics suggest that

- Medicare will confront a mere 2 percent reduction, which is peanuts, given the fact that year after year its budget reaches for the stars.
- Money available to the National Institute of Health, which funds medical research, will be cut by 5 percent.
- Space operations at the National Aeronautics and Space Administration (NASA) will also be cut by 5 percent.
- The largest cuts are supposed to come from military budgets, which are national defense and therefore untouchable.

Even the 2 percent reduction of Medicare funds is theory rather than fact. Some analysts suggest that Medicare cuts with the sequester will not be higher than 0.25 percent of allocated funds and the Obama Administration can always count on the support of labor unions to go on strike against a deficit reduction plan by Congress.

It happened in the Netherlands the first days of March 2013 when a euro 4 billion ($5.2 billion) package of additional austerity measures aimed at enabling the country to hit EU deficit targets in 2014, led to a bitter clash with trade unions. The assault against the plan started with Holland's largest labor federation attacking the cuts as stupid and ill-advised.

Superficially, people look at austerity plans and sequesters as totally different things, but down to basics the notions propelling them tend to converge. The idea is to blow open policies and practices underpinning inaction on debt issues and stop further financial bleeding by

- Trimming entitlements, and
- Putting budgetary deficits up for repayment.

All this has to be studied under real life conditions which involve plenty of headwinds: payroll tax increases, delayed tax refunds, higher gasoline costs, you name it. These have had a discernible impact on the citizen's spending practices and on taxable income, translating into declining ability to repay the debt.

The worst enemy is inaction. With no alternative solution in sight, on March 1, 2013 president Obama had no alternative to ordering the start of $85 billion in government spending cuts, beginning a potentially decade-long wave of belt-tightening. The Office of Management and Budget sent Congress a detailed list of program cuts and government agencies notified their employees and informed affected government contractors.

Everyone will feel the pain of these cuts which have been "a solution by default," rather than one properly planned. They were intended to be so onerous that Congress and the president would not let them occur, by coming up with a debt control plan ahead of the March 2013 deadline. Moreover, everybody knew that the sequester is an inefficient way of cutting government spending. It was not designed to address the soaring cost of health care entitlements, even if the share of US GDP consumed by Medicare alone is projected to rise:

- From 3.7 percent today
- To 6.7 percent in 25 years.

Another weakness of the sequester is that it provides no prioritization, as guide to budgetary reductions. The FBI, Center for Disease Control, Food and Drugs Administration, and Federal Aviation Authority would temporarily lay off 10 percent of their workforce, causing chaos throughout the country. By contrast, health care and pensions will steam through unscathed. It would have been more rational if the sequester was not looking only after the symptoms of the disease:

- Spending

but also what created the illness:

- The reasons for spending.

Like in France, Italy, Spain, and plenty of other western bankrupt countries, the underlying problems are home grown. Hence the urgent need for thorough reexamination of all public expenditures, with no sacred cows escaping the slaughter; making a 10-year projection of government revenues on the base of different scenarios of tax income; and comparing receipts against expenditures, looking at primary and full budget surpluses and coming to a conclusion on which expenditures have to be cut with a sharp knife.

The sequester is not doing this. It just orders the aforementioned $1.2 trillion savings over 9 years. That's not enough. To increase transparency, the analytical steps I am suggesting should be extended to the level of the single individual benefiting from Medicaid, Medicare, and Obamacare—with emphasis on his or her use or overuse of common funds.

An example is the data which hit the public eye in February 2013. In the average, over his lifetime of health care service each beneficiary of Medicaid contributes to the common purse of Medicaid $110,000 and uses the system's common funds to the tune of $333,000. Has anyone searched to find how a system which rewards its "clients" to the rate of 300 percent the money they cash in, can survive?

That's worse than a Ponzi game and economists have plenty of reasons to worry about what happens next. The challenge is not just inflation, which for the time being in the United States (but not in Britain) is subdued; though the inflation worry is not totally absent. With inflation already forecast to be above target for 2 years, a growing number of economists abandoned the camp wanting more QE and joined the opposite side.

In conclusion, the advent of flat sequestration is a low point for Washington, giving everyone the message that congressmen—both representatives and senators—have lost their ability to make up their mind. They take too lightly the risks which accompany rising public debt. But there is at least one thing the sequester did right. It hit the nation's discretionary expenditures. Almost all forms of so-called *discretionary* spending that Congress gets each year will be cut equally and indiscriminately. Well done. Nothing hurts the politicians more than losing access to the pork barrel.

10.2 Don't Let Grandparents Steel the Young Generation's Money

Stan Druckenmiller has been one of the best-performing hedge fund managers during the last couple of decades. Based on his experience he has this warning for young Americans: don't let your grandparents steel your money. In the background of his advice are the mushrooming costs of Social Security, Medicare, Medicaid and Obamacare—with unfunded liabilities of $211 trillion:

• As this overhead is growing and growing, and it has to be serviced, it will bankrupt the nation's youth, and
• Everything counted it represents a much greater danger than the $16 trillion of public debt currently being debated in Congress (Chapter 11).

"While everybody is focusing on the here and now, there's a much, much bigger storm that's about to hit," Druckenmiller said in an hour-long interview he gave to Bloomberg News, adding that: "I am not against seniors. What I am against is current seniors stealing from future seniors." To his opinion, espoused by many other knowledgeable people, unaffordable and unsustainable spending will bring a crisis worse than the financial meltdown of 2008, when $29 trillion was erased from global equity markets.

People who care for their country's and their currency's survivability say that what's particularly troubling is that skyrocketing government expenditures are more and more related to programs for the elderly. The US government budget went out of control, even before the first baby boomers (those born in 1946) started turning 65 adding themselves to the retired. In parallel to this imbalance which has created unfunded liabilities of $211 billion came up a plain un-American credo: "Spend Now, Earn Later."

An example of "spending without limits," associated to poorly planned and badly executed big government policies, is Obamacare (officially known as the Affordable[3] Care Act (ACA)). By mid-2013, with a few months to go before the main feature of the 2010 US health care law takes effect, the White House was confronted by mounting bureaucratic challenges of a sweeping legislation. Critics argued that this is evidence of

- A poorly designed, and
- Hastily passed health care policy.

The new rules are promoting "spending without limits" as the state exchanges will (for one year) be able, in cases where the information is not easily available electronically on a federal database, to waive the requirements that they verify the income of individuals seeking tax credits.[4] Sampling procedures adopted by the Obama Administration's do not solve the problem of dependability, unless accompanied by severe penalties for false declaration (which is not the case). Simply auditing a small sample of randomly selected files is a half-baked solution.

The end result is that, for reasons of its own doing, the Obama administration is now coping with an untenable situation and it is being blamed for incompetence. This incompetence also led to a breakdown in the normal legislative process, as on July 18, 2013 Congress stroke out two chapters from Obamacare's 600-page regulation. By way of lousy management, in three quarters of a century we have gone a long way in terms of spoiling the nation's financial resources.

Publicly supported pensions and health care were invented almost simultaneously, in 1936, by the Roosevelt Administration in Washington and the Leon Blum government in Paris. The idea was sound *if*, and only *if*, they were kept away from politics and their deliverables were always kept in a zone of expenditures which was affordable and, in the long term, it could be honored.

This has not been the case. "We must be conscientious that in France social policy and demagoging policy are always being confused," said George Pompidou a former president of France.[5] Back in 1964, Pompidou foresaw that the simple train of social measures being taken will outrun before too long the country's financial possibilities. This proved to be the right estimate. The so-called *French model* failed when the entitlements it guaranteed could no more be financed by

- Economic growth, which currently stands at zero or worse, or
- A steady devaluation of the currency: the *Franco-Italian model*, since France adopted the euro.

In a letter George Pompidou wrote to Charles de Gaulle, then president of the French Republic, he clearly stated that reforms which go against economic realities always fail.[6] This is precisely the condition western governments are confronting—America above all others because its economy is so large and so is the size of its problems.

This underlines the tensions between Republicans, who see the expansion of Medicaid ordered by the 2010 Affordable Care Act—the unaffordable big government initiative. Plenty of Americans, particularly the young, now appreciate the 2010 Act was not studied in terms of its affordability. As it stands, it would add a lot to the already sky-high budget deficit.

Politics, however, blur the people's mind and Democrats who want "more Medicaid and Medicare" at any cost. Under the ACA, states are mandated to expand their unbalanced and uncovered Medicaid programs, which provide health services to the poor, children, and disabled—the criterion being incomes below 133 percent the poverty line. That meant that in one shot the federal government promised to pay all of the cost for 3 years[7] for:

- An estimated 16 million new patients with unfunded liabilities.
- An unwarranted cost representing $5.3 trillion at the average of $333,000 the typical Medicaid client takes out of the system.

Companies, too, could pay a heavy price for the political wrangling, and the issue became so fraught that even the Chamber of Commerce has opted to stay out of the fight. Hospitals are among the most concerned. "One of the biggest things every hospital is going to pay attention to is the expansion of Medicaid," said Steve Glass, finance chief of the Cleveland Clinic. "Medicaid is the worst payer because it pays below cost but it's still better than someone who doesn't have any insurance at all."[8]

While the argument about "paying below cost" is open to debate, there is an even more important question which needs to be addressed. In simple terms: What's the value of the health care the common citizen buys with the money of a highly indebted sovereign. Is he or she paying two cents for something worth one?

If voters were rational they would examine every government-sponsored action should be examined under this criterion of cost/effectiveness, because in the last analysis they will foot the bill through higher taxation. Here is an interesting example on what can happen. In 2012, the US government spent $116 million minting pennies which since 2006 has cost more than a cent to produce (mainly due to the price of zinc, the coin's primary ingredient).

Because for small coinage costs exceed value, in Canada the government recently ditched its steel-based penny. Relegated to jars and lost behind cushions, the penny has failed to perform its primary function: facilitate commerce. Vending machines and parking meters don't accept it. Penny critics note that fiddling with them adds some two seconds to each transaction, costing the economy many millions of dollars on an annual basis.

The more the cost of the penny increases, the more zinc industry lobbyists pressure the government. The coin's demise, they say, would cost consumers, as merchants would round prices up to the nearest nickel. "Economists disagree," says an article in the *Economist* which suggests that "shop keepers might in fact round down in order to avoid moving from a price of, say, $9.99–$10."[9]

Similar spoilage but at grand scale is happening with health care costs. The numbers are astronomical. There are simply good reasons why the United States spends way above publicly supported health care expenses in Britain, Germany, France, Italy, and Spain—or for that matter a high multiple of what is spend in neighboring Cuba more or less equal longevity (Section 10.3). This is a go-for-broke policy, which

- Makes no sense, and
- It is going to cost dearly the next generations of American citizens.

So far American politicians have not been brave enough to say, in no uncertain terms, what Stan Druckenmiller stated about grandfathers and grandmothers stealing the money from their grandsons and granddaughters via unfunded liabilities (the $211 trillion stuff). Using their very powerful lobby the seniors keep on getting more and more transfer payments from the younger generations to their own. That's no more the pay-as-you-go system Social Security and public health care used to be in the United States or anywhere else.

In 1990, Social Security, Medicaid, and Medicare accounted for 34 percent of the government's expenditures. This hit 44 percent in 2011, a mere 21 years down the line, according to statistics compiled by the government's Bureau of Economic Analysis. In 2011, the cost to the federal government has reached a cool $3.7 trillion, and it keeps on growing almost without bounds.

In 2010 in the United States, there were 40 million people 65 years old or over, according to the US Census. According to the Department of Health and Human Services, by 2020 that number is expected to hit 55 million—a significant increase which will reflect itself into the ongoing government deficits making it all but impossible to balance the budget.

To the opinion of Lawrence Kotlikoff and Scott Burns, authors of "*The Coming Generational Storm,*" by 2030 there will be about two workers per retiree, down from 3.4 workers in 2000. Similar statistics (indeed, even worse) prevail in western Europe. In future seniors are taxed at the same rate as today's working population, they will get (at best) less than half of the benefits that our present day seniors are getting. This has been Druckenmiller's message.

As for the unfunded liabilities the way to bet is that they will be reaching for the stars, hitting $1 quadrillion. Eventually the market will wake to the fact that behind commitments made by the central governments of western democracies is only hot air.

When this sips down the market's mind, its response will not be mild.

If the reader does not believe that, left unattended, the present unfunded liabilities of the United States can grow to $1 quadrillion, *then* he or she should use Italy as proxy of the rise of US public debt. In both countries, the political and economic situation has shown similar (as well as disturbing) long-term implications, with common ground the tendency of modern democracies to pile up debt by making unaffordable spending promises—essentially, by lying to the voters.

Mario Monti, Italy's former prime minister, said that much without *ifs*. . .and *buts*. The fact that he spoke his mind was not appreciated by the voters. Monti ended a poor fourth in the February 2013 elections. For a little more than a year (late 2011 to late 2012) his government and its reforms won the approval of the markets—but not of the voters, with the result that Monti trailed to an undistinguished position.

Like Italian politicians of the Berlusconi class (Monti's nemesis), American politicians responded to the economic crisis by lifting the debt ceiling, ignoring the debt ceiling, making permanent tax cuts, and introducing new taxes with any coherent plan. The keyword is spending. To put the size of the current QE3.5 program of the Fed into context, when the US stock exchanges closed for a week in response to the 11 September 2001 terrorist attacks, the Federal Reserve injected $34 billion into markets. That's less than 2 weeks expenditures of the current QE3.5 *permanent* program.

This ratio helps to dramatize the level of the current public debt crisis in the United States. Section 10.3 will bring to the reader's attention statistics of runaway health care costs around the globe and also demonstrate that there exist no miracle solutions. Miracles are the things we don't understand, said Isidor Isaac Rabi, the physicist of the Manhattan Project.

10.3   Case Study on Health Care Expenditures and Their Incoherence

The danger of a default gets a boost when unsustainable debt levels become chronic and nothing is done to turn around the situation (other than words and very light commitments). For any economy a default would be a social, logistical, economic, and political challenge of the first order. The government would in effect have to engage in a massive effort not only trying to find the money to pay for the essentials but also deciding which payments

- It is willing to make, and
- Which it chooses to halt for lack of funds.

In early- to mid-2011 Tim Geithner, Treasury secretary, has been warning Congress about the dangers of failing to raise America's borrowing limit. Barack Obama himself stepped in to spell out the implications of a default. On August 3, 2011, the day after the final deadline, the US government was due to send out some 70 million checks. This is not just a matter of Social Security checks, Obama commented. These are veterans' checks, these are folks on disability. But with the arguments about raising the US debt limit still ongoing, he said he could not guarantee that the checks would be posted.

Veteran check and health care deals come out of the same purse. For how long can the US government, or for that matter any government, guarantee that it can keep on paying the ever rising health care expenditures? Health care has been one of the entitlements whose infinite continuation is typically taken for granted. That's wrong. There are reasons why economists and politicians have entered the debate regarding the

- Efficacy,
- Drawbacks, and
- Continuity of the current system.

The big question is not one of just developing some more refined version of publicly supported health care. It's one of continuing to pay ever increasing costs in a low growth economy. The whole system has to be reexamined bottom up, including its details, to restore its credibility and assure that what is retained is affordable.

This means major cuts in order to be able to promise that what remains in health welfare will not be subject to new and steady cuts. Given lower than hoped for federal revenues, how will the government confront the entitlements without the ax? Solely by imposing new taxes on the wealthy? Fiddling with the idea of a balanced budget is meaningless *if* economic growth weakens while health care and other entitlements costs are rising.

Obamacare, Medicare, Medicaid, and all other health care plans for an aging society are an excellent ground where to apply the principle of sustainability. This is not a subject born last night. The budgetary pressures arising from health care paid by the common purse have been a cause for concern for a long time. But reforms have always been half-baked while the need for timely and comprehensive real policy reform remains high. Until this takes place, risks to long-term fiscal sustainability will continue being elevated because

- The liabilities related to health care require a substantial increase in government spending, and
- The United States, as well as most other western countries are in a weak fiscal position with high debt-to-GDP ratios—but lack the will to take downsizing measures.[10]

While particularly expensive is the long-term care brought to the foreground by an aging society, the overall concept of nanny state health care lacks a rational analysis in terms of costs and deliverables. A generally held notion is the higher are health care expenditures, the longer the life expectancy. Such a notion is *utterly wrong*.

An excellent study published by Crédit Suisse brings this issue in perspective. Its basic premise is that no country has yet figured out a sustainable solution to health care financing. All developed nations are coming under cost pressure, though some much more than others, but "good health care" is more than just a matter of money: above all, it requires out of the box ideas.[11]

So far new ideas are in short supply. Statistics are however revealing particularly the lack of correlation between health care costs and longevity, suggesting that *if* it is to rein-in skyrocketing health care costs, *then* everything connected to *health* (not only to health care) should be on the table. Table 10.1 provides statistics on health care costs per capita and GDP per capita, in 9 countries.[12]

In the first decade of this century, among western countries the steepest increase in health care costs has been in Spain, Britain, the United States, and Switzerland (the latter particularly in hospital spending). The four are followed by Japan, Germany, France, and Italy (in this order). While in statistical terms the smaller increase in percentage points was in Italy, it has been an extravagant and unaffordable 147 percent in 10 years.

The usual excuse for spending and spending is that "health is precious." Table 10.2 brings to the reader's attention the fact that health care costs and life expectance don't correlate. On equal life expectancy of 78 years, the United States spends 1377 percent more money than Cuba. Is it that the Cubans are world masters in health care? Or is health care money spoiled the big way in the United States? Short of unprecedented spoilage these figures simply don't add up.

Spoilage is a many-headed curse. India's 1.2 billion inhabitants use about $10 of packaging per person annually, compared with $40 a head in China, $100 in Brazil, and $400 in the United States.[13] I lack statistics on the cost of packaging in Greece prior to

Table 10.1 Per Capita Health care Costs and Life Expectancy in Nine Countries

Country	Health care Cost Per Capita in US$[a]	Life Expectancy (years)
United States	8360	78
Cuba	430	78
Switzerland	5390	82
Japan	3200	82
Britain	3480	80
Russia	1000	68
India	130	65
South Africa	940	52
Burkina Faso	90	50

[a]In *purchasing power parity* (PPP) and constant US dollars, costs are rounded up to the last digit.

Table 10.2 The Rise in Health care Cost Per Capita in a Decade and GDP per Capita, Expressed in PPP and Constant US Dollars

Country	Health care Cost Per Capita in 2000[a]	Health care Cost Per Capita in 2010	Increase in a Decade (%)	GDP per Capita in 2010	Health care Cost as % of GDP per Capita in 2010
United States	4700	8360	178	42,080	19.9
Switzerland	3210	5390	168	37,580	14.3
Germany	2670	4330	162	33,410	13.6
France	2540	4020	158	29,460	10.3
Japan	1970	3200	162	30,970	10.7
Britain	1830	3480	190	32,470	10.7
Italy	2060	3020	147	27,080	11.2
Spain	1530	3030	198	26,970	11.2
Russia	370	1000	270	14,200	0.7
Brazil	490	1030	210	10,090	10.2
China	110	380	345	6820	5.27
India	70	130	186	3040	4.3

[a]All figures are rounded up in their last digit.

WWII, but based on remembrance my guess is that it was not far from that of today's India—while at the present time it is nearer to that of the United States, which means spoilage of resources.

Health care specialists who are not afraid to express their honest opinion suggest that what people eat has more to do with longevity than money spent on health care. The speed with which obesity has risen to global epidemic proportions is staggering, as are the consequences for patients and health care costs. The dramatic growth trend in obesity rates seen over the past decades is expected to continue as citizens in western nations go for fast food and emerging countries are increasingly opting for high-calorie unhealthy western diets.

Moreover, the trend in urbanization lessens the amount of physical activity. The switch from bicycling or walking to the automobile has been one of the factors contributing to obesity. The physical environment is another big factor while zoning laws and market conditions have created "food deserts"[14] where whole neighborhoods have no access to fresh produce unless they drive to the supermarket.

Spoilage in personnel cost is another of the debt hydra's heads. In late 2012, the US postal service pleaded with Congress to vote a law permitting to end Saturday deliveries and restructure its health care plan for retired employees. This asking for indulgence revealed that most of its recent $16 billion annual loss was due to health care benefits the postal service had provided.[15]

There is no evidence that US postmen live much longer than their colleagues in Cuba in spite of 2000 percent higher health care costs to the taxpayer. Something similar can be stated with the 80−82 years life expectancy. The big spender in this case is Switzerland. Though 36 percent lower than in the United States (Table 10.1), per capita health care costs in Switzerland are 68 percent higher than in Japan (an aged society) and 55 percent higher than in Britain. Yet, Britain's National Health Service (NHS) is known for its inefficiency.

In the 65−68 bracket of life expectancy, Russia spends on a per capita basis 77 percent more than India on health care. Similarly, at the level of 50−52 years life expectancy, South Africa spends on health care 1044 percent more than Burkina Faso (inefficiency aside, another reason may be that in South Africa 17.8 percent of people are infected with HIV).

These statistics are suggesting that the more money the government taxes the more it spends on publicly supported health care without any change in life expectancy. Such statistics give plenty of food for thought. Something is basically wrong with the way the publicly supported health care system is set up and operates. Abuse is known to be rampant. In France, 50 million people have the right to a health care chip-in-card which pays their medical expenses and pharmaceuticals, but 60 million cards are in circulation.

Abuse of public health care benefits is surely accompanied by mismanagement, and other more esoteric reasons which have not been as yet properly researched. Finding out "what" and "why" is most urgent because unless all background factors influencing health care costs are found and corrected nothing will stop them from rising at high pace.

As these statistics document, there is no time to lose in bringing health care costs under lock and key. The public budget does not only to address health expenditures, there are as well other entitlements requiring a great deal of funds— pensions and education being examples. It is simply impossible to give to anyone of them the lion's share of the sovereign's annual income.

What is true for government is also true for companies which have assumed health care expenditures for their employees. No surprise, therefore, that some of them are shifting health costs to their workers. Examples are: Sears, the retailer, and Darden Restaurants, which operate Olive Garden and Red Lobster restaurant chains.

This switch hit the public eye in September 2012 as the aforementioned companies unveiled a "defined contribution" health insurance plan which would give employees a lump sum of money and allow them to choose from a variety of choices in a menu of insurance options. This is an emulation of the change many companies made from traditional pension schemes to the 401(k) program (in the case of the United States) that give employees greater choice while assuming more risk.

Precisely because of this risk component to be assumed by employees and workers, the possibility of private exchanges becoming mainstream has raised concerns among consumer advocates. Their main objections are that low-wage workers will be at risk:

- *If* they choose their plans poorly, and
- *If* the health care money given by their firms does not keep pace with medical costs.

Some years ago similar objections were made as companies altered their pension plans to a defined contribution basis. To the opinion of those against the switch shifting responsibility on to workers as a way to cut costs, the defined contributions health care is unlikely to work because doctors and hospitals have incentives to make them spend more. To the contrary, the pros say that with a defined contributions plan employees and workers will benefit from greater choice and the option of purchasing a less expensive health insurance.

Curiously enough, absent from argument advanced by the critics is whether sovereigns and the companies can afford to pay wholesale the rising medical, hospital, and pharmaceutical costs of their citizen and of their employees. There is plenty of proof that the way the now classical system has worked is unsustainable. In a manner not dissimilar to that of pensions, the population health care dynamics have changed. Not only a great deal needs to be done to bend the curve of rising health care costs but also a new solution has to be found in *cost sharing* in order to avoid that the whole health care system goes bankrupt.

"People who have high cost sharing tend to use less services, don't take medication or go to the doctor," says Tim Jost, a professor at Washinggton and Lee University School of Law. "if there is anyone out there who thinks this care is going to be free, they're probably in for a bit of a surprise."[16]

10.4   A Bankrupt America Needs an Age of Austerity, Says Mort Zuckerman

Economic growth in the United States continues being slow despite all the money thrown at the problem by the Obama Administration as well as the Federal Reserve's quantitative easing and its other unconventional policy tools. The bigger uncertainty is what the government will do with its own fiscal challenges. Back in January 2012, a poll by PWC found that 48 percent of American company CEOs thought that over the next couple of years the situation will get worse, not better. As far as the US economic outlook is concerned there has been concern about diminishing visibility which made the CEOs uneasy.

Nothing has changed during 2012 and 2013. What was true then, continues being the case today. Companies want clarity in economic outlook, not uncertainty. Lack of clarity leads to indecision, with the result that senior management holds back investments which damages the economic outlook. The longer the distrust continues, the deeper the economic impact. Distress is exported:

- The main economies in the world are interconnected much more than one might think, and
- When a big economy is in trouble, its affiliation and adversity may affect all the other.

"... this is being called the most predictable crisis in US history. For who could dispute, when our government must borrow $4.5 billion a day just to keep going, that our debt is now an existential threat?" wrote Mort Zuckerman[17] in a July 2012 article, "... knowledgeable people in finance are aware that the Fed has been buying 70 percent of all new Treasury paper, making the government by far the largest client of its own debt. This is possible only by increasing the money supply and the balance sheet of the Fed itself, a practice that sooner or later must blow up."[18]

Zuckerman's advice is that the US government adopts a long due policy of austerity. Being a pragmatist Zuckerman appreciates that since taxes cannot be raised enough to recover the ever increased expenses, the United States has no choice but to enter its own age of austerity by way of long-term spending reductions. And he is right when he says that the scale of deficits and debt, demands nothing less if the country is to save itself from default.

Compare this with the Fed chairman's congressional testimony in early February 2012. After a vague reference to supposedly improved economic conditions, Ben Bernanke went on to stress that the sluggish expansion has left the economy vulnerable to shocks and economic developments must be monitored closely because the outlook for the United States remains uncertain. This is not too different from what Zuckerman wrote, but instead of following his own advice in September 2012 Bernanke engaged in QE3 and in December 2012 in QE 3.5.[19]

Reconciling the Zuckerman and Bernanke approaches presents a dilemma. We can claim that one is right and the other is wrong. Or we can consider the possibility that the Federal Reserve is motivated by more than the state of the US economy, and therefore saying one thing and doing another is not as contradictory as it might seem. But whatever else may be motivating it, is it enough to justify throwing more liquidity in an already overliquid market?

Somehow it seems to have escaped the Fed chairman's attention that in the longer run "more of the same" is an unhealthy economic policy. As its debt mountain continues rising, the United States will eventually have to decide between another rating downgrade due to overspending or risking a recession due to an emergency in cutting the deficit.

This challenge is not as far away as the neo-Keynesian economists hope. On June 13, 2011, Bloomberg's ticker carried a statement by Bill Gross, of PIMCO, that the United States is in worse shape than Greece. When Gross expressed this opinion, Greece was at the brink of bankruptcy.

This is by no means an isolated way of looking at the coming peril. Interviewed on July 2, 2012 by Bloomberg News, David Cote, Honeywell's chairman, had an advice for Washington. The monitor asked: "As a successful businessman, given Honeywell's results, what would you have done to redress the American economy if you were running the government?" Without a glimpse of hesitation, Cote answered: "I would declare bankruptcy."

What was meant, though not explicitly stated in this exchange, is that there is no question the status quo can continue with budget deficits a daily ritual and an ever increasing cost of endowments. While taxes may rise, as the last two decades of sovereign spending habits document public expenditures will rise faster. Alternatively, the quantity and quality of public services will shrink to make the ends meet. In the aftermath, the citizens

- Will no more have the right to public services beyond a bare minimum, and
- Will need to provide for a significant chunk of costs associated to education, pensions, and health care by themselves.

Critics may say that the opinions expressed by Gross and Cote are pessimistic views of the future of the American economy, but one should not forget that there were reasons for them. "Free university education for all" provides an example, albeit from the other shore of North Atlantic. In Europe, university studies are largely featherbedded by the sovereign (an exception is Britain where college fees were established in the Blair years). In the United States, the fact that universities spend beyond their means is reflected in student loans which hit $1 trillion and in ever increasing tuition fees. Between the mid-1970s and 2012:

- College tuition in the United States increased an average of 1200 percent, while consumer prices grew by "only" 400 percent, and
- Over the same period, the universities' administrative overhead practically doubled from 5 nonfaculty employees per 10 faculty members, to parity.[20]

This is quite a substantial increase in administrative costs in education, and it provides evidence that the business of *homo bureaucraticus* is kicking. The same is true of administrative costs in health care, with the result that taxpayers are charged for a booming bureaucracy, exactly the sort of thing an overindebted society does not need.

Administrative costs have to be cut with a sharp knife, even if this is sure to encounter political resistance, while all other costs have to be examined from the viewpoint of their deliverables based on firm evidence. The budget must be balanced and to do so no stone should be left unturned. *If* public debt continues its current course, *then* outright bankruptcy will be an option. The government could write off trillions of dollars at a stroke, but this will have a huge negative impact on the economy with end result a total loss of confidence.

Bankruptcy might also happen by default. Debt reduction via hyperinflation is another option, leading to forced downsizing of federal debt at the expense of common citizens[21] and investors. This, too, will negatively affect the economy and have a global wide impact. Most significantly it would imply heavy taxation of the poor, as is always the case with inflation.

According to his critics, with QE1, QE2, QE3, and QE3.5 Bernanke allegedly tried to engineer the latter alternative. Drastically devaluing the dollar is still another option, which will most likely ignite a wave of competitive devaluations, like the one that preceded WWII. This solution is far from unthinkable, as there is precedence to it. In 1933, President Roosevelt fixed its value of the ounce of gold at $35.00 against the then prevailing rate of $20.67.

Financial history books write that prior to making up his mind on this *de facto* 43 percent devaluation of the US dollar against gold, which affected all outstanding debt, Roosevelt asked the respected Democratic Senator Gore of Tennessee for his opinion: It will be stealing Mr. President, would it not? Gore replied. Stealing or not, this halving of the dollars' value did take place 80 years ago; hence, it is not unthinkable that it could happen again.

It is far from being clear which of the major alternatives will be adopted for pulling the American economy from the precipice. Much depends on political will. Factors which will probably impact on the final choice include:

- How fast the economy is moving towards the precipice
- How deep the drop is likely to be, if it happens
- Which people will be hurt by each alternative, and by how much.

Why not to consider another alternative: that of pulling the Swedish economy away from the cliff. It is interesting because of some striking similarities between the American economy in 2013 and the Swedish in 1993. In the post-WWII years, Sweden used to be famous for its generous welfare state and full employment. This was the envy of other countries. George Pompidou, the French president, once said that he wished France to be a kind of Sweden by the Mediterranean. The system worked, or at least gave the impression of doing so, by

- Taxing the Swedish citizens at very high levels,
- Leaving no room for maneuver in case of hard times, and
- Ignoring the fact even a prosperous economy can get into deep trouble.

In his predictions contributed to the *Financial Times* A-List on the big challenges of 2012 (written on January 3, 2012) Jeffrey Sachs, of Columbia University, has this to say about events down the line: Barack Obama will be reelected because of his consistent strategy to stay one step towards the center of the right-wing Republican party. But the presidential elections will do nothing to reinvigorate American society. Government will remain corrupt, incompetent, and shortsighted. Let's see how the Swedes handled that problem.

10.5   Sweden's Near Bankruptcy in 1993 Provides Food for Thought

The majority of people running western governments find it difficult to understand that *if* their electoral promises materialize *then* the result would be catastrophic for their country, even if it helps them individually to sustain the image of exceptional politicians who stick to their word. Yet, the economic realities are those they are. It is better to decelerate debt issuance and reverse gear than to press on the accelerator, because the latter leads straight against the wall. Sweden provides an excellent example on, and precedence to, the challenges today confronting the United States.

The Swedish government's nightmare came in the 1993 fiscal year, when the budget deficit soared to about 14 percent of GDP. To make matters worse, Swedish banks lost at this time so much money, that only a deep-pocketed government could help keep them afloat. The prediction of a study group of economists, headed by professor Assar Linbeck, was that worse was yet to come. It proved true, and it was left to a right-wing government, a rare bird in Swedish politics, to save the day.

The Linbeck study blamed several decades of socialist government mistakes and reckless endowment policies for Sweden's plight. Sounds familiar? It is precisely so. Today, each one of the mistakes identified by Linbeck and his associates finds its counterpart in the United States. As far as Sweden is concerned, the post-WWII period were the years when

- The welfare state was constantly expanding,
- The power of the trade unions was entrenched, and
- High wage settlements put the country on the road to economic precipice.

All this led to a dismal economic record which in our days is by no means unheard of. Every one of the aforementioned problems now affects not only the American economy but also all other in the industrial countries—with Italy, Spain, and France in the frontline. Yet, most surprisingly, nobody really studies the pre-1993 Sweden as a model of what *not to do*.

What not to do is to try to appease the market by throwing money at the problem, and by keeping the cost of money near zero over the medium to longer term. That's the Bernanke policy. By contrast, in 1993 the president of Riksbank (Swedish central bank) did quite the opposite, and who would argue with success?

The Riksbank brought the overnight interest rate sky-high and through this action it pruned the system, while remaining vigilant about the appearance of the next symptoms. It's attention was not grounded in preserving and possibly amending a system which had failed, but in identified and closing the gap between measures taken and their practical results.

Contrary to what socialist-inclined economists had expected, the recovery of the Swedish economy proceeded speedily and was complete within a couple of years. The economic policy lesson from Sweden 1993 is that when the time comes for tough decisions the government should not flunk the test. The longer term should never be lost from sight. Even if the right decisions are unpopular in the short term, they have to be made. Seeing them through is more a matter of will than of ability.

"If you postulate a system that depends upon one country always following the right policies, you will find sooner or later that no such country exists," says Paul Volcker. "The system eventually is going to break down ... there is no easy way out of the burdens of leadership."[22] Integral part of that burden is steady watch and readiness for action, without cornering oneself to a road leading nowhere.

There exists in economics, particularly in econometrics, a mathematically unproven put powerful multiplication law. Its nature and impact is suggested through practical experience and anecdotal evidence. What it states is that, past a certain threshold, the mass effect tends to create an exponential curve:

- The more sovereign budgets get out of control and deficits grow, the greater the amount of red ink in the coming months and years because the system gets fractioned, and
- The more speculative are the markets the more the upturn or downturn will amplify and accelerate, reaching changes which are unexpected, discontinuous, and abrupt.

The economic situation the United States confronts today is a year or two away from "Sweden 1993." In the time preceding the Swedish debacle, proposed "solutions" were half-baked at best, lacking consistency and decisiveness. They were developed by politicians thinking of their careers and by bureaucrats dreaming of spending "more" of other people's money.

This is one of the reasons why Stockholm 1993 and Washington 2013 + correlate. Another reason is the "unknown unknowns." In the United States today three factors suggest that, percentage-wise, annual increases in the deficit in the near future may be way beyond those of Sweden in 1993:

- The next big stimulus promoted by the US president is still an unknown,
- The sovereign's deficit will skyrocket if pensions, health care, and other commitments which are not yet provisioned are added up,[23] and
- The compound effect of interest to be paid on the accumulated US deficit will rise exponentially if interest rates escape the Fed's control, as they might.

Clear minds in America have seen well in advance the coming impasse. In a seminal book on his experience with US deficits, published in the 1980s, former White House Budget director David Stockmann demonstrated that unless the entitlement programs are radically cut the federal budget can never be balanced.[24] To Stockmann's opinion runaway net expense categories include

- Social security,
- Medicaid, Medicare,
- Interest paid on borrowed money,
- Defense outlays, and
- Subsidy-related government expenses.

More recently the current account, too, has been singled out as a source of anxiety. No country can run a trade deficit forever. It can borrow a lot before it goes broke, but at some point the world's financial markets will clamp down on its finances just as they clamped down on Mexico. As Lester Thurow says: "The question is not whether an earthquake will occur. It will. The only question is when."[25]

The US current account deficit has been a long-standing drag on the dollar. In 2006, at the height of the credit boom, it reached $800 billion or 6 percent of GDP. Though the deficit has been reduced as the credit crunch which followed the 2007/2008

economic and financial crisis has lowered imports, it still stands at over 3 percent of
GDP, largely because like Euroland, the United States remains a major energy
importer.[26]

In a way quite similar to "Sweden 1993," the 2013+ US scenario will be dominated by the widening gap between booming sovereign expenses and fiscal contraction. Economists say that estimating the economic impact of fiscal contractions is
made more difficult by the uncertainty surrounding the size of fiscal multipliers.

In addition, a big unknown is the speed with which households react to a potential increase in taxes, and on whether they will perceive the change in policies as
transitory or permanent. There are as well adverse effects on confidence that may
arise, if businesses and consumers start to perceive the risk of an abrupt fiscal
change and restrain their spending plans.

Most Americans, even those benefiting from oversized entitlements, are afraid
of an abrupt fiscal change because they can see that the US government's deficit
and debt are unsustainable. Not only policies to correct these imbalances are not
advancing but they are not even on the table. Closely related to this is the fact that
neither the White House nor Congress have defined what they want the United
States to be in the twenty first century. Have the politicians who run the US fortunes decided where the nation is going? And, if yes, do they have a strategy to
reach that goal?

Benjamin Franklin was the first member of the Constitutional Assembly to
come in contact with citizens anxiously waiting outside the assembly hall to hear
what kind of regime was decided by the Founding Fathers. They rushed to ask him
and Franklin answered: "A democracy, if you can keep it."

Benjamin Franklin's "*IF*" is today's Number 1 question for every American;
evidently also for the president and for Congress. A democracy under an
unsupportable weight of debt is not a democracy. If proof is needed, look at ancient
Athens at the time of Pericles. He loaded the city-state under his watch with debt
and exploited the Athenian empire to pay from it. The other member states of alliance revolted, and this led to the 30-year Peloponnesian War which brought to an
end of ancient Greece.

10.6   Everybody Will Suffer from Currency Wars

Twenty years after "Sweden 1993" Bernanke's Fed applied precisely the opposite
policy of near zero interest rates over long stretches of time, and failed to move
forward the American economy. Sweden was lucky to have at the helm of the central bank a person capable of deciding swiftly, taking risks and at the same time
being in charge of assumed exposure through moves which were:

* Drastic,
* Short lived, and
* Effective.

Sweden 1993 was a complex social, political, and economic crisis with more than one sector to be looked immediately after. Bernanke, too, confronted a double whammy. But the impact of his decisions, targetted the market, not the American Society at large. Therefore, the US economy did not see a rapid revival. Massive QE failed in its goals. Unemployment unwind only slowly and the prospects of economic activity remained subdued. That took care of Goal No. 1 in Bernanke's policy. In addition, when one examines the decisions taken by a scholar of the First Great Depression, he cannot escape the thought that a competitive devaluation of the US dollar has been Goal No. 2 of the Bernanke's Fed policy. This, too, has failed.

Back in 2010, led by Brazil, emerging economies accused America of instigating a currency war. The occasion was presented in 2010 when Bernanke's Fed bought heaps of bonds with newly printed money. Investors rushed into emerging markets in search of better returns, and has been instrumental in lifting their exchange rates.

The issue of currency wars has been on and off for over 3 years. In February 2013, the Group of Seven issued a statement intended to calm spirits about "currency wars" but ended up causing more confusion than clarity. While the G-7 statement chided government intervention in currency markets, it also supported an effort by Japan to combat deflation. (Competitive devaluations in Britain and Japan were a key theme during that period of time.)

True enough, there is plenty of hypocrisy in the devaluation argument. Devaluing one's currency against the global financial and payments system is the objective of every government overtaken by budgetary deficits, creeping uncompetitiveness, and a mountain of unfunded liabilities (Section 10.2). QE in Britain and QE in America had practically the same rationale:

- Bring the currency down, and
- Offer the local industry a competitive edge by way of cheap currency rather than higher productivity.

In Britain this policy has succeeded, becoming the legacy Merwyn King left behind as he quit the governorship of the Bank of England. In a few days the pound fell by an appreciable 9 percent and it continued falling in the following weeks, albeit slowly.

It helped that under the Gordon Brown government the British banking sector was obliged to come clean on losses and be subject to needed recapitalization which made the sovereign majority owner of big British banks. Also, that under David Cameron every effort was made to accelerate needed structural reforms that might encourage higher investment by the private sector.

So, the British made it leaving Bernanke in the dust. Devaluation, of course, will not solve single-handed a sovereign's problems, but it might succeed in boosting overseas demand for British products to bring about the rebalancing that the economy needs to have and improve Britain's dismal current account.

One swallow, however, does not bring spring. Even after the 9.0 percent devaluation of the pound, data suggest that manufacturing remains uncompetitive relative to services, with the net rate of return on capital in manufacturing being a mere 4.7 percent—a small fraction of the rate of return in services.

This knocks down the argument that the real exchange rate of the pound was overvalued, a notion which has been debatable. What is true is that with demand abroad weak, manufacturers needed all the help they could get and a significant devaluation boosted their fortunes. In other terms while the fall in sterling could be economically helpful, the economy would as well require other measures all the way to

- Structural reform, and
- Higher productivity.

The lesson America can derive from the competitive devaluation of the pound is that it has been helpful to the economy, but far from providing "the solution." It takes more than a devaluation to put the currency and the economy on track to competitiveness—and no doubt if Bernanke had succeeded with his $ devaluation he would have done nothing to kill the monster of $211 trillion in unfunded US liabilities.

A similar lesson can be derived from the other devaluation which took place more or less within the same time frame: That devaluation of the yen, from 77 to the dollar (September–October 2012) to 95 (March 2013). The yen has been another strong currency which capitalized on geopolitical changes to give the Japanese industry an edge in the global market. Investors and speculators who judged right the magnitude of the yen's fall made a fortune. George Soros is said to have made $1 billion out of it.

Shinzo Abe, the new Japanese prime minister, promised bold stimulus to restart growth and vanquish deflation. He also called for a weaker yen to bolster exports. Since the end of September 2012, the Japanese currency has fallen 16 percent against the dollar and 19 percent against the euro. The steeper fall was in February 2013 when it became clear that Abe meant to exercise his power.

In currency exchange terms the Japanese and the British hit their goal, but the Americans did not profit. No matter what Bernanke does it is not possible that the dollar devalues against itself. The luminaries who invented the different devaluation theories as the neat way out did not understand that the dollar can only then devalue against the global financial system *if* it abandons its privileges.

From Bretton Woods times, all important global commodities are denominated in dollars. This gives the US currency a king-size advantage in the international market. Abandoning it by way of substituting the dollar by a basket of currencies is an option—one highly unwise from the American point of view. Here is then the top choice Bernanke and company have are confronting:

- Keeping control of the global currency and trade infrastructure, but dropping the dream of dollar devaluation, or
- Abandoning the privilege of pricing in $ important global commodities (hence infrastructural control) and aiming at dollar devaluation.

Trying to do both at the same time is a policy which has failed so far, and will continue failing. It's like planning to kill two birds with one well-placed stone. Neither should it be forgotten that the dollar is refuge money. Every time something happens in the global political or financial landscape the dollar's exchange rate goes up, no matter what Bernanke may be saying or doing. Uncertainty always favors the dollar.

Take the WSJ Dollar Index[27] as an example. In September 2012 it reached a low 69, then hovered around 70 till January 2012 when it took off. January to March 2013 the WSJ Dollar Index rose 5 percent, almost in straight line, helped by the chaotic result of Italian election and their impact on the euro—confirming one more time that, aside the other economic damages which it creates, Bernanke's dream to talk down the dollar through massive QEs remains just that—a dream.

There are plenty of issues weighting against the dollar's devaluation, Bernanke is desperately trying to achieve through quantitative easing. In addition, as we already discussed in connection to the British example, devaluing a currency does not necessarily lead a country to higher exports. Countries with traditionally strong currencies, such as Switzerland, Germany, and Japan, have a much more important industrial sector than countries with traditionally weaker ones, such as France, Britain, and the United States.

Neither is it true that exporting more assures that a country will grow faster. Exports are a complex issue where not only prices but as well the need for the product (for instance: oil), innovation, productivity, high quality, and cost control play important roles.

There exists as well the historical fact that if every industrial nation tries to devalue its currency in the end there are only losers. This "beggar-thy-neighbor" policy has led to the First Great Depression. Faced with recessions, many countries introduced protectionist measures in the form of tariffs[28] which ultimately backfired, and international trade crumbled, leading to recessions and depressions. The $211 trillion in uncovered liabilities is daunting, but it has to be solved within the US economy, not outside of it through QE.

End Notes

1. *Financial Times*, March 4, 2013.
2. A sign of desperation by the US Congress regarding the control of government expenditure.
3. No kidding!
4. Concerns on how the government will verify personal financial information on the new state-based health care exchanges have kept on mounting. In these exchanges uninsured Americans are expected to shop for individual and small group health insurance plans.
5. *Le Figaro* Magazine, September 28, 2012.
6. *Idem.*
7. After which the states would have to pay for up to 7 percent of the cost.
8. *Financial Times*, February 26, 2013.
9. *The Economist*, March 2, 2013. Other countries have eliminated the 1 penny and 2 penny coins. An example is Finland which dropped the 1 cent and 2 cent euro. In 1857, the US ditched the half-cent, then worth nearly as much (in real terms) as today's dime.

10. After the 2010 restructuring of government expenditures following the bailout and austerity drive, Greece stands out as the country where the outlook for aging and health-related expenses *might* be brought in control.
11. Suisse C. Global Investor (GI) 2.12. Health care. Entering the Digital Era. Zurich, 2012.
12. The author is indebted to Dr. Thomas C. Kaufmann, equity analyst global pharma & innovation, Crédit Suisse, in his collaboration in structuring the two tables and in providing the PPP statistics.
13. *Financial Times*, January 11, 2013.
14. *The Economist*, January 5, 2012.
15. *The Economist*, December 1, 2012.
16. *Financial Times*, May 7, 2013.
17. Editor-in-chief, US News & World Report and chairman of Boston Properties.
18. *Financial Times*, July 25, 2011.
19. Chorafas DN. The changing role of Central Banks. New York: Palgrave/Macmillan; 2013.
20. *The Economist*, January 12, 2012 and other sources.
21. Particularly those financially weak.
22. Volcker P, Gyohten T. Changing fortunes. New York: Times Books; 1992.
23. If FASB Statement 106 is applied, as it should have been the case.
24. Stockmann DA. The triumph of politics. New York: Coronet Books; 1986.
25. Thurow L. The future of capitalism. New York: William Morrow; 1995.
26. This may change in the coming years as the United States is in its way to become energy sufficient.
27. A gauge of the $'s exchange rate against seven of the world's more heavily traded currencies.
28. For instance in the United States the Smoot–Hawley Tariff Act.

11 Public Debt, Balanced Budgets, and Current Accounts

11.1 The Debt Ceiling

Chapter 10 brought to the reader's attention the fact that economic reasons, social policies, and political motives are often closely intertwined. One of the manifestations of this intimate linkage is the *debt ceiling*, periodically reset by Congress; it's an American specialty. Prior to a statutory ceiling on public debt, the Treasury had to obtain congressional approval every time it wanted to borrow money.

The idea of having a debt ceiling as a barrier is interesting, particularly so if its resetting takes place after a relatively long period of time and has as a prerequisite a deep examination as to *why* the public debt has risen, with measures taken to correct the slippages. This is no longer true of the US debt ceiling, if it ever has been. Instead:

- The debt ceiling is a legislative policy administered in bits and pieces, and
- Requests for its raising do not lead to the control of national indebtedness, or even to hitting the brakes to public debt.

Critics say that the debt ceiling led to profligacy rather than to cost control. Interestingly, the 1917 ceiling was set at $11.5 billion, less than 0.7/1000 the level of $16.4 trillion where it stands today. Moreover, its first version created on the Second Liberty Bond Act was better than the second, set up in 1939. The first version imposed differing limits for different categories of borrowing, which eventually waned and were forgotten.

The second version of the US debt ceiling has been lifted nearly 100 times since its inspection, with varying degrees of political bickering. In 1979, political squabbling led to a small technical default. Then, as in several subsequent upgrades, the limit was raised only at the last minute and interest rates ticked up as a result of the ambiguity which followed the delay.[1] Figure 11.1 presents a snapshot of how the debt ceiling operated during the last 15 years.

- In the last 3 years of his administration, Bill Clinton had one upping of the statutory debt limit;
- Over 8 years, George W. Bush asked six times for raising the debt ceiling;
- In his first 4 years, Barack Obama had five uppings, two of which were major, and a new one is around the corner.

Public Debt Dynamics of Europe and the US. DOI: http://dx.doi.org/10.1016/B978-0-12-420021-0.00011-7

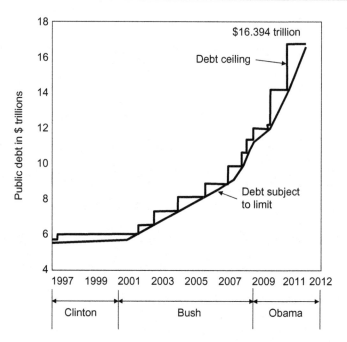

Figure 11.1 The skyrocketing US debt ceiling.

There is no better way of documenting who is the biggest spender. It is *as if* Bush Jr. and Obama have been in competition to one another on who will dig deeper the US public debt hole. This rush to bigger debt contradicts the Dennis Healey principle (Healey was chancellor of the Exchequer in Britain under the labor government) which states: "If you are in a hole stop digging."

Both Obama and Bush dug deeper the hole they were in and into which they brought the American public. Many economists criticize Washington's inability to control budgetary deficits because of social services and the (vein) effort of reflating the economy. The latter is just an excuse. As successive sections of this chapter demonstrate, there are expenditures which could be easily avoided but are not. Foreign wars are an example.

The $9 billion Washington spends every month on the war in Afghanistan exceeds what it has spent in nearly 3 years to help the millions of Americans whose homes are under water.[2] For every worker Obama failed to retain, there were more boots on the ground in Afghanistan. For every home foreclosure he could not stop, there have been massive Predator attacks against the Taliban.

Neither is the 12-year beat in Afghanistan Obama's only unnecessary spending spree. Up to December 31, 2011, the equally unnecessary long-term military presence in Iraq had cost the American taxpayer over $1 trillion. It is as if nobody is paying attention on how well money authorized by the statutory debt limit is being spent. It is *as if* the debt ceiling attracts and promotes spending habits. Clinton kept the federal budget nearly balanced, but Bush Jr. added one deficit to the other:

- The federal budget went out of control under Bush Jr., and
- Deficits and debts skyrocketed under Obama.

As far as the future of the American economy is concerned, as well as the dollar's stability, the exponential rise of the debt curve in Figure 11.1, under Obama, is frightening. Still the public reelected him to continue his good work of demolishing economic, financial, and currency stability. Also destabilizing is the fact that Congress sets the ceiling on how much the country may borrow from its citizen without asking penetrating questions to those who authorize runaway expenditures.

Critics say that by now raising the debt ceiling has become the nearest thing to routine. This does not go unnoticed by the markets. In mid-2011, when the debt ceiling was raised after a political fight, trading in CDSs on Treasury securities picked up. The price of protection against default, as measured by the CDS spread, rose to the point that 1-year credit protection became almost as expensive as 5-year protection—which is typically seen in distressed markets where investors price in an imminent default.

Economists outlined several consequences of a default. These include the dumping of US government debt by foreign holders, and downgrade of the US triple-A credit rating (which did not take long to be pronounced by Standard & Poor's). Other projected effects are a run on money market funds (as the one that followed the collapse of Lehman Brothers in 2008), and a wave of acute deleveraging.

Put under pressure from several sides in August 2011 Congress gave in, without questions asked on future deficits and overruns. Interviewed on CNBC on August 2, 2011 Bill Gross, of PIMCO, said that the economic situation of the United States has not improved by the bill which raised the debt limit. This was a classical *releveraging* measure. Other Wall Street experts expressed the opinion that the bill raising the statutory debt limit was a fraud. Of the $2.1 trillion of reduction in government expenses supposedly agreed to by the Obama Administration, some $880 billion, or 42 percent of the promised budget cuts, came out of the military budget—and they had no chance to materialize.

In addition, Wall Street had expected budget cuts of $4 trillion instead of an uncertain sum of $2.1 trillion. We don't take that serious anymore, said a broker. It will have to be revised in the not too distant future, commented another market operator. Both market specialists proved to be right. Practically, all the interviewed Wall Street experts pressed the point that the negotiations which led to the lifting of Uncle Sam's debt limit were characterized by *short-termism*, pointing out that:

- Economic growth needs a long-term plan, and
- It's an illusion that one can promote economic growth in the short term.

Economists said that though in exceptional cases in the short-term budgetary deficits may be necessary, in the medium to longer term economic growth promoted by deficits makes no sense. Others criticized the fact that Congress did not censure the Administration for its deficits, and therefore, there is no reason to believe that the federal government's budgetary imbalances will be taken care of in the future. Government is the only big spender in town, said an expert.

One of the most important concerns Bill Gross expressed during the August 2, 2011 CNBC interview is that the consumer has disappeared as the financial moving force of the economy. This is in stark contrast to what was the rule prior to the 2007–2014 economic crisis, where consumers represented 71 percent of spending in the US economy.

With employment still high in spite of zero interest rates and the Fed's unconventional measures, US households are afraid to spend because of uncertainty about the future. To the opinion of financial analysts, quite recently the Fed has been prepared to fill the gap with another quantitative easing (QE3)—this too with fairly uncertain prospects. "Stimulus is a dirty word," said one of the interviewed specialists, "but it is not dead."

What Gross feared the most was a continuing currency depreciation, with inflation hiding behind it. Between the lines of the interview he gave to CNBC, it was easy to see that PIMCO was moving funds out of US dollar, investing in Canada, Germany, even Mexico, and in commodities. Neither was Gross alone in these concerns.

Other critics said that the repetition of ineffectual central bank measures was unwise as the Fed has been falling short on achieving both of its two mandates, namely, price stability and full employment. In spite of QE1, QE2, QE3, QE3.5, and Twist, the unemployment rate is still far away from the Federal Open Market Commission's (FOMC) estimate of the long-term structural unemployment rate of 5.2–6.0 percent. As far as price stability is concerned, the different QEs, Twists, and buying of Treasury bonds had become a Damoclean sword over its head. To put it mildly, the Bernanke doctrine of central banking was judged by the best of all critters, *The Economy*, and found faulty.

11.2   US Public Debt Is Over $16 Billion. Who Is to Blame?

In August 2011, Standard & Poor's, the independent rating agency, downgraded the US credit rating by one notch from AAA to AA+ . In the aftermath, the stock market plunged. This was a symptom of loss of confidence, more than a political, economic or financial reaction, even if the slow pace of economic recovery and wayward public finances weighted on the downgrade.

A triple-A credit rating is not God-given, but neither should it be discarded lightly because it tells a great deal on how well an entity—sovereign or company— is being managed. In addition, once the higher rating is lost, it is rather hard to get it back. Psychologically, the bragging rights attached to it are probably as valuable to the owner as the cheaper borrowing, because the highest rating of creditworthiness enhances an entity's prestige.

Let's face it; not only is the United States a debtor country but also the federal government now borrows 30 cents of every dollar it spends.[3] America also imports nearly 40 cents of merchandise for every dollar in demand. Even more ominous is the fact that since the early years of this century, under the Bush Jr. Administration, the government has turned a blind eye to the country's skyrocketing fiscal deficit.

To make matters worse, Bush Jr. decreed hefty tax cuts, allegedly to stimulate the economy, even if the budget was in deficit. The sure outcome was an increase in the national debt. To support the president's (questionable) action, Alan Greenspan, then chairman of the Federal Reserve, sent copies of his forthcoming testimony to members of the Senate's Budget Committee, and found out that several senators were not pleased with what they read.

Ron Suskind describes one of the meetings which took place. Senator Ken Conrad, the Budget Committee's senior Democrat, complained that there was no $5.6 trillion surplus.[4] "If the government would just engage in honest accounting and take appropriate notice of its long-term liabilities, there would be no surplus...these surpluses are fictional," Conrad said to Greenspan, adding that: "If you endorse these tax cuts, Alan, you're going to unleash the deficit dogs. All bets are going to be off... What you'll do is throw fiscal responsibility out the window."[5]

According to Suskind, the then Fed chairman excused himself by saying this was not *his* tax policy, while admitting that distributing the surplus in an economically correct and safe way was his responsibility. But there was no surplus. The evidence subsequently provided through statistics is that in his 8 years in the White House, Bush Jr. run on deficits which added on an already sky-high public debt. In retrospect, what there has been at the Administration's side was lack of political will to:

- Face the facts, and
- Reduce the deficit.

Flooding the market with liquidity by working overtime the central bank's printing presses and destabilizing the currency through mammoth budget deficits is like putting a dagger in the steering wheel. It makes the consequences of monetary policy's failure potentially lethal. The dagger is supposed to encourage safe driving, but accidents happen just as frequently at government level as they do on the turnpike.

At least at the time these lines are written (April 2013), there is no question about the technical ability of Washington to make good on its debts. Less sure is the resolve of the political system's willingness, let alone readiness, to resolve America's economic and financial problems—all the way from economic growth to the *reasons* why unemployment is high. Neither is there any urgency of ending the (frequent) increases of the nation's debt ceiling.

In 2011 and 2012, the increase in US public deficit-to-GDP ratio has been a mind-boggling, 8.5 percent per year, and it is forecast to stay at this level in 2013. This or worse will be the case unless major, meaningful, and honest reductions in public spending are agreed—which is not in the cards.

Economists who want their country to get out of the yoke of rising public debt have concluded that ill-advised political decisions are the reason why fiscal policy is not delivering the desired boost to the real economy, no matter how much money the Fed throws to the market. To the contrary, economists who do not challenge the negative economy status quo, the wrongly labeled Neo-Keynesians, have come to the opposite conclusion.

To the so-called Neo-Keynesians' opinion, the irresponsible public deficit spending witnessed in the last 6 years, which has sent the public debt to a stratospheric $16.4 trillion, or 110 percent of GDP, is not enough. Actually, this is a flawed reasoning and so is the concept of throwing more money on the fire. Debt-loving economists say that:

- *If* deficit spending is not functioning,
- *Then* it is because more of it is needed.

But does it make sense to spend more and more public money, without first earning that money? After years of the US economy's stalling and subtrend growth, it is time to admit that the path taken by the Bush Jr. and Obama Administrations leads to a dead end. The deleveraging and healing processes will be long and involve painful adjustments. America is in the midst of the world's largest debt crisis.

The US Treasury now owes the public over $11 trillion plus more than $5 trillion to foreigners—and that does not include what households owe—which is another 110 percent of US GDP—and what companies owe which runs upward of $8 trillion, or nearly 60 percent of GDP. It adds to 280 percent of GDP.[6] Income from the next 3 years has been already consumed prior to being earned.

Like France, Italy, Spain, and Greece, the United States is a very heavily indebted nation, raising the question: who will bear the burden of adjustment. The answer is no other than the American public. There is no way to "bill foreigners" or tax only the wealthier members of society. Everyone must participate including the beneficiaries of most of government spending such as public employees and recipients of the so-called social spending. Other questions too will have to be answered.

- Will the government act soon, raising taxes and cutting spending, or wait for another credit rating downgrade?
- How strongly will the US government reduce spending when it starts doing so? Will entitlements be looked at as sacred cows?

Shakespeare has written that three things don't come back in life: the time that passed by, the word that has been said, and the opportunity which has been lost. There is no time to lose. To the opinion of Mohamed El-Erian, the CEO of PIMCO, the US economic situation is terrifying. The first decade of this century was lost by squandering wealth and borrowing as if there was no tomorrow. The result has been:

- Incomplete recovery,
- Economic stagnation, and
- High unemployment rate.

For the American economy, the 8 years of the Bush Jr. Administration have been an unmitigated disaster: irresponsible tax cuts, unnecessary but ruinously expensive wars, failures of banking regulation, the *fiesta* of subprimes, and housing boom and bust. This does not mean, however, that the Obama Administration did any better.

In the Bush Jr. and Obama years, the money made even by those who had a job was dwindling. Figure 11.2 dramatizes this point with reference to the median income of American citizens. Taking the 1982 median income equal to 100, the rise to peak median earning (nearly 125) is in the second half of the Clinton Administration. The median dropped under Bush Jr., recovered a little, and moved all the way south under Obama since his first year in office.

Experts suggest that this is largely the result of economic downturn under the Obama Administration, with the skyrocketing budget deficit and economic stagnation being major reasons. Because of economic uncertainty, Obama renewed the Bush Jr. tax cuts, reduced taxes, and broadened unemployment benefits. As a result, in 2012 public deficit run to 8.5 percent of GDP—even if, according to what the government said, the US economy has been "in recovery" for over 3 years.

America is deeply in debt with a great deal of unfunded liabilities. Alan Greenspan says there is no painless solution to the US debt problem.[7] Plenty of other financial analysts and economists agree with him. At the end of the day, nothing is more illusory than to deny a problem's existence and pretend that somehow numbers have lost their connection to reality. The challenge is political.

The bipartisan compromise, brokered on New Year's Eve by Joe Biden, the US vice president, and Mitch McConnell, the Republican Senate minority leader, has

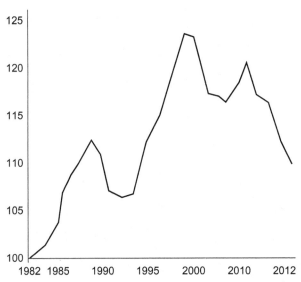

Figure 11.2 American median real income over a 30-year time frame, with 1982 = 100.

not improved a single bit the US budget deficit. It just replaced an immediate fiscal cliff with two other greater and more demanding tasks:

- Statutory debt ceiling, and
- Deep spending cuts.

US government spending formally hit the ceiling on December 31, 2012, but the Treasury has been able to buy some extra time through creative accounting. This demolishes the reason for which the debt ceiling was created in 1917 by act of Congress (authorizing the second loan to fund the American military and industrial effort in World War I). While this represented a transfer of responsibility from Congress to the Treasury department, the ceiling itself provided the legislators with oversight by:

- Imposing limits on maturities,
- Watching over interest rates, and
- Barring the Treasury from borrowing beyond totals originating from loan acts (see also Section 11.1).

Such a functional setting was fairly neat, but it changed over time as individual limits were removed and replaced by a total borrowing ceiling. Eventually, congressional authorization turned into a routine. But as it has been upped many times at increasing frequency, the debt ceiling turned itself into a political power tool. (Section 1) The same is true of spending cuts.

By all likelihood, negotiations on spending cuts and debt ceiling will be protracted in a political game where each party, the White House and House of Representatives, accuses each other of inflexibility and bad faith. All that has been provided by the New Year's Eve 2013 compromise is an increase in taxes for the higher income earners without counterparts (see also in Section 11.6 the impact of events which took place in January 2013.)

Leftist legislators have asked for abandoning altogether the debt ceiling, "because it works against seniors (for their entitlements) and juniors (for their education)". To put it mildly, this is highly irresponsible because it makes fun of debt.

This is by no means a call against taxes, but one for government responsibility. Entitlement and other social costs, which the American economy cannot afford, have to be trimmed to a sustainable level. Rather than paying for "more entitlements," an increase in US taxes is urgently used to retire the colossal public debt which is crashing the economy.

Americans pay on average 29 percent of their income in taxes. In Europe, the average is 42 percent and goes up to 50 percent in some countries. The 13 percent difference can provide a torrent of money to bring public finances into shape (even if some 47.5 percent of the population pays no taxes, if what Mit Romney said during the presidential campaign is correct). Let me repeat my statement. An increase in taxes, preferably for everybody not just for the so-called *rich*,[8] should primarily aim to retire the public debt.

11.3   Balanced Budgets Do Not Come As a Matter of Course

When in the mid-1950s, in one of the hick-ups of a prosperous American economy, economists said that the federal budget had to be balanced, President Dwight Eisenhower answered that he agreed. He also remarked that this will not be achieved just by trimming here or there different expenses. Whole chapters had to be left out.

This is true. The question is: "Which chapters?" Logically, it should be those fastest growing and/or able to be privatized. The challenge inherent to this approach is that the fastest going expenditures happen to be untouchable. Here is how the tax dollar is channeled into US government expenses:

- *Entitlements*: 14.4 percent of GDP and fast growing; their share was 7.6 percent in early 1970s, almost half the present one.
- *Defense*: 5.0 percent of GDP; significantly downsized from 6.4 percent in early 1970s and mid-1980s.[9]
- *Net interest on debt*: "only" 1.6 percent of GDP because of near zero interest rates. With free market interest rates, it was double that amount in the 1980s, on much smaller public debt.
- *Other federal expenses*: 4.4 percent of GDP; over the last 30 years these fluctuated between 3.5 percent and current level.

Eisenhower was right when he said that trimming the different expense chapters here and there barely scratches the surface; it does not confront the main problem. In the 1950s, the main problem was the military—industrial complex. Today, it is entitlements which, for many people and households, have become permanent second and third income. This is particularly true of Medicare and Medicaid (providing health care for elderly and poor, respectively), the new add-on of Obamacare, and Social Security (pensions).

Obama has proposed cutting Medicare fees to hospitals, nursing homes, drug manufacturers, and other providers. There is plenty of air in this statement, made for partisan purposes. The proof is that it did not convince Medicare's/Medicaid's own actuaries, who think this will not work.

Other politicians have proposed a screening of means to decide on Medicare coverage. This will be open to abuse, aside the fact that it involves moral risk. The better-off households are asked to pay the major share in taxation, and at the same time, they will be cut off the nanny state's goods. The better approach is that:

- The politicians explain to the public the reasons for redimensioning unaffordable and unsustainable entitlements, and
- Those administering social net programs look like a hawk at every dollar being spent, with violators brought to justice.

It is a sound policy to look at the facts rather than living in the clouds. With health care and retirement being socialized, violations in health care and pensions should be legally defined as tax evasion cases. Nearly free of cost medication is an emulation of tax relief or negative taxation, depending on the case.

In France, the amount of public health care's (part of social security) participation to the cost of medicine depends, *inter alia*, on the cardholder's age. A lady in her twenties paid for the medicine in a pharmacy with a chip-in-card. Examining the personal data, the pharmacist found the cardholder had menopause. The young lady admitted that this was her mother's health card. Entitlements' fraud is widespread, and it has been globalized:

* Ignorance of the inner workings of a system and lack of steady control are the two main reasons leading to such fraud and to faulty judgment regarding public health care's affordability.
* When an expense item in the government's budget represents 15 percent of GDP, it cannot be managed through a policy of bits and pieces.

In his seminal book *The Affluent Society*, John Kenneth Galbraith had foreseen this course of events.[10] He also diplomatically hinted on the necessity to put the administration's finances again on the rails by eliminating those public expenses whose last drop can break the camel's back—but even Galbraith's disciples have forgotten his advice.

The generally held opinion of "trying to do better" in cost control by increasing productivity has short legs. Industries like health care, education, and government services have not been able to increase their productivity the way manufacturing industry used to do. Services are a different game than factory production, and it is precisely these low productivity sectors which loom larger in:

* The modern economy, and
* The need for public financing.

The unstoppable rise in government costs accompanied by large budget deficits is present in both the western economies and in developing countries. In 1991, Taiwan's debt as percent of GNP was 6 percent. It grew to 12 percent in 1999; zoomed to 25 percent 2 years later, and it now stands at 40 percent (which is also Taiwan's legal debt ceiling). Other developing markets have had a similar experience with the hydra of government debt.

* A bigger and bigger government spends and spends, and
* Cancerous growth continues without questions asked regarding its sustainability, *as if* there is no limit to spending.

Some economists and several politicians say "our country is rich and can afford the extra spending," but they fail to explain what it means "the country is rich." The way to bet is that it has resources which could be sold, at least as long as they last. Is this true? In the early part of this century, Tony Blair's government sold whatever was sellable of British assets, and this left only trivial assets for sales by David Cameron and his government. Is Britain a "rich" or a "poor" country?

"Nationalizations" and "privatizations" are supposed to be the opposite of one another. In reality, they work in unison. In the 1980s, in France, François Mitterrand nationalized plenty of banks and insurance companies. In the 1990s, the Baladure government privatized at a fraction of their nationalization cost. Experience shows that, in the general case, sales of state "assets" may only generate limited revenue because of a weak economic environment. Or, the privatizer "assets" are unappealing and no investor is interested in them.

For instance, the sale of Greek government "assets," in compliance to bailout clauses, included a railroad deeply in the red that no investor wanted to touch even with a mile-long pole, dry deserted island which could easily cost 10 times their purchase price to provide with basic services, and other propositions unattractive from an investment perspective. No wonder therefore that the original idea that such "assets" could command euro 80 billion ($104 billion) proved to be an overstatement by more than order of magnitude.

Alternatively, there exist state assets which can be sold at short notice because there is demand for them, but the government finds reasons to delay or outright refuse putting them on the block. This is true not only in matters involving state property but also in acquisitions of private companies judged strategically important which can prompt a government veto. A few years ago, a Chinese state-owned oil firm wanted to buy an American oil company. Washington objected.

In January 2013, two Russian bidders emerged as frontrunners in a flagship sell-off expected to raise more than euro 1.5 billion for Athens, putting the Greek government in a dilemma as it seeks to meet privatization targets set by international lenders. Gazprom and Sintez (a private natural gas company) wanted to acquire Depa, Greece's state-owned natural gas company. The government hesitated after warnings by the EU and the United States against opening the Greek market to Russian interests.[11]

This leaves as the major (if not the only) source of debt reduction sufficiently large budget surpluses. This should be used first to stabilize the debt-to-GDP ratio and then reduce it. While deleveraging goes on, contracting more debt is counterproductive. But it can happen. When in April 2010 the EU offered to Greece the bailout, the public debt stood at about 160 percent of GDP. After 2½ years, in spite of PSI which (applied a 73.5 percent haircut on private lending to the sovereign), this ratio is 178 percent. (unofficially, at end of September 2013 it stands at 190 percent of GDP)

A substantial drop in revenues, compounded by a number of bank bailouts, economic stimulus, and nontraditional central bank interventions[12] beef up public debt. This is also true of failure to concentrate on questionable government finances. Japan makes an interesting case study on this issue because of its long history of rising debt-to-GDP ratio and, by consequence, the flattening out the formerly prosperous Japanese economy.

In 2007, when the most recent economic and financial crisis started, the debt-to-GDP ratio of the United States stood at 65 percent. With the crisis, however, came a cyclical downturn in federal receipts coupled with substantial spending on ineffective fiscal stimuli. This double whammy led to a rapid increase in the US budget deficit, which zoomed in 2008 with the salvage of big banks, AIG, Fannie Mae, and Freddie Mac. Budget deficits exceeded 10 percent of GDP in 2009 and again in 2010; were slightly reduced to 8.5 percent in 2011 and 2012; but unofficial estimates suggest another big leap forward in the deficit as 2013 comes to a close.

Excuses can always be found for failing to exercise restraint in budget deficits and even more so for not targeting budgetary surpluses. In Japan, the government justified big spending on account of expenditures related to the consequences of the big earthquake, tsunami, and nuclear catastrophe of March 2011. Indeed, debt ratios continued rising steadily to 2013 and (most likely) beyond.

In the United States, where there has been no tsunami or nuclear power plant problem, the excuse has been that of reflating the economy (which proved to be highly unsuccessful) and provision of social services with Obamacare a new big spender. Neither country bothered to see to it that expectations about budgetary constraints are fulfilled. In the absence of watch over sovereign expenditures, the result has been rapid increase of outstanding debt. Between 1990 and 2012:

- Mandatory spending by the United States increased by well over 200 percent, and
- Discretionary spending increased by about 180 percent.

According to the IMF between what the Obama Administration said to Congress about the 2012 budget, which includes an annual deficit for 2012 of somewhat over $1 trillion (what its economists had estimated), and the real 2012 deficit, there is a difference of $1.3 trillion, nearly 9 percent of the 2012 US government budget.

Worse yet, US global imbalances[13] are still on the rise while China, Germany, and Switzerland, to mention only a few, have been featuring positive current accounts over many years. Since 1983, when the US current account turned negative, the gap is still widening with the result that among western nations America has become the largest current account deficit country.

If nothing is done to redress the balances in the coming years, the situation will get worse because the cost of entitlement, particularly health care expenditures continue to explode (Section 11.3). More, much more red ink is coming later in this decade, as the country's aging population will bring to bear steadily higher costs in an array of popular government programs.

There have been good reasons why the nonpartisan Congressional Budget Office warned that in a probable scenario of policy choices, federal debt would be running way ahead of receipts. The implications can be deadly, economists warn. The cost of servicing the debt could lead to a crowding out of private investments, a spike in interest rates and a fundamental diminution of American global power. This has been a very serious warning, but it does not seem to have had an effect on the Obama Administration's spending plans.

The United States has not even started its deleveraging process. Up to this time, its enormous public debt has only been shifted from one year to the next. Economists say that it will take at least 15 years of consistent effort to bring American balance sheets (government budget and current account) back on track.

11.4 The Current Account Balance Has Much to Do with Discipline and Competitiveness

Nations have an internal and an external public debt. The latter consists of the money they borrow to buy from other nations, as well as the expenses their citizens do for tourism. These sums are reflected in the *current account*, may eventually amount to large amounts. When current account deficits are intermittent and contained, there is nothing unusual about them. Questions are raised when:

- Negative balances become persistent, and
- They continue growing because no real effort is made to bend the curve.

The gap in trade and tourism may be significant. America *imports 40 cents for every dollar sold in its stores.* This has become chronic, and it is very dangerous. It is not easy to maintain a persistently positive current account, but neither is it wise to let negative current account balances accumulate because it is very difficult to reverse established trends when they run out of control.

Current account deficits which are relatively small, closely watched with policies adjusted in a way to reverse deficit trends (provided there is the will to do so), are generally considered to be affordable. This, however, is in no way the "normal" way for managing a nation's foreign accounts.

In the course of the past three decades, the better managed countries have exhibited massive, persistent current account surpluses. By contrast, those who consider current account discipline as being of secondary importance have seen also massive, persistent current account deficits and have thus accumulated net foreign debts. They allowed themselves to drift into a mountain of net foreign liabilities which they may not be able to repay.

China is an example of a country which by becoming the manufacturing center of the world became a global current account creditor.[14] America and France are chronic current account debtors. Though the Chinese may have slippages in their watch over their country's current account, the way to bet is that they will remain with positive balances while there are no reasons to believe that America, Britain, France, Italy, Spain, and other western countries will be able to persistently establish and maintain positive accounts.

Both internal factors (such as a wide public preference for the quality of imports or for the price of imported goods) and external factors like a sudden stop in capital inflows (for instance through Foreign Direct Investments (FDIs)) can play a role in shaping up the current accounts pattern. Corrective measures have in common that they conduct to a reduction in import activities and hence also on the current account deficit.

Solon has been the great law giver of ancient Athens (after Dracon). Bolstered by the Delphic oracles "Know yourself" and "Nothing too much," he was also concerned with reestablishing order in the derelict finances of the ancient city. He forbade export of all agricultural produce (except olive oil), and this brought better quality and lower prices to Athenian households. To balance the city-state's current account, he wrote a law against female luxuries, bringing the import of superfluous luxury items to a standstill.[15]

Current accounts are not being balanced with good words and peanuts. It takes discipline to bring financial order. In the absence of it, the woes of persistent current account deficits are recycled within a revolving balance of payment crisis, and global imbalances are widening.

On one hand, some countries have been running large, persistent current account deficits for several decades, accumulating large foreign debts. This is the case of the United States, Britain, and Spain. Other countries have been running large, persistent account surpluses, also for decades, piling up large foreign assets; the case of Japan, China, Germany, and Switzerland. The global recession in 2009 caused imbalances to build up more slowly, but:

- The deceleration was not sufficient to rebalance the global economy, and
- Imbalances are again on the rise, particularly in big economies like the United States.

Current account imbalances can effectively be corrected in two ways: through legislation and by way of greater competitiveness with emphasis on exports. In a highly technological society like ours, much more is necessary than a few laws which lobbyists will anyway assure that they go unobserved. High-cost plants which survive by subsidies and fail to export their produce must be closed, regardless of where they are and who their political patron is. A great amount of labor flexibility must be assured through restructuring for all of the industrial and service sectors. By closing uncompetitive plants, utilization rates at those remaining will rise, reducing the excess supply of products that:

- Has led to rampant discounting, and
- Put heavy pressure on profits.

Positive and negative balances which finally show up in the current account start with the pluses and minuses at industrial and service levels. Products which have been projected by capitalizing on fat R&D budgets but with scant support from engineering disciplines permitting their steady performance appraisal and cost evaluation do not succeed. When in 1977 Abe Karem arrived to America from Israel, the most promising unmanned aerial vehicle (UAV, drone) was Aquila. Yet, it's record was awful:

- It needed 30 people to launch it,
- It flew for just minutes at a time, and
- It crashed in average every 20 flight hours.

"It was insanity itself," says Karem. "It was obvious to me they were going to crash because they had 30 people doing something that could be done better by three."[16] There is always a gap between what the engineering discipline allows to do and what's being done—and this goes all the way from product design to company management.

There is no better recent example where high quality and low cost are the criteria for success than the smartphone. It was invented by Apple, but Apple only has 20 percent of the global market. Samsung has 30 percent (as of March 2013), Nokia a mere 5 percent, and "others" hold the balance. Provided that it is by majority manufactured in the United States, Apple's smartphone can contribute a great deal to the American balance of payment and that's where the "battle royal" lies.

It is not easy to beat Samsung Electronics in its game of lower costs and more advanced features. It made a big step forward after it unveiled its fourth-generation

Galaxy S smartphone in New York, mid-March 2013, capping its yearlong effort to strengthen its software capabilities to better compete with Apple. Such new software features include:

- A function that lets users control the smartphone screen with their eyes,
- The ability to wave their hands to scroll up and down a Web page or accept a call, and
- A built-in sensor designed to automatically monitor one's health.[17]

Products which cannot match these features on short notice will fall out of the competitive arena of new generation smartphones. Products die. The wheels of innovation, and of fortune, are not waiting for the laggards to catch up. This is widely known. Less known is the fact that laggards are negative contributors to the current account figures. If Apple wins the "battle royal," the American current account balance gets a boost. *If* Samsung wins, *then* the South Koreans gain a current account advantage.

Companies, too, die. Nothing is immortal. Bankruptcy may be the better way to prune a company's balance sheet and its contribution to the national current account. One of corporate America's best-known names, Eastman Kodak, was estimated to have had nearly $900 million in cash on hand when it last disclosed its financial condition, but that has not stopped its move toward bankruptcy protection.

In January 2012 the 123-year-old company, the greatest name in the photo and film industry, filed under Chapter 11 of the US bankruptcy code (which protects firms from their creditors while they try to reorganize financially). This has been a sad ending as at the end of the day Kodak lost the long fight to remake its film business for the digital era. Kodak's exports, "Made in America" no more contribute to the US current account.

American Airlines, too, filed for Chapter 11. Till January 2011, AA was the only big American international airline that did not seek bankruptcy protection. It racked up $10 billion in losses over the first decade of this century and had debts of $30 billion. But with $4 billion in cash on hand, AA—which blamed "the accelerating impact of global economic uncertainty" for its fate, but pledged to keep flying while it restructures—went through protection from creditors chores in its way to improve competitiveness.

A great deal of social questions are being raised by the shift toward competitiveness and greater productivity including questions which have to do with labor relations and the resistance of the labor movement to change—which works both against the workers and the national economy. The option is adapt or die. The following example comes from France, and it involves a British company and an American company and French work habits.

In a city in northern France, there have been 2 tyre factories of about the same size, making precisely the same products and located at either side of the main road: Dunlop and Goodyear. The two companies and their manufacturing facilities have been well-known competitors; and both were hit by the economic crisis of 2007–2013.

The management of Dunlop explained to its union that it was confronted by two options: Plan A, which meant closing down the company's French factory and transferring the work to other establishments the company owned in low cost countries and Plan B, which required thorough restructuring taking away some of the perks, reducing wages and salaries, and working three shifts to lower administrative overhead. In the latter case,

- Dunlop promised to bring work to its French plant from other of its factories abroad, and
- This would have helped not only the French workers who would not lose their jobs, but as well the French sovereign's current account which in recent years is permanently in the red.

The negotiations were not easy, but labor unions at the Dunlop plant saw that there were no better options, while company management meant what it said about closing the plant. The unions accepted the compromises to save most of the jobs. After the usual give-and-take they agreed to Plan B, employees and workers returned to work (albeit at lower salaries), and the Dunlop plant in France is always working.

To the contrary, labor union leaders at the Goodyear plant chose a confrontational approach. They rejected outright management's offer for restructuring, and asked the French government to keep the plant open under the prevailing labor contracts. Or, as an alternative to nationalize the Goodyear plant. Being itself against the wall in terms of finances, the French government rejected both requests.

The hard line at Goodyear's plant was engineered by a relatively young labor leader of the Confederation General du Travail (CGT) who had previously tried to get elected to parliament under the communist party banner[18]—and got less than 1 percent of the vote. By contrast, his stance made him a darling of Goodyear plant's workers, with an approval rate of 79 percent. Yes, but in the end the Goodyear plant was closed and all of its jobs went abroad. (We will return to this issue, and the way it impacts American unemployment in Section 11.5.)

11.5   "Too Big to Jail" Has Become the New Moral Code

In one of his books Leon Tolstoy has written that every family is miserable in its own way. In a quite similar way, each country and its citizen are happy or miserable in their own manner—a reason why it has been a deliberate choice to look into the ever more complex debt problems of Greece, Spain, Italy, France, and the United States country-by-country rather than as a group of western democracies whose topmost challenges are:

- Their mountain of unfunded liabilities, and
- The bleak future they leave to their children.

Along with Britain, the aforementioned western states share among themselves a sense of "victimhood" unknown in earlier times: the skyrocketing outlays for all sorts of unaffordable and unsustainable entitlements—along with the rush to find

the money to pay for them, *if* in no other way *then* through more public debt—
have taken precedence over other social priorities leading to misgovernance:

- Medicaid, Medicare, public pensions are payments for yesterday's events. They
  are expenses which do not contribute to the future.
- Education is the future's wheel of fortune, and the sad fact is that after nearly
  eight decades of excellence, the American university system confronts a funding
  crisis because so much money drains toward the past.

The demographics do not help. The population's aging increases the expenditures
and reduces the overall savings rate, hence capital accumulation. In addition, sovereigns got the costly (and irrational) habit of saving from bankruptcy self-wounded
enterprises—particularly big banks—by throwing at them taxpayer money in a
massive way with no questions asked. This introduced into western politics and business life, two unprecedented syndromes each with strong moral risk:

- Too big to fail, and
- Too big to jail.

Mammoth financial institutions control the western nations' wealth and buy political favors as well as protection the way it suits them best. It is no more the state
which calls the banks to obey the law of the land and code of ethics; it's the big
banks who tell the state where the line dividing right and wrong should be traced.

Eventually, the state wakes up and wants to see the accounts, but as of recently, it
does so in a way which does not upset the people under examination. There is as well
a new practice that solidly established itself in the years following the great economy
and banking crisis of 2007: none gets punished for violating the legal or moral code.

On March 15, 2013 Senator Carl Levin, of the US Senate, headed a committee
which examined the way JP Morgan Chase hid its losses of $6 billion from a scam
deal in its London subsidiary. The CIO[19] under whose watch these losses material-
ized was asked to deposit and all she said has been: "I was deceived by my people.
I am not responsible." With that cheap excuse, she was let go.

Nobody bothered to bring up her own betrayal of moral and managerial
responsibility. Neither were the senators informed, or *if* informed reacted, that over
the previous 2 years the lady CIO in reference had made a rumored $20 million
per year from high-risk derivatives gambled by her minions with her blessing—
precisely the stuff her "top trader" (the so-called "London whale") had accumulated
in London. The scandal blew in the face of JP Morgan Chase, its shareholders and
its customers.

Far from being a rare exception, this is just one of a thousand of similar cases
which have been conveniently forgotten, with nobody facing judgment for his or
her wrongdoing, let alone going to jail. On March 15, in the Senate hearings
Senator Levin said, "They (the wrongdoers) manifested the risk control model."
And that was it. Within no time, all the tralala was forgotten.

Neither is banking the only hotbed for unpunished fraud. In February 2013,
in France started one of the more pervasive food frauds in recent history which

pulled-in some of the better known names, like Ikea and Nestlé. At no time it spread like a brush fire all over Europe. Frozen food, like Italian lasagna (very popular with consumers) was labeled as containing beef meat; instead it had horse meat.

The media were all too happy to spread the news, but those responsible first kept mum; then different experts came into the show to explain that horse meat is healthier than beef meat; it might be so, but this was not the point. The case was one of plain fraud: horse meat costs a fraction of beef meat, and there were as well laboratories which stated that the quality of horse (and beef) meat used for frozen food was in doubt. As with the banking cases and plenty other cases of crossing over legal and ethical wires:

- Nobody has been brought to justice, and
- The fraud was simply forgotten; winner takes all.

This new moral code of impunity for the "too big to jail and their consort" prevails nowadays in both western Europe and North America. Its code of ethics is written in direct contradiction to the principles of ethical behavior which characterized western democracies. The new rule is:

- *If* money, good money, can be made in the cheap,
- *Then* why should one do an honest day's work?

With so many people "well-placed" making millions per year and the morals laxity which currently prevails, the workers are feeling left out of the economy even if they have a job. With this, they turn to the leveraging of their entitlements as their way to riches. Anachronistic labor unions make matters worse by insisting on clauses impossible to fulfill in the cut-throat environment of a global economy. The result is making US produce uncompetitive in the global market.

Even more curious is that in the rich, inert, easy-going western culture of the twenty-first century, the workers have turned against themselves, their jobs, and the economy. In a last ditch effort to understand how French workers do their daily job, and may be find a better solution than closing the Goodyear plant in France (Section 11.4), the president of the American firm holding the Goodyear label went to France and started with the workings at work early one the morning. He simply followed their daily routine.

At 9.00 a.m. the workers stopped to have a break, but to his surprise 2 hours passed and they were still not back to their workplace. He tried to understand what was happening and he was told that "this was the French way of working." To his question when they will be back to the manufacturing line, he got the answer "after lunch" because lunch was already so near. Needless to say that this left the American CEO only one way: GET OUT. Back to the United States, he closed down the French plant effective immediately.

The reader may rightly question what this has to do with American working habits. The answer is that it shares plenty of common thinking, because the virus of uncompetitiveness and of "I don't care less" has spread widely at both sides of the North Atlantic. It has also penetrated broader and much lower levels in the organization, turning technology into a tool of idleness (see the Yahoo example). The America of the early 1950s, which I knew and loved, is no more around:

- Today, nobody would deliver "a message to Garcia."
- "Coming up from under" is no longer a priority; the State Supermarket is expected to lift everyone up.[20]
- In many quarters, "excellence has been replaced by greed."
- Personal responsibility got a permanent leave, taking ethics along to a long journey.

A news item in *The Economist* documents the last bullet but I also have a personal example. Marissa Mayer, Yahoo's new boss, banned her employees from telecommuting without a good reason. The aim has been to force workers to inter-act more with colleagues, and most particularly to cut down on skiving. Like many other firms, Yahoo allowed working from home because in the digital era the label is "Communicate don't commute" and workers, especially those with families, like it. But a survey of American telecommuters found that:

- 43 percent sometimes watched TV instead of toiling, and
- Another 7 percent said they worked in only their underwear or in the nude.[21]

Standards of competence and of commitment always vary from country to country and over time. Like war, the economy and competitiveness are not all calculation. But never to my knowledge the work standard and work ethic in America were so low, leading to the conclusion that next to balancing the budget, Congress and the White House have to rethink very carefully the whole character of economic sustainability.

- How to weed-out lust and greed, and
- How to reinstate the guiding principle of an honest day's work.

If you don't keep challenging yourself, you start wasting away, said Lee Iacocca, of Ford and Chrysler fame. Issues have to be raised, spun, and tossed about to estab-lish a new framework for competitiveness at global scale. Most importantly, wrong-doers have to be brought to justice and punished whether they were presidents of banks which went bust, or watching TV instead of toiling.

11.6   Faculties Should Give the Example, and Students Must Put Up Their Best Effort

I head a Swiss not-for-profits foundation which for over two decades gives prizes to the best graduating PhD of a partner university. In 2000, I met with George Soros to learn about the failures one may do in granting awards, and the loopholes. To my question what's the big difference in attention between running a for-profits and a not-for-profits entity, Soros answered: "Be attentive not to be exploited by the beneficiaries and would-be beneficiaries." I took to heart that advice.

Over the years several problems happened, for nonqualifying candidates submit-ted for a prize to plain nepotism. As long as these mainly concerned east European universities, the Board handled them along the French principle "Bon pour l'Orient," without awarding a prize to a nonqualified person.

There has been one American university persistently submitting social scientists as prize candidates, which created a problem. According to its statutes, the Foundation only awards prizes to hard sciences. The partner university knew that and the partnership was resolved in common accord.

Then came the real surprise. It lasted not just 1 year (which might have been seen as an oversight), but 3 long years, and every year the nepotism was contested but the faculty was back to it. At the end, enough was enough. The following e-mail briefly describes this case, brings in perspective its background and suggests that the very high standards of the university faculty have bend:[22]

Prof. . . .
Associate Dean of Engineering Research
. . . . University

e-mail March 12, 2013

Dear Professor . . . . . . ,
I am in receipt of your e-mail of March 11, 2013 and deeply surprised.
Your questions wrap themselves around a case of *nepotism*, which is anathema to the Foundation.
The Statutes of the Foundation explicitly forbid the submission for a year's prizes of a file from the same person whose candidacy was rejected in a previous year's competition.
If I understand right between the lines of the Byzantine writing of your e-mail, what you want in essence is that a person which did not qualify last year for a prize (I guess a young lady) will be presented again this year.
It has to be *that* person. There is no alternative.
We don't work that way.
If you look up the 20-Year Anniversary brochure of the Foundation, you will see that over the years the Foundation found itself obliged to end its collaboration with 7 partner universities. The reason of 2 interruptions has been persistent nepotism − your case.

A Brief Historical Perspective
Throughout the years that Prof. . . . . . . was the Associate Dean for Research and Entrepreneurship at . . . . , there has been no single incident connected to the prizes.
In fact the stream of young Ph.D. graduates was so strong and so high that the Board of the Foundation decided to increase from 1 to 2 the number of prizes allocated to (your university).
The problems started right after Prof. . . . . . . unfortunate accident and your taking over. There was also a bad omen: You flying to Brazil, at taxpayer's money, a couple of days after your appointment.
Since then there has been only friction. An example is provided by the cases described in my letter to you of May 22, 2012.
Subsequently, in the absence of reply from your part, I wrote to you on June 7, 2012, asking for confirmation of 1 award only for 2013.
Your answer should have reached the Foundation prior to December 6, 2012 date of the Board meeting. There was plenty of time for doing so. Instead, you played cat and mouse writing after that deadline and again failing to respond to my correspondence.

The next act in the drama is your letter of March 11, 2013 from which I quote: "the mistake was by the College of Engineering, but not the students or faculty" Then by whom? The janitor?

It's a bad policy to take other people as *a priori* stupid or senile.

The next board meeting ...... will examine this case, which means that (your university) will not have candidates for the 2013 prizes of the Foundation.

Best regards,

DNC

To appreciate the puzzle relating to the surprising poor performance of several doctorate prize winners, one has to understand that though PhD stands for "Doctor of Philosophy," what it means is that its holder is a "Doctor of Research." Hence, an enquiring mind is capable of thinking (not just of being logical) and of concentrating on a complex issue to advance the current level of science. Or, to find a solution in other situations, less trained people find it difficult to penetrate.

Saddle, twenty years of experience with prizes to the "best of the class" PhD graduates at partner universities around the globe give a totally different pattern. A sample of about 600 prize winners is statistically valid, and what it reveals is totally different than theory suggests. The following letter has been address to the senior faculty of all of the Foundation's partner universities. The drift in learning is a sure and present danger to the western civilization.

Prof. ...

Rector

University of ...

June 8, 2012

Dear Professor...,

As an old academic, I am writing this letter to express my worry about the future the West's young generation prepares for itself. The subutilization of benefits derived from education is one of the key problems.

To make such worry comprehensible, allow me to start with some references from years past when young people found their way by compassion, vision and hard work.

James Cook left school at age of 12, to help his father on the farm. Sometime later, he began his professional life as a common sailor but worked his way up until he became one of the most eminent navigators, surveyors and explorers.

When he was young, Thomas Edison had to support himself by selling newspapers. Edison had none of what we now consider as academic credentials − but by being determined, imaginative, single-minded and practical he became the greatest inventor of his time.

Edison is also the author of the famous saying: "Success is 98 percent perspiration and 2 percent inspiration which − speaking from experience - was a guiding light for young people in the immediate post-World War II years, but today is all but forgotten. Instead of working for their education, students got the bad habit to accumulate debts since early age.[23]

Another example of reputable effort to come up from under is Konosuke Matsushita. He grew through hardship, turning his hardship into a source of learning and made it a driving force. Though he left school before the age of 10 to work as an apprentice, at age 20 he created his own company which became a giant in electrical engineering.

One of Matsushita's basic principles has been that it is not enough to work conscientiously. No matter what kind of job a person is doing, he has to think of himself as being completely in charge — with all this means in terms of:

- Quality of work, and
- Personal responsibility.

"The key to product development (at Matsushita Electric) was perspiration, not PhDs or big R&D budgets," says John Kotter of Harvard University, "Manufacturing was organized to keep costs as low as possible ... And the entire process was built on a willingness to:

- "Take risks,
- "Experiment, and
- "Learn."[24]

I could write two dozen examples like Cook's, Edison's and Matsushita's. Bill Gates was a college dropout, but made the third largest company in capitalization at NYSE. Steve Jobs has been a self-made genius and inventor, directing a swarm of projects and, till his last day, never failing in his capacity to deliver.

*   *   *

All this poses the question: What's the *added value* of university education?, and: Is it used in the *right way*?

Let me tell you about some of the happenings with the Foundation's prize winners, all of them Ph.Ds from renown universities. I look at these examples as warning signals which have taken place during the last half dozen years — not in the 1990s.

In two separate occasions the prizes' international checks issued by Crédit Suisse have been lost (and took an ordeal to recover them) because their beneficiaries deposited them in small, local credit unions. Would you not say that people who finished postgraduate studies and were considered to be the best Ph.D graduates in a given year, would understand that a small local cooperative is not fit to handle international payments?

One of the prize winners was told by his bank that it will take 2 weeks to clear the certified check, and he impertinently called (directly from Boston) the account executive of Crédit Suisse in Luzern, Switzerland, to have "immediately" *his* money cabled to him through Swift.

On another occasion, a prize winner wrote to the secretary of the Foundation: "Can you help me? I cannot deposit my check:" The problem was that he deposited it to the post office which in Switzerland does accept checks by commercial banks. The puzzle is that he did not even have the curiosity to find out *why* this is so, and search for a solution.

Delays in depositing the check to one's bank has been another curious issue. Certified checks are issued by the Foundation for the protection of the prize winner. For security reasons, one of their features is a deadline for cashing them. Six months is plenty of time for doing so, yet some prize winners take longer than that.

There has been a couple of other cases where postgraduate researchers needed assistance to find out their way on how to cash their checks, but I pass them over to focus on a different case. It concerns a prize winner who wrote to his university an urgent letter asking:

- Which was the organization giving him the prize?

This came as a surprise and shock. The least one can expect is that prize winners learn about the organization from which they receive a prize. A few of them, only very few, write thank-you letters. Now it is revealed that some don't even have the curiosity to know about the prizes until, three years later, they need that information for their career.

In fact, even then they cannot take the initiative and they ask someone to help them, *as if* research is not a Ph.D's competitive advantage and remit. Another query posed by the same person three years after receiving the award has been:

• Which are the criteria for giving the award?

It would not be unreasonable to expect that a prize winner is familiar with the criteria, since he applied for the annual award and was even prized. But this, too, seems to be too much to be expected by a Doctor of Philosophy.

It would seem to me that, like any other graduate, a PhD should do his own research and assume his responsibilities, rather than be waiting to get everything ready on a plate. I feel sorrow when seeing that young, educated people:

• Don't have the imagination to quickly grasp a problem,
• Are undecided about what to do or how to do it, and
• Wait for others "to help them" on simple, easy, straightforward issues.

This new-found policy of passivity by the young generation, and most particularly the educated elite, as well as the complaints associated to not getting what they are asking for:

• Is harboring ills for western society, and
• It has become a dangerous foreboding for the future.

Prizes, of course, are only one example. The reason why I take them as indicators is that these events are associated to the best educated people in our society. The underlying culture has become "help me" — and with it complaints which can be without bounds.

On February 12, 2012 the temperature in Verdun, France, was −12°C. In a supermarket reporters found a 90-year old lady doing her shopping. Surprised, they asked her if she does not feel cold. She answered that in the winter in Verdun the climate is cold. "I am accustomed to it," she said. "It is the young generations which are afraid of cold and complain about it."

Instead of being lost in a bucket of hot or cold water, young educated people should be masters in navigating in uncharted territories and in investigating anything unfamiliar or unusual which they find in their way. That's not only integral part of learning, particularly in higher education, it is also its *prime value*.

Emile Coué, a French chemist and philosopher[25], admired American initiative and effectiveness. "The French," he said, "like to argue about principle. The American mind, on the other hand, puts the principle to work and discovers its practical adaptability to everyday life. That's why this young nation is a success."[26]

• Success usually comes to those who are too busy looking for it.[27]
• What has happened to this spirit of imagination, initiative and effectiveness at both sides of North Atlantic?

If a PhD graduate does not have imagination and initiative he or she cannot do research. This is not only too bad for his career but as well a troubling message about his or her learning and ability to exercise judgment. As William Shakespeare put it in Hamlet:

"If it be now, it's not to come;
"if it be not to come, it will be now;

"if it be not now, yet it will come;
"the readiness is all."
Where is this readiness? Are we sure the next generation understands what it takes to be ready? *If* not, *then* it is not really able to be in charge of its own future.

                            *   *   *

If I share these concerns with you it is because I am really worried about the self-reliance and planning skills acquired by young people presently graduating from institutes of higher education. One day these will be the persons running companies or the government. But as quantity has displaced quality, they will not be up to the job.
If the current remiss continues, the second raters will be taking over. This is already happening in public administration, and in some cases in business. For instance, it has occurred in General Motors after Alfred Sloan, and in IBM after Thomas Watson, Sr.
Bureaucracy, which is the antithesis and deadly enemy of science, is an increasingly attractive featherbedding profession. In the early years of this century, in loud and lousy rallies, university students paraded in the streets of Paris against the *"Contrat Première Embauche"* by the French administration. Journalists asked a sample of these students what's their plan for their future, and 3 out of 4 answered "to become government employees".[28]
Young scientists don't anymore seem determined to be entrepreneurial and get results in their life, which has been the foremost endeavor of many of their predecessors. Just some kind of *"petit travail tranquil"* will do, provided it is secure for life and well paid.

                            *   *   *

To help in getting the best out of the young scientists who compete for the Foundation's prizes, in its meeting of June 6, 2012 the Board decided to implement − starting with the 2013 prizes - a clause which is in the Foundation's Authentic Act. This requires that in the file submitted to the Board, along with his or her CV each prize candidate includes a *one-paragraph* answer to each of the following two themes:

• His or her plan for a professional future[29], and
• How he or she will contribute to the well-being of the society in which they live.

Ambition and the attitude of questioning the "obvious" will be welcome. "Many people search for security, as for me I prefer the questioning attitude. If we have no doubts, where will be security?" asked Goethe.
Even something which sounds impossible will be well received if the prize candidate is truly decided to reach his goal. The way Aristotle had it: "Probable impossibilities are to be preferred to improbable possibilities" − which in practical terms translates that in contemplating his career one better thinks "out of the box".
It will be, indeed, most interesting to read how a prize winning PhD graduate thinks of his future, and how he or she will use the just obtained doctorate as an asset. This requires skill and strength, but if they do not challenge themselves young people will be wasting away.
Yours sincerely,
DNC

                            *   *   *

These are the facts. A commentary will be redundant.

End Notes

1. The 1979 political squabbling meant that the Carter Administration could not keep its payments on schedule for a sliver of short-dated bills.
2. Financial Times, October 24, 2011.
3. The Economist, January 12, 2013.
4. Half of that was supposed to be Social Security and Medicare.
5. Suskind R. The price of loyalty. New York, NY: Simon & Schuster; 2004.
6. Without even counting social security, health care and other federal commitments—or the deficits of states of union and of municipalities.
7. Bloomberg News, December 6, 2012.
8. "We must tax the poor, they are the more numerous," said André Tardieu, the radical-socialist French prime minister in 1930.
9. When President Reagan rearmed America.
10. Galbraith JK. The affluent society. London: Penguin Press; 1970.
11. Financial Times, January 11, 2013.
12. Chorafas DN. The changing role of central banks. London: Palgrave/Macmillan; 2013.
13. Global imbalances are defined by persistent current account deficits and surpluses.
14. Chorafas DN. Globalization's limits. Conflicting national interests in trade and finance. London: Gower; 2009.
15. Zarleng S. The lost science of money. Valatie, NY: American Monetary Institute; 2002.
16. The Economist, December 1, 2012.
17. Wall Street Journal, March 15–17, 2013.
18. In France and in Greece, there is still a Communist Party.
19. As an anagram, CIO stands for Chief Information Officer, and it is a misnomer. The right title would have been "Chief Destruction Officer" (CDO) of the bank's wealth and that of its customers, because under the CIO's watch take place wild bets like that of the London whale.
20. Right? Wrong, but people believe it is right.
21. The Economist, March 2, 2013.
22. In Europe, too. There have been cases of faculty accepting envelopes with money to give doctorate degrees to young people who don't worth it.
23. In the United States alone, student loans stand at $1 trillion.
24. Kotter JP. Matsushita leadership. New York, NY: The Free Press; 1997.
25. The principle of Emile Coué has been that physical, moral, and spiritual improvement could be attained by daily repetition of "Day by day in every way I am getting better and better." Coué's teachings have been widely used (and distorted) by Sigmund Freud.
26. Davenport WW. Gyro! The life and times of Lawrence Sperry. New York, NY: Charles Scribner's; 1916.
27. According to Henry David Thoreau.
28. Ronald Reagan, the late US President, is famous for having said that the most dreadful sentence in English language is: "I am from the government and I am here to help."
29. MIT prize winners already do so in regard to this question.

12 The Merger of Quantitative Easing and Politics Is the No. 2 Suspect

12.1 "Bernanke Should Show Humility at the Fed," Says Senator Bob Corker

The advice Josef Stalin gave to Yuri Zhdanov, son of his one-time designated successor, worth writing in golden letters and having it displayed at the desk of every central bank governor, president, or chairman: "It is said that you spend plenty of time in politics, but believe me politics is a dirty business."[1]

It's an expert's opinion, coming directly from the horse's mouth; that of a master of politics (and of terror). Politics is a combative sport, and few engaging in it really succeed. Playing politics and providing for currency stability are not at all the same thing. The banker's most important duty is that of economics and financial stability while full employment (where, quite evidently, the word "full" is a lie) is the politicians' job.

True enough, no two central banks (or reserve institutions) are alike in terms of their charter, mission the authority they exercise; as well as in terms of and their independence from the whims and priorities of their government. But if in the post-World War II years a general statement was to be made establishing what a central bank is supposed to do regarding its primary functions, then these would have fallen into four main classes:

1. Deciding on monetary policy,
2. Issuing money with congressional limits,
3. Being a lender of last resort, and
4. Acting as the government's commercial bank.[2]

Some reserve institutions also assumed other duties, the most important of them being bank regulation and supervision. This has been a subject leading to discussions and controversies, with critics saying that bank supervision distracts the central bankers from their topmost responsibility for monetary stability.

What the last couple of paragraphs mean is that, in practice, each central bank has its own specific objectives. An example is the Federal Reserve which, following an act of Congress dating back to the late 1970s, has the added responsibility to look after employment.[3] That was a political mission which contradicted the Fed's

Public Debt Dynamics of Europe and the US. DOI: http://dx.doi.org/10.1016/B978-0-12-420021-0.00012-9

original and topmost duty of monetary policy independence from government goals and directives. Such a contradictory Fed mission led to loss of its independence. (We will see why later on in this chapter.)

Other western central banks have followed the same path. The Bank of England and ECB are examples. Indeed, the best kept secret among western central banks in the twenty-first century version of their duties is that what you hear is not what you get. Although QE, LTRO, OMT,[4] and other unconventional central bank programs have arguably reduced tail risks to markets:

- Economic growth in the United States, Britain, and continental Europe has been unsatisfactory, and
- The unprecedented expansion of central banks' balance sheets is not made to assure economic stability.

The fact that the Federal Reserve expanded its balance sheet from $800 billion in September 2008 to $3000 billion in September 2012 is evidence that politicians and central bankers have merged into one lot, and they are in no way eager to explain to the public what they are doing. Moreover, what they are doing is not necessarily the most rational in assuring a sound monetary policy which guarantees the value of the currency and with it the financial stability.

An often heard excuse is that economic developments have left behind old monetary policy and regulatory duties. Though no economist openly challenges the fact that monetary policy should be and remain a central bank's basic assignment, pseudo-Keynesian and political voices add other obligations which distract the monetary institution's attention and dwindle its independence.

Most of all, it is the change in central bankers' personalities that damages most of their institutions' standing.[5] In an article, he published in the *Financial Times* under the title *Bernanke should show some humility at the Fed*, Bob Corker, a Republican senator from Tennessee and member of the US Senate Banking Committee, says that the blame cannot be solely debited to Congress:

> *It would be helpful to have a Fed chairman who acted with a greater sense of humility about what monetary policy can achieve. Mr. Bernanke's ... unwillingness to stand up and say that there are limits to what monetary policy can accomplish is disturbing, to say the least.[6]*

Corker is right in his opinion that America needs a Federal Reserve that helps rather than hinders its economy's transition; a Fed which pays attention to savers rather than being wholly reliant on leveraged consumers.[7] The need the senator identifies is that of a central bank which serves as a utility to the US economy: "not an enabler of some perverse financial system addition."

This is by no means a one-person's opinion. In the campaign which led to the selection of the Republican challenger to president Barack Obama, Rick Perry, the governor of Texas, stated that it would be almost treasonous for the Federal

Reserve to print money. Perry's statement stirred up a debate and highlighted the political pressure surrounding Ben Bernanke. In the governor's words:

> *If this guy (Bernanke) prints more money between now and the election . . .*
> *we would treat him pretty ugly down in Texas. Printing more money to play*
> *politics at this particular time in history is almost treasonous, in my opinion.*[8]

It takes people who stand by their opinion, and are not afraid to express it, to explain to the American public the risks embedded in the wrong-way monetary policy by the Fed (and other western central banks). It takes courage to explain why and from where these risks rise and what may be the most likely outcome when official pronouncements and the resulting numbers don't add up.

Jan Tinbergen, a Nobel Prize winner, has become known for his rule that "for each policy objective, at least one instrument is needed." In his testimony to a panel of the US House of Representatives in early 2012, Bernanke implicitly admitted that the Fed stepped over that rule. Though it more or less brought prices under control, it struggles with high unemployment. And as some economists put it:

- If your only policy choice is to print more money, you will have to compromise on the two targets.
- If not, liquidity injections, which have been already too high, will also be inadequately restrained in the future.

Precisely because of the Fed's easy money policies and the fact that, like other western central banks, it has compromised its independence by assuming a political position, discussions about reintroducing the gold standard have returned to mainstream US politics for the first time in three decades. In mid-2012, drafts of the Republican Party platform called for:

- An audit of the Federal Reserve's monetary policy, and
- A commission to look at restoring the link between the dollar and gold.

This proposal followed on the steps of the Gold Commission, created by president Ronald Reagan in 1981. While that commission ultimately supported the status quo, it did raise the issue that return to the gold standard is still an option, particularly when there is no other restraint to the money printing machines of the central bank working overtime.

A politically motivated twenty-first century attitude by the reserve bank in sharp contrast to the 1956 decision by the Board of Governors of the Federal Reserve System that while relatively little is known about the safety margins in the finances of consumers who borrow on a short-term and intermediate term basis, the evidence of a trend over the past decades toward more liberal terms suggests that safety margins have shrank. This proved to be a prophetic statement because in the decades following 1956:

- First, consumer spending reached for the stars, and
- Then, the sovereign accumulated a higher and higher mountain of public debt.

The shrinking of safety margins and explosion of public debt led to financial instability and heavily weighted on the economic downturn we are in. Made at the expense of longer term stability, short-term decisions upset the balances. Still the excuse that "other western central banks are doing the same" does not wash, particularly as what they are doing is to take over fiscal policy from the government.

What has been until two decades ago reliable monetary policies by central banks became the nearest thing to a Ponzi game. Monetary institutions are willing to lend against poorer quality assets and for longer periods of time. This involved them in financial intermediation characterized by political aims. Filled up with assets of ever lower quality, their balance sheets ballooned.

Since 2008, the Federal Reserve has monetized about 60 percent of the increased Treasury and government-sponsored enterprises paper. "This all serves to give the happy appearance of a borrower living comfortably within its budget constraint," says a study by the Société Générale. "... governments have more tricks up their sleeves than the rest of us, like monopoly control of the seniorage industry. Since it jealously reserves for itself the right to supply the nation's medium of exchange, (sovereigns have) recourse to the most splendid of all budget constraint-avoidance maneuvers: if tax revenues, or the trust of honest creditors, are insufficient the government can simply print any money it needs."[9] What this proves, in its way, is that both Senator Corker and Governor Perry have been right in what they said. But is anybody listening?

12.2   Employment and Unemployment Are Political Issues, Not the Central Bank's Remit

In the short span between years 2000 and 2012, America has lost more than 5 million manufacturing jobs. By all evidence, these will never come back. Their loss has been a legacy of the Bush Jr. years, but both Clinton's and Obama's Administrations contributed to the delocalization of US jobs.

Neither is the loss of all these employment opportunities just a matter of delocalization, as some economists continue to maintain. The novelty which came up in the 2010−2013 period in the employment front is that many young people (55 percent in Spain and Greece and a great deal also in the United States) don't find a job because they are not qualified for modern industrial effort. The skills even college graduates acquired are simply not in demand. This has been a terrible failure in career planning.

Another effect of professional misorientation which has shown up in the same time frame is that young people whose skills were in the borderline of what industry demands have become in the meantime long-term unemployed. They loafed while in unemployment, they did not keep up with their training, and what little they knew has become obsolete.

This professional misorientation is a deep political fault, *not* a matter of monetary policy as Bernanke likes to think. The Fed funds rate may stay historically low as long as the Fed chairman pleases and the share of the reserve institution's Treasury holdings may be keep on being extended. These are monetary policy decisions having nothing to do with the roots of the unemployment problem in the United States, or anywhere else.

The evidence is that when by 2011 American manufacturing activity somewhat picked up, few new jobs have been created. Moreover, to compete in a globalized manufacturing environment, where every penny in cost counts, companies use automation as far as they can and cut out of their business bloodstream every superfluous cost dollar. Cutting costs with a sharp knife has replaced delocalization as senior management's focal point, but it does not help in job creation.

At the end of 2012, there have been 23 million unemployed in the United States, representing a little less than 8 percent of the working population (official statistics talk of 7.5 percent). Unofficially, however, there is talk of 28 million unemployed which rises to nearly 40 million if part-time and precarious jobs are included. All the big money spent by the Fed with QE1, QE2, QE3, and QE3.5 has been for nothing—if one counts by obtained results.

The situation is not any better in the European Union with over 20 million unemployed, or 11.3 percent of the working population. This is an average number. For the young, the unemployment statistics stand at 26 percent in France, 53 percent in Spain[10] and in Greece—despite all the money the ECB is spending with its LTRO, OMT, and other politically motivated anagrams.

Governments are still hiring workers and employees they don't need,[11] adding to their budget deficits and the mountains of public debt. Companies are not hiring because the economic conditions are bleak despite the torrent of liquidity thrown to the four winds by the Fed, Bank of England, and ECB[12]—or because of it as its most pronounced effect is to greatly diminish confidence at both sides of the North Atlantic.

Projections up to 2018 by the US Bureau of Labor Statistics are hardly encouraging. They indicate that American manufacturing employment will witness virtually no growth while many industries will continue to experience technology-based employment losses.[13] In the United States and Europe, unit labor costs are uncompetitive compared to those in developing countries, because they are also loaded with inordinate taxation relating to the social net: pensions and health care costs.

Ironically, as the US Bureau of Labor Statistics has it, half of the top 20 fastest growing occupations in America are health care related (see also Chapter 10 on health care costs). These are adding themselves to other costs to make factory produce even more uncompetitive in the global market. By 2018, two grades of health care workers:

· Home health, and
· Personal care aides,

are projected to grow to a level nearly matching today's care manufacturing total tally. Notice, however, that these jobs pay roughly one-third as much as those in manufacturing. The Fed's and ECB's wild money printing operations don't take such basic trends into account. But then they should not destabilize the currency and the financial market to play Heracles—because, by so doing, they feed rather than decapitate the mythical Hydra's multiplying heads.

When I say so in my lectures I am asked how this "feeding" is done. The answer is straightforward: through uncertainty about future economic conditions created by the western central banks' unlimited paper money printing. The top 10 problems cited in a survey by the National Federation of Independent Business (NFIB), a small-business lobby in the United States, include:

- Uncertainty over economic conditions, and
- Frequent changes in federal tax laws and rules.[14]

Other issues contributing a great deal to western unemployment have to do with working culture, which deteriorated greatly during the last three decades and continues doing so. Nearly everybody waits that a job is served to him or her on a silver platter. There is also a phrase coined in socialist France: "The right to work." There is no "right to work," but there is an *obligation*:

- To try hard to get a job, and
- To perform with full professional conscience while at it.

Has the reader heard of Sidney Weinberg? Seeking employment while still in his teens (back in 1907) he went to the top of a 25-floor building (which at that time was the tallest in New York) and asked every company at every floor if it was looking for a worker. He got 23 refusals, but he did not give up.

At the second floor was a, then, relatively small investment bank: Goldman Sachs. Weinberg asked the same question, if work was available, and the chief clerk hired him to assist the porter at $3 a week.[15] The teenager got the job. He worked during the day and studied in the night and weekends. He stayed for sixty-two years with the firm rising to become chairman and CEO for the last four decades of his employment at the firm.

Any young fellow or young lady who waits for the government to "find him or her a job" should read the life of Weinberg, as well as of Andrew Carnegie (who also started at $3 the week and became the king of steel and a well-known philanthropist); of Captain James Cook who left school at 12 to work and became one of the best-known explorers and cartographers; of Konosuke Matsushita who also had to leave school at a very young age but early on in his life made one of the giant firms in electrical engineering and electronics.

What Bernanke thinks that he accomplished in the US unemployment front by flooding the market with liquidity and destabilizing the currency? Does he believe that it is enough to keep the presses working overtime? Is he prompting the young to do their damnedest to get a job and work hard at it? Or is he only throwing newly minted money at the problem so that they remain unemployed forever?

Unfortunately, most unfortunately, in our western society, the search for a job and its diligent maintenance lies low in their list of priorities. By contrast, rent-seeking is near the top. *Rent-seeking* is the way economists describe all efforts on the part of special interests to benefit by influencing political decisions, asking for money without doing any work.

At the root of the trouble is a combination of entitlements and other benefits indiscriminately offered by the welfare state. The result is one of social distortion and of lower ethics. The irony is that this often happens in the name of "free enterprise." Profits are often determined by way of:

- Winning government contracts,
- Receiving subsidies,
- Getting higher tariffs and quotas,
- Having competition suppressed, and
- Managing to have regulations eased.

In conclusion, unemployment is too deep and complex an issue for central banks to solve by operating at the money end of the problem. Bernanke should have known that much. Presumably he does not. The issue is nearly 100 percent political. *If* the western economies are unable, unwilling, or both to touch the gilt-edged welfare benefits that strangle them, *then* high unemployment is here to stay. *If* on the home-front governments cannot cut social costs, which hurt their companies' competitiveness and jeopardize society's longer term well-being, *then* it is not realistic to expect that the Fed or any other central bank would solve the problem for them.

12.3   Money Is Always Invested, but There May Be Bad Investments

Except for money hidden in mattresses, there is no such thing as cash in the sidelines. Money is always invested in something: bonds, equities, commodities, real estate, and deposits paying an interest rates. Other things equal, when investments in one sector (s) of the economy grow rapidly, this means that in another sector they are going down. And when interest rates are kept rock-bottom for too long, in their search for yield, investors assume inordinate risk of which quite often they are unaware.

This is not only characteristic of individual investors but, as well, of institutional: pension funds, insurance companies, university endowments, and more. It therefore came as bad news when at its January 26, 2012 meeting, the FOMC[16] decided that low interest rates will stay till end of 2014, which meant for 3 more years. Worse yet, as 2012 neared its end, a new Fed decision has been that near zero interest rates will stay till end of 2015; once again another 3 years.

Prior to the first of these statements which pointed to a longer accommodative policy, the market expected a first rate hike in early 2014. Following it, investors adjusted their plans to reflect the FOMC's new language. As longer date Treasury yields reflect expected short-term yields sometime in the future, the 10-year Treasury yield fell by 14 basis points to 1.91 percent after the announcement, then it rebounded to around 2 percent.

That policy even deceived the market's expectation, and there was a second deception. Many analysts thought that the Fed was so focused on inflation that it would tighten as soon as it topped 2 percent, no matter how high unemployment was. Bernanke dispelled that notion by emphasizing the Fed's attention to unemployment without any reference to the impact a rising inflation may have on Fed policies.

This wrong-way priority in central bank decisions started at end of 2008, and it became unstoppable. After so many years of fed funds rate at about zero, four quantitative easing programs and an extended operation Twist, the resulting ballooning of the Federal Reserve's balance sheet (Section 12.1) is a precursor to another bubble.

Critics say that most damage will be from a mixture of politics and arrogance which dominates current monetary decisions. This damage will have much to do with the fact that balance sheets at monetary authorities are likely to stay bloated for some time. The way Robert Parker, a former senior banker at Crédit Suisse, put it in an article in the *Financial Times*:

> *Over a period when banks are deleveraging, when consumers are increasing their savings and reducing their borrowings, when companies are running historically high levels of excess liquidity and when fiscal policy is having a negative impact on GDP growth, it is difficult for monetary policy to be effective except as a backstop.*[17]

The way other economists look at the problem, while inflation fears have moved back into the economic landscape, a polarized policy at the Federal Reserve is unlikely to provide further monetary stimulus in 2013. For instance, nothing happens in economic growth or US competitiveness by additional Treasury purchases by the Fed, on top of its current pace of buying mortgage-backed securities (MBSs). Other western central banks which, quite likely, also engage in more monetary policy stimulus on top of the considerable expansion of their balance sheet they have already done, can expect the same minimal to zero results.

A return to the fundamental view of central banking in line with its historical origins is not yet in the books, even if it has become evident that focus is on just one objective: kicking up the economy deprives the western economies of the basic services to a monetary institution. There are as well, other mishappenings.

Audits made at central banks come up with negative findings for their governors. An example is the audit conducted in the Fed by the Government Accountability Office (GAO) of the US Congress. GAO found problems with Federal Reserve loans which were not covered by appropriate collateral. Neither is this a *one-tantum* case. An Italian banker characterized the collateral in the vaults of ECB as being more garbage than that found in the streets of Naples.[18]

The western public is not particularly thrilled by the central banks stance on economic policy and the stability of the currency. A widely held view in the United States is: "All the Fed has done is to help Wall Street." Common citizens and managers of small to medium enterprises object to the fact that there is a growing gap in central bank support for Wall Street and for Main Street.

For their part, many economists hope that monetary policy will become more supportive of financial stability. The market, too, thinks in this way but some of the projections being made over the last few years turned out to be wrong, for instance, that the Fed will refrain from QE3 because, contrary to QE1 the QE2 results were minimal and investors did not believe in the wisdom of QE3. Bernanke, however, continued to flood the market with liquidity.

Analysts looked at the Fed chairman's August 31, 2012 speech, kicking off the Jackson Hole Conference of the Federal Reserve Bank of Kansas City, as an opportunity to explain what mechanisms the Fed would use in the near- to medium-term future. The more general expectation was that he lays out a path of moderate easing able to address the transmission mechanism of monetary policy rather than simply providing additional liquidity to the market.

Others believed that Bernanke's Jackson Hole speech will provide the inspiration for a Fed program through which credit institutions would be rewarded for meeting targets related to their business behavior:[19]

- Increasing bank lending,
- Writing down principal for outstanding loans, and
- Accommodating distressed mortgage refinancing.

It did not turn out that way. Instead, on September 2, 2012 Fed officials set out their views on a third round of quantitative easing, with Bernanke hinting at more action along that path. James Bullard, president of the St. Louis Fed, said "middling" economic data meant that the Fed could afford to wait, stating that: "The most reasonable expectation is still that the economy will improve in the second half of the year and that it will improve further in 2013."[20]

In a paper presented to the world's assembled central bankers at Jackson Hole, Professor Michael Woodford of Columbia University implied that the Fed was going about easing policy the wrong way. The way newly minted money was invested was not the best possible. Woodford argued that:

- The effectiveness of quantitative easing was limited, and
- It was wishful thinking for a central bank to imagine that it could boost the economy without getting involved in the allocation of credit to specific sectors.

Woodford also stated that forecasting low interest rates for a long time without making a commitment to them could have a perverse effect, because people could reasonably assume the central bank was deeply pessimistic about the outlook for growth in the American economy.[21]

Indirectly, Bernanke allegedly admitted that QE1 and QE2 created just 2 million jobs. This was less than a fifth, the then prevailing unemployment, and it was small game compared to the destabilization of the currency. As for the unexciting speech the Fed chairman gave at the Jackson Hole Conference of 2012, it was interpreted as meaning that his personal wish was to proceed with QE3 (which he did anyway).

To the opinion of financial analysts, Bernanke does not want higher end yields, and this not only because an increase in the cost of financing will impact negatively on business activity. The more important reason is that the $16.4 trillion of public debt will weigh heavily on the interest the Obama Administration has to pay, and therefore on the government's budget deficit.

A quick look at the behaviour of dollar interest rates suggests that this is a plausible hypothesis. In June 2011, the Fed completed QE3 as the yield on 10-year Treasury bonds stood at 3.1 percent, following a spring decline below 3 percent. At that time, Washington debated raising the debt ceiling, and this issue led to partisan politics.

The debt ceiling was raised in August 2011, near the deadline. By then, the interest rate on 10-year Treasuries had fallen just north of 2.1 percent. A month later, the Fed announced Operation Twist and the 10-year yield dropped to 1.70 percent, after the Fed committed itself to keeping rates rock-bottom until mid-2013. By July 2012, the interest on 10-year Treasuries dipped below 1.40 percent, but the market turned around and interest rate rose to nearly 2 percent.

- In August 2012, the Fed extended Operation Twist until end of that year, with a commitment to keeping rates low to late-2014.
- In September 2012, Bernanke launched QE3 and heralded his intention to maintain low rates until mid-2015. Rates dipped again.

To assure that interest rates on 10-year Treasuries stay low, in December 2012, the Fed chairman announced an open-ended QE with outright Treasury purchases replacing Operation Twist (more on this so-called operation QE3.5 in described in Section 12.4). Throughout these milestones, "unemployment" has been used as the weeping boy. The true reason for throwing so much liquidity to the market lies in the maintenance of an accomodative economic policy.

With the exception of Neo-Keynesian economists, others said that such a tandem of QEs was not the solution, and therefore, the law of diminishing returns hit a policy stuck in the search for elusive full employment. Critics compared QE3 to "monetary heroin," with several Fed governors wanting to prevent that from happening. Allegedly, the central bank's chairman acknowledged it is uncharted waters, but saw no other way to follow. His tool box has only one tool, printing money, said one of the critics.

12.4   Twisting the Treasury's Refinancing and QE3.5 Releveraging

With the so-called *Operation Twist* which started in September 2011 and finished at end of December 2012, the Fed got itself into the public debt controversy and the US Treasury's refinancing operations, particularly their term structure. This term structure is disquieting in the short term when, reportedly, it is due the majority of US debt. As the majority of US debt on the market falls due within the next 3 years:

- Creditors have to be found in the coming months and years for very large sums,
- The abandonment of long-term refinancing comes at the potential price of considerably higher interest rates in the future, affecting domestic politics, and
- Terms on which the market will provide credit is not simply a quantitative problem, but also a qualitative one should there be concerns about the creditworthiness of the debtor.

Each one of these consequences is affected not only by national economic factors but as well by international ones, the two most important being the continuing willingness of Asian countries (Japan, China) to keep on buying US debt and Euroland's crisis exemplified by the state debt showdown by Greece, Portugal, Italy, Spain, Cyprus, Slovenia, and eventually France. (Mario Draghi's policies at ECB did not provide a solution to these outstanding debt problems. It only *temporarily* calmed the market.)

The fact that neither the American nor the European economy got going with all the liquidity their central banks threw to the market and its players, is disquieting. As a result, it highlighted an important way in which western economies appeared to have changed, while central banks continue to administer the old remedy of trying to be market-friendly.

Through *Operation Twist*,[22] the Fed decided to combat slowing growth by buying long-term Treasuries while selling shorter duration debt. Twist reminded investors that the central bank is ready to turn to provide accommodation. The Fed:

- Purchased 6 to 30 years Treasuries,
- Sold short term up to 3 years Treasuries, and
- Aimed to convert a total of $400 billion up to 2014 bonds which had to be refinanced.

This practically means the Federal Reserve decided to replace $400 billion of short-term debt in its portfolio with longer term debt, while aiming to reduce borrowing costs for the government (Section 12.3) as well as banks and other entities. It did so by exerting slight upward pressure on short-term rates while keeping long-term rates low. The result on the long end of the curve, however, is only tentative because there exist several factors that put pressure on yields. The three most important are:

- America's exposure to Euroland's debt crisis via the banking system,
- Possible credit crunch whose likelihood is far from being zero, and
- Uncertain investor sentiment at any major center of the globalized economy.

Operation Twist was said to be a monetary policy tool that does not necessarily involve money creation as such, and rightly or wrongly it is thought of as neutral for the currency. Both assumptions are wrong, even if they can be found in the background of the Fed's decision.

The target of Twist has been to lower the yield of risky assets by lowering the yield on risk-free Treasury bonds well into very long maturities. With this, Bernanke aimed to deter private savings and to encourage spending and investment. With 71 percent of the money greasing the wheels of the American economy coming from consumers, higher spending and investments have a positive impact on growth. But, they are also bad for the currency because they contribute to widening the US trade deficit.

In addition, lower yields over the whole yield curve reduce the incentive to buy US bonds by investors, including foreign investors. This means that the Fed will need to intervene in the Treasury bond market even more than at the present time.

According to other economists, Operation Twist should be seen not as a stand-alone event but as part of a global process affecting interest rates. For example, US 10-year yields fell back to 2 percent after an early December 2011 press conference by the ECB, while the EU "summit" held that same month also disappointed investors who were hoping that either:

- The ECB would openly come to the rescue Euroland countries,[23] or
- The next "summit" would decide to form a fiscal union.

Critics expected Operation Twist to have a rather limited impact on asset classes even if the central bank extended the average maturity of its US Treasuries portfolio. Moreover, the FOMC announced that it would rollover maturing securitized US government agency debt. Indeed, QE3 targeted MBSs aiming to support the mortgage market by way of exercising downward pressure on mortgage yields.

On December 12, 2012 Bernanke announced his 3.5 round of quantitative easing to take the place of Twist which was expired at end of 2012. QE3.5 consisted of throwing to the market an extra $45 billion per month of newly minted money primarily directed to the purchase of MBSs. Together with the $40 billion of QE3, the Fed was flooding the market with $85 billion of new liquidity per month—or 1020 billion per year, roughly the US government's deficit.

The deeper result of this decision is that Bernanke used the central bank as substitute to the Obama Administration's fiscal policy, probably foreseeing that investors and foreign governments will buy less and less US Treasuries at about zero interest rate. "It's zero rate forever," said an economist, since 15 out of 19 members of the FOMC voted to keep it that way till 2015.

Many economists were looking in the Fed announcement for a limit to the zero rates, but in this regard, the wording has been very vague. It set as a barrier US unemployment falling below 6.5 percent committing itself to zero interest rates till then as well as to continuing buying of MBSs. In his speech, which followed the December 12, 2012 announcement, Bernanke looked at the $45 billion of extra liquidity as the best possible way. In contrast, several economists and financial analysts suggested that:

- Unemployment has just been an excuse, and
- The real aim is to provide the Obama Administration with fiscal firepower.

Apart from other negatives, an evident downside is that the Federal Reserve's balance sheet gets bigger and bigger, becoming a bubble. "The market will force the Fed to exit," said a financial analyst interviewed by CNBC. One of the interviewed economists put his thoughts in this way: "Prior to this policy, a person retiring with $1 million could expect an income of $40,000 per year. With zero interest rate he gets nothing. This depresses savers and hurts their living standard." To the opinion of still another expert: "Zero interest rates over seven years are going to change the American economy forever."[24]

Looking at Twist and QE3.5 from a currency perspective, economists point out several aspects which, in sum, are more negative than positive for the US dollar. They are chipping away its armory which consists of an impressive 86 percent of all foreign exchange transactions still being made in American dollars.

This 86 percent figure is under attack by Federal Reserve actions such as Twist and QE. By contrast, one aspect of Twist that should be positive for the currency is that the government (and real-estate lenders) were to lengthen the duration of existing debt, therefore being able to better confront changes if inflation expectations change or other economic stress shows up.

This may be handy at a time the US dollar loses ground as the world's reserve currency. Not long ago, the then Chinese prime minister Wen Jiabao and Japanese Prime Minister Yoshihiko Noda promoted the use of their own currencies in bilateral trade, rather than using the US dollar as intermediary. China already has similar agreements with some of its trading partners like Brazil.

Japan and China, Asia's two main industrial powers, hold so much American public debt that if bilateral agreements in local currencies become a trend, this would impact US interest rates at some stage. Quantitatively speaking, among themselves, Japan and China own a whopping $2.1 trillion of US Treasuries which represents a cool 13 percent of total US debt, larger than the Federal Reserve's US debt holdings.

Economists say that bilateral currency deals can start a ball rolling. In addition, the more the assets are issued in Chinese currency, the deeper becomes China's financial market. Another negative for the dollar has been that holdings of US Treasuries by foreign central banks had fallen by a record amount of $69 billion over the 4 weeks prior to January 2012. (If Bank of Japan had not bought Treasuries to weaken the yen against the dollar, the statistics would have looked worse.)

Globalization promoted free capital mobility elevating it to "fundamental right." It should not be forgotten, however, that Bretton Woods restricted financial speculation and attacks on currencies, which today have become a second religion. Indeed, John Maynard Keynes considered as the most important achievement of the conference the establishment of the right of governments to restrict capital movements. It is curious that the self-proclaimed Neo-Keynesians refrain from making reference to this and other important policies of Keynes. They only spouse deficit spending.

In conclusion, Twist and its successor QE3.5 have been more politically oriented than a monetary policy might warrant. Not only the so-called unconventional tools provided massive liquidity to the financial system, beyond reasonable needs and limits, but also bought unprecedented amounts of government bonds hurting the currency without really helping the recovery or reducing unemployment. This has its own risks. As an article in the *Economist* commented: "More power of central bankers means less for politicians. Hardly surprising, them, that a backlash is starting."[25]

12.5 An Unwarranted Worst-Case Scenario

According to Strategas Research, a think tank, total US government debt has risen 42 percent over just 3 years: 2009, 2010, and 2011. Weak growth and inflation have played a part but Fed largesse, both realized and expected, accounts for a large chunk of it. The central bank is walking the thinnest of tightropes with plain disregard to the Copernican thesis, expounded in 1526 by King Sigismund of Poland: "Money loses its value when it has too much multiplied."

Printing paper money without limits is like becoming drug addict. It's an unwarranted practice getting its users over many difficult moments, but it is fatal to those who persist. Only the analphabets of economic conditions and currency behavior are unable to grasp that age-long truth; whether we talk of people or of the economy, drugs kill.

This drug addiction allegory is bad news for the US economy and for the West at large because, quite unfortunately, it has become a more general trend in western economies. The desire to repay debts and repair balance sheets is easier to find among companies and households than among sovereigns. The approach most usually adopted by governments is that of always:

- Rescheduling debt,
- Raising the debt limit, and
- Trying to push the day of reckoning at a forward but unspecified date.

This is ludicrous. The problem lies precisely in the role central banks play as *deus ex machina*, which has been totally unhealthy. The money supply is growing more prodigiously than ever. The Fed's policy to flood the market with liquidity and keep the cost of money rock-bottom over a long stretch of time has damaged the free market as well as Bernanke's reputation as scholar of the First Great Depression:

- In sequel to purely political decisions, the Fed's risk manual continues getting frayed at the edges, and
- Part of the bad news is that the central bank's chairman proved to be consistently wrong by following unconventional policies which are incapable to deliver.

There is a delirium in ballooning the monetary base by turning the handle of the printing press, merrily but unconsciously of its disastrous aftereffect. This is done by central banks accepting no connection between printing money and its depreciation. In turn, this means that they are not in control of the country's monetary stability. That's the typical socialist practice.

Socialists, Winston Churchill has said, are like Christopher Columbus. When they start their voyage they don't know where they go, and when they arrive they don't know where they are. Margaret Thatcher had an even better definition: Socialism lasts as long as other peoples' money is lasting. When the central bank is part of the socialists' game and it keeps on minting paper dollars, other peoples' money would not last for long. Then comes the day of reckoning.

The socialist state has already established itself in western democracies and ruined the sovereign budgets through unsustainable entitlements. Nowadays, it set for itself a second objective: pressing into the shortest time frame of fallacies and errors regarding currency stability. This has been Lenin's strategy for conquering the western democracies, which he expressed in a short sentence: "If you wish to destroy a nation you must corrupt its currency."

Bernanke is no Benjamin Stark, Marrinner Eccles, Arthur Burns, or Paul Volcker. He is a theorist with a transparent socialist inclination who is not made out of central bankers stuff. The policy he is following at the Fed is indeed a losing battle because the US debt-to-GDP level is so high that America's credit has been downgraded by US-based independent rating agencies. Printing lots of paper money, over and above that, evidently makes matters worse.

Since some time, a growing number of economists have been suggesting that the United States is living beyond its means and that with so much paper money minted overnight without real assets to back it up, the dollar's dominance is threatened. Financial markets are also uneasy about the longer term, as with its spending programs the Obama Administration is playing with fire.

The argument that the Federal Reserve, as well as Bank of England and ECB have plenty of time to absorb the huge liquidity they threw and continue throwing to the market lacks conviction. According to well-informed opinions, monetary policy decision makers have been looking to exit quantitative easing since its inception in 2009, but political reasons don't allow doing so.

Each time central banks look for the exit, the government bond market sells off and they are forced to do more of the same. As the paper money piles up, there is no reason to expect that "next time" it will be different. It is more likely that a *worst-case scenario* will resemble hyperinflation in the Weimar Republic. According to Adam Fergusson, by early 1924, hyperinflation in Germany was rising so rapidly that legal tender billion mark bills became obsolete by the time they were printed. The Reichsbank stocked them in 300 railroad cargo wagons.[26]

This is what happens when a nation's money is looked upon by the market, investors, and common citizens as a joke. At the center of the hurricane were the sovereign German politicians, Allied reparations, and Reichsbank—the monetary institution. This crisis started in 1920 with an elusive economic revival, and kept on building up over the following couple of years.

Left unattended, as the Weimar Republic's government could only make ends meet by the Reichsbank's benevolence to print more and more money—which somehow resembles the western world today—hyperinflation became, so to speak, institutionalized. The German government's income was a mere 30 percent of its expenditures. In the United States today, the government's income is 70 percent of its expenditures (Section 12.1) and as expenses for endowments continue rising Weimar comes in many peoples' mind.

We are not yet there. But who can say so in a few years? Phillip Cagan defined hyperinflation as beginning in the moment price rises first exceed 50 percent per month.[27] That's where we may be heading, unless politically difficult decisions are now made, at long last, to bring the budgetary deficit and start paying back the debt. Paul Ryan, House Budget Committee chairman, is right when he asks for a "big down payment on the debt crisis" and for focus on fiscal deadlines.

Moreover, as the case of Weimar Republic documents, a tragedy parallel to hyperinflation would be its effect on ethics. Speculators and profiteers will spring all over the globalized financial market, causing an increase in uncertainty and unbearable pain to common people. No economic discussions will pacify the anxiety of citizens because they know from experience that such discussions lead to nothing that is concrete.

Pretending that the debt issue could be solved without downsizing entitlements and increasing taxes is as childish as insisting that the current unfunded liabilities of sovereigns would fade away on their own will or as a result of unstoppable high-speed printing of paper money. If anything, the Bernanke model has been faulty as it worsens an already bad situation.

The more the Fed buys Treasuries the more money the government has to spend, while at the same time it tries to raise the statutory debt limit. On May 12, 2011 when a major jump in statutory debt limit was in discussion (Chapter 11), the Fed chairman warned that using the national debt limit as bargaining chip may lead to a Lehman-type meltdown of the US economy.[28]

Critics answered that what the Federal Reserve Chairman forgot to say is that such a meltdown is promoted by his policies of flooding the US and global market with newly minted dollars in a desperate effort to face single handed the huge US government deficits which continue to grow.

"I am very much concerned about the fiscal cliff," said Alan Greenspan in an interview he gave to CNBC on October 23, 2012. "Each of the two political parties has its position and the parties do not really talk to each other. They need to talk to reach a compromise." A month and a half later, Greenspan was quoted by Bloomberg News as having said that: "There is no painless solution to the US debt problem."[29]

Congress, the White House, and the central bank are the three parties with topmost responsibility to fix the debt, rather than doing matters worse by delaying the big down payment on the debt crisis Ryan asked for. The American economy, which has espoused socialism *à la Française*, can no more afford the State Supermarket (into which has been the outgrowth of nanny state) and its voracious appetite for money. Even less sustainable are the increases in "benefits" contemplated by Obama.

This does not mean that there should be no tax increases. Having balanced the budget through the downsizing of expenditures, the new tax money should be strictly used to pay down the colossal public debt of $16,400 billion. There is plenty of room for doing so by adopting a top tax bracket which prevails in other developed countries. For example:

- 50 percent in Britain (with projected reduction to 45 percent)
- 45 percent in Germany
- 50 percent in Japan

In America, the current top level tax rate is 39 percent, and an increase will probably leave it below that of other western countries.[30] A precondition however is that the Federal Reserve is part of the deal and stops sailing very close to the wind, often to the wrong side of it. This means that it:

- Ends the policy of zero interest rates,
- Abandons quantitative easing, and
- Refrains from buying the 70 percent of bonds issued by the Treasury, which allows the government free reign with a skyrocketing public debt.

In May 2011, Charlie Rose interviewed Singapore's founding prime minister and elder statesman who criticized those central banks ready to flood the market will newly printed money. Lee Kuan Yew[31] said that the US dollar still holds a global position because all important commodities are dollar denominated, but it is losing value against other currencies. To his opinion, if the United States continues along the current path, it will become a deeply indebted country and the huge amount of currency floating around will create a great deal of inflation.

Singapore's elder statesman might have added that when the currency is destroyed, the nation's resources would be shot away to nothing, as it has happened with the Weimar Republic. Given the way we are going, the question is not "*if*" but "*when*" the bill will be presented. This issue of unsustainable indebtedness will linger in the public's mind,[32] just as that of uncovered banknotes will haunt central bankers and sovereigns for years to come.

12.6 Financial Stability and Systemic Risk

The focal point of *financial stability* is that of providing assurance that there is not another crisis or another bubble, and *if* one is building up it will be taken care of without delay. Too much liquidity, way above what the market needs, is a way bubbles build up. Financial stability and the avoidance of systemic risk correlate. *Systemic risk* is the risk that the failure of a very large financial entity, or an accumulation of failures, can tear the fabric apart and lead to a domino effect with the one economy pulling another into the abyss.

When leveraged deals go right, the result may be spectacular. When they go wrong, they may wipe out plenty of capital and goodwill. New financial instruments as well as unconventional monetary policy measures magnify the danger of systemic risk, because of several reasons compounding upon one another:

- Policy makers navigate in uncharted waters,
- Ways to contain them look "evident," but turn out to be disastrous,
- The deals' size is usually large, and the task of stopping the slide is oversize,
- The opaqueness surrounding the journey diminishes visibility, and
- The consequences are not well known in advance hence measures risk being ineffective.

Derivatives are not the only source of possible inordinate exposure. Quantitative easing by central banks provides another example of going way out on one leg. And there is always the tendency to confuse team playing with the urge to avoid the expression of contrarian opinion, which condemns decision makers to one-way thinking.

"It is not an easy thing to vote against the President's wishes," said Henry Wallich (a fed governor in the Carter years). "But what are we appointed for? Why are we given these long terms in office? Presumably, it is that not only the present but the past and the future have some weight in our decisions. In the end, it may be helpful to remind the President that it is not only his present concerns that matter."[33]

On the surface, the origin of systemic risk is simple; it gets complex as the globalization of banking and financial markets ties the players together so effectively that shocks in one place can have severe implications in other far-away places which till then seemed untouchable. Speaking at the eighth International Banking Event on May 7, 1996 in Frankfurt, the then Federal Reserve Chairman Dr. Alan Greenspan pointed to the likelihood of significant market disruptions and the potential for systemic risk. This, he said, had become a worry in the mind of every banker.

What is particularly startling, Greenspan stated, is how large the expansion in cross-border finance has become relative to the trade it finances. The discrepancy between the real and the virtual economy—the goods being traded and financial aggregates—is not necessarily the result of out-of-control financial speculation. It is a consequence of the change in the nature of output that has become progressively more conceptual and less physical.

- Measured in tons, the weight of GDP today is only modestly higher than some decades ago,
- The huge rise in price-adjusted value is more the result of the development of expansionist ideas than of the transformation of physical resources.

In a startling change from past generations, a much smaller proportion of the measured real GDP currently constitutes the classical physical bulk. This is an expression of a trend toward "physical downsizing," while the rising "virtual content" of output has become a major factor in financial exchanges. At the same time, the more virtual is the economy, the more it depends on confidence.

"There is no doubt in my mind," writes Volcker "that the two big devaluations of the 1930s − Britain in 1931 and the United States in 1933 − did place large pressures on their trading partners, deliberately or not, and set off further rounds of instability."[34] Deliberately or not, confidence was lost and this led to what became known as *beggar-thy-neighbor* policy considered to be one of the key reasons leading to World War II.

At global scale, loss of confidence can turn at no time into a systemic political crisis. In a similar manner, a systemic financial crisis is the result of loss of confidence in the banking industry at large, including the central bank(s). Theoretically, but only theoretically, bank liabilities are meant to be riskless allowing customers to assume they can get back 100 cents on the dollar on request. If anybody in the modern economy still believes so, he or she is living in a past world.

True enough, in the eighteenth[35] and nineteenth centuries bank liabilities consisted of privately issued notes convertible on demand to gold or silver (specie). But with the advent of paper money, in the case of panics the banking system did not have enough specie to meet all the redemption requests.

The abandonment of the gold standard after World War I made the specie issue irrelevant, at least for private citizens. To the contrary, the Bretton Woods agreement preserved specie for the central banks. They could ask for the conversion of paper money to gold, if they so choose. In terms of their monetary policy, this kept the reserve institutions in their line of duty. Since 1971, however, Bretton Woods belongs to history.

Bringing the amassed paper money back to its issuer and asking for gold was a great disciplinary tool. The unwanted consequence of its cancellation has been a flood of newly minted paper money. "Looking back, the performance of the world economy in the first twenty-five years of Breton Woods was exceptional," says Volcker. "... convertibility of currencies was restored, exchange controls in Europe were relaxed, exchange rate changes among industrialized countries were limited in number and, by prewar standards, relatively small."[36]

Monetary discipline made the difference as Bretton Woods turned from symbol to substance, but with the end of the agreement this discipline was lost. Tremendous changes have taken place over the following four decades, but only after the economic and banking crisis which started in 2007 we began to appreciate their deeper implications. One of them is that the nature of the systemic risk has changed; another that the tools which we were using in the past have become substandard but we hardly know the aftermath of so-called unconventional tools newly added to the central banks' arsenals, particularly when:

- They are used time and again in a massive way, and
- The results which they produce are, at best, questionable.[37]

Bernanke's Federal Reserve started with quantitative easing, as an experimental tool, in late 2008, at a time when the dollar was rising sharply because of being regarded as "safe haven" currency. Investors rush to the US dollar when they are worried about the outlook for the global economy.

The increase in the size of the central bank's balance sheet significantly expanded the monetary base as the Fed bought assets from the financial system and credited the account of the counterparty from which it bought the asset by an equivalent amount of central bank money which did not exist prior to this transaction.[38]

The reasons for QEs in 2008 and in 2013 are not the same. The target in 2013 is to keep from rising the longer term dollar interest rates. As already brought to the reader's attention, if they do rise (which they will eventually do), the federal budget will be devastated. As Masaaki Shiraka-wa, governor of the Bank of Japan, told the Diet regarding his country's huge public debt: long-term yields could rise and that would be a problem for public finances.

We are living at the end of an epoch characterized by the dollar as global reserve currency, unit of money for transactions, and credit card whose balance is never to be repaid. The Fed is using the paper money weapon to fill the gap in Obama's budget, but this can work out only as long as there are counterparties accepting it. The way to bet is that the wider acceptance which dates back to Bretton Woods would not last long.

In retrospect, Bernanke chose the wrong policy in playing the eternal financier of US government deficits and protector of its mountain of public debt. "We have substituted central bank credit for the fiscal deficit of countries," said Greenspan in an interview he gave to CNBC on October 23, 2012. As the understanding of this substitution sips down business, industry, and foreign governments,[39] the level of confidence drops while systemic risk rises.

At the level commercial and investment banking, systemic crises are largely about obtaining cash. Much depends on the bank's ability to fund itself in the financial market, and this has much to do with its creditworthiness. Since the beginning of this century, such as constraint has been relieved through sovereign action, government uses taxpayer money to pull up from under banks "too big to fail." Big government and big banks merged their interests. Yet, there is an interesting reference in Adam Smith's *Wealth of Nations*, capitalism's bible, warning of the dangers of leaving the management of banking entirely to the self-interest of bankers.

It's all part of the socialization of America and of Europe. In his book *Mémoires*, David Rockefeller writes that when in 1964 he visited the Kremlin with his daughter Neva, Nikita Khroutchev told them that they would end up by living under a communist regime in the United States.[40] The extent and length of economic and social uncertainty we are now confronting tends to suggest that old man Nikita might, after all, have been right.

End Notes

1. Montefiore SS. Staline. Paris: Editions des Syrtes; 2005.
2. For instance, in payments, such as handling the payroll of public servants, retirees, war veterans, and so on.
3. The Humphrey−Hawkins Act of 1978 through which Congress rid itself from its responsibilities for employment by assigning to the Fed a broad and contradictory dual mandate.
4. LTRO, Long-Term Refinancing Operation; OMT, Outright Monetary Transactions.
5. Chorafas DN. The changing role of central banks. New York, NY: Palgrave/Macmillan; 2013.
6. Financial Times, August 29, 2012.
7. As well as on self-wounded banks.
8. Financial Times, August 17, 2012.
9. Société Générale, Cross Asset Research. Popular delusions, Paris; May 17, 2012.
10. Altogether the number of unemployed in Spain reached 6 million, by mid-January 2013.
11. Anecdotal evidence suggests that at Electricité de France (the French government-owned power company) one out of three people is superfluous.
12. As of January 2013 also by the Bank of Japan.
13. Despite some improvement in 2011.
14. The Economist, October 6, 2012.
15. Endlich L. Goldman Sachs. London: Little Brown; 1999.
16. Open market operations can be liquidity providing, liquidity absorbing, or have other goals. An open market operation is a financial transaction executed on the initiative of the central bank. Such operations include reverse transactions, outright transactions as well as the issuance of fixed-term deposits, debt certificates, foreign exchange swaps.
17. Financial Times, September 27, 2012.
18. Which are famous for accumulated household garbage at every corner and on the sidewalks.

19. In a way similar to the Funding for Lending program by the Bank of England.
20. Financial Times, September 3, 2012.
21. *Idem.*
22. Which, as these lines were written, ends in December 31, 2012 but is likely to be extended under its present or some novel form.
23. Which it did at a later day with OMT, but at time of this writing, OMT has yet to be tested.
24. CNBC, December 12, 2012.
25. The Economist, December 1, 2012.
26. Fergusson A. When money dies. New York, NY: Public Affairs; 2010.
27. Friedman M (editor). Studies in the quantity theory of money. University of Chicago Press, Chicago, 1956.
28. Bloomberg News, May 12, 2011.
29. Bloomberg, December 6, 2012.
30. It is interesting to notice that the top tax bracket in Russia is 13 percent, but without allowing any deductions for no matter which reason. Anecdotal evidence suggests that this 13 percent brings to the government as much as the 35 percent in the United States with a long list of deductions.
31. Lee is also famous for having aptly remarked that "America lost the war in the United States, not in Vietnam." (Rockefeller D. Mémoires. Paris: Editions de Fallois; 2006.)
32. As the present generation's children and grandchildren will pay for their parents' and grandparents' excesses.
33. Greider W. Secrets of the temple. How the Federal Reserve runs the country. New York, NY: Touchstone/Simon and Schuster; 1987.
34. Volcker P, Gyohten T. Changing fortunes. New York, NY: Times Books; 1992.
35. Save the Mississippi Bubble and the South Seas Bubble in the eighteenth.
36. Volcker P, Gyohten T. Changing fortunes. New York, NY: Times Books; 1992.
37. Chorafas DN. The changing role of central banks. London: Palgrave/Macmillan; 2013.
38. By contrast, qualitative easing is a shift in the composition of assets toward less liquid, holding constant the size of the balance sheet. Usually, a central bank takes assets with longer maturities from the market replacing them by an equivalent amount of shorter maturities from its own balance sheet.
39. Which still buy US bonds to keep their currencies from appreciating.
40. Rockefeller D. Mémoires. Paris: Editions de Fallois; 2006. First published in 2002 by Random House Trade Paperback, New York.

Part Five

Returns are Not Rising Forever

13 Storm Clouds over the BRICs

13.1 The Rise of Emerging Markets

In the 1960s, a French economist coined the label "Third World" for all countries that would not fall under the then popular "First World" reference to western nations. The First World consisted of America, Western Europe, and Japan. Successively, as a term, the Third World has been changed into "countries in the process of development," and later on became "developing countries" as well as "emerging markets."

Though the label "emerging markets" is nowadays common currency, there exists no solid block of nations behind it in terms of economic development, industrialization, family planning, and standard of living.[1] But there is a group of nations nicknamed BRICs—which stands for Brazil, Russia, India, and China. Three out of these four economies constitute this chapter's theme.

Of course, there are as well other countries in emerging markets, such as South Korea, Taiwan, Thailand, and Indonesia in Asia; Turkey and Egypt in the Middle East; Mexico, Chile, Peru, and Argentina in South America. These will not be individually examined in this text, but they are part of the broader references made in this introductory section.

If South Africa was added to the BRICs (to which it does not really belong), *then* they would make up 43 percent of the world's population.[2] As one of the experts interviewed by CNBC pointed out, there are no other economics that can compete with BRICs. China is already a major global player, and it grows faster than the Asian economies surrounding it.[3]

Another interesting fact about emerging markets, particularly in terms of a trend, is that in the course of the 6-year economic crisis (2007 to today) they have shown a high degree of resilience, even if they were not entirely immune to global economic weakness. For instance, in 2012 Asian GDP grew somewhat below 5 percent[4] compared with 6.6 percent in 2011. A 5-percent GDP growth is great when contrasted to Europe or to America. Even if in the years preceding the crisis emerging markets were accustomed to much more than that, the trend held.

Moreover, by mid-2013, downward revisions to emerging market GDP growth forecasts appear to be coming to an end. Analysts have started to expect emerging market GDP to increase to 5.3 percent in 2013, while Germany revised its 2013 growth forecast to a mere 0.6 percent. IMF projections also talk of moderate growth in emerging markets in the course of this year.

Public Debt Dynamics of Europe and the US. DOI: http://dx.doi.org/10.1016/B978-0-12-420021-0.00013-0

Even if the economy were not globalized, it is unavoidable that economic crisis in the richer markets will affect those ascending. Nobody has yet found a way to defy gravity. As the larger emerging markets are not able to compensate for the drop in economic activity in the western world, they therefore underperform. Brazil is expected to head toward zero GDP growth. India, too, has problems, and in the course of 2012, China gradually reduced its forecasts.

Nevertheless, despite growth projections well below those of the twenty-first century's first decade, the economy in several emerging markets has been supportive. Talk about structural reforms lifted some of the bigger emerging economies. Russia announced possible tax relief in the energy sector to encourage investment. By all evidence, China had a soft landing. India spoke of policy measures making it easier for foreigners to invest in the retail sector.

One would be justified in thinking that these are minor amends and in the end they may account for little depending on the intensity of the next crisis. As Japan reminds us, the export-led growth model is an unreliable one. Even if a policy of investment and infrastructure, followed by the better-off developing economies, is sound, it tends only to work in conjunction with exports—particularly when the country's consumers are not spending that much.

In that sense, the key risk to the near-term growth outlook for the emerging markets is external shocks from advanced economies. This is a double cutting knife because western economies also suffer—at least in regard to their household debt and current account (balance of payments)—from too much money flooding into the emerging markets. (A trend which is now reversing itself)

Developing economies certainly need to upbring their internal market, but this takes lots of preparation (including a psychological one of the consumers). It cannot be done at high speed. Analysts say that consumer growth will remain defensive in China, India, and Indonesia in 2013 even if it is especially supported by policy, for instance in China. Resurgent inflation is also a latent threat, and in this case, Indonesia and India are most vulnerable, limiting government policies to promote growth.

Theoretically, the Indonesian economy should have been strong because of the country's important natural resources, oil being one of them. But inland, the price of oil was kept cheap, with the result that it was overused and spoiled. Indonesia is no more the oil-exporting country that it used to be. Russia is a better example of how to leverage what is beneath the soil.

In 2012, the Russian economy grew faster than expected. GDP expanded as compared to 2011, mainly driven by positive real income growth. While economists expected that the Russian economy will slow down in 2013, one of the reasons being that the government is unlikely to commit to further salary increases, others look toward a positive economic growth in 2013.

As with China (Section 13.2), a crucial question is whether domestic Russian demand can offset weaker export growth. The uncertainty of an unqualified positive answer led analysts to the projection of a moderate slowdown in Russia in 2013; nevertheless a positive growth.

From a structural point of view, the emerging markets' strength has to do with their improving domestic consumption, relatively high savings rate and rather strong investments. From a more cyclical standpoint, emerging markets' balance sheets are healthier than those of major western economies, so there is no pressure for them to go through austerity like several European countries had to do, because of rising mountains of public debt.

Emerging markets, however, do have hick-ups. In the late 1990s, during the most difficult days of the Asian crisis, the IMF extended bailout packages attached with reform conditions that were, as usual, strict. The harder working nations profited handsomely from this support. Combined with significant currency devaluations, the Asian governments' implementation of reforms made it possible to quickly restore competitiveness.

In early 2013, Egypt confronts a difficult economic scenario (much of it its own doing), and asked for an IMF loan. The Egyptian pound fell. By contrast, Euroland's common currency sees to it that European countries cannot devalue to restore competitiveness. This makes it even more important to implement structural reforms with resolve, which is simply not happening.

Nearly all emerging countries have put their hopes in international cooperation, favorable tariffs in western countries, and global economic convergence. However, Morgan Stanley's Ruchir Sharma, head of the bank's Emerging Markets and Global Macro, says that international economic convergence is a myth. Part of his argument is that "... few countries can sustain unusually fast growth for a decade, and even fewer for more than that. Now that the boom years are over, the BRICs are crumbling; the international order will change less than expected."[5]

While the BRICs label (like the PIIGS)[6] might have been primarily a marketing concept which reduced the whole emerging market space to only a handful of larger countries, this was not a random selection. It was simple cherry-picking. Other emerging markets have more pronounced problems, and therefore, they are not particularly appealing in an investment sense. Their growth prospects are not appealing because of reasons ranging from social strife (the case of Argentina) and economic issues, all the way to heavy indebtedness.

This does not mean that the BRICs are free of such problems, a reason why in mid-2012 (as a group) they fell out of the wall relative to the S&P 500 index. Beijing and New Delhi are locked in long-standing border disputes. Russia is stepping up its military investments to counter China's; and Brazil finds out that economic trust is difficult to build after it is shaken.

In addition, it is not easy to promote mutual prosperity when economies run at different levels. The interests of a commodities exporter are not the same with those of an importer, particularly when downward revisions to emerging markets growth projections are a reversal of previous trends. This could change again as the IMF forecasts emerging markets growth rising moderately into 2013 and further into 2014.

Sentiment about China's outlook (Section 13.2) has improved, and there have been longer term structural policy measures announced in India and Russia. Still, for the time being there are more policy announcements than corrective actions. Analysts think that once announced measures are implemented, they should be helpful to the economies where they apply, provided that reforms make the labor market more flexible and facilitate economic restructuring.

13.2 The Ascent of China

In the twenty-first century, the Chinese economy expanded quickly beating forecasts and continuing to do so as western nations confronted the economic, financial, and banking crisis which started in 2007. China has been a fast-developing emerging country with plenty of room yet to grow. It invests a lot, and though such investments might not always generate good returns for the banks that lent the money, they do contribute economic growth.

China also depends on its hard-working population as well as the Chinese of the diaspora throughout most of Asia. For instance in Indonesia, ethnic Chinese make up just 3 percent of the population, but they control an estimated 70 percent of Indonesian business. China and other Asian countries are part of the entrepreneurial model which advises:

- Keep your company's produce cheap, and
- Press exports over internal market consumption.

In this century's first decade, China's internal market consumption was at the level of 20 percent to 25 percent of GDP; the balance has been going to exports. This cannot continue forever. To sustain growth, internal consumption should be at least 50 percent of GDP, but as long as the export boom lasted, it provided China with the hard currency it needed to pay for infrastructural and industrial equipment (which it could not otherwise acquire), as well as to create a war chest in hard currencies:

- In 2001, the western world had a 35 percent share of global exports, Japan 22 percent, and China 18 percent.
- A decade later, in 2010, these ratios radically changed: the West's share was down to 22 percent, Japan's down to 14 percent, and China's up to 39 percent.

This provides double evidence: of sound management of the economy and of persistent effort. The Chinese leadership followed Lao-tze's, the Chinese philosopher's, thoughts. He lived 2500 years ago and his motto was: "Ruling a great country is like cooking a little fish." A light touch is needed for a good meal; the result of applying this recipe to the economy has been growth.

The pace of this growth made economists wonder whether China can or cannot sustain its high rate of investments, as well as the destinations of its produce. Because export-oriented industries employ an estimated 200 million people, weakening exports figures are a big concern for the country's economy at large.

Critics say that Chinese growth is unbalanced because it is highly dependent on investment as a source of demand and driver of the economy. This argument has a point as between 1997 and 2010 gross investment rose from 32 percent to 46 percent of GDP, while household consumption somewhat fell.[7]

While there is indeed evidence that China's policy overemphasized investment, the pros answer that infrastructural works were not only necessary for social and industrial improvement, but as well for adjustment of the economy to a new production model—as consumer export markets are no more as strong as they used to be. Capital equipment is indeed a crucial part of the global market, most particularly in Southeast Asia where China is redirecting its exports.

- The high water mark for exports to America was in 2006–2007 representing nearly 22 percent of China's produce. On January 1, 2013, this stood at a little over 17 percent.
- In percentage of China's manufacturing the high point of export to the European Union was 21 percent in 2008–2009. By January 1, 2013, this dropped to 17 percent.
- By contrast, Chinese exports to Southeast Asian countries were a mere 7 percent in 2005, but rose steadily over the following years to reach 10 percent on January 1, 2013.

While today China's economy is not as dependent on exports as it used to be, foreign markets are important because, in the early part of this century China worked itself into becoming the world's largest manufacturing power. Its output of mechanical and electrical engineering surpassed America's in 2010,[8] now accounting for roughly 20 percent of global manufacturing.

- Chinese factories have made so much, so cheaply that they have curbed inflation in many of their country's trading partners.
- This is, however, a double cutting knife because a present-day China problem is that the era of low cost products may be drawing to a close while inland production costs are soaring.

This is not only true of labor costs. Increases in land prices, machinery, environmental and safety regulations as well as taxes, all play a part even if the biggest cost factor is labor as wages rose by 10 percent in 2012 alone. Coupled with export problems, this suggests that in 2013 economic growth will not return to a double-digit annual increase even if destocking continues.

The way an article in *The Economist* had it "some low-tech, labor-intensive industries, such as T-shirts and cheap trainers, have already left China. And some are employing a "China + 1" strategy, opening just one factory in another country to test the waters and provide a back-up."[9] The irony of this reference is that China is discovering firsthand the reasons which made western companies to delocalize.

This means that China's new leaders in the Politburo Standing Committee will face major challenges in the next years. The country's size alone will not be a problem. But to achieve sustained growth for a population of 1.4 billion, people will require continuing refocus from export-led growth to more balanced growth which capitalizes on the home market.

The good news for the new political leadership is that Chinese consumption continues to grow at a low double-digit level. The bad news is that still private consumption only comprises 34 percent of Chinese GDP, while 49 percent comes from fixed investments. Hence, the latter to determine whether China's overall economic growth meets or misses the nation's expectations.

Another piece of good news for China's economy is that in spite of growing production costs, China's exports are increasing again, particularly toward the

United States. All by itself, however, this is not enough. Not only the internal market must be sustained in a growth path but also investments have to be optimized in regard to the country's overall strategic plan, even if optimization is one of state capitalism's weaknesses.

- How can the state regulate the companies that it also owns?
- How can it stop them from throwing good money after bad commitments?
- How can firms in which the state is major shareholder remain innovative when innovation requires the freedom to fail?

Other questions, too, are pertinent to the Chinese nation's future. Will the new leadership be able to squash the tendency of managers in both "plain capitalism" and "state capitalism" to run companies to suit their own interests rather than the interests of their owners and customers? Or will the top brass be too distracted by other duties to exercise proper oversight? And how far will the politicians go in controlling the companies' mission toward a balance between commercial and the social requirements?

Neither are these the only short to medium term challenges. China is entering the group of countries known as "middle-income." Many governments get stuck in this setting and go on to experience much lower growth rates than they did prior to entering it. Another one of the BRICs, Brazil, was already a "country of the future" in the 1960s and 1970s—and so it is still is today. Countries fall into that trap when they stick to labor-intensive sectors which are more and more challenged by cheaper-producing countries.

- *If* a country is not ready or able to climb the ladder of quality and sophistication to reshape its industry,
- *Then* its per capita growth will stall and it will lock itself in middle-income like the silk worm in its cocoon.

Climbing up the ladder is a "must," but the decision needed to do so does not come as matter of course. A prerequisite is that the country opens its political system, as several smaller countries have done in Southeast Asia. Another prerequisite is the avoidance of micromanaging its currency because this has adverse fallouts.

China has relied on keeping its currency in a peg against the US dollar. This allowed it to export at cheaper prices than it would have otherwise, but it's a policy which also has downsides. This is particularly true of a country that has been importing large quantities of energy and other materials at higher prices than it could have otherwise. The aftermath is that of igniting inflation, of which China had its share.

Iron ore and base metals are a case in point. The country's share of global demand stands at around 60 percent for iron ore and 40 percent for base metals. In crude oil demand, China's share is 11 percent, less than that of base metals but still high. For every country, the optimal exchange rate for its currency is a balancing act; one difficult to define, let alone to achieve.

"Treasure the things that are difficult to attain," urges a Chinese proverb. It is sage advice but the proverb does not say "how." One has to find his own way. Back in March 2009, China's central bank tried to do just that. It suggested replacing the US dollar as the international reserve currency with a new global system to be controlled by the IMF.

At the time, analysts said that proposal was an indication of Beijing's fears that quantitative easing and other actions being taken by the Federal Reserve would have a negative impact on China. To replace the dollar-based global system, the People's Bank of China suggested expanding the role of special drawing rights (SDRs).

- SDRs were introduced by the IMF in 1969 to support the Bretton Woods fixed exchange rate regime.
- Since 1971, however, with floating exchange rates they had become less relevant even if they were still around.

Currently, the value of SDRs is based on a basket of four currencies: US dollar, yen, euro, and sterling, and they are used largely as a unit of account by the IMF and some other international organizations. China's proposal would have expanded this basket creating a new basis of SDR valuation which involves all major economies and also, setting up a settlement system between SDRs and other currencies.

It is appropriate to note that the Chinese are not the first to come up with the SDR suggestion. Joseph Stiglitz of Columbia University and former chief economist of the World Bank has also proposed expanding the role of SDRs to lay the foundation for a world currency. And in the 1940s John Maynard Keynes made a similar suggestion about the need for a world currency, but Keynes' idea was set aside as the dollar became *the* international currency.

Still the Chinese proposal of an IMF-led international currency was a bold move, which documents how far the country has gone in gaining self-assurance. More than two centuries ago, Napoleon Bonaparte, the French emperor, warned: "Let China sleep, for when the dragon awakes it will shake the world." China is now awake, but to shake the world it still has to take many crucial, and sometimes painful, decisions whose outcome is less than certain.

13.3 China Faces Important but Not Unprecedented Challenges

As far as unprecedented challenges in the Asian continent are concerned, let me start with the heavy artillery. China is the most populous nation in the world, and India comes right next to it. In both countries, life expectancy has zoomed. In India, it has reached 65 years[10] and stands somewhat above that in China. Longevity, however, is not just a piece of good news; it's a challenge whose impact may upset the most meticulously made plan which forgets to account for it.

The challenge is the cost of aging to the country's economic equation, health care and pensions included. Due to the fast growth of its population, Asia is in the frontline of the problems longevity brings along (Africa will be next). China, India, and Indonesia, which make up 40 percent of the world's population, are set to enter an accelerated phase of population aging over the next decade. Higher health care spending over the next few years will haunt the Chinese leadership, as it does that of the United States and Europe.

Chinese health care expenditures grew by an impressive 18 percent per year over the last 5 years. That's one of the highest rates in Asia, sparked by the start of health care reforms in 2010 and progressing at an accelerated rate.[11] The reforms' impact has been particularly significant in the government's contribution to total health care spending. It matters little that China still spends only slightly over 5 percent of GDP on health care, compared to 16 percent in the United States. The pace is all-important. Let's not forget that:

- The United States too spent on health care "only" 5 percent of GDP years ago, and
- According to current estimates, due to a combination of increased health care spending and other social reforms, the Chinese health care costs could grow by 20 percent a year over the next 5 years.

The rapid rise in health care cost as well as its aftermath is in no way "news" to the western countries. Practically, all of them know very well what rapidly rising entitlements mean in terms of public debt. That's precisely why developing nations must watch over (and control) health care costs with the greatest attention. *If* this fails, *then* those responsible for managing government expenses and the economy are not doing their job.

It is to the interest of China to learn from the West's mistakes in unsustainable entitlements and in the social net. These are not age-old efforts; they have been made by western nations after World War II, most particularly in the 1960s and thereafter. Social costs must be limited to a level that is affordable and sustainable. Otherwise bankruptcy should be written as a clause of the constitution.

Errors made by other nations are important to the Chinese government which starts to build a social security network. The criticism made by westerners that "it still has a long way to go" is unfair. There is no reason for the Chinese to destroy their economy with the *nanny state*, the way western countries did. Instead, they should carefully study *a priori* the social net solution they adopt, keeping in mind that the western State Supermarket is the worst possible policy.

Nobody has provided evidence that a two-digit GDP share by health care is right. Matter of fact, it is wrong. The common citizens, and political leaders, too, must save for a rainy day rather than wait that the government provides everything to them at much higher cost.

As its name implies, "saving for a rainy day" requires a culture of *savings*. The Chinese excel in this, as the Japanese used to do in elder times. In 2012, household savings as percent of disposable income stood at 40 percent in China, compared to:

- 12.1 percent in Switzerland
- 11.3 percent in Germany
- 4.6 percent in the United States
- 3.9 percent in Italy

Experts project that China's high saving rate will start falling, as the population ages. Inland capital is already becoming less captive as savers are finding ways to take their money out of the country, contributing to downward pressure on the currency. This is one of the key reasons why China's bank deposits are now growing at a slower rate than in the past.

There is as well a redistribution of wealth. With the global economic downturn, the country's richest citizens have become less well-off: the number of billionaires has fallen for the first time since China opened to the West in the 1970s. From about 15 in 2006, the Chinese citizens worth $1 billion or more peaked at 251 in 2011, then fell to 231 in 2012. Anecdotal evidence suggests that also below the $1 billion net worth most of China's richer people saw their wealth shrink.

Phenomenal savings and plenty of rich households should be a boon for Chinese banks. This is not, however, self-evident. Though their nonperforming loan ratios look as being under control at an (official) average 0.9 percent, their asset quality seems to be deteriorating. There is as well the problem of rolling over local government debt, and the need for recapitalizing some Chinese banks with central government money.

- When the credit tide is high, liquidity is plentiful.
- When the steam goes out, the consequences can be unpleasant.

This is another challenge for China's leadership, in a climate of economic slow-down. Financial analysts say that despite the high level of coverage of nonperforming loans, Chinese banks are not necessarily fully equipped to face a cycle of worsening credit quality, though they can still capitalize on their strengths:

- Low level of loans to deposits, which sees to it that they do not have funding problems, and
- Relatively high profitability ratios, a trend which showed up over the past few years.

The downside is souring property loans. The infrastructural buildup discussed in Section 13.2 led to a boom in local government financing vehicles (LGFVs). By and large, these have been leveraged off-balance-sheet entities used to get around prohibitions on borrowing and, as such, they have copied all the bad habits of western "special investment vehicles" (SIVs).

According to regulators, at the end of 2011 bank debts of these entities were worth $1.4 trillion. Private estimates tend to be higher, suggesting that between 20 percent and 30 percent of LGFVs loans may be nonperforming. As for real-estate property, at government's initiative it is undergoing a forced cooling.

An article in the *Financial Times* points out that two problems can be symptomatic of deeper ones in the structure of a business, as well as in excess capacity in an economic sector: ". . . fresh credit only delays a reckoning. But, if the problem is disruption in exports, or a short-term dip in domestic sales — which could be the case for many Chinese companies — then the support of lenders becomes crucial . . . (and) Chinese banks are facing a step-change in their competitive environment."[12]

The banks may be but not the Chinese government which, capitalizing on current account surpluses, has put together the largest sovereign fund worldwide to the tune of an estimated $1.3 trillion. This is a time-and-a half bigger than the next in line of the United Arab Emirates (UAE), and more than double Saudi Arabia's.

While the *nanny* state's health costs, rapidly expanding social net expenditures and refilling of the banks' treasuries with taxpayer money are familiar challenges to western sovereigns, another challenge facing Beijing is specific to China (and for totally different reasons, also to India). This is the significant imbalance between the two sexes which is bound to have social and economic aftereffects. So to speak it is part of unwanted consequences.

Three decades ago, Chinese government decided there should be one child per family. But Chinese families like boys not girls. Today, many young men find it difficult to find a wife and it is estimated that by 2020 the gap will be 40 million young Chinese men without women.[13] In China, as in India, families play the lottery for boys by resorting to abortion, outright killing of newborns, or simply leaving them out in the cold to die. Anecdotal evidence suggests that to stop that practice, the Chinese government is now recording every pregnancy and also uses carrot and stick. A new rule sees to it that if the first newborn is a girl, the parents are allowed to have a second kid and they also benefit from subsidies. For instance, the family is awarded an annual pension for two daughters.

The government tries to break a millennium culture favoring boys, but it would not go away that fast. By contrast, a millennium Chinese (as well as European) culture dying out is that young people support their parents in old age. The reason, sociologists say, is that Chinese girls have got westernized, and they no more want to be slaves to their in-laws.

There is, as well, another social vice confronting China: corruption; stamping it out is a challenge well known in the West and in plenty of other developing countries. In a global fraud survey by Ernst & Young, the auditor, 39 percent of participating companies said corruption is common in countries where they operate. Raghavendra Rau of Cambridge University and Yan Leung Cheung and Aris Stouraitis of the Hong Kong Baptist University examined 166 high-profile cases of bribery since 1971, covering payments made in 52 countries by firms listed on 20 different stock markets.

- Bribery offered average return of an order of magnitude greater than the value of what was paid out to win the contract, and
- The returns being obtained depended on which officials are having their palms greased; higher ranking ones get bigger bribes but also deliver so much more.

As in most other countries, some individuals get rich in China through corruption and bribery. According to a number of publicly exposed corruption cases, serious bribery takes place in processes related to bidding for infrastructure contracts, approval of business licenses, and tax collection (among others). The media have reported numerous cases in recent years about multinational corporations bribing government officials to gain business favors. These came to light following official investigations by both the multinationals' home governments and by the Chinese authorities.

It is to the credit of China's new leadership that it made the stamping out of corruption a priority. Vladimir Putin did the same on his return to the presidency of the Russian federation. Neither task will be easy, but it has to be done. Hopefully, stamping out corruption will also become a policy in other countries which, during the last couple of decades, allowed themselves to drift into such practices.

13.4   The Japanese Economy—A Comparison

In the immediate post-World War II years, Japan was a developing nation. For hard-working Japan, the 1950s and 1960s were a period of rapid recovery and financial development. Some economists called it "the Japanese miracle" as the country's economy successfully resumed its pre-war strength and set a new pace of industrial and financial relations with the world.

For a large part of the country's rapid recovery, economists credit the government's active industrial policy which encouraged strategic companies by administrative measures. These included preferential allocation of scarce resources, tax relief, and the opportunities offered by an undervalued currency.[14] (This advantage, however, turned into disadvantage as the yen stayed too long undervalued leading the Japanese banking industry to global overexpansion and eventual collapse.)

In the economic landscape, an important factor in Japan's quick recovery was the steady and successful control of inflation. Following American advice, the Japanese government imposed a *strict budget balance*—a fact from which both the United States and European countries, as well as their central banks,[15] should have applied to their own policies particularly in the aftermath of the economic and banking crisis which started in 2007. But they did not.

- Japanese inflation was running at 50 percent in 1948, prior to this strict balanced budget policy.
- After the new policy was in place and wage increases were restricted, inflation turned to deflation (to a negative 10 percent), but the country's economy zoomed up.

The benefits the Japanese economy gained with the balanced budget policy is a first class reference for China as well as the United States, Britain, France, Italy, Spain, Greece to name but a few. *Financial stability* and hard work saw to it that the Japanese recovery proceeded speedily and by the mid-1950s the country was well in its way of full economic recovery. But times have changed.

Allow me to recapitulate what has just been stated. The first lesson the Japanese miracle taught to the country's industry and political leadership has been the advantage of generating its own reserves. The second lesson following the wild global expansion in Japanese bank lending which led to the collapse of 1991: that once a market, or an industry, loses its credibility, restoring it takes a very long time—*if* it comes. The difference could not be starker.

- The 1960s was the decade of the *Japanese miracle.*
- The 1990s have been the decade of the *Japanese premium.*

To borrow, Japanese companies had to pay an extra premium over prevailing interest rates, because lenders had lost their confidence to the country as its economy fell from riches to rags. Over the following two decades, Japan's problems have been compound by an aging society, by mounting global competition and by loss of competitiveness. It is as if one recounts Euroland's current problems.

At Wall Street, in the first years of the 1990s, securities analysts suggested that the reason why the United States abandoned its trade war against Japan was that the latter faced financial collapse. There was a rumor the Federal Reserve even made an offer to help with expertise in bailing out Japanese banks that got into deep liquidity trouble.

In regard to the *Japan premium*, financial history as well tells us that the wholesale banking markets cannot effectively handle risk premiums. In the United States, too, big banks that went into trouble, like Seafirst and Continental Illinois, could one day raise billions and the next they could not find a cent. This also happened to the big Japanese banks as: Foreign lenders thought that something pretty nasty lurks in Japanese banks' spreadsheets, and there were reasons to think so. The news about Daiwa, the failures of the coops, and the shaky trust banks gave to foreign financial institutions nightmares about even bigger monsters.

The Japan premium added to the woes not of one but of all of Japan's credit institutions. By early December 1995, it reached 25 to 100 basis points over the (now discredited) LIBOR. Matters were made worse by the fact that after years of "good news only," the markets no more believed the Japanese banks answers, or those of the government.

The powerful Finance Ministry's reputation was tarnished because it failed to prevent the country's banks from piling up so many risky loans, and because it refused to provide information on each bank's status, while it was common knowledge that bad loans had soared. Critics said that the Finance Ministry only expected its pronouncements on the safety of lending to Japanese banks to be treated as a self-evident truth. The market did not like this strong-handed approach.

With the Japanese economy descending to the abyss, the government made the mistake of engaging in deficit financing to bring itself and the economy up from under. Over a period of 22 years, this proved to be a severe mistake, and it constitutes another important lesson which can be learned from the Japanese experience. Yet such a wrong-way policy has been adopted by the United States, Britain, and Continental Europe after the economic crisis of 2007.

- In 1991, the Japanese public debt-to-GDP ratio stood at slightly over 60 percent.
- In 2013, it is nearly 240 percent and rising, while the Japanese economy continues being in and out of a coma.

Correspondingly the US debt-to-GDP ratio which was also 50 percent at 1991 just past the 110 percent in early 2013, without any results to crow about. No major good news is carried by the wires, let alone news commensurate to the wider and wider indebtedness. Throwing money at a problem never really solves it, though it may make it worse.

Statistics seem to suggest that Japanese companies got more results by reducing their leverage, than from the government's high spending. This is also true in US business, or even more so. In the mid-1990s, some years after Japan's huge downturn, Japanese corporate-bond yield were only 16 basis points higher than government-bond yields. By contrast, in late 2008 the corresponding spread in

America has been 350 basis points. This huge difference cannot only be due to the fact that the Fed keeps the Treasuries' interest rate rock bottom. The reason, some of the experts suggest, is that the underlying problems are different:

- Japan's problem was a deflationary environment and moribund investment.
- America's problem has been a rising fear of default and illiquidity.

This explanation is difficult to swallow. If the Bernanke Fed did anything, since 2008, it is to provide liquidity, liquidity, and liquidity through unstoppable quantitative easing and huge purchase of Treasury bonds. Economists who care about financial and monetary stability disapprove of this policy, and investors seem to vote against it with their money. They prefer the corporate bonds.

Still another lesson to be learned from Japan's experience is that of problems created by the rapid aging of a population. This clearly interests Europe, America, and China, in that order of urgency.

In 2013, about 25 percent of the Japanese population is over 65 years old. The United States features not quite half that percentage (some 12 percent). Many Japanese now work after reaching 60, and many of those who do not would like to. The official retirement age has been raised to 65, and according to experts the population aging problem will not be solved unless Japanese work until perhaps 70 or 75 years old.[16]

While there is really no Japanese unemployment to talk about, the cost of labor skid. In 2009, 8 years after the economic debacle, wages in Japan suffered their sharpest drop since tracking began (almost two decades earlier). Retirement age has been increased but at the same time Japan has been a lifelong employment country, and employment takes precedence over the maintenance of salary and wage levels.[17]

In the post-World War II years, during Japan's ascendancy as an industrial power, its companies featured lifetime commitment between company and worker, which meant that employees have more stability in their careers. While this lifetime commitment has been recently weakened, its presence is still felt. (The way a Japanese executive had it, he wished he was born American. When times are tough, the workers are fired, and when times are good, management gets all the bonuses.)

Clearly, an aging Japan has not one but several problems to run after. One of them is that governments became short-lived. As one administration after another tried to fix the economy's ills by spending even more money, and failed, the political aftereffect is cacophony. This started in the mid- to late 1990s. The way an article in *The Economist* put it: "...discord in the cabinet, and a woeful absence of discussion about the budget next year and beyond, have left many worried. Foreign allies are wondering what the new government stands for. Investors are beginning to vote with their feet...."[18]

This commentary talks volumes about the importance of political and financial stability. Since 1991, Japan has run continuous fiscal deficits and the international rating agencies downgraded its debt. With its bonds yielding from a tiny 0.1 percent to 2.1 percent, the downside risk of a bearish bet is limited but the upside potential neither looks that great (except for the carry trade).

The irony of course is that in spite of the economy's travails, and of its own problems, the Japanese government still enjoys some of the lowest borrowing costs in the world. The explanation most frequently heard is that Japan has not been dependent on foreigners for finance, as only a 4 percent of its bonds are owned by nonresidents, and there is a long record of deflation.

Several economists however suggest that even if the carry trade is another potent reason for the attraction of low-yield Japanese bonds, economic discrepancies cannot last forever. The day of reckoning may not be that far away as more citizens reach retirement age, Japanese households are no longer saving as they once did, and the Government Pension Investment Fund, one of the biggest holders of government bonds, has stated that it has no massive new money with which to buy more sovereign debt.

13.5   "Abenomics," the Falling Yen and Longevity Risk

The image of Japan given in Section 13.4 is that of today. Though the Abe government might turn things around, such an outcome is by no means a sure bet. Western sovereigns as well as those of developing nations will therefore be well advised to study the rise and fall of Japanese economic and industrial power as a most instructive case study, starting with the reaction of the IMF.

The IMF warned Japan of what in technology we call the "butterfly effect": the prevailing conditions are such that even a minor happening like a butterfly moving its wings can create a chain reaction. In a similar way, a highly indebted country in a leveraged world can reach the point where even a small rise in borrowing costs (let alone a spike) could create havoc in the financial market and:

- Once market confidence is lost,
- Monetary upheaval follows on its heels.

With the massive devaluation of the yen, which was his political program, Shinzo Abe took a huge gamble and did not care of the warnings. He knew that Japan was losing its state buffers one by one: the trade surplus had evaporated; post-Fukushima the nuclear industry, which provided Japan with cheap energy, was in disarray; the work force was shrinking every year; the savings rate had fallen to 2 percent from 15 percent in 1990; from the banking industry remained only a shadow of its past glory; and in the international market the yen was expensive, very expensive.

Could it be that the solution to Japan's deep economic problems passed through a cheap yen? Postmortem, economists and financial experts said that the significant fall in the yen and the rise in stock prices triggered by a change of government created the feeling that Japan is moving again and in the right direction—toward:

- Economic recovery, and
- Economic expansion.

This was the impression, but in reality, Japan remained highly exposed to swings in its currency. While in recent years manufacturers shifted production overseas, there were other headwinds to complain about: labor and environmental laws, curbs on energy consumption, high taxes, and tight trade. Most damaging was the servicing of a debt equal to 240 percent of Japanese GDP created during 22 years of a spending spree to restart the economy without getting it done.

Adam Posen, a former member of the Bank of England interest rate setting committee and a Japan expert, says fiscal stimulus ceased to be any help a decade ago and is now counterproductive. Posen advised Japan to rely on monetary policy alone to right the ship but while he bought the monetary policy argument at his exchange rate end, Abe wants to try still another stimulus.[19] This may have political implications. Several Chinese economists and business leaders have criticized this move saying:

- It would hurt export competitiveness in other countries.
- It could trigger large capital inflows to China, and
- It could push up inflation.

By contrast, Christine Lagarde, of the IMF, was supportive. Her thesis has been that the huge monetary stimulus plan unveiled by Japan made sense and its aftereffect can be positive by helping to boost global growth at a time when the outlook is starting to improve. In a year's time, we shall see who is right.

From engineering the conditions for a falling yen to sticking to his stimulus, Abe's message has been: "Japan is back." In February 2013, given the country's troubled recent history, he carried these three words as a banner to Washington for his meeting with Barack Obama. "Japan is not, and will never be, a tier-two country," the new Japanese prime minister said. And as an article in the Financial Times had it, not long ago, a Japanese leader would have risked mockery with such assertions."[20]

The pride surrounding what might be a national rebirth carried the news, and little attention was paid to another statement—even more vital to the future not only of Japan but for the whole world: *Longevity Risk*. Longevity-related health care costs and pensions for old people have put the economy under stress beyond any previous experience, and if the trend continues, it will bring disaster.

It is not quite 10 years that insurance companies addressed themselves seriously to the aftermath of longevity risk. Till then, living longer was considered to be one of medicine's wonders, and of the pharmas laurels. Nobody spoke of the fact that there are costs attached to it, probably unaffordable and unsustainable. As I emphasize in my book *Household Finance*:[21]

- On the one hand, an aged society requires long-term treatment and those receiving it desire that it is immediate and of high level, and
- On the other hand, costs have escaped control because health care practices grew like wild cacti. They have *not* been designed for an aged society.

Taro Aso, Abe's 72-year-old finance minister and deputy prime minister recently joked that old people should "hurry up and die" so that they did not drain the public purse.[22] He presumably made that statement as a joke. If so, it is a joke with more truth in it that has even been said. Our society simply cannot afford to be all things to all persons. The public debt we confront today is direct result of trying to do too much in the most clumsy and unsuccessful way. Longevity risk is the new God-size challenge.

Congratulations Taro Aso. This is real straight talk, and it contrasts to that of all other hypocrite finance ministers around the globe who hide the truth from the people. Our society has to make a choice: does it want to support the young *or* the old? It can finance half-decently one of these two groups (I don't even expect to do it well, but do it nevertheless).

Octogenarians and beyond should have no more the right to live on "entitlements." Longevity risk might have been a worrisome subject for the life insurance industry. Now it is building up as the Waterloo for sovereigns. Its skyrocketing expenses will destroy the social system as we know it—or this system should be the subject of a major overhaul which leaves no cost unchallenged: kiss the entitlement goodbye and don't depend anymore on state pensions. You will hear more, much more, about that challenge during the next 10 years.

13.6   Japan and China. Is There an East-Asia Syndrome?

Syndrome is a medical term for a collection of symptoms with common cause which, however, is not quite understood. The US syndrome of zero interest rates for an estimated half dozen years (or longer) has in its background the symptoms of the 2007 economic crisis, 2008 deep banking crisis, skyrocketing public debt, flooding the market with liquidity, search for full employment, and plenty of unorthodox moves by the sovereign and reserve bank working in unison. By contrast, in Japan the sovereign created the syndrome it now confronts single handed, since the Bank of Japan has followed prudential monetary policies.

Borrowing a leaf from the book of medicine, there is usually a perceivable period of time between an unwanted outcome, for instance, obesity, and a person developing of other symptoms. Something similar might be happening in economics, as well. The Japanese economy's downhill slide which started in 1991 has led to the so-called *Japanification* of interest rates, a syndrome widespread in the western world though not in developing countries.

As the case of Japan, the United States, Britain, and Euroland illustrates, when interest rates go to zero they do so for reasons of deep economic weakness, and difficulties in getting out of it. There are reasons keeping them at zero for a long period of time and the symptoms are still around us. Yield would be a scarce commodity in coming years in the West as it has been for over two decades in Japan. All this happens at the worst possible moment as demographics create a lot of demand for savings (Section 13.4).

There should have been no metastasis of the interest rates' Japanification syndrome to West, given the near zero interest rates record of delivering a pitiful economic resurgence in Japan. This is an easy and ineffective way out of an economic, financial, and banking crisis, and it is followed in the longer term by reserve institutions and governments unable to deal with crisis conditions.

Where the Japanification syndrome has succeeded is in making speculators out of formerly careful investors, and this can hardly be regarded as an achievement. One of the visible aftereffects of Japanification is that Tokyo's main stock market index has been for low stretches of time a shadow of its former self—which talks volumes about investor confidence. The country which, in the 1970s and 1980s, was on its way to financially conquer the world through superleverage:

- Slipped way down the global league, and
- Amassed the largest public debt-to-GDP ratio ever recorded in peace time.

Contrary to the American economy and the economies of Europe, China has not caught that syndrome, but nothing guarantees that this will not happen in the future if the economy escapes prudent planning and control. To a worrying mind, the similitude between Japan and China during the phase of steep rise as player in the global economy gives food for thought.

It would as well be proper to remember that when the Japanese downturn came in 1991 (paradoxically) there was a belief in Tokyo that there is no imminent crisis. Eventually nothing forced Japan's policymakers out of a paralysis, while everyone rushed to put the blame for deflation and rising debt elsewhere than his courtyard.

This can happen to all nations, and all of the BRICs (as well as other developing countries) should be aware of the risk. For years, Japanese politicians thought the real problem was low productivity growth in Japan, which kept wages low and suppressed demand for goods and services. With such a prevailing political thinking, it is most curious that in 2010 and 2013 the Japanese government favored an increase in the consumption tax in its medium term plan for fiscal reform. An even greater policy blunder was done in 1997 by the then government when it started with consumption tax hikes which ended in a double whammy:

- Bending the curve of a mildly rising GDP, and
- Sending south the (also mildly) recovering TOPIX banks index.

Another major mistake made both by Japanese governments and some of the bigger Japanese companies, was to sacrifice quality to expediency. The torrent of recalls by Toyota is an example. An even better once can be learned by studying the disaster of the Daiichi nuclear plants. China should learn a basic lesson from that case.

Let's return for a moment to the fundamentals. Right after WWII ended, Japan made a major effort to turn quality into a competitive weapon, and it succeeded. But in the (nearly) seven decades since that time, the top management of Japanese companies changed two or three times over, a new generation came to power and the high quality policy waned.

On March 11, 2011 a vast social, economic, and material damage was created by the 8.9° Richter scale earthquake and 10-meter tsunami which followed it. Theoretically, the tsunami and earthquake were the reasons for the nuclear catastrophe. True enough, they contributed to it, but a much more potent factor has been the low-quality syndrome. The most fundamental causes for the Fukushima major nuclear accident were:

- Faulty nuclear plant design (from its location at seashore to light construction),[23]
- Wanting damage control facilities and slowly delivered services, and
- Above all, opaqueness and mismanagement by Tokyo Electric—the company blindly supported by a corrupt political class.

The easy answer has been the switch of Japan out of nuclear power. This, however, further weakens its industrial competitiveness as clean energy takes a leave and the cost of power rises. Though it is not clear how big the bill may be, the case of France and Germany can be taken as a proxy. In France, 80 percent of consumed electricity originates in nuclear power plants. Germany is (unwisely) phasing out its atomic power production. As far as the manufacturing industry is concerned, power costs in Germany are 20 percent higher than in France.

Like Germany, China got cold feet after Fukushima and slowed down its nuclear power program betting, instead, on coal. This is unwise even if the use of coal is now rising worldwide and projections are that by 2020, or so, coal will nearly equal oil as energy source. Fear can induce people to do many funny things—and going backward in energy production is one of them.

The Daiichi plants at Fukushima are a problem, and the better answer to this problem is first class engineering, reliability in design, and top quality control in operations. The return to coal will unavoidably bring more environmental pollution as the medium is rich in CO_2 and China has more CO_2 than it can possibly handle. As for the alternative of wind power, this is just a way to spend money—despite what long-haired greens and other theorists may say about its wonders.[24] (To the contrary, solar energy solutions have merits, but for individual installations, not for massive energy production.)

Quality deteriorates over time, if it is not properly and steadily maintained. This leads us to another East-Asia syndrome: infrastructure. Both China and Japan are confronting it but at two different ends. From transport to telecommunications, China needs to build a vast infrastructure (Sections 13.2 and 13.3). By contrast, the Japanese infrastructure, put in place in the 1950s and 1960s, is decaying. (The same is true of the American infrastructure, like the roads and bridges network constructed by the Eisenhower Administration in the 1950s.)

The Chinese government and the Abe Administration in Japan have big infrastructural plans, less known is whether these are conceived in a way to generate returns commensurate to the investments which need to be made. If political choices carry the day, this will add to either and both countries' public debt without generating output—a case is much more severe in Japan where the national debt stands at 240 percent of GDP and, by all evidence, infrastructural works will be done through deficit financing.

It is also proper to bring to the reader's attention the syndrome of political and financial stability. For four and a half decades after WWII, Japan had stable governments. Political instability started in the early 1990s after the crash of the banking industry, the stock market, and the real-estate market. Today, China has political stability, and it should be keen to preserve it.

China should also use the economic and technical history of Japanese events from 1991 onward as if they came from a once-in-a lifetime laboratory experiment. With the switch from the Japanese miracle to Japan premium, the country fell off the track. In September 2012, it slashed its second-quarter growth estimate while South Korea unveiled a new round of fiscal stimulus, underscoring the vulnerability of both economies to a slowdown in China, their most important trading partner.

This has been a major economic event at a time globalization is still alive. Much of the weakness came from crisis-hit European Union, China's biggest trading partner. Chinese exports to the EU fell almost 13 percent in August 2012 compared with a year earlier. The way economists look at this problem is that, if the weakness in the European and American economies continues, China too will be stalling leading to downward revision of its GDP growth and raising fears that the world's second biggest economy is heading for contraction in spite of the heralded soft landing.

There is no overstatement in suggesting that economic policy and fiscal policy process in the United States, Europe, and Japan are beginning to resemble a bumbling football match punctuated by individual goals, poor refereeing, and shots sailing over the crossbar. At least in America and the EU, governments try to "snatch defeat from the hands of old glory" while until the last elections Japan was playing for time in the hope that time heals all sorrows. Instead:

- Japan's ongoing fiscal deterioration remains worrying, and
- The cold comfort is that the country's dysfunctional fiscal policy has yet to spark a new financial market unease.

Nevertheless, surprises are always possible. According to the 21st Century Public Policy Institute, a Japanese think tank, by 2050 the debt-to-GDP ratio could reach a staggering 594 percent unless Japan significantly improves its primary balance. While this "594 percent" is a projection, the current fact of a 240 percent public debt-to-GDP ratio has created doubts and uncertainty.

13.7 The First Letter in BRICs: Brazil

Brazil is a country of 192 million people with a GDP of over $2.5 trillion. Over the last three decades, the Brazilian economy had its ups and downs. From 2007 to 2011, it had a top performance while the western countries' economies moved south, but the economic news from Brasilia is not so brilliant in 2013.

The 2007–2011 performance, the years of fat cows, is documented through foreign direct investments (FDIs) in the Brazilian economy as well as its currency's rise in the foreign exchange market. In 2007, there were 221 deals of $34 billion in total value; in 2008, 234 deals of $71 billion; 2009, 189 deals of $52 billion; 2010, 259 deals of $79 billion; in 2011, a whopping 350 FDI deals of $86 billion. FDIs in Brazil collapsed to 80 deals of a mere $16 billion in 2012—the year the country's economic problems started.

By May 2012, the Brazilian real had weakened against the dollar, and analysts were of the opinion it was likely to weaken further as market sentiment remained weak. This is precisely what has happened, as the central bank did not defend the currency from weakening further. In fact, the Brazilian government wanted to weaken the real. In parallel to this, by 2012 South America's biggest economy has slowed to a crawl, after a decade of robust commodity-led growth, pushing Brazilians into a debate on whether to embrace a state-led economic model or to return to policies of real devaluations.

This has not been an easy choice. Even by the end of the first decade of this century, Brazil still carried the stigma of the Latin American debt crisis of the 1980s and of Argentina's default of 2001. Over several years, Brazilian government bonds were rated as junk and its debt yielded more than a 10 percent interest.

• Brazil however did not default, and
• In 2008, its bonds were promoted to investment-grade status.

The economic environment changed again after Brazils' "B" became the first letter in BRICs, a term coined by Goldman Sachs to identify the emerging economies with the best potential. Following some years in which everything seemed to fall into place for Brazil, its citizens and its government's policymakers were forced to rethink the country's strategic direction. The issue at stake has been:

• What kind of economy does Brazil want, and
• How big a role the state should play in this economy.

The Brazilian people put the bar rather high. They wanted to live in a consumer society like the Americans and have social services like Europeans, while their economy grew like an emerging market. These goals are evidently incompatible among themselves, but Brazilians were not alone in wanting a society able to profit from everything.

The choice of what "they want to be" is just as difficult and pressing for other emerging countries, too: Russia, China, and India being examples. At the same time, however, with the American, European, and Japanese models looking battered—and Soviet communism in total discredit—there were no brilliant standards left to guide policy choices. Neither is this problem of choice going away as the next few years will be critical for the direction of the world economy. Like it or not, policymakers and the public:

• Will have to navigate without a compass, and
• The direction in which they are going will be just as obscure.

Among major developing countries, Brazil just happened to be the first to hit the essence of this salient problem which is as much political as it is economic. Politically speaking around 2010 several countries, who once were reliable backers of America's geostrategic goals, went their own way. Brazil and Turkey, for example, sought to broker a deal with Iran over its nuclear program while America and other western nations pushed for new sanctions. This assertiveness was a product of:

- Their growing economic weight, and
- America's diminished clout in the global political and economic landscape.

Brazil wants the status of a bigger global role. But is it ready to assume the risks and burdens that global leadership requires? In the western press, the BRICs have been lionized as fast-growing superpowers-in-waiting which, at this point in time, is by no means the case as they still have a way to go till they get themselves free from red tape and are to muster the political will to take on global commitments—a domain where only China has so far given clear signals.

In all developing countries, government must start to confront inherited weaknesses, and to this, Brazil is no exception. The annual growth rate it enjoyed over several years looks excellent by western standards, but it is below both what Brazil needs to continue its recent social services claims and what China has achieved.[25] Moreover, some of the sources of the faster growth of recent years may now be exhausting themselves. To boost the economy, in mid-2012 the Brazilian government made a broader policy shift:

- From fueling a decade-long consumer-led boom,
- To increasing competitiveness and private investment.

Particular attention has been paid to giving a helping hand to local manufacturers. The government's action included reducing the rates industry pays for power, offering to private companies licenses to build and operate roads and railways, and unveiling plans for upgrading major airports and ports. Still a lower overseas demand for commodities, falling investment, and rising household debt saw to it that Brazil's growth slowed.

Brazil's efforts were further handicapped by the fact that during the years of rapid growth Brazil became an expensive place to do business. The government blames the currency exchange rate for this, but it is no less true that the bureaucracy itself and its policies are responsible for much of the higher cost.

The tax burden rose from 22 percent of GDP in 1988 to 36 percent in 2012, while the tax system remained too complex. Businesses face a mare's nest of regulations, and the minimum wage is 3 times that of other developing countries, for instance Indonesia. Therefore, Brazilian manufacturers are struggling.

In addition, the state has started messing around with nationalistic signals for business. An example is the rule that 65 percent of equipment for the deep-water oil industry must be produced at home. This practically guarantees that developing the new oil and gas fields will be slower and it will cost more than otherwise.

Like in other countries, including both industrialized and developing, the government also sets for itself conflicting goals. Dilma Rousseff, Brazil's president since January 2011, wants to eliminate the fiscal deficit, but has started to cut taxes for favored industries. Critics also say, her effort to drive down costs is too timid, and as costs are rising, investors start looking for lower cost and higher growth markets in Latin America.

All this leads to a changing economic climate which is also documented by the fact that in the first semester of 2012 demand for loans was nearly 8 percent lower than during the same period in 2011. With defaults rising, banks have been tightening their terms. Bad loans in Brazil hit a record high in May 2012, adding to fears that the country may be heading for a deeper than expected slowdown—putting to test government efforts to stimulate borrowing to try to reignite the country's stalling economy.

The good news is that altogether the Brazilian banking industry is in rather good shape. Its strengths are a rather balanced amount of loans compared to deposits, high profitability ratios, and sound level of coverage of the nonperforming loans. But there are two weaknesses: high level of costs and a growing level of nonperforming loans.

One of the slowdown's victims has been Brazilian retail sales. Unexpectedly, in mid-2012 they fell the most since the onset of the financial crisis, raising fears for one of the remaining bright spots in the country's economy. This is bad news for the government inasmuch as the Brazilian consumer (thanks to rising wages and greater access to credit) was one of the main drivers of the country's growth over the past decade. Concerns are now being heard that the country's model of growth may be reaching its expiry date as Brazilians struggle to take on more debt, but rising defaults prompts the banks to tighten lending.

An unknown factor of the Brazilian economy is the level of inflation in the coming years. Economists say that emerging countries have never believed the notion that the average price of goods in their economies would magically fall, year after year. While it was possible that there would have been a bit of pressure on prices in some countries altogether for the emerging markets the conditions were inflationary. Between 2007 and January 2012,

- In Russia the price level increased by 59 percent,
- In India by 55 percent,
- In Brazil by 30 percent, and
- In China by 20 percent.

This inflation represents a substantial erosion of wealth for anyone who kept local cash under the mattress. While a relative decline in oil prices helped to ease some of the near-term inflationary pressure, the currencies of weaker emerging economies currencies have prevented them from realizing the full benefit of lower materials prices.

Within a global environment characterized by less confidence than in earlier years, Brazilian authorities watch carefully for unfair foreign competition. On September 20, 2012, following Ben Bernanke's QE3, Guido Mantega, Brazils' finance minister, warned that the Fed's "protectionist" move to roll out more quantitative easing will reignite the currency wars, and this will have potentially drastic consequences for the global market.

"It has to be understood, that there are consequences," Mantega told the *Financial Times*, adding that the Fed's QE3 would "only have a marginal benefit (in the US) as there is already no lack of liquidity . . . and that liquidity is not going to production. . . instead (it is) depressing the dollar and aimed at boosting US exports."[26]

From his viewpoint Guido Mantega is right, but this is not enough to solve Brazil's developing economic problem. As of January 2013, most market analysts project that consumers will be using much of their income to restructure their balance sheets paying off loans with which they had bought cars and house appliances. Economists suggest that to get the country moving again, the government:

• Must do the utmost to improve competitiveness, and
• Abstain from micromanaging private enterprises.

This means working against the current as analysts are slashing their predictions in view of the fact that Brazil is seeing its worst growth performance in a decade or more. A bad surprise was the fall in investment, despite the government's efforts to lower business costs. A tax on foreign-currency inflows and the central bank's interventions led to a fall in the strong real of around 20 percent against the dollar in 2012. But economic turnaround is not yet on call.

In conclusion, in spite of being a member of BRICs, Brazil's economy performed worse than expected particularly in the third quarter 2012, having grown by less than 1 percent compared with the same period of 2011. This comes after a range of measures introduced by the government to try to lift output which did not yet bear fruits. And the fact the global economy still hangs on a fork is not promoting Brasilia's hopes for a rapid recovery.

13.8   Is India's Economy Another Falling Star?

In his lecture on "India's Dilemmas," in the first days of January 2013, Kaushik Basu, chief economist at the World Bank, dramatized his point by quoting impressive (or, rather, depressing for India) statistics. In 1950, South Korea and India had the same income per capita. Today, South Korea's is 22 times India's.[27]

In 2012, the Indian economy grew by 5.3 percent which (as absolute figure) is not bad, but it does not support the hypothesis of a catch up, apart from the fact that it compares poorly with growth in China. Worse yet, the projection for 2013 is not much better. Government economists talk (hopefully) of GDP growth of 6 percent, but India observers say that it would not be much better than 5.5 percent.

These references reflect the fact that India's economic growth has been in decline since the first quarter of 2011 when it stood at about 9 percent. It was 8 percent in the second quarter, less than 7 percent in the third and 6 percent in the fourth. It fared worse than expected in the first quarter 2012, and the bad news continued to indicate the slowest growth in almost 8 years, falling far short of the government's target of 9 percent.

One of the reasons for the decline is lack of confidence, the Indian economy's longer term growth will depend on the government's ability to promote investment and continue liberalizing the highly regulated internal market. Because of stiff opposition to such measures, this demands plenty of political courage. Half-way solutions will not do because there is plenty of lost ground to cover, particularly when India is compared with the "Asian tigers" or with China—because of the billion-plus population, increasing military capabilities and value as a trading partner.

Critics say that the most important reason for the troubles confronting the Indian economy in the second decade of this century should be found in political fragmentation and weak leadership in New Delhi. *Inter alia*, these are eroding federal power relative to India's states, but the greater challenge can be found in negative news related to India's growth prospects because of:

- Steadily high inflation,
- Large current account deficits, and
- Persistent fiscal imbalances.

These are problems well known to the United States, France, Italy, and Spain (among others), and they have much to do with the decline of their economies. One, however, would not expect to encounter them also among the BRICs. A weak administration and poor macroeconomics is a double whammy, which has a debilitating effect on the economy as well as negatively affects market sentiment.

There was a time when India's future and its fortune looked quite different. There was hope of rapid economic growth after the negatives were overcome. After independence came the hardship, the split with Pakistan, the exchange of populations, the rebuilding of the nation—and with it a wide-ranging educational effort. It has not been easy, but there was a tomorrow.

In the early 1950s, Neil Jacoby, Dean of the School of Business Administration at UCLA and economic advisor to Dwight Eisenhower, was asked by the president to visit India and identify promising projects to which the United States could contribute. Jacoby met with Nehru and the Indian prime minister invited him to come along to a visit to a hydroelectric dam under construction.

Nehru was proud of the Indian infrastructure in the making. What impressed Jacoby was the thousands of people moving around and carrying earth. This can be improved he said to the Indian prime minister: "Earth-moving equipment can significantly better worker productivity; you would not need all these thousands of people." "But it is for them that I am making the dam," answered Nehru.[28]

Finding jobs, particularly in a large country in the early years of its independence, is always a challenge. If properly planned and executed, large infrastructural projects can deliver several times their cost. Not only they provide work opportunities but they are as well the structural elements in building a nation.

Another major challenge is education. Down to basics this is a lifelong project which takes much more planning and effort than a hydroelectric dam. The first goal is to lift-off analphabetism, which is more easily said than done. Difficult enough in a country of small dimensions, it is a colossal task in one (then) of half a billion people with resources[29]—both human and financial—in short supply.

Nehru's solution was to bet on the new generation. It made sense. The question was "how"? His answer was to institute learning centers to which went kids from the villages. If my memory is correct, the schools offered 5-year studies. The kids went into the educational cycle at 7 or 8 years of age and returned literate enough to their villages at about 13.

The Indian prime minister's hypothesis was that the literate kids would pull their village out of illiteracy. It did not happen that way; indeed 5 years after they had come back, the kids had rebecome illiterate. That's what I learned in 1966 in my meeting with the University of Calcutta, which was asked by the government to look for an alternative educational strategy.

If I were to express an opinion about the greatest handicap which impeded India's progress in the intervening years, this would be the absence of family planning and corresponding rapid rise of the population. In neighboring China, Mao was right when he instituted and enforced the "one kid per family" policy (Sections 13.2 and 13.3). Drift is always a bad counsel. Let me put it this way:

- It is easy to make kids. Every cat and dog is doing it.
- But it is very difficult to educate kids, teach them a profession to make them self-standing and, as such, contributors to their country's future.

The building of human capital is not achieved by making people dependent on the State Supermarket for their living. It requires a long-term plan, consumes plenty of effort, and calls for significant investments. A developing nation does not have the resources to be everything to everybody. Even developed nations, the United States and EU's member states, who tried to do everything spreading them thin, have failed though:

- They have more resources than India, and
- They did not have to confront a stupendous population increase from 500 million to 1.2 billion people in a matter of a few decades.

One of the effects of massive changes whose impact is often (and conveniently) forgotten is that the price of quantity is being paid by quality. In the 1980s Indian entrepreneurs worked hard, targetting quality and performance; but today, there is a visible drop in quality. It is as if people don't care anymore for the work they are doing, and management has lost control.

Moreover, in the subcontinent live in effect "two Indias" side by side. The one is the well-educated 15 percent or so of the total population (Indian friends say 20 percent), which is at par with America and Europe.[30] Though no more illiterate (as in the time of independence), the lion's share of 85 percent lives as a nation in the side and finds it difficult to lift itself from its shoestrings.

Typically, the 15 percent is mainly urban, while the 85 percent is mainly rural, but this is by no means an absolute rule. Neither is this dichotomy a matter of casts, though for evident reasons the untouchables find themselves by large majority in the 85 percent. It needs no explaining that the 85 percent are, so to speak, the underprivileged. High birth rates are one of the main reasons why it is so difficult for them to collectively improve their lot.[31]

The message the preceding paragraphs convey is by no means a one-tantum observation. I had the opportunity to confirm it over more than a decade, from 1978 to 1989, as I was frequently in India for my seminars. Make no mistake about it: 15 percent of the about 1.2 billion people is a large population of 180 million, with a relatively high economic standard, which moves the nation forward but cannot make miracles:

- Its members are presidents of western banks, university professors, and other professionals.
- Among its members are global entrepreneurs like Tata and Mittal and billionaires inside and outside India, and
- The pinnacle of political power in India also comes from this 15 percent, but I am not sure they pay due attention on how to carry along the other 85 percent.

Add to this the usual inefficiencies as well as corruption which comes with big government, and you find that during the last decade the Indian economy has lost the sprint it had in the latter part of the twentieth century. The advantages India gained from exporting information technology services faced competition, energy prices soared, and the global economic crisis which started in 2007 did not help.

While some economists blamed political infighting and negative attitude toward foreign investments for India's continuing slowdown, the most important reason has been that its economy lost its competitiveness. Along with putting the brakes on growth, inflation remained a big concern, and so did the significant rupee depreciation.

As if to make matters worse, monetary and fiscal policies remain in a deadlock, inflation reduces the scope of interest rate cuts, and budgetary imbalances increases the already high fiscal deficit. Add to this the aforementioned population explosion in and the "two Indias," and there is no wonder that growth has taken a hit. In several respects, this is a well-known scenario from western countries.

Another one of western viruses which infected India is that politicians have little incentive and no will to deliver essential structural and labor changes or to enact lasting reforms. A ray of hope lies in the fact that in recent elections Indian incumbents who worked to improve economic outcomes are finally throwing out of office poor performers. This is at least the message carried by the media.

For its part, worried about the stagnating economic situation, the Indian government seems to be on the verge of undertaking policy reforms to shore up investor sentiment. To the contrary, the Reserve Bank of India largely stands back, observing the development with the control of persistently high inflation remaining its major concern.

Here is how a study by UBS has looked at this issue "... inflation is easing gradually in Asia, and ... most governments in the region can afford to continue to ease monetary policy to support growth ...One notable exception is India, where inflation remains sticky due to a weakening rupee and a high public deficit."[32]

This commentary was published in mid-2012, but a year down the line the situation had not improved. As the same analysts were to comment: "Our cautious stance stems from India's persistent current account deficit, which constrains the (Indian currency) appreciation potential, and also exposes the currency to sudden capital outflows amid risk aversion."[33]

                    *   *   *

As of mid-2013, the Indian economy's growth has slowed to half the rate during the boom years but inflation flared up. At 10 percent, annual inflation is worse than in other major economies, while the government's failure to reform dragged down the rupee.

With a high fertility rate, every year millions of young people have to find jobs. Reigniting the growth to create them requires radical deregulation of protected sectors like obsolete labor laws, mammoth state monopolies, and the bureaucracies that go along with them. As for India's infrastructure: roads, ports,power production and distribution they, too, require an urgent and major overhaul.

In conclusion, after Brazil, India is another member of the once-hot BRICs quartet which reports relatively poor economic results. Following several years of relatively good performance, its economic growth is well below what is needed to raise living standards as fast as hoped.

Let's end this chapter with a last thought. Until western economies return to health, developing countries will be feeling the pressure, but they should not remain just spectators. There is plenty they can do for themselves. Properly managed and assisted India's 85 percent (we have been talking about) may become the economy's blessing—the motor that drives the other 15 percent.

End Notes

1. Family planning, infant mortality, hunger, and standard of living correlate, though because of taboos most authors and lecturers fail to make this point.
2. Aljazeera, March 27, 2013.
3. CNBC, May 5, 2013.
4. More precisely, 4.7 percent in the average.
5. UBS CIO WM, November 22, 2012.
6. Portugal, Ireland, Italy, Greece, Spain.
7. Financial Times, January 11, 2013.
8. Also in 2010, China became the world's second largest economy.
9. The Economist, March 10, 2012.
10. Crédit Suisse, Global Investor, 2.12, November 2012.
11. In 3 years it matched the aggregate spending during the 6 years prior to health care reform.
12. Financial Times, September 19, 2012.
13. This has had another unwanted aftereffect: "wife trafficking." Very young girls are abducted to be sold as brides. Kidnapping is, reportedly, a big and profitable business. Families allegedly hire private detectives when the police does not find their daughter.
14. At 360 yen to the US dollar. It hovered between 77 and 87 yen to the dollar.
15. Chorafas DN. The changing role of central banks. New York, NY: Palgrave/Macmillan; 2013.
16. Tell that to the French, and don't mind what you hear as a reply.
17. Another characteristic of Japanese business is that salaries are based on length of service rather than performance, and there is no big difference between the salaries of the highest- and lowest-paid staff of the same age.
18. The Economist, November 14, 2009.
19. The Bank of Japan announced it aimed to double its monetary base over 2 years.

20. Financial Times, March 4, 2013.
21. Chorafas DN. Household finance, adrift in a sea of red ink. London: Palgrave/Macmillan; 2013.
22. Financial Times, March 21, 2013.
23. Chorafas DN. Quality control applications. London: Springer Verlag; 2013.
24. Chorafas DN. Energy, natural resources and business competitiveness in the EU. London: Gower; 2011.
25. In 2011, Brazil's GDP grew only 2.7 percent versus 7.5 percent in 2010.
26. Financial Times, September 21, 2012.
27. Financial Times, January 11, 2013.
28. Quotation from Jacoby's reference in a postgraduate seminar I was attending at UCLA.
29. This was India's population in the early 1950s. Today it stands at 1.2 billion people.
30. A great lot of this top 15 percent Indians have made excellent careers primarily in the United States and also in Britain and in Germany.
31. The only Indian politician who had the courage to actively work for birth control was the younger son of Indira Gandhi. Unfortunately, he did not live long enough to establish a firm family planning policy.
32. UBS Chief Investment Office, Wealth Management Research, June 21, 2012.
33. UBS Chief Investment Office, Wealth Management Research, December 5, 2012.

Part Six

Which Therapy? Where are the Doctors?

14 Iceland, Latvia, Ireland, Britain, Germany, and a Taste of Fantasy Economics

14.1 Iceland Comes Up from Under

Prior to its descend to the abyss in 2008 due to business expansion without limits and associated gambles by its three bigger banks, Kaupthing, Landsbanki, and Glitnir, Iceland was one of the richest nations in the world (in terms of income per head). The bankruptcy of these three mismanaged banks saw to it that this is now history, one of the calamitous results of financial deregulation.

The election which took place in Iceland right after the deep banking crisis had much to do with the punishment of the wrongdoers as well as with public acceptability of austerity needed to turn around the disaster left by the banking scam. But even if the measures which followed were largely about economic restructuring, fiscal consolidation, and debt reduction, the legal consequences should not be overlooked because they are a lesson for other, bigger countries.

Within 3 years after heaven broke loose, Iceland became the first country to put on trial for the crisis the political leader under whose watch the deep banking crisis took place. Bringing to justice is a solution highly recommended to all nations who have the misfortune to be led by politicians who accept (and often cover) acts which are corrupt and damaging to their nation's fortunes.

The small northern Atlantic nation also offers live evidence of the advantages of an indebted country to simply let its banks collapse and default on their loans. The citizens who have been asked to underwrite against their will the banks' huge losses would like to know through evidence presented to the court:

- How often government officials are driven by conflicts of interest (if not altogether personal greed) rather than loyalty to the nation which elected them, and
- How many decisions, including those affecting the economy of the nation, are made by financial people motivated by personal reasons rather than the public good.

These queries reach deep into the soul of a nation and of its leadership. Unanswered questions still remain all the way from the 2007 subprimes scam in America—for which nobody was brought to justice—to the blow up of the Greek sovereign debt which reached for the stars in 2010, and so many other cases. Precisely because of this reason Iceland's travails, as well as its recovery from the shock of the banking crisis, matters much more than might suggest the size of its small economy with a 320,000 population.

On trial went the man who ran the country from 2006 to 2009—the calamitous years of Icelandic banks running wild. "It is one of the big things that need to be dealt with ... before the country can return to normal," said Steingrimur Sigfusson, minister for economic affairs.[1] The former prime minister faced 2 years in jail if found guilty. Most significantly, however, this was the first of a series of legal procedures against people allegedly responsible for the crisis which led to a 700 percent increase in unemployment.

For its part, the trial of the Icelandic bankers began in early 2012, in sequel to a wide-ranging criminal investigation conducted against reckless financiers responsible for the country's economic collapse. In February 2012, Iceland's special prosecutor's office charged Hreidar Mar Sigurdsson, Kaupthing's former chief executive, and Sigurdur Einarsson, the bank's former chairman, with fraud and market manipulation.[2]

"This is an important step for the country," said Olafur Hauksson, the special prosecutor. "The public has been calling for justice to be done, and I think it will be a relief to see the courts dealing with these cases."[3] The Icelandic public seemed convinced that criminal charges against politicians and the banks' alleged looters and mismanagers will matter little if the economy does not continue to improve. Hence, in parallel to disciplinary action, it did its utmost to:

- Capitalize on Iceland's natural resources, and
- Boost the economy to recover the citizens' standard of living.

Ethical standards require that wrongdoers, including politicians and bankers, are always brought to justice and from there, it found guilty, to prison. But nowadays in the West (though not in Iceland), the State Supermarket issues indulgencies. Nobody who has the inside track to the system's benevolence is being punished. To this benevolence, Iceland is an exception.

It used to be quite different when ethics had a place in the western world. In their book *Free to Choose*, Milton and Rose Friedman make reference to the Bank of the United States which on December 11, 1930, at the time of the twentieth century's Great Depression, folded up. The Friedmans say that this was a tragic event to the bank's depositors, but justice was on the heels of wrong doers.

Two of the owners were tried, convicted, and served prison sentences for acts which were technical infractions of the law."[4] Technical infractions are a lighter case of malfeasance. Today, even very serious infractions go unpunished because in a society of widespread entitlements people came to admit the "right of looting" as God-given. All but forgotten is the old wisdom that:

- A society unable to eradicate malfeasance becomes its victim, and
- A society which lacks the courage to lift itself up from its abyss is condemning itself to oblivion.

The Icelanders acted the right way, on both bullets and they did not throw Molotov cocktails when the government said that everyone has to pay the cost of the damage. Since the collapse of the Icelandic economy in 2008, the average household has suffered a 30 percent fall in purchasing power. It became difficult to make ends meet as household debt exceeded previous percentages of disposable income, and corporate debt previous percentages of GDP. All parties, however, worked hard and eventually they were able to restructure their balance sheet.

Unlike the citizen of Club Med countries, the Icelanders did not descend to noisy (and useless) protests down the streets. Wisely, they decided to rebuild their economy rather than wait for somebody else to come to the rescue. Even the loans offered by IMF and Scandinavian countries were small, and therefore they could be easily repaid. The Icelandic economy shrank by 7 percent in 2009 and by nearly 4 percent in 2010, but by 2011 it turned the corner.

The island nation's recovery has been led by fishing and tourism, helped by the boost to competitiveness from the 50 percent devaluation of the krona against the euro in 2008. Icelanders did their best to attract tourists. They did not go on strike to screw the tourists—like Greeks did from taxis to ferries—and the fact that inland prices remained fairly stable, in spite of the devaluation, did help as tourist numbers reached record levels.

The lesson learned from this experience is that the more sure way to recovery is working harder. As for the country's new government, it abided by the IMF's guidelines providing a model of crisis management. The GDP expanded by a respectable 2.5 percent in 2012. This contrasts starkly to the contraction in Euroland's Club Med wounded economies.

The Icelanders are right in believing that a nation cannot borrow their way out of trouble. While it is true that growth is essential to restore fiscal sustainability and prune the sovereign balance sheet, growth can never be created by handouts. Handouts end in pockets. Growth requires both public and business confidence, investments stimulating the economy and structural reforms.

14.2 Contrarian Opinions on Iceland's Escape from the Abyss

Iceland's example of coming up from under in four short years is a lesson for all of Europe, and most particularly for Greece, Portugal, Spain, and Italy. Politicians have to face up to simple truth: past is past, but its legacy has to be confronted. In doing just that, governments find out that nearly every method has advantages and downsides.

European countries were accustomed to set the terms of engagement with most of the rest of the world; therefore, economic and social structures were framed accordingly to that principle. Today, however, it has become hopelessly outdated. The rise of developing countries turned the old rules and assumptions on their head; many of them were scraped, others are still around. Until mid-2012 Iceland's, Latvia's, and Ireland's examples could be looked at as the new paradigm of coming up from under in a severe economic and financial crisis; also as a reminder that half-way measures don't work.

Not everybody is in accord with the thesis I have presented. "Is there an Icelandic model for dealing with failing banks? My conclusion is mostly no," says Már Gudmondsson, governor of Sedlabanki, Iceland's central bank. "There is lot of misunderstanding about Iceland."[5] As Section 14.1 brought to the reader's attention, in 2008 Iceland's three largest banks whose total assets are 10 times the size of the Icelandic economy were permitted to fail. Here we have two models, in one go:

- Ireland protected and bailed banks out.
- Iceland forced losses on bondholders and other bank's creditors.

Revealed postmortem, a downside of Ireland's method is that, according to the OECD, Iceland spent more as a percentage of GDP than any other country (apart from Ireland) in rescuing its banks. Allegedly, the banking crisis cost Icelandic taxpayers 20–25 percent of GDP, largely because of the loss in value of collateral that the three collapsed banks had pledged to the central bank when the latter was trying to save them. There have as well been other consequences.

Critics for instance say that trade improvements from the falling Icelandic currency have not been as important as many predicted. To the opinion of the central bank's governor: "The level [of the currency's exchange rate] does give stimulus to exports, that is absolutely true. But export growth has been lower than you would expect given the depreciation. Even if you depreciate the exchange rate you can't create more fish."[6]

Gudmondsson has put his figure on a crucial issue associated to the result expected from a major devaluation, which economists tend to forget. If Greece, Italy, Spain, and France were having their own currencies and they devalued—rather than being constrained by the euro—would they have solved their problems? For instance:

- Would the market rally to buy goods "Made in France"?
- Will their exporting industries be ready with an aggressive strategy to benefit from this devaluation?

Following the 9 percent devaluation of the pound in recent past, in Britain the discussion has been that if there are limits to what can be achieved through genuine QE, there are also limits to benefit from weakening the pound. Three cheers for a sinking pound, suggested Martin Wolf, the economist, in a *Financial Times* article. Really? Answered other economists, who contested Wolf's thesis.

The question several economists posed to themselves has been: How would the British economy react to further weakness of its currency in a globalized world? We are not in the late 1920s and early 1930s of competitive devaluations among western nations. For those who look at a cheaper currency as a salvation, the input from Iceland is not positive, let alone data from the pound's 25 percent devaluation in 2007–2008.

In terms of the real traded goods balance, in the course f the 2007–2008 event, the capital and intermediate goods balances have proven to be insensitive to the currency move. More precisely, the real trade balance in cars improved while that for consumer goods declined. Neither had a 25 percent devaluation an impact on British appetite for Chinese consumer goods.[7]

If 25 percent devaluation sounds "small," let's return to that of the Icelandic krona. Right after the crisis, it fell by more than 50 percent against the euro. This evidently boosted the cost of imported goods, lifted consumer prices, reduced incomes, and (evidently) increased unemployment. Financially, the Icelanders say, the sinking krona has been a double-edged sword—as most Icelandic loans were linked to inflation.

Last but not least, when Iceland imposed capital controls after the property bubble burst, which was the alter ego of its three bigger banks collapsing, the prevailing political opinion was that the measures being taken will be only temporary. They were not. Moreover, the fact of splitting the Icelandic big financial institutions into "good" and "bad banks," dented the confidence the common citizen had to the banking sector.

There have been as well collateral issues. The stabilization of the currency provided an important reason for control over the movement of capital out of the country, while the government also targeted legacy foreign investments in Icelandic securities. The next unexpected consequence was that capital controls had a negative impact on the economy:

- They discouraged outsiders from investing, and
- They made it harder for Icelandic companies to sell their bonds overseas.

In 2008, FDI collapsed and it remained about a quarter below the precrisis level. Summing up, the restrictions and controls imposed by the government to redress the country's financials hit hard the common citizen. The fact that instead of being temporary controls became sort of permanent was one of the reasons which led to the debacle of the governing socialist party in the April 2013 election. Hence, yes, Iceland is still a good example but not as good as it seemed to be a couple of years ago.

14.3   Latvia Is Much Better-Off than Argentina

The case of Latvia proves what has been said in Section 14.1 about the "will and the way" the Icelanders found to bring their economy up from under. In 2008, the Latvian economy suffered from massive overheating, confronting the government with the option of devaluing the currency.[8] The decision has been to hold the peg, and to do so without going hat in hand to richer nations for loans and handouts. The way has been:

- *Internal   devaluation*,   which   facilitated   what   the   Latvians   called "equitable austerity," and
- A proportional cut in wages and public expenditures, while prices dropped without creating a depression.

Latvia has not been a member of Euroland to ask for handout from the ECB and from Brussels.[9] Like Iceland, it has been able to withstand alone the shock of a massive bankruptcy of its big banks, and come back to a normal economy paying its debt to IMF and to Sweden ahead of time—indeed, almost 3 years earlier than the deadline.

In a nutshell, the Latvian recipe has been smaller income cuts for the poorer segment of the population and higher taxes for the more wealthy, accompanied by substantial structural reforms. The exchange rate of the currency was not changed, and no massive loans were contracted. The shakedown was not that long. In about 2 years, the economy started moving again.

According to the opinion of several economists, it was not austerity that caused the output fall in Latvia, but the liquidity freeze of September 2008. From 2000 until 2007, the country's GDP had grown by an impressive 83 percent, which was unsustainable. This annual (nearly) 12 percent rise, however, provided a cushion for 2 years of output fall. In retrospect, the Latvian government was right to believe that a devaluation:

- Would not have helped, and
- Might have caused mass bankruptcies.

Indeed not only Latvia but as well Estonia and Lithuania, the other two Baltic countries, have successfully undergone internal devaluation. Wages and GDP per head shrunk by a quarter or more in order to regain lost competitiveness. The successful result sharply contrasts to the Argentinean experience (more on this later) as well as to what has followed the euro crisis.

Greece, Ireland, and Portugal have imposed swinging budget and wage cuts and other unpopular reforms on their voters. To come up from under, Spain and Italy now have to do the same. None of them learned anything from the Baltic and Icelandic experiences. Instead, they thought that they have a rich aunt in Berlin who should pay for all their profligacy and misconduct.

The failure to study all of the options, their costs and aftermaths is a serious mistake. Used properly, lessons from a past experience worth a great deal. While one should never uncritically cut and paste bygone circumstances to apply them to the new realities, plenty can be learned from what was done and not done, provided there is no:

- Omitting of inconvenient facts,
- Falsifying of results to make a point,
- Using misleading metaphor, or
- Manipulating of financial statistics.

All four events have happened in Argentina from 2001 to 2012 which is a paradigm to avoid. Successive governments did almost everything wrong. They defaulted, turned their back on alternative solutions at an early stage, adopted an aggressive position with their creditors, spent many years defending extensive litigation, and ended by being excluded from the international markets.[10]

They also made a joke of currency stability, even if a template which adorned the lobby of Argentina's Central Bank, proclaimed that its "primary and fundamental mission is to preserve the value of the currency." At the end of March 2012, this template was removed after the Argentinean Congress approved a government bill that gives the bank a new, wordier mandate:

To promote, to the extent of its ability and in the framework of policies established by the national government, monetary stability, financial stability, jobs and economic growth with social fairness.

Sounds familiar? Here we are with another central bank turned into employment Santa Klaus. Ben Bernanke finds imitators. Like the Fed, the monetary institution of Argentina lost its legal independence and became the piggy bank of the government. Conflicting goals given by parliaments and governments to central banks are a dime a dozen these days.

As for the Argentinean people they are *de facto* condemned to deal with this drama and uncertainty. So are the citizens of Greece, Portugal, Spain, and Italy whose governments asked Euroland for help rather than choosing the much safer self-help like Iceland and Latvia did.

Since the 2001 default of the South American country arranged nothing for long-suffering holders of devalued and restructured government bonds, analysts advise setting very low expectations regarding Argentina, assuming:

- Another default,
- Protracted legal and political battles, and
- Losses from current trading values.

There has been no economic rebirth as in Latvia and Iceland whose choice was to take their fortune and their future in their own hands. By contrast, Argentina's default sparked social unrest and runs on banks. It dirtied the country's name and that of western banks that pushed its bonds down the throat of their clients. (A case in point is 60,000 middle class individuals in Italy, advised by their banks to buy Argentine bonds as the best retail investment.)

Club Med countries, but not the Baltics or Iceland, have confronted a similar problem to that of Argentina, with overcoming entrenched opposition to structural changes, supported by corrupt politicians. The other disturbing similarity between Club Med countries and Argentina is the resort to short-term liquidity fixes for long-term solvency problems. This means that the moment troubles brew up, investors rush out of the same door and the countries depending on short-term financing are cut off the capital market.

Long-term financing for longer term commitment is the way to successfully recover one's freedom of action. This must be translated into the common economic language, to be learned and used by *all* its member states. There exists always a unifying power of a common language. As Latvia and Iceland demonstrated, an important element of a common economic language is how to suffer and recover all alone.[11]

Working along these principles, the people of Latvia labored to recover their wealth. The economy resumed growth, expanding about 5 percent in 2012, the EU's best figure. With a 2012 budget deficit of only 1.5 percent and public debt at 42 percent of GDP, Latvia's finances are the envy of many countries. But there is also a puzzle.

On January 31, 2013 Latvian lawmakers flew in the face of public opinion by declaring a path for the Baltic nation to apply for Euroland membership starting January 1, 2014. According to a December 2012 poll, two-thirds of the country's citizens oppose this move, and some parties wanted to sink the plan with a referendum. There was a protest rally in Riga. "Latvia should not provide aid for ailing euro-area nations" was one of the panel's slogan. "If the EU collapses, it will be easier to recover without the euro," stated another.

But there exist as well embedded interests, while Estonia provides a precedence. The Latvian government's bet is that adoption of the euro will boost private direct investments in a country where more than 80 percent of loans and more than 40 percent of deposits are denominated in lats, and where labor costs have been brought down to competitive levels.

This does not change the fact that if Latvia now joins the euro, this will be at the worst possible time—at a time the common currency has a clear reputation problem in most European countries. Among the profligates, people associate the euro with austerity and forced structural reforms. In Northern Europe, the "transfer union" and bailout fatigue see to it that people no longer look at it as gateway to increased prosperity, trade, absence of exchange risks, and the common market.

14.4 Ireland Is in its Way to Win the Battle of Austerity

Ireland is the only member state of Euroland which, at least so far, provides a positive answer to the question creeping up on everybody's mind: whether austerity and structural reforms are really working. Contrary to the case of Iceland and Latvia which took all alone the tough road and reached their goals, the Irish response talks of the ability of countries that have received bailouts to return to a healthy economy.

Economists who looked into this question started by defining the meaning of a country's ability to come up from under and set as criterion its return to capital markets. Is it able to convince lenders that it is again trustworthy? Can it borrow longer term from banks and other private investors, at reasonable interest rate roughly resembling what it paid historically?

In 2005, prior to the economic and financial crisis, Ireland was able to borrow for 10 years at 3 percent, or a little less. Then, its ratio of debt to GDP zoomed, as it assumed euro 64 billion ($85 billion) of bank debt and it went through the EU/ECB/IMF bailout. The crucial question is: As of 2013 where does the notional 10-year borrowing cost stand? As of January 2013, it has been 4.3 percent—about 150 percent of what it were prior to the crisis.[12]

There are no miracles. Only hard work provides deliverables. For 2013, the Irish government established its sixth consecutive austerity budget. In the 5 years since 2008, nearly euro 29 billion ($38.5 billion) worth of spending cuts and tax rises have been implemented. Critics say that by strong-arming Dublin into a deal, Euroland safeguarded the interests of its banks[13] via the Irish public purse. That may be true, but it is no less real life that—unlike southern Europeans—the Irish are in their way out of the public debt pit.

By mid-2013, the news from Ireland are relatively good. Instead of getting into political bickering and destabilizing public opinion—as it has happened in Italy,

Spain, and Greece—Irish politicians got to work in order to rebuild the economy, and so did the common citizens. As a result, Ireland has a good claim to being a model of adjustment through structural reform and austerity.

- It met its deficit-cutting targets,
- Recovered much of its export competitiveness, and
- Supported the right conditions for growth of the Irish economy, albeit slowly.

In the aftermath, Ireland regained market confidence. This in no way means that risk has miraculously disappeared. As a major exporter, Ireland is exposed both to recession in the rest of Europe and to a slowdown of the global economy. It also faces the burden of its collapsed banking industry which is a drag on its economy.

Like the American and Spanish real estate market, the Irish helplessly watched the rapid fall of house and other real estate prices. Indeed, prices tanked more than in the other two countries. Experts say that the housing market has not yet bottomed out, though the restart of the American housing market tends to suggest that an inflection point may not be far away.[14]

Some economists say that Ireland's problem is totally different than that confronting the Club Med countries. This opinion is only half-right. It is right as far as the origin of the troubles is concerned. It was the Irish banks and not the entitlements that brought the economy down. But it is wrong in terms of the real estate market which was overleveraged.

The British government's willingness to offer support for Ireland suggested worries about possible fallouts on British banks. The Bank for International Settlements estimated that British financial institutions accounted for almost 30 percent of European banks' total exposure to Ireland (estimated at euro 309 billion ($412 billion)).

The Royal Bank of Scotland and Lloyds Bank were at top of the list of British banks at the cliff of falling Irish real estate prices. More than 40 percent of Lloyds' £27 billion ($43 billion) exposure was through commercial property, with impaired loans accounting for over two-fifths of that amount. Both British lenders expected impairments to remain high, and so did other European and American credit institutions with direct or indirect exposure to Ireland.

The argument that without support by the EU, ECB, and IMF, the measures would have been even more severe is not quite true. The Irish government and the people were determined to confront their challenge. The 4-year plan for recovery included:

- Income tax increases,
- Deep cuts in social welfare, and
- A reduction of 10 percent or more in the minimum wage.[15]

With the exception of smaller parties, like Sin Fein, which engaged in fantasy economics to increase their followership, particularly among the young, the country's political leadership understood the challenge. Both major Irish parties appreciated that unless politicians are prepared to dig into the pockets of middle- and upper-income families, government finances will not get under control; neither can recovery have a chance without cutting back all sorts of entitlements.

There was, of course, the risk that any serious effort to curb long-established middle-class benefits sets off a public backlash, but this did not deter Irish politicians from doing their duty. Compare this with the risk of full fallback to *dolce vita* that threatened Italy after the fall of the Monti government at end of 2012; also remember that Italy is a country both too big to rescue and too big for the euro to survive its possible departure.

The demanding task associated to the Irish austerity decision was particularly stark, since many families depended on the social safety net as an essential feature of western society since World War II. But, by all evidence, the Irish public understood that this has been largely built on providing unsustainable benefits—from health care to relatively comfortable pensions, augmented by:

- Child subsidy,
- A number of special deductions, and
- Even winter heating allowance.

As the Irish found out through their experience, the right level of austerity is a balancing act. Too little fiscal consolidation could roil financial markets, but too many risks further undermining the recovery and, in this way, could also raise market concerns, said the IMF in its Fiscal Outlook, in April 2012. Economists added that the debt dynamics of wounded countries are not helped by the global slowdown. When growth is a scarce commodity, only those who take very seriously the need to get out of the hole stand a chance.

Like the Icelanders and Latvians, the Irish appreciated that they had to cut state expenditures. To the contrary, the Spanish do not. The way Marco Annunziata, chief economist at General Electric, looks at this issue is, Spain is simply doing what it needs to justify the euro 100 billion ($130 billion) promised from the EU to shore up its teetering banks. "Madrid's austerity measured send a very important signal that, just as Spain is receiving additional support from the Eurozone, it is in turn making an additional effort to keep its fiscal policy on track," says Annunziata.[16]

The excuse that conditions in Spain are tougher than in other countries does not wash, because all wounded Euroland member states confront an unholy combination of challenges. Their banking industry suffers because of its past lending mistakes, as well as the fact that it massively bought government bonds without due care about credit risk exposure—and sovereigns are co-responsible for this aberration.

This difference between Ireland and Spain in righting the balances is very interesting because the countries share among themselves some of the underlying problems. In both, the real estate industry has collapsed, and they are both confronted by a bloated, mismanaged, and wounded banking industry. The difference lies in human capital.

Ireland has shown that austerity and structural reforms imposed as the price of bailouts can work. A sustained return to the bond markets (discussed in the opening paragraphs of this section) would boost confidence. This has also happened with unit labor costs which came down sharply, making the economy more competitive. In turn, competitiveness enhanced Ireland's allure for foreign companies, which continue to favor the country for manufacturing and services. (A role is also played by its low corporate tax rate.) Hence the forecast is that in 2014, Ireland might be able to leave Euroland's bailout program.

14.5   Britain Tries to Put its House in Order

In a statement made on March 27, 2012 Citigroup said the Netherlands is no more a "core" country of Euroland.[17] With the exception of Germany, no European Union member is anymore a "core" country of the EU—surely not France which lost its AAA credit rating and, by all evidence, not Britain which also lost an A in rating, is not part of Euroland and still faces large budget deficits in spite of its government's effort to bring them under control.

Theoretically, the principal cause for this persistent deficit is the collapse in sovereign revenues. This cannot be explained entirely through the loss of tax income because of banking woes, property-sector collapse, and the forfeit of taxes due to increased unemployment. These are contributing factors but not the whole story. Neither has the persistent budget deficit been caused single-handed by the need to bail out the banks in 2008 and 2009—which was a one-off increase in expenditure.[18]

Practically, the shrinking of sovereign revenues has been matched (even exceeded) by an increase in expenditures, in spite of the British government's effort to reign over them. One of the more serious and persistent reasons is that 60 percent of government expenditures is exempt from the cuts made by the Conservative–Liberal coalition. The sacred cows include military spending and the wasteful National Health Service (NHS). Since it saw the light right after World War II, NHS exhibited a voracious appetite for "more money," which can turn an austerity budget on its head.

All British political parties share the blame for this state of affairs, which in the post-WWII western countries "is a norm," but lacks any good sense. The government's original figures on "savings" were published not by George Osborne but by Alistair Darling when his March 2010 pre-election budget became public. The Labor's "solution" was to assume that departmental expenditure and gross income would grow in line with the general inflation level of the whole economy, while deficits would hide behind inflationary figures. These became known as *Darling estimates*.

Labor's 2010 light budget raised fears about Britain's economic health which David Cameron exploited by reminding his audience about Britain's humiliating 1976 bailout, under another Labor government, by the IMF. To Cameron's words: If we continue on Labor's path of fiscal irresponsibility, at some point, and it could be very soon, the money will simply run out. The thinly veiled implication was that Britain and its government will go bust.

Gordon Brown could, of course, have answered that a default under his watch would not have been a "first" for England. Edward III defaulted on debt to Florentine lenders in 1340. To save his reign from default, Henry VIII seized the

Catholic church's lands and was also debited with reneging on financial obligations. In more recent times, Britain in effect defaulted in 1932 in a "voluntary" reduction on the interest it paid on war loans.[19]

The core of the matter is that the former dynamics of western economy have run out of steam (and out of cash). All of the EU as well as the United States find themselves in a deteriorating economic climate. As if this was not enough, practically every western government, including Germany's, has been obliged to engineer banking support packages which focused attention on:

- How weak western banks are, and
- How difficult and slow it will be to get again credit freely flowing.

Britain is neither the "good" nor the "bad" exception among western sovereigns. Many other governments are in a more unfavorable situation than they hoped for. Year-after-year entitlements become more expensive, while with growth weaker than projected future revenues are lower pointing to either:

- A de facto abandonment of deficit reduction objectives, or
- The need to enact more cuts and more taxes with every new edition of the budget.

How much "more" is the theme of a wide-ranging debate, because the frame of reference on which rests the debt weighting on the government's shoulders continues to change. The concept underpinning the public sector is slowly but surely enlarged to include not only unaffordable new entitlements but also avoiding bankruptcies of highly leveraged credit institutions (which is a false target), as well as other newly found obligations.

It used to be that public sector debt was restricted to sovereign gearing. On such a premise, the government's ability to finance itself without wealth confiscation or bankruptcy was measured in terms of creditworthiness. Because of the aforementioned reasons, however, this is no more an adequate definition. Governments are searching for a better one to define a believable strategy for growth.

Credibility is the name of the game and central to it is the recognition that because sovereign expenses are so far ahead of income much of what may be painstakingly gained in one year's "austerity" might be lost next year. Therefore, there is need for persistent discipline in managing public finances. With:

- Deep-rooted review of all ongoing commitments, and
- Public explanation of what it means to be snowed under public debt.

Whether in Britain, America, France, or other western countries, the challenge is more profound than merely announcing budgetary cuts then getting back to business as usual. The worst of all solutions is entrusting the state with "new powers" and "more responsibilities."

Pruning the bloated sovereign balance sheet and restoring the economy to sustainable growth is what the Cameron government had tried to do by means of growth-enhancing structural reforms and cost cuts, while sticking to fiscal consolidation plans. The bad news is that health care and other entitlements continued to increase upsetting government plans and suppressing the green shoots of recovery.

Osborne, the chancellor of the Exchequer, admitted that the country has deep-rooted economic problems but maintained that the government was "dealing with our debts at home and the debt crisis abroad." Britain's credit rating may not mean much to the majority of the population but investors grew increasingly wary even of the threat that the triple-A rating may be cut. Moody's and Standard & Poor's have both rated Britain AAA since 1978 but that materially weaker economic growth led to a rate cut.

Evidently, not everything is negative. Back in 2007 the trade surplus of London's City stood at nearly 3 percent of Britain's GDP (more than that with insurance). Even after the descend to the abyss of 2008/2009, the City's trade surplus in 2011 was nearly 2.5 percent of British GDP. Critics, however, do not fail to remind that who says "financial industry" says leveraging.

The 2012 British downturn is incorrectly labeled "double dip" because it was milder than that suffered by the other European nations. The contraction hinged on construction activity is notoriously volatile. Still Britain ended below its cyclical peak in 2008. There is no guarantee that under a more expansionary fiscal policy the economy would have done significantly better.

Seen with hindsight, the effort of the coalition government to put Britain's public house in order has hit against the hard rock of undiminishable public expenditures. To this are added headwinds from Euroland as well as from the United States, and households deleveraging which continues to damp demand and (by all probability) will be doing so for some time to come.

Not all sectors of the economy are equally affected. A mid-2012 £38-billion ($61 billion) development boom in London's most expensive neighborhoods has been spurred by rampant demand from European and Asian buyers; some of the former moving away from turbulent Euroland economies. (François Hollande, the French president, added to it by his announcement to tax incomes of euro 1 million, or more, per year at 75 percent.)[20]

Upmarket real estate investments are, in their way, a sign of growth. The pipeline of expensive housing projects in planning or under construction in Britain's capital has increased by more than 66 percent during 2011, flourished in 2012, and continues as long as there is political and financial stability, but may fade with a radical change in government. Investors from overseas seek stable investments, away from economic and political turmoil.

Compared to other safe currency havens, like the Swiss franc, Norwegian and Swedish krone, Japanese yen, and US dollar, the pound has been rather cheaply valued leaving upside potential. The dark cloud is the return of business confidence which is not growing in the European Union. It has become volatile and bends with every new bout in the debt crisis.

In conclusion, there are good reasons to support the thesis advanced by some economists that (everything counted) Britain provides one of the relatively safer harbors in the West's debt storm. As the European sovereign debt crisis deteriorated, Britain pulled out of the crowd. There exist, however, reasons for caution given the gap between market optimism and economic reality in the West. The negative effect of the printing presses (at Bank of England) working overtime is illustrated by the fall in 10-year yields on government debt to below 2 percent, the lowest levels since the 1890s.

14.6   Germany and the Policy of Fiscal Discipline

A short time prior to the outbreak of World War I, the total face value of paper reichsmark in circulation was 2.7 billion. This was less than half the coinage German citizens were encouraged to trade-in in exchange for paper money. In November 1918, after the WWI armistice, the amount of paper marks stood at 27 billion, an order of magnitude higher.[21]

Two years later, in November 1920, the mass of paper marks reached 77 billion and from there on its growth accelerated—most evidently with no real assets to back it up. The sovereign who might have guaranteed its paper money was in a coma, but the German central bank marched in. As prices zoomed, even strikes for higher wages made not much sense. The workers discovered that the misery result-ing from the strikes fell largely upon themselves.

Let's leap forward by nine decades. To make ends meet, the United States, Britain and Euroland's sovereigns, and central banks chose the soft option: the printing presses. As with the German hyperinflation of 2003, deficit financing acquired its own momentum and became unstoppable. In November 1920 when Berlin's hydra of inflation established its kingdom, the exchange rate of the British pound was 240 marks. Three years later, in October 1923, the number of marks to the pound was equal to the number of yards to the sun. As Daniel Lloyd George, the WWI British prime minister, noted words like disaster, ruin, and catastrophe had ceased to rouse any sense of genuine apprehension any more.[22]

Not unexpectedly, the trauma can last for centuries like that of the Fourth Crusade which looted Constantinople and destroyed the last vestiges of the Byzantine empire. Who can blame the Germans for being unwilling to see the results of their labor and their wealth being utterly ruined and their economy devas-tated for a second time within 100 years?

By 2013, while the American public debt crisis continues unabated (Chapters 10 and 11), in Europe the Club Med sovereign debt crisis (Chapters 4 through 9) remains the greatest threat to financial stability in the old continent. Matters are made worse by the multiple transmission and contagion channels that are inherent within a closely integrated economic and monetary union.

Since its onset in 2007−2008 Euroland's crisis has largely dictated the risk situ-ation. The German financial system has undergone significant changes because of the crisis, but it lacks the breadth and resources to carry nearly the rest of Euroland on its shoulders all alone.

The German government is fully justified to maintain fiscal discipline and walks carefully on Euroland's financially and economically mined terrain. The large majority of the citizens want it to be that way. Business is divided. Big firms tend to favor further support for indebted Eurozone members, since for them these are "markets." *Mittelstand firms*[23] oppose it.

A short time prior to German's vote empowering the EFSF lobbyists for the country's biggest companies wrote urging parliamentarians to vote "yes." By contrast, family firms said Germany must refuse, the reason being that small and medium company owners are personally liable for debts and other liabilities.

If there was a political union of Euroland member states, the situation would have been more transparent and, may be, better managed. With 17 jurisdictions each looking to protect its own interests, the risks not only to Euroland but also to the German financial system are high. The European sovereign debt crisis is still in full swing, dictating the level of exposure.

Economic exposure has broadened in the course of 2012 and came to a head at various times in the year, with doubts cast over longer term survival of the monetary union. To be effective, crisis management measures require plenty of funds, and as the EFSF funds did not suffice, Euroland instituted as well the ESM. Germany contributes:

- 29.1 percent of EFSF's capital, and
- 27.2 percent of ESM's capital.

If two other European support mechanisms are added to this lot: EIB and European Financial Stabilization Mechanism (EFSM), *then* altogether:

- Germany contributed euro 427 billion ($555 billion), or 7.6 times its annual intake from household taxes,
- France, euro 331 billion ($430 billion), or 7.3 times its annual household taxes, and
- Britain (which only participates to EIB and EFSM) euro 43 billion ($56 billion).

What is Germany getting in return? The answer most often one hears is a large market for its exports. Yes, but Germany exports to the EU roughly are 40 percent of its produce, much less than other EU countries' statistics:

- France, 50 percent
- Italy, 45 percent
- Spain, 55 percent

On a percent-of-exports basis Spain, Italy, and France (in that order) benefit more than Germany from the common market. But Germany pays more. Some economists say "that's all right" because Germany has long been the economic powerhouse of Europe. This is a sort of twisted logic which also forgets that Germany is not immune from the global financial crisis.

Much of Germany's industrial might comes from its strong manufacturing sector, which has meant that unlike many of its neighbors, the country did not have to inorderly rely on the financial services industry or the property market. Experts however warn that the German economy, which heavily depends on trade with China, may be highly exposed to any future trouble in the Asian markets.

Neither can Berlin do as it pleases without taking account of its citizens' opinion. Most German citizens are unhappy with having to bail out the southern European countries. They are far from being convinced of having to give them their money. The majority have found it difficult to give up the Deutschmark. It was a symbol of the country's recovery, and joining the euro was for them a sacrifice.

In exchange for this they wanted a financial and currency stability pact. They got it on paper, but not in reality. The ink on the *Stability and Growth Pact* was not yet dry when every member state started gaming it—particularly France but as well Germany's socialist government. Then came out a new version whose rules were so diluted that it was worse than nothing. Euroland's debt crisis followed on the heels of "Euroland without financial stability" rules.

Angela Merkel wanted a new pact: the *Fiscal Compact*, with reformed budgetary rules and emphasis on balanced budgets. Seen from the perspective of Stability and Growth Pact experience, however, there is a risk that the Fiscal Compact may fall short of the mark by a margin:

- In Euroland, every jurisdiction is still on its own, and
- Fuzzy assessment criteria will not detect problematic developments in time.

It makes plenty of sense for the Fiscal Compact to call for all of Euroland's 17 members to insert a binding clause into their constitutions to set a ceiling on public borrowing, intended to make balanced budgets the norm. To be binding (at least theoretically) such a commitment has been put into national legislation, but it is highly doubtful that this will have any effect.

These are as well loopholes, like the absence of a rule to systematically include off-budget funds. (This was envisaged, but it is not implemented.) Another loophole is lack of rules not just to list the values for the agreed key figures in stability reports but also to show detailed (but standardized) calculations enabling to produce cross-member state comparisons extending beyond agreed ratios. Therefore, even with the Fiscal Compact:

- Creative accounting can continue having a field day, and
- The bad habit of massaging official statistics by some member states may not come to an end.

Personally, I see it unlikely that independent member states will coordinate their budget plans and seek to negotiate a common corporate tax base. To do either and both feats, Euroland's governments have to at least trust one another and reconcile differing priorities—which they are not ready to do. Instead, they choose the easy way out:

- Let Germany pay for all of us, and
- We launch "jointly guaranteed" Euroland bonds to help the most debt-strapped members of the monetary union.

For evident reasons, Germany is strongly opposed to the idea of guaranteeing borrowing for profligate Euroland states. Even with much closer economic and fiscal harmonization, this will be highly risky for its economy and a very poor initiative indeed, as it will discourage Club Med countries to do whatever is needed to rid themselves of heavy public debt.

In addition, Germany is no longer the country with low public debt-to-GDP ratio that used to be, and it simply cannot afford to increase its national debt just to pay for other states. In the mid-1970s German debt-to-GDP ratio stood at about 18 percent; it rose to 40 percent in early 1990s with unification and reached 60 percent by 2000. In 2013, it has been about 83 percent (still a tentative figure). That's better than over 110 percent (and fast growing) for the United States, but it is way beyond the 60 percent implied for membership to the euro.[24]

The federal government has also to look after its own citizens' needs, not only those of foreigners. Pensions is a case in point, and even more so health insurance. Beyond that is local government finances and the gapping holes opened by the derivatives gambles of German banks. Deutsche Bank's assets, for example, are greater than 100 percent of Germany's GDP, and early August 2012 saw a sharp deterioration in Deutsche Bank CDSs. Should Deutsche's CDS widen, it would signal significant financial stress within Germany.[25]

With its own problems to look after, Germany does not want to hear about a "transfer union" pooling national debts. Neither it wants, at least for now, a breakup of the single currency. These are two positions very difficult to reconcile even *if* one starts redesigning European institutions (which will be a hopeless task). Just new ways to enforce budget rules will not resolve the crisis nor ensure it does not recur. Euroland's problems have been caused by the laxness of countries that piled up debt and lost competitiveness.

14.7 Mervyn Le King, Mark De Carney, and Fantasy Economics

Since the great banking crisis of 2008, the priority at Federal Reserve and Bank of England has been to demonstrate how dependent are the western countries' financial, social, and political structures on money printing. This has created the illusion that fast running printing presses at central banks make sovereigns more solvent than they really are, and that budget constraints are really elastic with their breakup point a safe distance away.

This is nothing else than *fantasy economics* and coexists in competition with another fallacy: Many people still think that money is backed by real assets which guarantee its value. Right? Wrong. The value of money lays in the trust its users place in central bankers and sovereigns to keep it up and protect it as a store of wealth and means of exchange.

As Karl Brunner, my professor of economics at UCLA taught his students: *The value of the money derives from the fact that it is limited in supply.* This is not what two of the major western central banks believe in these days: Federal Reserve and Bank of England. With its LTRO and OMT, the ECB has joined them in their policies against monetary stability. With Abenomics the Bank of Japan has done the same.

Over the last 6 years, the Fed and Bank of England have printed enough money to buy over 60 percent of the issuance of their respective government securities. Contrarians are asking: What would bond yields in America and Britain look like without such wild purchases of sovereign debt? And the answer is: Probably similar to those of Club Med.

Rather than "masterfully navigating" the financial crisis and avoiding another depression, the unimaginative and easy solution of fast running printing presses has been the one already invented by successive French governments. In the 1980s, when he was president of the Fifth Republic, François Mitterrand used it, and thereafter he had to devalue the franc three times in a matter of a few years.

Anecdotal evidence suggests that Mervyn King might have been a French central banker where he got his experience with QE, rather than having learned it from Bernanke (who allegedly found it in books about the Great Depression). Collateral damage is widespread. The British pensions industry claims that it has been badly hurt by the Bank of England's:

- Quantitative easing, and
- Rock-bottom interest rates.

The National Association of Pension Funds (NAPF) has been one of the most prominent critics of the Bank of England's £375 billion ($600 billion) of gilts purchases since 2009. By driving down long-term interest rates, QE has caused pension liabilities to rise.

To NAPF's opinion, QE forces businesses to divert money away from jobs and investment and into filling pension fund deficits.[26] (The Bank of England's response has been that QE's impact was neutral on fully-funded defined benefit schemes though retirement plans that already had problems prior to the financial crisis were likely to have seen negative deficits increased.)

Another reason for caution, if not for outright worry, is that the effects of QE on the real economy appear to be far more limited in what is considered to be their "positive side," while laying down the preconditions for a zoom in inflation. To some opinions, the 5 percent inflation recently experienced in Britain is just the *hors d'oeuvre*. And with the Bank already owning more than 40 percent of the British government bond market, there is clearly a limit to how often the trick can be repeated.

Mervyn King has been sensitive to this argument. The central bank admits that its policy has costs as well as benefits, and not all of them are easy to track. There is subtle recognition of the fact that whatever the Bank of England may be doing happens in an environment of disorderly high leverage among credit institutions and of a great deal of uncertainties about the sovereigns purse.

With oversized balance sheets stuffed with dubious assets but real liabilities, there is a potential for enormous losses. Something new is definitely needed, and it has been invented. Here comes Mark Carney, another hypothetical French Republic central banker who made his schooling as investment banker at Goldman

Sachs (as well as formerly governor of Canada's central bank and newly appointed governor of the Bank of England).

Carney is the inventor of a new economic theory on how to flood the market with newly printed paper money. Forgetting that the first and foremost duty of central banks is *monetary policy* and along with it *currency stability*, Carney announced his version of money of the mind: *nominal gross domestic product spending* (NGDPS).[27]

Theoretically, NGDPS was intended to deliver financial stability in spite of its many enemies: populist politicians, the Berlusconi species, nineteenth century socialists of all colors and hues, and so on and so forth. That's the folk to whom currency stability is anathema. To the contrary, inflation is their credo as well as that of the State Supermarket's.

Worryingly, all of a sudden the Bank of England will be sounding much more hawkish, because with NGDPS the printing presses will be turning at so much higher speed than with QE. This will turn monetary policy on its head. It might, just *might*, also lead to a monetary policy crash that is appalling and unprecedented. To appreciate why the NGDPS affair should be looked at with mistrust, we should take a look on its pillars:

- Replacing inflation targeting with nominal GDP level targeting,[28] and
- Setting a growth objective of 4 or 5 percent per year, without questions asked on whether the economy can follow.

Men, financial institution, and whole nations are no more satisfied with the sure but slow way of earnings coming from cautious industry. Wild risk-taking, subprimes-type, is the name of the game. Society is falsely informed by the printing presses and their political bosses that such games with currency stability can only bring profits since all hazards will be guaranteed by the central banks' QE, NGDPS, LTRO, OMT,[29] or whatever other anagram comes along.

Another popular delusion espoused by a horde of politicians, particularly populist and socialist, is that with paper money presses running full time, the voting public's optimism will rise and all by magic everyone will become rich. The great central bank lottery will finance from now on the State Supermarket, and common citizen can make a fortune under the NGDPS regime, without ever searching for work.

As one piece of crazy ideas hides another, the NGDPS apostles are even able to provide assurances about the sunny future: thanks to NGDPS, countries will be able to address the public debt problem, as they should, without fear that austerity will cost jobs. That's one of the miracles one of NGDPS' apostles wrote in an article.[30]

Who believes in that crap will believe anything. Aside the fact that NGDPS will produce inflation, there exist technical flaws in using GDP as basic monetary policy instrument. Unlike the consumer price index (CPI)[31] which is rarely revised, GDP is not only actively restructured but also takes years till its revisions are implemented by the different countries—which means that, in the global economic landscape, it is a heterogeneous metric.

It also happens that after the "final" GDP version has been published at the end of a revision cycle,[32] the index can be further manipulated if a new methodology or standard is introduced. This is true of both nominal GDP and volume measures, making NGDPS a moving target which is a negative for a policy instrument, particularly at a time of crisis.

Over time, however, Mark Carney's views have become much more realistic. In his first big speech as the new governor of the Bank of England he explained that he leaves all policy options open, and plans no actions in the current environment. If the situation requires, Britain's central bank might enter another round of QE or use other simulative measures; but he would also not hesitate to tighten standards by implementing macro prudential measures to stop a bubble. Carney as well calmed down worries that the Bank of England will revise the inflation target somewhat haphazardly in the future.

Cicero, the great Roman senator, author and orator, used to ask: "To whom it profits?" All this commotion is happening at a time when central bank balance sheets are set to increase further, most particularly those of the Federal Reserve and of the ECB. The Fed plays the leading role in global quantitative easing. The ECB may well be out of lack with its OMT operation if Spain and Italy ask it to massively purchase their (untrustworthy) sovereign bonds. The combined requirements stand between euro 2 trillion and 3 trillion, the money Mario Draghi does not have even in his wildest dreams. There are two options:

- When Spain and Italy call his hand he either has to retreat, losing face while ECB and Euroland go to the *oubliettes*.[33]
- Or, he prints and throws to the market an unprecedented amount of liquidity ballooning the ECB's balance sheet and asking the Germans to pay for it.

Most likely, the Germans will refuse to pay other people's bills, as they recently did with Cyprus, and opt out of Euroland. This is still an event waiting to happen. When the time comes, we shall see what takes place. Another adventure, however, has already occurred, and it is far from being to the credit of politicians, central bankers, and regulators.

Under pressure by governments, on January 8, 2013 the Basel Committee on Banking Supervision announced that the implementation of Basel III[34] will be delayed for another 4 years. Not only the target date changed from 2015 to 2019 but also the liquidity conditions have been softened. Sovereigns and the banking industry teamed up to get the extra delay, as self-wounded credit institutions are not in a position to meet the core capital requirement and liquidity rules.

Worse yet, the original prudential rules of Basel III have been eased reducing by so much the effectiveness of bank supervision. With central bankers and regulators abandoning their caution, pressing ahead for tearing down the walls of the city, the way is open for another repetition of the 2008 severe banking crisis. Delays beset governments and big banks whose time is up. There are obstacles and potholes on the road. Fasten your seat belts.

*   *   *

Deleveraging with discipline is what Iceland, Latvia, and Ireland did with fair amount of success. The task is doable. Britain, too, has tried to rid itself off the Labor government's high indebtedness but the coalition faces internal difficulties (such as redimensioning the NHS) as well as external constraints from the EU—a reason why Cameron seeks to repatriate powers.

Plato's *Republic* has an allegory of people described as prisoners in a cave. Since childhood they live in half darkness and can only see shadows of two-dimensional objects projected on the cave's walls. From this experience, they conclude that the shadow theater is indeed the real world. Rare is a person who can free himself from such a widespread make-believe environment, but when he explains to the others their mistake they are not able to understand.

The two-dimensional vision dominates and, joined by central bankers, politicians face an electorate forcing them to head down two tracks at the same time. The one is paved with debt and entitlements; the other with remnants of past glory mixed with hope for better tomorrow. But as with the people in the cave, hopes and illusions are not reality. And the drama continues, because resurgence does not come out of leftovers.

End Notes

1. Financial Times, March 30, 2012.
2. Just like Haarde, the former prime minister, the two bankers denied the charges.
3. Financial Times, March 30, 2012.
4. Friedman M, Friedman R. Free to choose. Orlando, FL: Harvest/Harcourt; 1980.
5. Financial Times, February 4, 2013.
6. *Idem.*
7. It is not the intention of this section to take a position pro or against devaluation. But it is important to bring to the reader's attention that criteria and results associated to devaluation have changed.
8. Pegged to a basket of western currencies. Lats were overvalued, as the exchange rate was higher than that of the British pound.
9. Curiously enough, however, it now wants to join Euroland. More on this later.
10. Judge Thomas Griesa, who presided over much of the Argentinian bonds litigation in the US branded Argentina's maneuvers "immoral," turning the writ of American courts into a "dead letter." He also reminded plaintiffs that they have rights but may not have remedies (The Economist, October 22, 2011).
11. More than 350 languages and dialects were spoken throughout the Indonesian archipelago at time of independence. President Sukarno realized that to unify the country, the people needed a common vocabulary in order to unite their lands and the cultures into one nation. Bahasa Indonesia was that language, and it became highly successful. Bahasa was easy to learn, and by the early 1970s, the majority of Indonesians spoke it, even if they still used local dialects in their communities.
12. Portugal has even further to go to qualify for the "return to normal" criterion. Its 10-year borrowing costs today are nearly 7 percent, about 200 percent the level prior to the crisis.

13. Deadly wounded Irish banks had borrowed heavily from other European credit institutions.

14. As in Spain, Irish house prices dropped also in 2012.

15. In the boom years, this had become one of the most generous in Europe.

16. Financial Times, July 12, 2012.

17. In the first quarter of 2011, Holland had a problem in maintaining its traditional budget discipline, and in the fourth quarter of 2011, Dutch GDP dropped by 0.6 percent.

18. The £114 billion of direct bailout costs lie on the government's balance sheet, not in its fiscal accounts. Moreover, the British taxpayer might end with some profits when the banks are privatized—which was a better strategy than putting public money into private banks' coffers.

19. This has been a distant forerunner of the 2012 PSI and its "voluntary."

20. This has been made into law, but it was rejected as unconstitutional by France's Constitutional Court.

21. Fergusson A. When money dies. New York, NY: PublicAffairs; 1975.

22. *Idem.*

23. Medium-sized, owner-managed companies which often address global niches.

24. Nobody is anymore observing this 60 percent, but it has not been officially revised either.

25. UBS Commodity Connections. Q312, Issue 7, August 2012.

26. Financial Times, September 3, 2012.

27. Chorafas DN. The changing role of central banks. New York, NY: Palgrave/Macmillan; 2013.

28. The pros say that this is not so. The central bank will target both inflation and NGDPS, but if central bankers go after two incompatible goals, they will reach neither.

29. Chorafas DN. Financial boom and gloom. The credit and banking crisis of 2007–2009 and beyond. London: Palgrave/Macmillan; 2009.

30. Financial Times, January 2, 2013.

31. The CPI, too, has been attacked and some economists wanted to replace it with another index which proved unstable. Hence, they returned to the CPI.

32. For instance, in the United States, the 1968 System of National Accounting (SNA) was revised in 1998 and revised again in 2008. Its longer term usage, therefore, lacks consistency.

33. A subterranean and obscure hidden place, where what is in it is simply forgotten.

34. Chorafas DN. Basel III, the devil and global banking. London: Palgrave/Macmillan; 2012.

15 Ineptocracy and the New Policy of Grabbing

15.1 Is Public Debt Good or Bad?

Publishers use consultants to advise them whether a book proposal should or should not be published. This is a sound practice. The consultants, or reviewers, are usually well-learned academics or professionals who develop a sound opinion on a new manuscript's worth (both from a scientific and for a marketing viewpoint). Quite often, they also contribute ideas for improvements to the contents and structure of the proposed work.

One of the publisher's consultants who reviewed this manuscript suggested that public debt has also positive features, and these should be brought to the reader's attention. The consultant is right. Up to a point, but only up to a point, public debt may have positive fallout. But nothing is cast in advance. "Win" or "lose" depends on:

- Whether the money of the public debt is used for productive activities or just for consumption,[1]
- The sovereign's ability to manage the new debt he has assumed over and above the old, and his readiness to pay it back when due,
- The austerity plan put in place to make money available for debt servicing and repayment, and
- The likelihood of an explicit default if the debt cannot be repaid as well as a plan on what happens next.

There may be a case that a new public debt has to be subscribed by an already bankrupt country, or there is war. Under the fascist regime, the Italians thought of themselves as the owners of the Illyric coast, particularly around Dyrachion where Cesar had landed. Invited by nobody, Mussolini sent two Italian geometers to fix the border between Albania and Greece. A Greek hothead shot them. The Italian dictator demanded $50 million in compensation (big money at the time)—or he would occupy the Island of Corfu.

In short, in 1935 a bankrupt Italy was pressing a bankrupt Greece to get an international loan. It is not easy to obtain a big loan when your creditworthiness is flat,[2] and as the negotiation went on and on, the glorious Mussolini army landed on Corfu. In a cruel century like the twentieth, this has been the most ridiculous military event on record. Finally, the Italian dictator got the $50 million of extortion money he asked for, and the military comic opera ended. Greece had to increase its

Public Debt Dynamics of Europe and the US. DOI: http://dx.doi.org/10.1016/B978-0-12-420021-0.00015-4

already high public debt, after all. But the story is also a reminder that tragedy has a comic dimension.

There can even be a worse scenario. The money borrowed by increasing the public debt is spent on luxuries, an extremely unproductive "investment." This is a case which bothered lawgivers since antiquity.[3] Today, a greater worry is that newly contracted public debt is spent for health care under social security protection in Europe; Medicaid, Medicare, Obamacare in America; and so on and so forth. Health care is an entitlement,[4] but these are yesterday's expenses providing absolutely no return. The loan, however, is a future commitment and has to be serviced.

When big social plans like Medicare, Medicaid, Obamacare, and Social Security come in and press on increasing the public debt, what in other days used to be small incremental (and, therefore, more or less controllable) steps in new public loans become a tsunami. *Deficit dynamics* take over. At the same time, because deficit dynamics is a new discipline and there is not enough research in this domain, spending is accompanied by failure to address the unsustainable old fiscal position in a credible and prudent manner. This:

- Threatens the long-term prosperity of the country, and
- Poses a near-term risk to the sovereign credit rating, as lawmakers repeatedly refuse to address ever-widening budget deficits.

It is rather difficult to understand how elected officials leave themselves with virtually no margin for error as they seek to navigate between short-term fiscal cliffs and an expanding longer term national debt crisis. This is precisely where *ineptocracy*[5] has its heyday. Second-rate politicians (who run the nation's fortunes (and misfortunes)) hide the problems under the carpet with the result that these accumulate. They become more complex and the solutions sought after require tough decisions which are not forthcoming.

A person may be lacking experience for the job he or she is expected to do, or simply the challenge confronting him is beyond his ability to comprehend and manage. The argument: "I know what I did was wrong, but had to do it because of orders from above," does not wash. This is Eichmann's dirty excuse. When confronted with such situations, ethical persons must stand up and say: No! (Section 15.4).

But there is the vanity of power for the sake of power and money; even borrowed money means power when the amount is big. We have spoken of this in Chapter 1 when discussing about gifts difficult to refuse. These are masquerading as easy terms loans the (pseudo) donors don't even want to have them repaid. What they want is to see them accumulate in the borrower's account, since this way the borrower keeps on being on the hook.

A different way of making this statement is that the idea of contracting public debt might have had some noble roots, but ineptocracy saw to it that the money has been used for nonproductive activities (see also Chapter 2). If the inept political leaders fail to redress the deteriorating public debt, this will surely cause a negative market reaction, leading to widening risk premiums and perhaps even triggering a fresh wave of banking woes.

If the country which goes through such turmoil is a major player in the world economy and in the global financial markets, *then* the aftereffects could well serve as catalyst to another global economic and financial crisis. The deeper irony attached to all this is that the winners of the new global financial turmoil will be the same select group of big banks expert in manipulating safe-haven assets.

The transition in public debt exposure we have seen in this section has been from a rather comfortable environment of small public debt packages which have outgrown themselves, almost unconsciously, into a leveraged environment of large dimensions carrying along with it a huge amount of risk. Gigantism has its own dynamics and, at least so far, we have not been patient enough to learn how to deal with its many unknowns. Let me rephrase this statement:

- *If* well studied in advance, a small, marginal change in public debt might be beneficial.
- But *if* the public debt system is neither small nor properly studied, *then* we are confronted by a mountain of unfunded liabilities weighing on the economy which is by no means a subject that could (let alone should) be handled lightly.

A major part of the challenge confronting sovereigns and their advisors is that nowadays the will of politicians, central bank governors, and others in the so-called *high places* is no more oriented toward doing one's homework. Decisions have become a sort of rule of thumb largely served by a hit and run approach. In Section 15.3, I take the case of Unilever, Goldsmith, and Lipton Tea to explain what I mean by a well done homework and the benefit derived from it. As an example, this has been a deliberate choice.

15.2   Ineptocracy Increases the Complexity of Sovereign Bankruptcy

Some of the deeper roots of social disparities can be found in government debt, not in one but in several countries around the globe, which keeps rising. Most economies now agree that the aggressive monetary expansion of the last 6 years will have to be unwound at some point. This means that people will pay for it—and not necessarily the people who benefited while the public debt wave kept on growing. Bank deleveraging will also be a headwind to economic development, and the same is true of ineptocracy.

Section 15.1 explained that *ineptocracy* is the system of government where the least capable of leading a nation, of executing public functions, or of running business enterprises are in charge; and to whom the other members of society are subservient. This system works by the accumulation of public debt which quite likely will be paid through the confiscation of the wealth of the community's common citizen. Ineptocracy brought along with it an innovation. Until quite recently:

- The guiding principle characterizing the government's catchment area used to be: *tax*, *tax*, and *tax*.
- This having reached a state of near saturation,[6] the slogan changed into *grab*, *grab*, and *grab*.

The March 2013, Cyprus event which involved the IMF, ECB, and EU, provides the evidence on the *grab policy*, but contrary to a general belief this is not its first instance. Also known under the names; *state gangsterism* and *banksterism*, this policy is a shame. Tomorrow, however, the ineptocracy behind the system may well see to it that it becomes the "normal" state of affairs in society obliging the common citizen to run for cover.

Section 15.1 stated that bureaucracy and ineptocracy are not exactly the same. Their correlation comes from the fact that the great protector of ineptocracy, and opponent to change, is the huge bureaucracy which in the post-World War II years has been rising *en masse* with one goal: perpetuate the *status quo* which is its baby and manna from heaven. This does not mean at all a more efficient society whose success is uncertain because politicians and the entrenched bureaucracy buy public opinion, and votes, by:

• Spending other people's money, through tax or grab, and
• Assuming obligations like pensions and health care by way of unfunded liabilities.

To confront the massive outlays made necessary by extracurricular activities, like the salvage of big banks, sovereigns went deep into debt. Both in the United States and also in Europe, central banks were happy to provide the money by printing it, while at the same time, they extended their authority into the sovereign's turf.

There has been no "Stop!" signal in that road because the show was run by ineptocracy which found it difficult to understand that with interminable money printing of money sovereigns and central banks are essentially in a lose-lose game. The market may wake up to the risks slowly, but unless there is a reversal in monetary policies:

• Inflation will grip the economy, and
• The sovereign's default will follow.

The self-proclaimed Neo-Keynesians say that by printing all the money it needs, a sovereign will not default. This is total nonsense. Printing money nonstop leads investors to losing part of their wealth through currency debasement. In late February 2013, in Britain, after Moody's downgrade, the pound suffered a 9 percent currency exchange loss. Sterling was already weak and the downgrade reinforced sterling's plunge to the lowest level since July 2010. A few weeks later, on April 19, 2013 Fitch stripped Britain of one of its AAAs.

Credit downgrades have the effect of putting an economy in the spotlight and thereby influencing market sentiment. Currency devaluation in today's global economy is like a truck zigzagging between lanes. There may be no accident in switching lanes once or twice, but the accident is sure to come if that practice becomes a habit. In the real economy, this raises two issues which have not been properly studied in terms of aftermath because:

1. Western sovereign risk is poorly known in its medium to longer term implications.

Indeed, an important handicap in effectively handling western sovereign bankruptcies is that there is no such thing as a bankruptcy regime for governments. Both the "ability to pay" and the "willingness to pay" play an important role in the dynamics of sovereign debt, and so does the psychology of the population which will be asked to come up with the money. This psychology has an important impact on the risk of a sovereign defaulting making it of a different nature from the risk of company defaulting.

2. Little research is done in this vast area of crisis management, where exposure is generally understated.

The current crisis has created a major shift in the evaluation of sovereign risk. To measure the associated risk, analysts used CDSs which fill a gap in metrics but are not exact instruments.

Both CDS pricing and the rating of creditworthiness have pro-cyclical bias. A worsening of ratings, or of CDS prices, leads to a higher interest rate, and this aggravates the sustainability of the debt. There may as well be a deadly embrace, as CDS pricing relies on agency ratings while rating agencies increasingly issue CDS-implied ratings as market-inspired. To this is added the variable role of the IMF as:

- Lender of last resort, and
- Ultimate crisis manager.

All of the above reasons see to it that economists, analysts, and auditors who tried to use experience from corporate bankruptcies in sovereign bankruptcies have found that this is hardly doable. The road taken in analyzing a corporate bankruptcy may be twisted but the milestones are at least clear: balance sheet, profit and loss statement, current assets, current liabilities, liquid assets, inventories, fixed assets, accounts receivable, accounts payable and, at the end, the decision on whether the company is or is not solvable.

There exist many unknowns, but they are not of the magnitude present in a sovereign bankruptcy, which involves the (highly uncertain) political will to restructure (including labor laws), public reactions to an economic plan which may be "too austere," prolonged strikes which typically make an already bad situation worse, or the downfall of a common currency followed by polyvalent economic consequences.[7]

While these are the issues generally discussed in economic literature, there is another important difference between a company trying to avoid bankruptcy and a sovereign: It is the ability to influence the psychology of the market toward one's viewpoint. This is done by luring the citizen (or market players) by creating a temporarily sustainable hope that steady improvements are in the way.

Companies help the price of their shares go north by increasing their dividend. This is an old policy for company boards, which in normal times is forgotten, but then it is reinvented. Nowadays, it has been adopted by boards who appreciate the market's message: pay higher dividends and your shares will rise. (As of April 2013, the proportion of cash flow returned as dividends and buybacks to shareholders in US nonfinancial companies is close to record highs.)

The surge in shares may look odd in light of the economic statistics. Besides that, in 2012, global growth slowed to its weakest pace since the 2009 recession, as the world's economies have lost steam simultaneously; America and China included. But because financial markets are forward-looking, investors have been betting that sustained monetary loosening will keep going the world economy (see in Chapter 12 the discussion on quantitative easing).

In contrast to this, an important reason for caution in a sovereign default lies in the gap between financial market optimism and economic reality. That gap is wide in Euroland. The single currency is an added headache, and uneven economies are still in deep trouble (the IMF expects Euroland's economy to shrink by 0.2 percent in 2013). Not only member states on the periphery are stuck in recessions, but even some of those in the core are looking weak.

Few people, even among the experts, properly appreciate that financial markets and the global economy are different from one another. Financial markets can have strong years at the same time that the economy has weak years. The opposite also is true. There is little evidence that economic growth bears any relation to financial market returns, because financial markets' prices are determined by future expectations of a number of factors such as:

- Earnings,
- Quality management,
- Political decisions, and
- Central bank action.

It is no exaggeration to say that more often than not investors' optimism ignores the fact that many politicians who are being shockingly irresponsible and their actions or inactions are the biggest short-term danger facing the world's economies. The only way a highly indebted sovereign sliding toward bankruptcy has to do some public opinion uplifting is fake promises about employment and entitlements—the latter largely unfunded. Lies however have short legs, and therefore, this is the worst possible option even if it is still practiced widely.

15.3   Western Living Standards Have Become Unsustainable

Ineptocracy saw a rapid development in the post-WWII years while easy money made available through the "democratization of lending" without bounds, and corresponding socialization of risk, led people to the belief that there is nothing wrong with living on debt. More and more individuals and families have been able to borrow, so that in America, Britain, and France household debt is at the level of about 120 percent of annual family income.[8] Worse still, an important amount of this debt has been subsidized by the sovereign.

Easy mortgages is one example. Under the Clinton Administration they created opportunities for all sorts of crooks and speculators, as mortgages were sold to families who could not afford them and they were sure to default. The lowest (CCC) credit quality of mortgages became the one most rapidly growing, the infamous *subprimes*, immediately repackaged and sold to investors as "assets" with credit rated AAA by rating agencies. This:

- Expanded the frontier of lending and borrowing,

- Influenced the financial markets in a perverse way, and
- Led to the *subprimes* cataclysm with the severe economic, financial, and banking crisis, which started July–August 2007 and continues unabated.

An easily definable characteristic of the socialization of risk has been the government-undertaken salvage of self-wounded banks after the speculative hurricane passed by. An early example from the late 1980s has been America's Savings & Loans, which today pales compared to the massive pulling up from under of derelict big banks both in the United States and in Europe. To do so, sovereigns used inordinate amounts of taxpayer money. In effect, by standing behind big banks, even if they were high stakes speculators, governments removed the oldest franchise in banking: *safekeeping*—which had started being chipped away in the 1930s with deposit insurance.

Another financial development of the last decades of the twentieth century worth noting is the reinvention of unsecured debt. Junk bonds, which essentially mean junk loans, played an expansive role in the boom of the 1980s and 1990s. With the socialization of risk, not only did creditors lend more freely than they had in the past, but also the sovereign intervened more actively than it had ever done to absorb the inevitable losses.

Still, of all the spending schemes (and there have been a great lot of them in the posy-WWII years) none exceeded the voracity of capital than *entitlements*. The French term tells it all: "les acquis sociaux"; these have been the presents (or acquisitions) by common citizen as a result of intense social pressure. The 99 percent of the population benefited from them, and saw entitlements as its compensation for the awfully (and wrongly) overpaid 1 percent.

"Social conquests" yes, but can the economy afford them? At the end of the day somebody will pay for them; by now we all know that this somebody will be next generations of western citizens. Fathers and grandfathers leave the public debt mess to their sons and grandsons. Till then,

- They remain the unfunded liabilities of the sovereign, and
- As they continue growing, they may well suffocate the state.

No sovereign that I know followed the wisdom of James Goldsmith to thoroughly study the file of new "social conquests," prior to committing himself to them. In the 1960s, President Johnson, at the spur of a moment, decreed that America is a rich country and can simultaneously pursue the war in Vietnam and expensive health care services. He launched Medicare and Medicaid, and we all know what has followed in terms of unfunded liabilities.

Contrast this unstudied approach to the case of Unilever and Goldsmith (to which reference has been made in Section 15.1). This is an interesting case study because it documents the high ground gained by thorough research against the ineptocracy which characterizes Medicare/Medicaid/Obamacare and similar unstudied decisions.

First a brief background. In the 1990s, James Goldsmith, the Franco-British financier, wanted to take control of Allied Suppliers. While it did not actively participate in the takeover, Unilever helped him to reach his goal. The payoff would have been the sale to Unilever of Allied Suppliers' Lipton Tea interests, at a price to be decided through adjudication after the deal was complete.

When he heard a date had been set for the hearing in connection to the Lipton Tea adjudication, Goldsmith summoned his financial advisers and told them that he had no intention assigning somebody else to represent his interests at the hearing. He himself intended to appear and directly deal with the case.

Following this, and anxious to get as much as he possibly could from the sale, Goldsmith spent a whole week going through every single argument that could be used. He knew that Unilever only expected to pay £10–12 million for the tea interests which he had valued at higher price. His challenge, and the very nature of his homework, was to find and provide the proof that Lipton's worth was much higher.

Big-headed, as big company executives usually are, Unilever managers thought the matter would quickly be decided in their favor. The executive delegated to appear at the adjudication had studied his papers only on the night before the hearing. He was no match for Goldsmith and his thorough analysis of facts and figures. After 3 hours of Goldsmith's evidence, it became clear to everyone around the negotiating table that Unilever were going to end up paying much more than they had expected for Allied Suppliers' tea interests; may be up to £20 million.

So it was. Sir Robert Leach, the adjudicator, decided that Unilever should pay £18.5 million for Lipton Tea. As it was confirmed at the time of the original deal, his decision was not subject to appeal. The £7.5 million difference between what Unilever thought it would pay (an average of £11 million) and what it paid was the direct result of Goldsmith's homework, and of the fact he had taken his challenge seriously.

Today we seem to have totally drained the inventory of people who take their work seriously, whether they are chiefs of state, ministers of finance, governors of central banks, or presidents of transnational institutions. So either there is no homework done at all, or it is relegated to the ineptocracy and we go from one snafu to the next, often repeating the same mistakes.

This, quite evidently, has dire consequences both on public debt and on the standard of living of the common citizen. Second rate politicians had the crazy idea to tell the voting public that everybody has "the right" to "free medicaments" and "free everything" else. Could the economy afford such unstoppable "free" gifts? Cheap populist policies have been a reversal of the gradual development (albeit with ups and downs) which for centuries characterized the rise of western society improving the standard of living of western citizens.

Fake promises, populism and ineptocracy took over, unfair competition flourished, miscalculation followed, and at the end, the western countries landed themselves in serious economic trouble. In the second half of the twentieth century, the United States, Europe, and Japan prospered largely by buying primary commodities at low price, then shipping and selling manufactured goods to each other, while less developed countries continued to concentrate on low cost goods.

Globalization, however, brought in a sense of global competition, and this prescription for one-sided economic growth could no more deliver. New players came in, targeted the soft underbelly of Western economies, capitalized on the lack of leadership and the advent of ineptocracy in the West, and managed to master the upper ground.

The lazy West with its "free" medicaments got once again indebted to buy the low cost (but fair quality) goods of the new massive producers. Borrowing a leaf from the Western book of financial dominance, China and the other major emerging countries were not bothered by this indebtedness. They knew that eventually too much debt will mean Western slavery to the East (Chapter 2). They were therefore ready to buy the Treasury Bonds of the United States. As of March 2013, the major foreign holders of Treasury securities have been:

- China, over $1.2 trillion
- Japan, $1.1 trillion
- Brazil, $0.28 trillion
- Taiwan, nearly $0.2 trillion
- Switzerland, $0.19 trillion

Practically, everyone knows that this cannot go on forever. The West searched for a new supremacy through financial globalization, but this was suddenly interrupted through the excesses which led to the great economic, financial, and banking crisis (starting in July/August 2007). Right after, the standard of living in western countries bifurcated toward the:

- Very high, and
- The low level.

Essentially what has happened crashed the middle class which was and is the pillar of democracy. It also wiped out a swarm of jobs in Western countries which migrated East. A report by Bank of America Merrill Lynch states: "Roughly 95 percent of net job loss during the recession[9] was in middle-skilled occupations. Since the recession, job growth has been clustered in high-skilled fields inaccessible to workers without advanced degrees or in lower paying industries. The United States now has larger patches of affluence and poverty, while the middle-class is shrinking."[10]

Fat cats, particularly big bank bosses and those of other king-size firms, saw their salaries doubled and got a shower of bonuses which exceeded the salaries. To the contrary, salaries and pensions of those who do not belong to the new money aristocracy shrank down to 50 percent of what they used to be. Disparities characterizing our society is the theme of Section 15.4.

15.4 Lack of Ethics and Ineptocracy Lead to a Dark End

Fedor M. Dostoyevsky, the Russian author of the human soul, was opposed to the movement of his epoch (mid-nineteenth century) which professed that major social events and social developments could be preprogrammed. To Dostoyevsky's opinion, there could be no recipe for the creation of "the new man"—the way socialism and communism professed. "The basis of ethics is individual freedom," Dostoyevsky said.[11]

Nowadays, in our society, individual freedom is in hibernation while ethical behavior has taken a leave. Lack of ethics, not insurmountable technical challenges, has been behind the tragic accident of BP Houston's refinery. And again, some years later, lack of business ethics was the reason for 2010 explosion in the Deepwater Horizon rig that killed 11 men and caused the worst offshore oil spill in American history.[12]

In neighboring *Mejico lindo*, Elba Esther Gordillo, the leader of Mexico's powerful teachers' union, was living a dream life, making other people wonder how she is able to maintain her lavish lifestyle on a public servant's salary. On February 26, 2013 Gordillo was arrested and charged with embezzling $159 million from union and school funds.

The attorney general said Gordillo and two other union officials "had spent the money on designer clothes, art, property and cosmetic surgery. That was the Mexican schools' and union members' money", if you don't mind. Some of the funds were transferred to companies abroad before being used to buy houses in San Diego, and as an article in *The Economist* had it, "This may not be the full extent of the swindle."[13]

Scams come sometimes in disguise. It is lack of professional ethics when, on April 8, 2013, in an interview to the *Financial Times*, Jean-Yves Hocher, Crédit Agricole's CEO asserts: "We are well positioned,"[14] when it is widely known in the market that his bank is bleeding blood since years—and that bleeding is unstoppable. Lack of ethical concern is also shown in the repeated assertion that: "Crédit Agricole aims to turn round its lossmaking investment bank by further shrinking its activities and costs, in order to focus on becoming a European debt house"[15] (whatever that might mean).

In making such statement, Jean-Yves Hocher forgets that since the most unfortunate purchase by Crédit Agricole of Crédit Lyonnais—a bankrupt bank specializing in scams, employing gamblers and with an amount of accumulating liabilities unknown and incalculable—his predecessors tried to do what he plans, and they have failed miserably.

Lack of ethics leads to the rogue behavior of banks, and this has spread all the way to central banking. Commercial banks tackle their intrabank counterparty loan risk by collateralizing the debt with government bonds. As the sovereign risk increases, it is prudent to ask for more collateral. But like a rogue trader, ECB and the Federal Reserve are doubling up their risk by relaxing the rules for collateral (the ECB lowered it from 20 to 12 percent).

It has been lack of professional ethics when, in September 2012, in an effort to cut off the tail risk of a Euroland implosion, EU officials were quick to tout its differences from previous schemes: the central bank's intervention would not only be "unlimited," like OMT,[16] but it will also be conditional on a struggling country living up to Brussels-mandated economic reforms. The decision on whether it lives or does not live "up to mandated reforms" is left up to ineptocracy, with plenty of room for special favors and nepotism.

In the wake of the late February 2013, chaotic Italian elections, economists, investors, and analysts were concerned that the strings attached to OMT to assure its proper usage, once hailed as the program's strength, may in fact be its Achilles heel. Without a government, Italy was without the kind of credible policy decisions needed to gaining access to ECB assistance—unless there has been another special favor.

Critics regard as lack of ethics and of the ECB's statutory obligations that of the euro 208 billion ($270 billion) the ECB deployed with the SMP government bond buying program, by far the greatest share: a king-size euro 99 billion went toward buying Italian debt.[17] This has happened at a time when Berlusconi, as prime minister, had failed to implement structural reforms explicitly detailed by Jean-Claude Trichet, the ECB president who initiated the SMP program.

Nobody should of course expect that the bending of ethical values is something happening only in Europe. In a letter to the Economist Balakrishna Adiga of Bangalore laments India's plight: "The biggest obstacle is corruption. We are fast becoming a cleptocracy. Dynastic politics and crony capitalism are helping India achieve a landmark which it can ill afford: most corrupt nation in the world."[18]

Whether we talk of Greece (Section 15.6), Italy, India, or any other of the better known countries, cleptocracy, nepotism, and ineptocracy have become a sort of new universal Para Olympics. Nepotism has characterized the relationship between ECB and the Italian sovereign, if one also counts the "other euro 103 billion" said to be transferred from ECB to the Italian Treasury (as anecdotal evidence has it).

The better way to describe the situation in which we find ourselves and have difficulty getting out is one of permanent economic drift. Yet, there are Italian leaders who foresaw the inevitability of descend to the abyss. Two decades ago, clear minds called for a change in course. But they were not heard. Back in July 1990, the late Italian philosopher Dr. Vittorio Vaccari wrote in *Operare*:

> *The frenzied pace of contemporary living, the fleeting nature of intentions and commitments, the slavery to consumerism, the indulging tolerance of permissiveness, the capricious adoring of fashion, the idolization of the unnecessary, the celebration of vice..., all of these mask a wound of contemporary humanity, a wound that plagues the human heart. They act like an anesthetic.*
>
> *Thus in the course of a few short years, man has become indifferent to the ideals of civilization and to the values that throughout history have promoted, reinforced, and upheld civilization.*[19]

Lack of ethics and ineptocracy see to it that a sense of balance is not observed even by those who preach social justice and aid to the poor. When in 2007 Nicolas Sarkozy, of the French center-right UMP party, was inaugurated at Elysée, the bill of the festivities has been euro 1,123,000—way too high. Five years later, the cost of the festivities for the inauguration of François Hollande of the Socialist Party, reached euro 4,502,000; a 400 percent increase. That Socialist bill included:

- 17,000 bottles of champagne,
- Hors d'oeuvres and petits fours,
- Sumptuous dinners,

- Expensive wine, whiskey, and other alcohols,
- Floor and other decorations,
- Free transport of personalities, and so on and so forth.

The Socialist Party's care for the poor was forgotten. The top brass of the left-leaning political establishment celebrated its return to presidential power and that called for thousands of bottles of champagne and sumptuous dinners at taxpayer's expense. Who said that Socialism was dead or dying? It is not only alive and well but also entertaining.

When it comes to throwing sand in the voters' eyes, and make them forget the extravaganzas, the politicians are inventive. To amuse the gallery, they find all sorts of stories, some of which may even be true but ballooned. Such is the case of the global fiscal fraud guesstimated at $25 trillion,[20] which allegedly escapes taxes.

In 2009, after the G20 London summit, Nicolas Sarkozy, then president of France said that the fiscal paradises were taken care of.[21] Four years later, not only the so-called *paradises* are kicking but also the worth under their wings is growing. Indeed, they are thriving.

Trade in drugs and counterfeit and contraband goods is another "industry" sovereigns and their consorts—a few of them theorists, the others card-carrying members of ineptocracy—proudly announce to have wiped out. Interviewed on April 16, 2013 by Bloomberg News, an expert on illegal trade on drugs and goods said that it generates $90 billion per year. Catch them, if you can.

With the western economy in dire straits, the time has come to abandon the grandiose pronouncements and concentrate on serious homework, the way James Goldsmith has shown that should be done when one is decided to win (Section 15.3). The "take it easy" time is past. The European Union needs a lot of uplifting. Like Concordia, the cruise ship, its reputation has fallen on the rocks.

15.5 Bail-In Is Blessed by the Masters of Indecision

Pushed and pulled by the EU, ECB, and IMF, and desperate to get a loan, the new Cyprus government grabbed the money of depositors in the country's banks. This has been a clear break with 500 years of European tradition in banking and finance. Led by the internal and external forces of ineptocracy (including those which chose their residence in the IMF, EU, and ECB) Europe violated the sacrosanct guaranty of deposits.

Labeled the "Great Euro Bank Robbery," this has been one of the most Byzantine twists on record in finance; quite likely an unavoidable aftereffect of poorly studied (or totally unstudied) "solutions" invented by the European Union during the last few years. While hard evidence is missing, rumor has it that originally the Great Euro Bank Robbery fiasco was supposed to be "a very intelligent approach" killing three birds with one well-placed stone:

- Punishing the Russian oligarchs for their alleged money laundering,
- Providing a way to justify a loan to Cyprus, which did not make unanimity among EU members,[22] and

- Being an experiment which could open the door to a solution of Spain's and Italy's crises.[23]

None of the three objectives has been reached; all three remaining in dreamland. EU's bail-in was a measure of rush and unpreparedness in confronting the challenges associated to Cyprus' public debt but not to the debt of the "too bit to fail" Italy and Spain. The Great Euro Bank Robbery has its supporters and its nonbelievers, but the new bail-in provisions have their own set of problems.

Classically, the banks' senior bond risk premium has no risk layer reflecting the event of bail-in, which is creating downside risks for senior bond valuations. Critics remark that the action by Euroland, ECB, and IMF made the institution of much wider and credible deposit insurance a necessity.

Critics moreover add that as bail-in risk rises, it makes evident that the Cyprus decision was made in a rush, and the market has ceased believing what the EU, ECB, and IMF say that this has been a unique event. Not only the bail-in will be institutionalized but also in 2015 (instead of originally stated 2018), the EU will implement:

- The Recovery and Resolution Directive (RRD), and
- Details institutionalizing the bail-in grab of depositors money.

A study by a major investment bank which looked at this issue came to the conclusion that "the bail-in of investors in senior bank bonds of a systemically important financial institution, would be a plausible case." The analysts raised the probability of such an event occurring from the formerly lower end of the 10−15 percent range to 20 percent or even higher, emulating the Cyprus grab.

For some time, the old and new methods of refilling a wounded bank's treasury will probably coexist. In January 2013 due to a large loss on derivatives, the Italian bank Monte dei Paschi di Siena needed a second bailout, a first capital injection having taken place in 2012. However, Italy did not force losses on any bond class despite the total bailout amounting to euro 7.7 billion ($10 billion), nearly the debt of Cyprus. (Anecdotal evidence suggests that the EU complained to Monte dei Paschi that no attention was paid to the RRD in the making—which talks volumes of the impertinence of the new grab policy pushed down the throat of financial institutions.)

With the institutionalization of the bail-in, the market will evidently ask for higher premiums to cover that extra risk. Some experts think that when the EU's Recovery and Resolution Directive is fully implemented, it will be possible to price in risk more accurately, but critics doubt whether the RRD bank resolution framework will achieve more credibility than today's piecemeal approach given the many uncertainties remaining in the market not only in connection to the bail-in but, as well, to many other projects—the often tooted but never well-defined banking union being an example. All these half-baked notions and projects have come out of the hands of the same masters of indecision. In essence with RRD:

- The distinction which existed so far between cash in the bank and bonds has been blurred, and
- Grabs of deposits by the government joined taxation as a way to increase sovereign income and then spend, spend, spend.

One of the opinions I heard in the course of my research is that from the beginning of the deep economic, financial and banking crisis which started July/August 2007 in the United States and spread to Europe, in the short space of half a dozen years, Euroland managed to create an internal grand depression like 1929. Then, having lost the sense of direction, its politicians made a bad situation worse by legalizing the grabbing of deposits.[24]

Grabbing *per se* is not the only problem. One of the more scary aspects of the Cyprus IMF/ECB/EU "loan" conditions is the very light way key decisions have been made. Homework has taken a leave[25] and personal responsibility went along. The situation is very serious, said Dominique Straus-Kahn, the former boss of IMF, in his September 19, 2011 interview by TF1, the French TV station. To his opinion, if things continue as usual in 25 years from now (which is more or less "tomorrow"), Europe will be a desolate continent.

- Democracy will be in decline (it already is),
- Unemployment will be high, and
- The social net will drift out of control.

To Strauss-Kahn's mind, America's future will not be better. Tough decisions and rigorous measures are urgently needed at both sides of North Atlantic, but they are not forthcoming. The citizens seem to simply not understand the depth of the public debt problem and the way it affects them, neither are *the politicians* aware of the volcano on which they sit.

Public opinion, and the political leaders who try to manipulate it, refuse to recognize that one must accept his losses particularly if there is plenty of them. Hence the search for ill-studied unorthodox "solution" and for inertia, both classical signs of the reign of ineptocracy.

The worries of Strauss-Kahn are corroborated by Jim Rogers, the American investor. In an interview he gave to CNBC, Rogers put his opinion on the current situation and its risks in these terms: "It's pretty scary what's going on in Europe, especially when they're taking money out of people's bank accounts ... with Cyprus, politicians are saying that this is a special case and urging people not to worry, but that is exactly why investors should be concerned... the IMF has said 'sure, loot the bank account', the EU has said 'loot the bank accounts' so you can be sure that other countries when problems come, are going to say 'well, it's condoned by the EU, it's condoned by the IMF, so let's do it too'."[26]

We are far away from the time when the sovereign cared for his subjects, and the institutions he made aimed to help the common citizen (albeit, not always). The drift did not start last night. By the 1960s, when the WWII damages were repaired, European governments chose the easy solution of generalizing "for free" university education (at great costs), so that young people can study what attracts their fancy and don't take to the streets.

- The quality of university education dropped,
- The chosen subjects were irrelevant to modern industry, and
- Today a mass of university graduates are unemployed.

The policy has been spend, spend without appropriate control. Spend and spend piled up debt.[27] Higher taxes were supposed to do a miracle. But as the reader is already aware, taxing has limits, and sovereigns found themselves both swimming in red ink and making commitments without provisions. There exist as well other rotten fruits of ineptocracy which inhibit society's effort to renew itself:

• An oversized financial sector with lobbying and iron-clad political connections,
• Banks too much focused on trading short term for quick profits and bonuses, rather than providing service to their community,
• A population accustomed, through decades of practice, to the good times and to spending beyond its means, and
• Politicians who at best are masters of indecision, and at worse take the lobbyists' words and harm their country.

Mario Monti, Italy's former prime minister, suggested that governments need to educate their parliaments. I would agree provided the first subject is ethics and the second effectiveness. The third should be to open the mind of members of parliament and of the senators on the further-out perils of debt—as well as the personal responsibility and accountability associated to:

• The decisions one takes,
• The motions he or she votes for, and
• The laws he or she votes for or against.

Educating the parliamentarians is nearly synonymous to increasing their ability to see through little more complex situations and their aftermaths, hence improving their potential. There is nothing more important than developing the human potential of the country *if*, and *only if*, it is done the right way which is far from being the general case.

Based on his long experience in politics and government, Nikita Khrushchev put it in this way: "I've known plenty of highly educated people who had no brains, and I've known people without formal education but with good heads on their shoulders."[28]

15.6   The Parliament Votes in Favor of Democratic Cleptocracy

For good or bad, western man gave himself a lot of power over his destiny. His secret has been science as well as persistence in what he was doing till a successful end. The sequel is beautifully described in *IF*, Rudyard Kippling's poem. At the same time, however, man and the human race as a whole failed to provide itself with an evolving, refined set of ethical values and moral standards with which to plan and control the newly found power.

Instead, man increasingly surrounded himself with the illusion that he was searching for the external truth. The deep things in science are not found because they are useful, they are found because it was possible to find them, Robert

Oppenheimer taught his students. And they are not necessarily used because they are needed. They are used because once found they have to be used.

Oppenheimer had good reasons for his statement. One of the principles in the scientific effort is that results must be visible. We should not let them hide for eternity. If we do so, there is no continuity of effort and, therefore, no more results. "I start having doubts about scientific truth when the atomic bomb was thrown on Hiroshima," another nuclear scientist suggested.

At the same time, however, this urge for visible results brings in perspective some of the rotten parts of man's values. We find that *humility* is the exception not the rule. Credos are often invented for the deception of the masses. "Jedem das Seine"[29] was written at the gate of Buchenwald. Deception has always been at man's service. Walter Lippmann believed that heroes are incarnated; devils are made by the same mechanism.

Every system perishes of its own excesses, Pericles stated in one of his speeches to the Athenians, adding that any in-depth appraisal of human society is bound to uncover lots of excesses. That's the environment in which we currently live, which widely misses ethics, trust, and confidence because of events which took place in the recent past. Outraged at the excesses that led to the economic and financial crisis, society is deeply cynical about:

- Favoritism,
- Nepotism,
- Ineptocracy,
- Wild spending,
- Bailouts,
- Indulgencies, and
- Grabs of other people's equity supposedly safely stored in a bank.

"Wisdom cannot be bought," says Edith Hamilton. "It is the reward for righteousness."[30] The prerequisite for righteousness is personal accountability for what each one of us has done (or has not done, but should have done). People must be directly accountable for whatever they do not only in front of God but also in front of the Court on the High Street.

Nowadays, however, "in front of the Court on the High Street" has become questionable as a universal principle because a growing number of people in the so-called *high places* have become *too big to jail* (Chapter 11). Since the 2008 descend to the abyss of the banking industry, due to its self-created deep wounds, the "Geithner doctrine"[31] made the preservation of big banks a top government priority no matter the consequences. The sovereign shields the wrongdoers from the Courts.

In an article he published in *The Financial Times*, Neil Barofsky points out that "Aside from moral hazard (this) has also meant the perversion of the US criminal justice system. The US faces a two-tiered system of justice that, if left unchecked by the incoming Treasury and regulatory teams, (it) all but assure:

- "More excessive risk-taking,
- "More crime, and
- "More crises."[32]

The government's benevolence toward big banks is easily demonstrated not only through the use of taxpayer money to refill their treasury but also by the stunning dearth of criminal prosecutions. According to the Geithner doctrine, a correct (albeit more aggressive) stance against big financial institutions could have a negative impact on the stability of the financial markets.[33] Another "principle" is that wrongdoers should not be bothered in their work—a funny way of thinking which makes the biggest and wealthiest amongst them not only too big to fail but also too big to jail.

To a considerable extent, this polarization of society was foreseeable. In the 1930s José Ortega y Gasset, the Spanish political economist and philosopher, had warned that with the rise of the mass society will come the birth of a new kind of politics—*the politics of organized pressure groups*, with which the West:

- Has no real experience,
- May find it difficult to adapt, and
- May fall victim of exchanging democratic freedoms for the straitjacket of consumerism.

Other political economists compared the advent of the mass society, and the changes it bring along, to eighteenth century England which saw the birth of a new sort of economy, one based on exploration and conquest of faraway lands with raw materials. This planted the roots of a global empire which found employment for large strata of the population. The day for Western empires is, however, gone.

With the victors of WWII having mastered the upper ground, the perception of greater wealth (though in most part a *fata morgana*) made large parts of society comfortable. Endowments filled the gap of the common man's income, and slowly but surely the new generation got featherbedded. No wonder therefore that plenty of problems are now confronting us, as Western society learned to live with no responsibilities but plenty of demands beyond the sovereign's means. No elected politician has had the guts to ask his or her electorate:

- "What do you think our country is, our daddy?"

At her time Golda Meir, a true political leader who left a mark in history, had answered that question. As she relays it in her seminal book *My Life*: "The government," I told the nation repeatedly, "cannot do everything all at once. I can't wave a magic wand and meet everyone's demands simultaneously: eradicate poverty without imposing taxes, win wars, go on absorbing immigration, develop the economy and still give everyone his dues. No government can do all this at one and the same time."[34]

Nowadays, with ineptocracy at the lead, I have never heard a politician asking his electorate: "Do you really think that every citizen can go asking for 'free' lunch, 'free' health care, 'free' medicaments, 'free' higher education for his kids, 'free' everything any time he or she wants to have it?" They don't. Their overwhelming desire is to rise in the hierarchy of ineptocracy and from there of cleptocracy.

The depth of ancient Greek tragedy has been divine punishment of people who tried to rise above the Gods. Today, it is not Zeus and his consort at Mount Olympus but the wider public which elects and judges the political protagonists, giving its preference to those who preach spending-and-spending even if it is the citizens' own money or simply more debt. This has evident consequences which tear to pieces the very fabric of society, eventually leading to:

- Uncertainty and frustration,
- Wider public dissatisfaction, and
- A change in public ethics for the worse.

After having expropriated loans and deposits, increasingly sovereigns look at the PSI (Chapter 4) and Cyprus grabs as the way to ease taxation's weight: You can be sure that in a few years, grab, grab, grab will become the sovereigns' new policy—no questions being asked and, if asked, no answers being given. Challenging the grab will become the *new* "les majesté" of Louis XIV fame.

The way a longer established practice had it, it was the citizens who tried to cheat the state in response to taxes, health care benefits, pensions to people who died 10 years ago and other goodies provided by the nanny state. Now, it is the sovereign searching for whatever hits his fancy to cheat his citizen and keep them subservient.

A "haircut" on bank deposits is the beginning. Higher up in the hierarchy of state gangsterism are the so-called *thalassodania*[35] given without collateral to all sorts of political friends. This is not a hypothesis; it happened 2009—2011 when George Papandreou Jr. was prime minister of Greece. The loans were given by banks to the Socialist Party (Pasok) and to a select list of political friends and entities. The mid-wife has been the Ministry of Development in the name of "developing a friendly environment for strategic and private investments" (I.T.I.).

All this was illegal and had to be legalized. No worry, the politicians thought of it. A new law voted on April 10, 2013 by the Greek parliament legalized the theft of public money for the benefit of the country's two main political parties and their friends. Ironically, the new law has been introduced by three members of parliament from the New Democracy (the center-right party), not by the Socialists who let others pull the walnuts from the fire.

A nation which had suffered already over 3 years of austerity was stolen euro 400 million in plain daylight by the same people it had elected to safeguard its integrity and respect its laws. This vote in itself confirmed that democracy has become a damaged brand. As per established parliamentary practice, to hide it as much as possible, the new law of looting[36] was attached to another, irrelevant legislation.[37] According to the clauses of democratic cleptocracy law, the banks which have given loans to political parties:

- The Socialist Party (Pasok) to the tune of euro 200,000,000 ($260 million), and
- The center-right New Democracy also for euro 200,000,000 ($260 million)

will not be subject to pursuit by the law if they don't ask back for their money. They can discharge that obligation to at the expense of the Greek taxpayer who, most evidently, has not been asked if he agrees to pay that high bill. And that's not all. According to that law of democratic cleptocracy and shame other organizations of private and public law (for instance the Music Palace) will also benefit from the indulgence provided they are not-for-profits. Since when political parties became not-for-profit organizations? Or is this a new mode of grabbing public money under a democratic cleptocracy regime?

End Notes

1. The Third Reich had two budgets, a system invented and implemented by Hjalmar Schacht: A consumption budget which had always to be balanced and an investment budget which was in the red with interest paid by the profitable projects to which that money was supposed to be invested. It did not turn out that way as the "development" budget was used for armaments.
2. At the time, Greece was just coming out of the ill-thought and even worse executed war in Asia Minor, which ended in a catastrophe.
3. For instance Solon, the lawmaker of ancient Athens.
4. Chorafas DN. Household finance, adrift in a sea of red ink. London: Palgrave/ Macmillan; 2013.
5. *Ineptocracy* is a composite word from "inept" and "autocracy." Applied experimental psychology teaches that the more inept is a person for the job he or she is doing, the more autocratic. Ineptocracy should not be confused with bureaucracy because not all bureaucrats are inept.
6. Too much tax kills the tax, said Jacques Chirac prior to being elected president of France. But right after his election, he forgot his own principle.
7. Chorafas DN. Breaking up the euro. The end of a common currency. New York, NY: Palgrave/Macmillan; 2013.
8. Chorafas DN. Household finance, adrift in a sea of red ink. London: Palgrave/ Macmillan; 2013.
9. Read: the deep economic, financial and banking crisis engineered by the subprimes.
10. Bank of America Merrill Lynch, 2Q12 Retail Quarterly, September 6, 2012.
11. Souslova A. Mes Années d'Intimité avec Dostoievski. Paris: Gallimard; 1995.
12. The government accuses BP of "wilful misconduct." If found guilty, BP faces fines under the Clean Water Act of almost $18 billion, in addition to even larger sums it has already shelled out.
13. The Economist, March 2, 2013.
14. The Financial Times, April 8, 2013.
15. *Idem.*
16. Outright Monetary Transactions.
17. Financial Times, February 27, 2013.
18. The Economist, April 13, 2013.
19. *Operare*, Torino, Number 3, July–September 1990.
20. VSD, No. 1859, 2013.
21. *Idem.*
22. With a GDP of euro 18 billion Cyprus needed a loan of euro 17.5 billion. The forced contribution by depositors reduced the EU loan to euro 10 billion.
23. Right or wrong, the name of Christine Lagarde was associated to this "experiment."

24. Anecdotal evidence suggests that in March 2013 secretive Spain has already proceeded in a "haircut" (read confiscation of deposits) on deposits in its own banking system.
25. For a concise description of what is meant by a serious homework see the work of James Goldsmith in Chapter 3.
26. http://www.cnbc.com/100600824; March 31, 2013.
27. In America, much of the financing of university studies has been done by president Johnson's Student Loans outfit which finds itself today with a debt of $1 trillion.
28. Khrushchev Remembers: The Last Testament. London: André Deutsch; 1974.
29. "To each one his dues."
30. Hamilton E. The Greek way. New York, NY: WW Norton; 1930.
31. A label coined by blogger Yves Smith.
32. Financial Times, February 7, 2013. Barofsky is former special inspector-general of the TARP and currently senior fellow at NYU School of Law.
33. Let me laugh.
34. Meir G. My life. New York, NY: G.P. Putnam's Sons; 1975.
35. Greek word meaning "loans given in the high seas" without records kept.
36. Adding insult to injury socialist and center-right newspapers did not publish the law of shame. It was only briefly announced at noon, prior to the vote, by the state TV but the evidence exists in the parliament's and the government's archives. The only newspaper who dared public the new "law" was AVGI of the Communist Party.
37. A usual parliamentary practice known as "piggy-backing."

Case Study and Conclusion

The Trickery Associated to the Birth of the Euro

A public debt which reaches for the stars is bad enough in itself as it destabilizes sovereigns, leads to banking industry excesses, and hurts the common citizen's standard of living as well as his hopes for the future. Even worse, however, is the sight of a western society which loses its bearings as it transits through higher and higher levels of public debt.

Lofty sermons about democracy change nothing when democracy has been turned into cleptocracy (Chapter 15), the common citizen's deposits are looted by the sovereign, government decisions are based on incomplete evidence, structural unemployment continues to increase, the quality of western culture deteriorates, and so does the future of western countries is in the hands of largely incompetent politicians. All the while:

- Governments and citizens fail to connect,
- Nobody seems to be in charge, and
- Confidence is a precious commodity which cannot be bought or is anywhere to be seen.

Animal spirits dominate. Just prior to and after the unwarranted gift of euro 400 million of public funds to political parties, the opinion in Athens has been that the famous "troika" was informally informed about the intentions of democratic cleptocracy and shame, and it gave a tacit approval. *If* this is so, *then* the troika's members should be rotated because they grow roots in Athens.

Evidently, this does not relieve the IMF, ECB, and EU from their part of responsibility of what has taken place under their watch, but it poses the question:

- Is the European Union a creaking network, or a system which is still doing useful work?

What is needed for the good of Greece, of the other "Club Med" countries, and of the EU as a whole is law-setting by a new Draco, the toughest and most straight-talking lawmaker of ancient Greece's.[1] There is an urgent need to establish tough ethical laws and watch over their execution. The more this problem of giant

---

[1] Draco laid down the first written constitution of ancient Athens so that nobody would be unaware of the laws. They were posted on wooden tablets (axons) where they were preserved for almost two centuries. The laws were harsh, but any citizen could make appeal to *Areopagus* for injustice. Draco also introduced the lot-chosen Council of Five Hundred, which played a large role in Athenian democracy.

public debt is pushed into the future the more the lure of democratic cleptocracy gains ground, the more the common citizen's losses will mount, while those who think of themselves as "well connected" (which means with strong political support) will profit.

Democratic cleptocracy and other scams evidently raise the question: Is there an official and independent audit authority in this EU, like the GAO in the United States and La Cour des Comptes in France? Nothing has been heard of a powerful European auditor, yet there is plenty of dubious happenings to be sanctioned, particularly the aforementioned creeping democratic cleptocracy which came to the public eye with the:

- Private sector involvement (PSI),
- ECB Cyprus ultimatum, and
- Vote by the Greek parliament handing to the two main political parties euro 400 million of public money.

An independent EU Accountability Office should have been most inquisitive in establishing what has happened to the billions of haircuts from PSI which have ruined the Greek, Cypriot, and French banks (among others), while it did not benefit Greece. It would have, as well, focusing its duty to find out personal responsibilities behind the ECB's Cyprus ultimatum. Ultimatums to EU member states are outside the statutory rights of the ECB.

The Stability and Growth Pact admits an upper limit of 3 percent of GDP to annual budget deficits for Euroland's member states (more on the hilarious history of this 3 percent later on). At 10.6 percent, Spain's 2012 budget deficit was the largest in the European Union. On April 22, 2013 Eurostat, the EU's statistics agency, reported that swollen by the cost of trying to salvage its banks Spain's 2012 deficit widened from 9.4 percent in 2011 and was worse than Greece's 2012 budget overrun.

Functions like that and sanctioning of overruns is classical work for an independent auditing office whose mark of distinction is the thoroughness with which its findings are researched, analyzed, and deployed. Without the analytical services of an accountability entity, the EU citizens are being gamed not in one but in many of the duties the huge, highly paid, and full-of-lobbyists Brussels bureaucracy is supposed to perform.

The same is true about the political meddling in European community affairs and the resulting misguided policies. Take membership to the euro as a case for auditing and you will find in it plenty of rights and wrongs in personal accountability. But no voice was ever raised by EU auditors to sanction the behavior surrounding the use of the euro which went against all logic—even if at the time this has happened "too big to jail" was not en vogue.

When in the 1990s the qualifications for euro membership were discussed, a critical question has been whether highly indebted countries like Belgium should be admitted. The technical opinion was negative, but the decision was political: Belgium's public debt was high in respect to its GDP, still it joined the euro.

There was as well the case of Italy. Technically speaking, its euro candidacy was found wanting: Italy had a public debt of 120 percent[2] of GDP, double the upper limit of the Stability and Growth Pact. The governor of the Bank of Italy said that the country was not ready for the euro, particularly in the domain of fiscal discipline. Germany, too, thought Italy was not ready to join the euro, but the French (wanting a partner to weight against Germany in the "soft euro" side) insisted that *if* Italy is not admitted to the euro *then* France will not participate either[3].

Feedback and control have been another issue of contention. The first opinion was one of automatic sanctions if the sovereign budget's deficit is greater than 3 percent. However, according to Jacques Chirac, who succeeded François Mitterrand as president of France, "this was the work of German technocrats." The French were against automatic sanctions. In one of its mistakes, Germany gave in when the Stability and Growth Pact was ratified, even if it stipulated that *politicians* should not decide whether or not there are sanctions.

Ottmar Issing, chief economist of the Bundesbank and (later on) of the ECB, objected, saying that a regime or jury where potential sinners hold judgment over actual sinners cannot function.[4] The politicians, however, carried the day. The time plan for the euro was set, though everybody knew it started with:

- Incomplete preparation,
- Arbitrary guideposts, and
- Plenty of opportunity for errors.

The famous 3 percent limit in annual budgetary deficit of Euroland's member states provides an evidence on how ill-studied, incomplete and superficial euro's rules and regulations are. What is written in the following paragraphs is a mockery of the common currency, revealed postmortem. By all likelihood, few people know its existence.

Yet, this 3 percent limit to budgetary deficits by Euroland's member states plays a vital almost daily role in negotiations between Brussels and individual Euroland governments. Even people expected to know about the 3 percent because it's part of their business, are in the dark as demonstrated by a recent public case.

Karine Berger is the national secretary for the economy of the French Socialist Party. In an interview she gave on February 13, 2013 to the RTL television station, she was asked what's the role of this 3 percent and her answer has been: "With a deficit of 3 percent the public debt starts shrinking."[5] It needs no explaining that this is patently false, and Berger's decisions are made on wrong premises. Any deficit, even one as small as 1 per million, increases the public debt. It does not decrease it.

[2] Today, public Italian debt stands at over 127 percent; in other terms it increased during euro membership.

[3] In fact, this is the famous trap François Mitterrand and Giulio Andreotti set for Helmut Kohl with the (infamous) Stability and Growth Pact which has never been applied (including by Germany).

[4] http://www.wdr.de/tv/diestory/sendungsbeitraege/2012/1105/euro.jsp.

[5] Le *Canard Enchainé*, February 27, 2013.

More colorful is how this 3 percent was invented. According to Guy Abeille, who worked for the French Ministry of Finance in the 1990s, and was present in the Franco-German negotiations which led to the common currency, this deficit limit of 3 percent has no real substance. When the more profligate French ministers objected to the trimming of the budget, a couple of their colleagues at a corner of the table guesstimated that 3 percent will be enough to calm them down without creating a negative reaction by Germany.[6] That's "scientific management" (of which the French are so proud) turned on its head.

Even if in terms of its foundations, the euro is a castle built on sand and, more than anything they did, the founding fathers were bent over to please the *pico palino*;[7] it did not take long till it became clear that almost every country who rushed to join the Euroland bandwagon found it difficult to fulfill the entry criteria. In a 1997 Brussels finance minister meeting, Jean-Claude Junker, the president of Ecofin, was confronted by German and Dutch requests to exclude some countries from the euro, such as Spain and Portugal. But the political will was to include them, and Junker gave in.

To their credit, there is an absence of evidence that in trying hard to join the euro, Spain and Portugal used a scam Italian strategy. To cover their country's huge annual budget deficit—which in 1991 was over 11 percent and in 1996 it stubbornly persisted at nearly 8 percent—Italy's authorities cooked the books. With the help of investment bankers, they engaged in a series of tricks with derivative financial instruments. According to the *Financial Times*,[8] the three men directly responsible for this frolic were:

- Draghi at scam's time director general of the Italian Treasury and now president of the ECB.
- Vincenzo La Via, Draghi's protégé, at the time boss of the debt department. In 2000, he left the Italian Treasury but in May 2010 he returned as director general.
- Maria Cannata, then a senior official involved with debt and deficit accounting, and presently boss of the Treasury's debt management agency.

The derivative instruments Italy used in 1996 to masquerade its accounts mandated up-front payments made by counterparties (typically go-go banks). This reversal in normal practices allowed it to reduce its publicly reported debt and deficit ratios, thereby meeting the criteria necessary to join the euro.

A big question is: Was the hoax a tightly kept secret which surfaced only in June 2013 with the news that Italy risks potential losses of billions of euros on derivatives contracts it restructured at the height of the Eurozone crisis? Plenty of red ink is being suggested by a confidential government report that sheds light on the tactics that enabled the debt-laden country to enter Euroland.[9]

---

[6] *Idem.*

[7] Literally, the little, little fellow and, by extension, everybody else.

[8] Financial Times, June 26, 2013.

[9] An Italian Treasury report (obtained by the *Financial Times* in London and *La Repubblica* in Rome) details Italy's debt transactions and exposure in the first half of 2012, including the restructuring of eight derivatives contracts with foreign banks with a total notional value of €31.7 billion and with potential losses at the €8 billion level.

Experts who examined what is revealed by the Treasury report are of the opinion the reason for the 2012 restructuring has been to permit the cash-strapped Italian Treasury to delay payments owed to foreign banks (which are not named). Allegedly, the transaction was done in a hurry and at disadvantageous terms for the Italian taxpayer.

As required by law, this report about the deceit was submitted in early 2013 to the Corte dei Conti, Italy's state auditors. Concerned by the amount of red ink, the auditors requested the finance police to intervene. In April 2013, the Guardia di Finanza visited the Treasury's debt management agency asking for more information, including details of the original derivatives contracts behind the euro entry hoax.

Absolute secrecy, however, is not a likely course of action in a Mediterranean country, where the going motto is "two men can keep a secret if one of them is dead." Alternatively, there are those who believe that the racket which preceded the introduction of the euro has not been for 17 years a closely held secret. The roots are somewhere else.

The awkward questions for Draghi, head of the ECB and director general of the Treasury at the time of the racketeering derivatives deals, were raised back in 1998 when Helmut Kohl, the German chancellor, warned that Italy is "dressing up" its accounts and would not meet Maastricht treaty criteria to join euro. But as masters of deceit, the French and Italians had their way. The French wanted a partner as profligate as they are, and the Italians were desperate for membership to the euro club.[10]

On June 26, 2013, the way a report by RAI News had it, this second thesis has been supported by Italian Treasury officials. According to this source, to cover Italy's annual budgetary deficit and qualify it for joining the euro, the country indeed used derivatives—but this was made known at the time to the EU executive, and Italy received its approval and its blessing. The antithesis between these two versions of what *really* happened in 1996 leaves two possibilities:

- The Italian derivatives swindle of the mid-1960s was indeed a well-kept secret, and in 2013, the top brass of Italian Treasury is lying.
- The vertex of the European executive and the then "leaders" of the Euroland nations were aware of what was going on and had authorized it so that on January 1, 1999, Italy joined the euro.

This second thesis is further supported by the fact that deceit by cooking the government's books had found imitators within the EU. At twentieth century's end, Draghi had quit the Italian Treasury to become a big gun at Goldman Sachs,[11] the investment bank. It's precisely at that time that Greece needed his expertise to do not just one but two window dressings through a derivatives hoax.[12] In spite of huge budgetary deficits and an inordinate level of public debt, Greece was welcomed to the euro.

---

[10] They did not heed Graucho Marx' advice that "a club ready to have him as a member does not worth joining."

[11] Draghi's partner in deceit in 1996 seems to have been JPMorgan, not Goldman Sachs.

[12] Draghi's involvement in the Greek derivatives deals has neither been proved nor disproved, but critics say that the absence of an investigation is itself a most curious event.

Let's recapitulate. These two deceits which created a *fata morgana* of strong economies out of weak and shaky have contributed the big way to the euro's downfall. The Greek derivatives masquerade came first to the public eye, but the Italian was the first machination and is by far the more important. Moreover, it involved *a permission by the EU*.

Not only Treasury officials in 2013 but also at an earlier time other people known to be trustworthy—like Giulio Tremonti, the former finance minister—have said the European Union was aware of the scam and gave approval to Italy's use of derivatives to qualify for entry into Euroland.[13] Greece followed suit 2 years later and took most of the blame because its irregularities in government accounts became public in 2009, 4 years ahead of Italy's.

In terms of precedence, Greece learned from its neighbor and the fact some investment bankers were masters of cover-ups through derivatives made the *Italian Way* so much more appealing for another try. It even emboldened the officials' viewpoint. In the spring of 1996, in the course of preliminary discussions by EU finance ministers meeting in Verona, Italy, Yannos Papantoniou, the then Greek finance minister said to Theo Waigel, his German counterpart, that on the euro bills have to be Greek characters. The German finance minister responded: "You are not in it." The Greek replied: "You want to make a bet?"[14] They made a bet, and we all know what has happened thereafter.

Greece miraculously met the 3 percent barrier and sent the entry application and the statistics to Eurostat in Luxembourg. However, Eurostat could not control these numbers. No database mining was possible, as the vital statistics were handwritten. When the European Commission suggested giving Eurostat the power to go to member countries and control the vital membership numbers, the big member states (Germany included) were against, saying that this is too big an interference in their sovereignty. Greece essentially delivered statistics which nobody could really know if they were right or wrong.

In April 2000, the head of the Hessische Landeszentralbank had enough and insisted during a press conference that Greece is not meeting the entry criteria and should be delayed by at least 1 year as it does not fulfill the Maastricht clauses. As a reaction to this statement, the Greek drachma and the Athens stock exchange went south. The Greek finance minister immediately called his German counterpart demanding that such public statements are not repeated. The German finance minister called the Bundesbank president and told him to shut up the critic.

The politicians had decided that Greece will be allowed to join the euro,[15] but the Greek sovereign knew that it had to do some face-lifting. Even if the political

---

[13] Moreover, in 2001 Gustavo Piga, an Italian economics professor, caused a storm when he obtained a derivatives contract taken out in 1996 and accused EU countries of window-dressing their accounts. Piga did not identify the country or the bank involved. Their names were only recently revealed.

[14] http://www.wdr.de/tv/diestory/sendungsbeitraege/2012/1105/euro.jsp.

[15] Information available at the time adds another picturesque detail. Western European politicians (read: French and German) were in accord that Greece was not ready for euro membership. They wanted British membership. London said: "No!" Frustrated by the negative answer, they invited Greece to join the euro.

will for euro entry had turned positive, the numbers remained dismal. Goldman Sachs was ready and willing to provide all its expertise to turn black into white and other feasts reserved to financial alchemy. Indeed, it made not one but two interventions to hide Greek debt:

- One before Greece joining the euro, to enable the country's membership, and
- The other right after, in 2003, as it became necessary to hide once again the desolate economic results.

In February 2001, the debt agency founded by the Greek government to manage the euro entry contacted Goldman Sachs and allegedly gave it the mission to hide euro 2.8 billion in debt. The American investment bank's London office sent one of its best specialists: Antigone Loudiadis, whose strength was one of finding "creative solutions" to difficult financial problems.[16]

While forbidden by law, the beautification of national accounts was marching on: sell debts now, pay back later. But there were no miracles. The swap deal on which Goldman Sachs and the Greek government agreed did not cancel the debt; it only transferred it into the future.

In March 2003, Athens again required the services of Goldman Sachs in order to hide debt. This time it was an interest rate deal which did not go as smoothly as the first one. Postmortem, a fatal error was found in creative accounting. The interest rate of the deal was not fixed, and as market moved in the opposite direction than the one the wizards had guessed there was plenty of red ink. It does not matter. Client pays it all. Goldman Sachs made $500 million on this deal.[17]

The good news is that Greece was not alone in face-lifting its accounts. Indeed, it found itself in good company. In April 2003, the European Commission in Brussels felt obliged to open a deficit procedure against Germany and France. Chancellor Schröder, who had just implemented the Agenda 2010, insisted that he could not apply such rigid reform program if Brussels makes it financially even more difficult for Germany. There was a heavy controversy between the Bundeskanzleramt and the Commission. Finance Minister Eichel went to Brussels to get going an alliance against the self-established rules of the Stability and Growth Pact in order to prevent sanctions.

Many Germans felt offended by their socialist government's curious initiative. The way Ottmar Issing saw it: Of all countries Germany, the country which had insisted on a pact, organized a political majority against the application of the sanctions.[18] This was simply embarrassing; a deadly stroke against the Pact.

In common accord, Germany and France broke the Stability and Growth Pact. It was more than simple tricking. It was the abandonment of common principles in

---

[16] Anecdotal evidence suggests that Goldman Sachs with this first "deal" generated fees of $300 million. The Greek government was not thrifty with taxpayer money. (http://www.efinancialnews.com/story/2010-02-22/loudiadis-greece-debt-deal).

[17] Rumor has it that the boss has been Mario Draghi, then at Goldman Sachs. Draghi orally denied his participation. The Greek taxpayer paid anyway.

[18] http://www.wdr.de/tv/diestory/sendungsbeitraege/2012/1105/euro.jsp.

the fourth year of the currency union. The larger two economies of Euroland have taught a bitter lesson to the smaller ones: "The rules we made are for you. We do what we consider right for our economies, but *you* obey the rules."

The rules said that Euroland's smaller economies were not expected to use favorable exchange rate swaps or other gimmicks to their advantage. That was cooking the books and had to be sanctioned. In July 2004, in Luxembourg, Eurostat's new boss controlled the Greek numbers and was puzzled by what he saw. Therefore, he sent some officials to the Greek Bureau of Statistics. The Eurostat inspectors obtained information which implied that part of the Greek military budget did not show in the national budget.

The statisticians who at the time were responsible for the numbers put the blame on the new government which changed the booking methods in 2004 by transferring huge sums to the past. This excuse became known among a wider group of statistical offices creating the impression that Greece tricked its way into the euro.

Frictions followed. Mid-April 2013 EU member states were clashing over plans to centralize the handling of failing banks, as Germany warned that Euroland is running out of road to adopt crisis-fighting measures under its current treaties. At an April 12−13, 2013 meeting in Dublin, Wolfgang Schaeuble, the German finance minister, told his EU counterparts that there is not enough of a basis in the EU's current rulebook for:

- Building a common bank supervision authority[19], and
- Creating a fund for bank failures.[20]

This was not the opinion of other member states who had to profit from such a fund, like France and Denmark. Probably foreseeing a collapse of one or more of their banks both urged swift progress on putting in place a resolution system, amid concerns that Lisbon Treaty changes would open Pandora's box—apart from causing delays. This argument indeed rested on curious logic: "*If* it is difficult to change the Treaty, *then* let's bypass it, work outside it, and disregard the letter of the law." This is not yesterday's policy. It goes on for years, and it has left big chunks of present-day EU outside a legal framework, hanging on a fork.

As per established policy, the financing of the fund for EU-wide bank failures is another example of an initiative which has not been studied regarding to its implications. Who is going to provide the funds when everyone knows that the financial situation of the European banking industry, particularly of the big banks, is a bottomless pit? Don't count on the EFSF and ESM, if such an idea crosses your mind; they are already overcommitted.

In terms of preparedness, not only matters concerning the banking union but as well for the majority of its projects the EU continues to behave as if it were selling watches out of the back of a van. Schaeuble had good grounds when he opposed the motion of a stillborn banking union, saying that: "A banking union only makes

[19] To intervene at crisis-hit banks in Euroland as demanded by Mario Draghi of ECB and Michel Barnier, the EU's financial services commissioner.

[20] http://www.bloomberg.com/news/2013-04-13/eu-set-to-clas-on-bank-deal-as-g. . .

sense if we have mechanisms for the restructuring and resolution of banks. But if we want these European institutions, we need Treaty changes."[21] That's precisely what scares the other 16 Euroland members so that the EU, its institutions, and its acts continue living in the twilight between legality and illegality.[22]

The investing mood is confused with two very different futures of Europe either pulling itself together and keeping the euro going or "things fall apart and the euro comes apart," said on April 9, 2013, at the Bloomberg Link Doha Conference, J. Christopher Flowers, chairman and chief executive officer of a private equity firm.[23] Investors are also confused because so many politicians are simply lying, and they find it difficult to make up their mind while, after listening to the lobbyists, some become turncoats.

"A truthful man," Trotsky said, "has this advantage, that even with a bad memory he never contradicts himself. A disloyal, unscrupulous and dishonest man has always to remember what he said in the past, in order not to shame himself."[24] Liars are cowards, and

"Cowards die many times before their deaths."
William Shakespeare (1564–1616) in Julius Cesar

---

[21] *Idem.*

[22] For those institutions whose transactions, acts, and commitments fall outside the Lisbon Treaty.

[23] http://www.bloomberg.com/news/2013-04-14/ackermann-says-euro-destruction-....

[24] Trotsky: The Essential Trotsky. London: Unwin Books; 1963.

Printed in the United States
By Bookmasters